TRANSPARENCY WEAVING

A GUIDE TO CREATING SHEER TEXTILE ART

WITH 6 PROJECTS

REBECCA SMITH

SCHIFFER CRAFT
4880 Lower Valley Road • Atglen, PA 19310

Other Schiffer Craft Books on Related Subjects:

Tapestry with Pulled Warp: Inspiration, Technique, and the Creative Process, Susan Iverson, ISBN 978-0-7643-6760-1

Weaving with Wire: Creating Woven Metal Fabric, Christine K. Miller, ISBN 978-0-7643-6693-2

Tapestry Talking: Understanding the Language of Handwoven Art with 326 Works from Around the World, Micala Sidore, ISBN 978-0-7643-7141-7

Library of Congress Control Number: 2026932918

Designed by Christine Stuermer
Front cover design by Lindsay Hess
Front cover image: Rebecca Smith. *After Lenore*, 2021. Linen, wool, cotton, acrylic: 13 × 39 inches. Photo by Bob Smith.
Back cover image: Rebecca Smith. *Lacy Wavy Banner*, 2024. Linen, wool, cotton, acrylic, metallic yarn: 6½ × 47 inches. Photo by Bob Smith.
Photographs by Bob Smith: pages 4, 7, 8, 12, 31, 32, 35, 38, 49, 50, 61, 84, 99, 100 (top), 102, 118, 130, 133, 134, 138, 141, 142, 144, 146, 150, 152 (r), 156
Type set in FUTURA®100/Tisa Pro

ISBN: 978-0-7643-7243-8
ePub: 978-1-5073-0761-8
Printed in China

10 9 8 7 6 5 4 3 2 1

MIX
Paper | Supporting responsible forestry
FSC® C167893

Published by Schiffer Craft
An imprint of Schiffer Publishing, Ltd.
4880 Lower Valley Road
Atglen, PA 19310
Phone: (610) 593-1777; Fax: (610) 593-2002
Email: Info@schifferbooks.com
Web: www.schifferbooks.com

To my mother, who told me when I was a child
that I could accomplish anything I set my mind to.

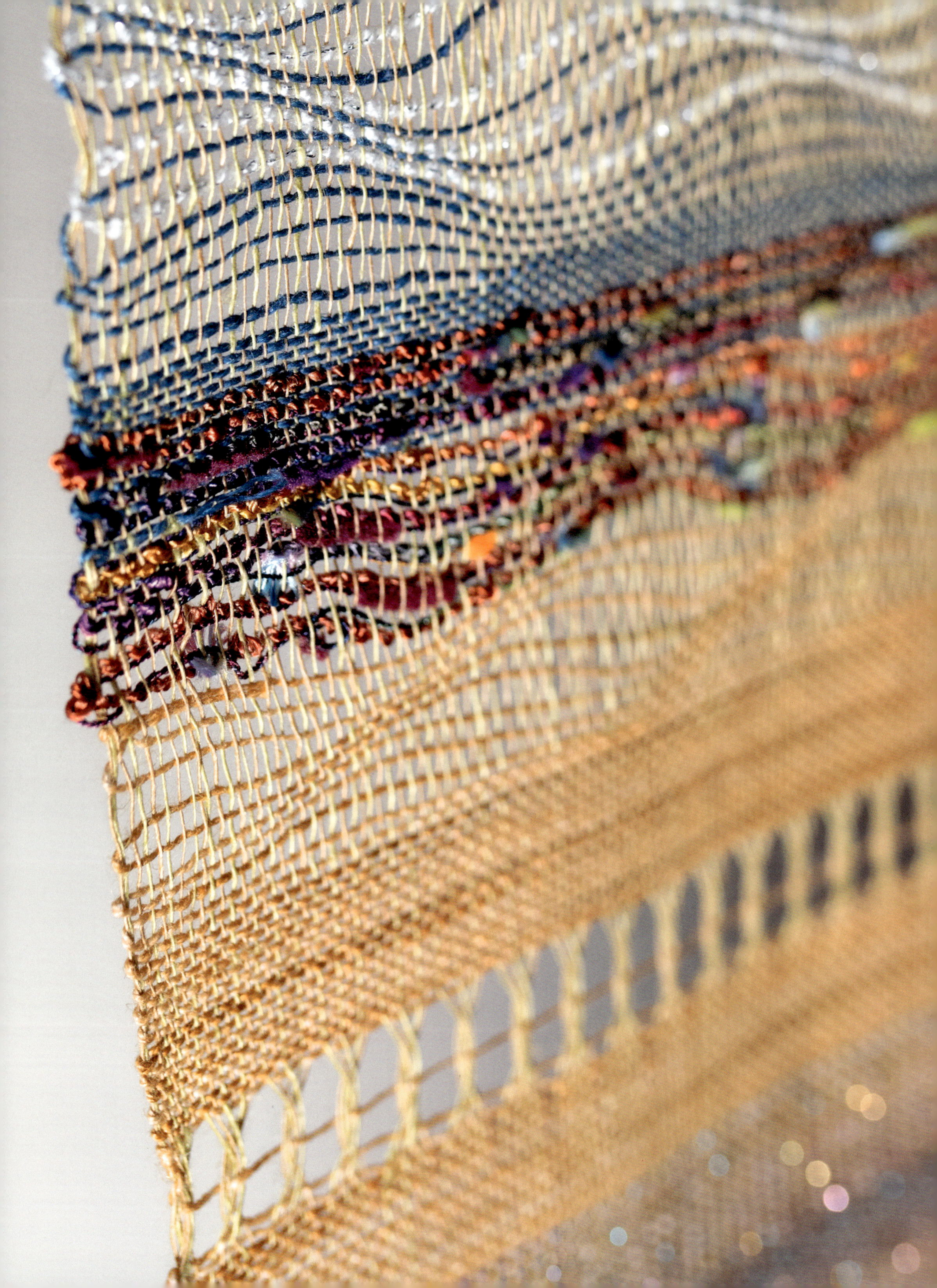

*"It's the creative act,
the energetic application of your imagination
to the materials at hand, that make weaving
or any other handcraft so precious."*

—LINDA LIGON

Rebecca Smith. Detail, *Lacy Wavy Banner*, 2024. Linen, wool, cotton, acrylic, metallic yarn: 6½ × 47 inches.

CONTENTS

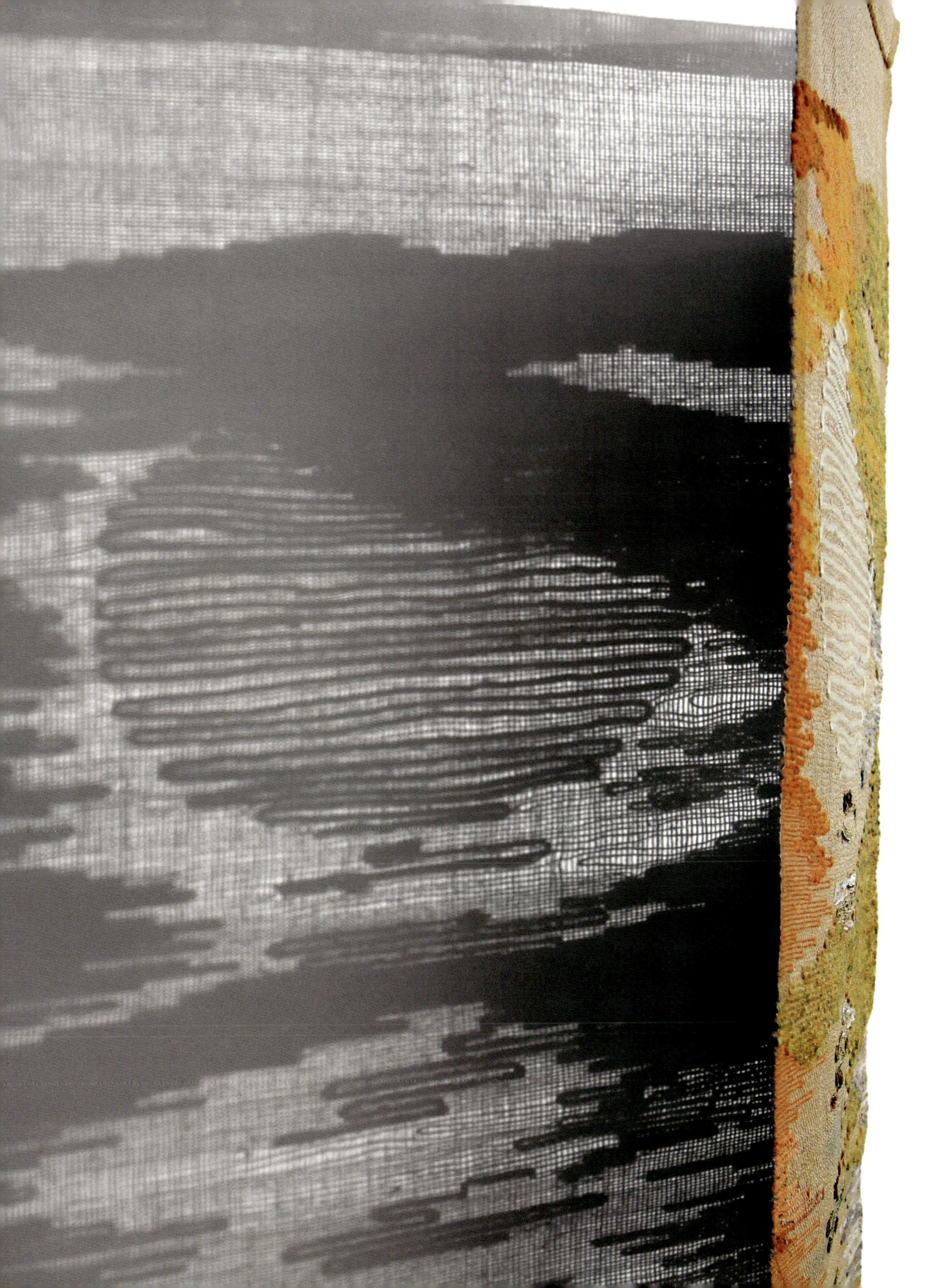

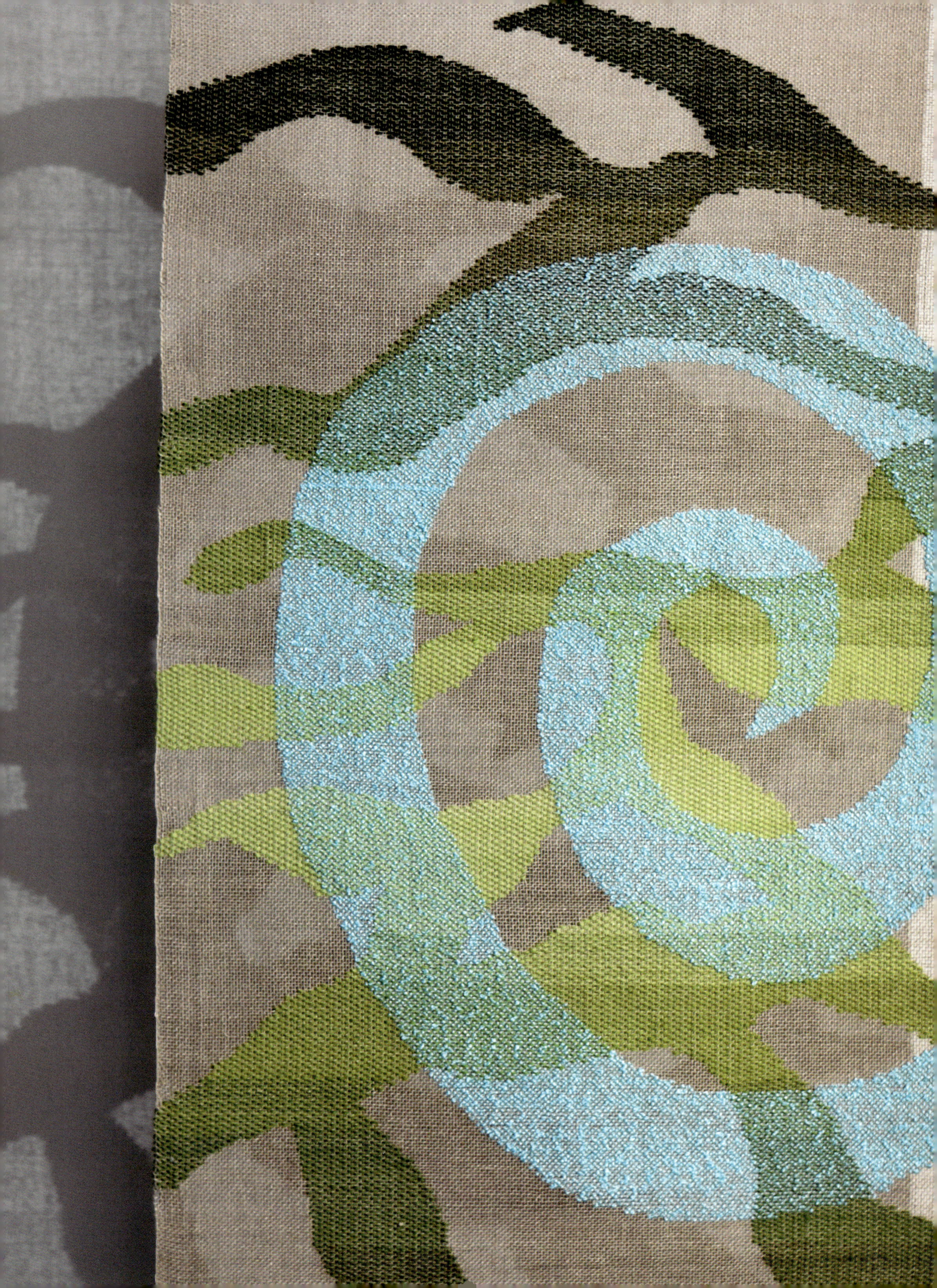

ACKNOWLEDGMENTS

I would like to acknowledge all the people who, in numerous ways, helped this book come into being. Christine Miller walked me over to the Schiffer Craft Publishing booth at HGA Convergence 2024 and introduced me to the editor attending the booth. Convergence 2026 found me in the Schiffer booth again, this time signing copies of my book. Thank you, Christine, for getting the ball rolling. And thanks as well to Sandra Korinchak and Kaylee Schofield, the two editors at Schiffer Craft who saw the project through from beginning to end.

Thanks to the digital age, I was able to reach around the world and gather information and materials to write about the history of transparency weaving. Special thanks to Emil Björck at Modernity Gallery, Stockholm; Anette Nilsson, photographer at Märta Måås-Fjetterström AB; Kathleen Mangan, executive director of the Lenore G. Tawney Foundation; and Brian Rusch at the John Michael Kohler Arts Center.

I am particularly appreciative of the six weavers who agreed to be spotlighted and shared their stories and photos with me. Thank you to Cyndy Barbone, Muriel Beckett, Boisali Biswas, Morgan Clifford, Kathleen Morris, and Helena Vento. I feel particularly indebted to Helena Vento, whose explorations with overlapping shapes inspired my interest in transparency weaving. Connecting with Inger Harrison Seitz was one of the highlights of my research. Thanks to Natalie Drummond for providing the contact information for Inger.

When I first turned to transparency weaving, Laura Viada encouraged me and shared her class notes and display methods with me. Laura taught transparency weaving at Convergence conferences in past years but willingly ceded the job to me when I told her of my plans to submit a teaching proposal for the 2024 conference. I am happy to be able to show some of Laura's beautiful work in this book.

I have mentioned several times in this book the lessons I have learned from students, who bring their own brilliant ideas to class. I am grateful to them for expanding my perspective. And, in a broader sense, I would like to thank all the workshop students who have helped me hone my teaching methods just by being in class. And more broadly still, since this book is the culmination of forty years of weaving experience, I am thankful to everyone who has contributed to my knowledge base.

My good friend and fellow weaver Susan Van Winkle reviewed the manuscript for technical correctness and clarity. I thank Susan for contributing her expertise and her admirable attention to detail.

And finally, thank you to my partner, Ruth, who has extended her unconditional love to me during this writing process (and at all other times as well!). Your sincere encouragement and your cautions against working too hard have helped me stay (mostly) balanced and sane during this project.

Rebecca Smith. Detail, *Entwined*, 2020.
Linen, wool, rayon: 20 × 36 inches.

INTRODUCTION

This is a book about transparency weaving, a weaving style with a long historical tradition and many modern and as-yet-untapped applications. To my knowledge, no books have been published on the subject since Doramay Keasbey's *Sheer Delight: Handwoven Transparencies* was published in 1990.[1]

My love of weaving transparencies grew out of my background as a tapestry weaver. Transparency weaving is only a short step removed from tapestry weaving. I suspect this book will appeal to a broad range of weavers, from tapestry weavers who wish to use their skills in a new format, to floor or table loom weavers who want to expand their repertoire to include decorative weaving.

Both tapestry and transparency weaving rely on a grid layout of warp and weft that the weaver manipulates to create patterns, pictures, or abstract designs composed of colors and textures. The challenge, technique, and ultimate beauty of this endeavor have captivated me for the past twenty-five years.

Weaving became my life's passion in 1985, a year before I was to begin preparing for my tenure defense at a major New England university. I was not an artist; I was a geographer. I saw an ad for a beginning weaving course at a small shop in Amherst, Massachusetts, called WEBS. Thus began my weaving career. I spent my tenure year preparing to open a fiber art gallery on Cape Cod. Thanks in large part to a book I ran across titled *Wishcraft: How to Get What You Really Want*,[2] I diagrammed a path to my goal that led me from knowing nothing about running a business, let alone a gallery representing a hundred fiber artists, to opening the gallery doors to the public on Memorial Day weekend in 1987.

My first love as a weaver was weaving rugs. I set up a 60-inch Swedish Glimåkra loom in the gallery and wove while customers browsed. I loved being a gallerist and I loved weaving commissions. I opened a second gallery in Alexandria, Virginia, to give me something to do the other forty-two weeks of the year between summer seasons on Cape Cod. And then, for personal reasons, I sold it all and moved across the country to my home state of California.

Everything happens for a reason, doesn't it? Shortly after I moved to San Diego, a friend in the weavers' guild suggested I take a workshop with Archie Brennan, the great Scottish-born tapestry weaver who brought his tapestry skills to the US and transformed the landscape of American tapestry art. The technical foundation I gained from what turned into three workshops with Archie Brennan was all I needed to make the leap from loom-controlled rug designs to the infinite variety possible in tapestry weaving.

Ever an explorer, I soon discovered that I was drawn to shiny objects and found a way to weave seed beads into tapestries as part of the weft. Not only are beads shiny, but they are also transparent, so I started incorporating a wire substrate into my tapestries to allow them to stand up and let the light shine through. There were no precedents in the weaving world for this combination of techniques, so I felt I had finally found my own authentic voice.

Between 2017 and 2020, the cumulative weight of world events such as climate change, political upheaval in the US, plastic pollution in the oceans, and the biggest of all—the COVID-19 pandemic, which began in 2020—made me feel that there was enough heaviness in the world and I needed a lighter form of expression. I remembered a book that had been on my bookshelf since the 1990s, Doramay Keasbey's *Sheer Delight: Handwoven Transparencies*. I found in the transparency technique a cure for the heaviness I was feeling. Throughout the pandemic, when everything in the world felt so heavy and dark, my transparencies gave me an emotional lift because they are light and airy and, somehow, refreshing.

The rest of the story is what this book is about. My curiosity as a former academic led me to seek information about the history of the transparency technique and its connection to other cultures and weaving styles. My role as a teacher forced me to hone my presentation of the skills and techniques required to weave transparencies. My inquiring mind and desire for innovation have driven me to seek answers to this question: What next? How can transparency weaving be expanded beyond its basic components to further explore light and lightness in weaving? These are the three cornerstones of this book: origins (where it comes from), technique (how to do it), and expansion (where can we take the technique). Like the linear act of weaving, the following chapters advance from past to present and then contemplate the future.

HOW TO USE THIS BOOK

A lot of this book is aimed at helping you learn to weave a perfect transparency. Some of the instructions go way beyond the basics and are in fact unnecessary if you just want to jump in and start weaving. Read enough to get the basics and then skip the rest, until later. But I would be remiss if I didn't include the more advanced topics. That would leave you to discover these things on your own, when I can easily share what I've discovered over years of practice.

After learning a little about the history of transparency weaving in chapter 1, you will get to the meat of the matter in chapters 2 and 3: What tools and materials are recommended, how to set up your loom, and the basic process of weaving to get a transparent effect. Chapter 4 looks at designing for transparency weaving. Chapters 5 and 6 will get you into the nitty-gritty of how to weave designs, which are basically just an assortment of shapes. In chapter 7 you'll learn how to dress up your design with weave effects that produce patterns and variations in density and, finally, focus on color. You'll go beyond the basics in chapter 8, where you will learn about weft-and-warp manipulations that are not part of traditional transparency weaving. Chapter 9 wraps it all up with ideas for how to finish and display your beautiful transparency.

The projects in chapter 10 encourage you to put into use the techniques learned in chapters 5 through 8. The project instructions do not guide you step by step so much as they offer possibilities of what *you* can do with the technique. Feel free to incorporate your own ideas and inspirations as you work through the book.

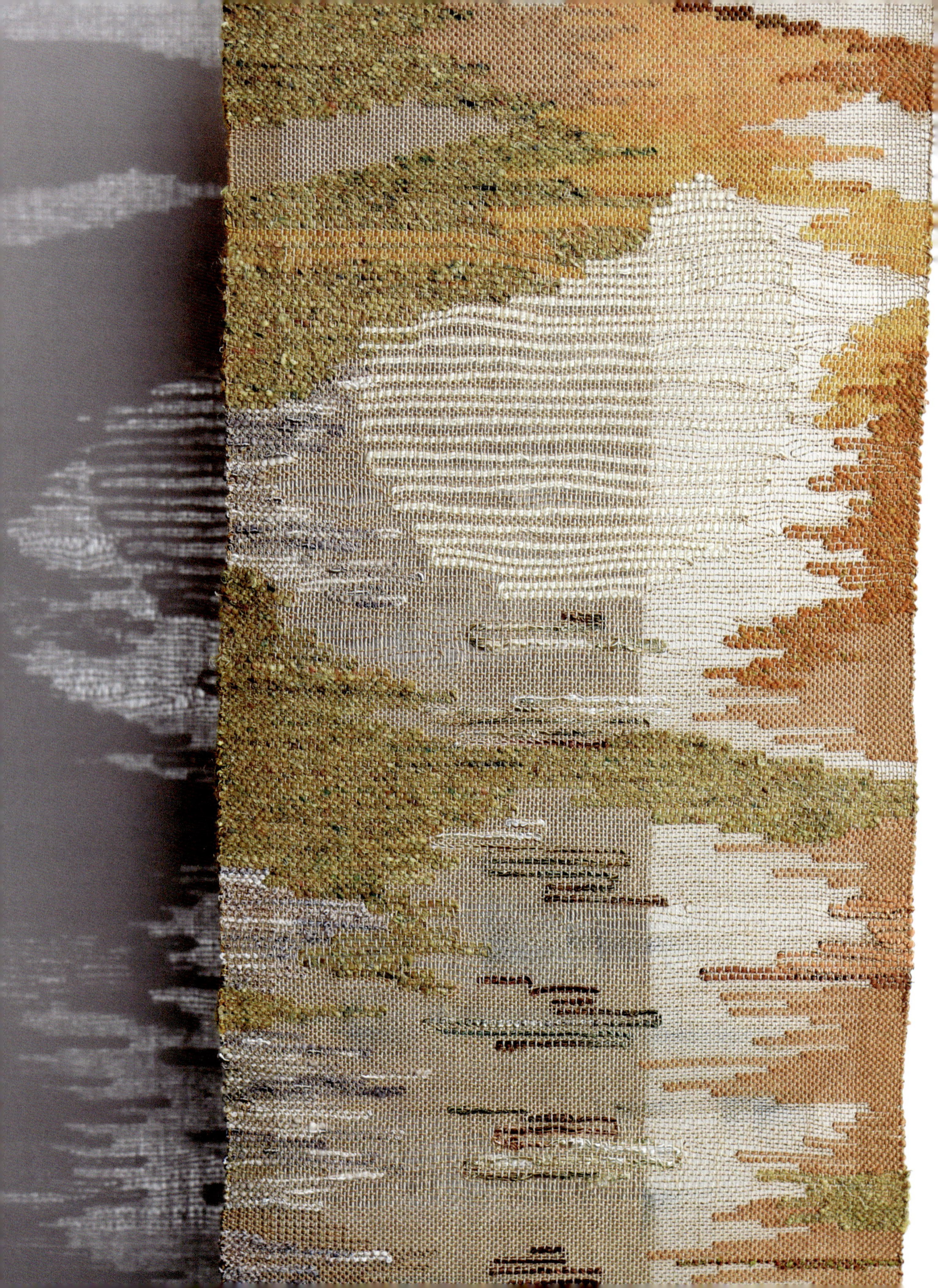

Chapter 1

WHAT ARE TRANSPARENCIES?

"What is essential is invisible to the eye."

—*The Little Prince*

Transparencies are a lightweight, delicate textile in which a sheer ground cloth supports opaque design elements. The design consists of heavier threads inlaid into the shed during the weaving of the ground cloth. The two wefts—ground weft and inlay weft—are woven simultaneously, distinguishing this textile form from others where a design is applied to an existing ground, as in needlepoint or embroidery.

A unique feature of transparencies is that the woven background—the negative space that surrounds the design elements—is see-through. Woven with widely spaced warps and a very light beat, the ground weft consists of tiny open spaces that allow light to shine through, similar to a window screen. When backlit by a window, the ground weave seems to disappear, while the inlay design, which was woven with heavier, more opaque material, comes to the fore and stands out.

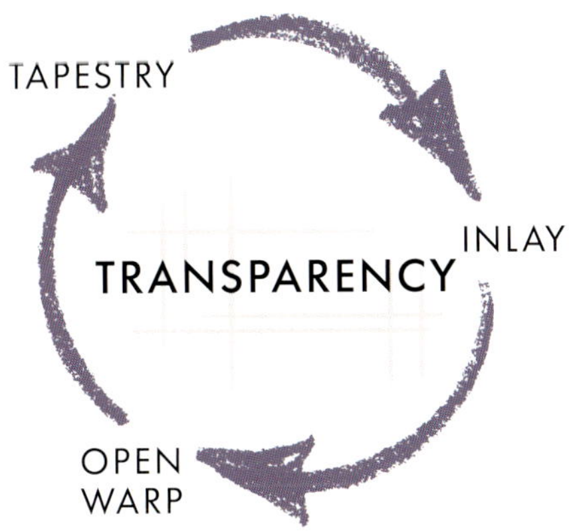

Transparencies feature a sheer, see-through ground cloth woven simultaneously with denser design elements. Rebecca Smith. Detail, *After Lenore*, 2021. Linen, wool, cotton, acrylic: 13 × 39 inches.

Where does transparency weaving fall within the wide spectrum of weaving genres, both historical and contemporary? The techniques utilized to weave pictorial and geometric motifs relate closely to the techniques utilized for tapestry weaving. However, whereas the design elements woven into tapestries are an intrinsic part of the woven cloth, in transparency weaving the design elements are introduced as supplemental weft through a process called inlay. Supplementary wefts are not an intrinsic part of the woven cloth: The inlaid design weft could be completely removed, and the cloth would still be intact. Inlay is purely decorative and has historically been used throughout the world for decorative cloth structures such as satin and brocade.

The common denominator that brings the disparate traditions of tapestry weaving and inlay together to create transparent textiles is the use of an "open warp" style of weaving. In open-warp weaving, the warp is spaced more widely than it would be for solid cloth, and the weft is beaten into place very gently to maintain a balanced weave, creating an open, sheer textile.

HISTORY AND CONTEXT

We can understand much about the development of the transparency weaving style by looking at the weave structure and when it emerged.

Transparent weavings owed early popularity to their use as a functional, utilitarian textile form. Following in the footsteps of tapestry weaving, which had been used for centuries to provide both warmth and decoration in castles and private homes, transparent textiles—textiles woven with the purpose of allowing light to transmit through them—first developed in textile studios in Scandinavia that were involved in the production of *portières* or room dividers. These large textiles were traditionally hung in doorways to control drafts.

During the first half of the twentieth century, several prominent Swedish textile design studios experimented with weaving structures similar to transparency weaving. Their motivations for moving in this direction were mixed. The impact of the Industrial Revolution on the textile industry most likely motivated weavers to find faster, cheaper ways to create their products. For some, it was a search for a more drapeable fabric that would hang better in a window or a doorway. And for some, the goal was to let light pass through the textile to create a more open feeling, consistent with the trend in home design toward more open, airy rooms.

Halv Gobeläng

The Swedish term halv gobeläng or "half tapestry" describes a group of textile approaches that arose during this period. The prime distinction between tapestry and half tapestry is the presence in half tapestry of a ground weft that separates rows of supplemental design weft. The term "supplemental," as mentioned above, means that the design weft is not part of the structure of the textile: If it were removed, the textile would still be a whole cloth.

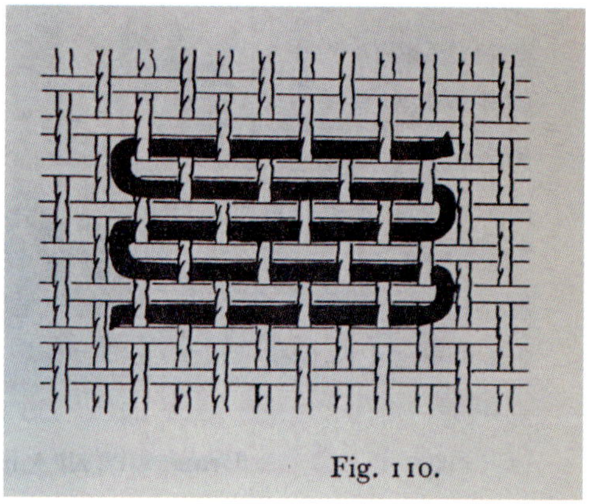

MMF weaving technique. Source: Ulla Cyrus, *Manual of Swedish Hand Weaving*, 1956, page 199.

Approaches to half tapestry all differed in the method used to weave supplemental weft. Märta Måås-Fjetterström, one of Sweden's most revered textile designers, originated a style that placed the design weft into the same plain weave shed as the ground weft. The "MMF" technique, named for her, was "specially developed with the purpose of filtering light through the weave."[1] Wool inlay patterns were placed by hand into a shuttled background of handspun linen yarn.

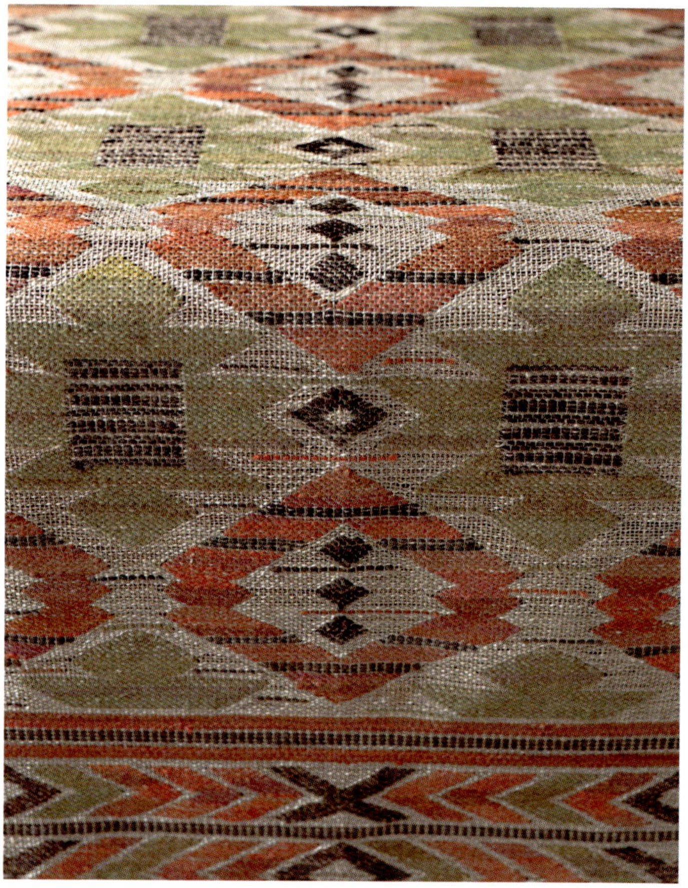

Detail of design by Märta Måås-Fjetterström. Early twentieth century. Courtesy of Anette Nilsson, MMFAB.

To create the transparent effect, parts of the design had no supplemental weft. These open areas formed borders that separated geometric components in Fjetterström's designs. The warp was spaced as it normally would be for tapestries and other weft-faced structures, which require space between the warps to allow the weft to settle in and completely cover the warp. By virtue of this fact, the areas lacking supplemental weft are open, with gaps between warps and between rows of ground weft.

Fjetterström's approach to inlay differed from most other types of supplemental weft, in that the inlay weft is woven in the same shed as the ground weft. Most types of inlay, such as satin or brocade, weave the inlay weft in a separate shed that creates floats over several warp threads, allowing the inlay to stand out on the surface of the cloth.

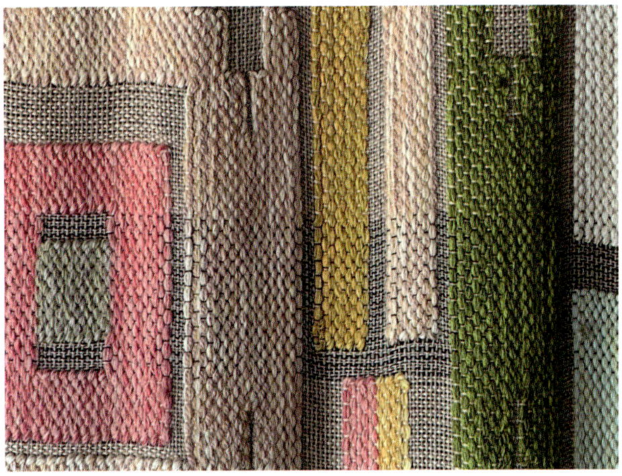

Detail of drapery by Agda Österberg. Likely woven 1963–1975. Courtesy of Anne Whidden.

One such pattern of inlay is called ryssväv in Swedish, or Russian weave in English. Examples of this technique can be found in the work of Agda Österberg, another Swedish textile designer active in the mid-twentieth century. Österberg employed ryssväv and similar halv gobeläng patterns to weave wall hangings and draperies that were semitransparent, allowing light through the areas surrounding the supplemental weft designs.[2]

Woven on an open-weave background, ryssväv features areas of supplemental weft woven in a different shed from the ground weave. The supplemental weft floats over three warps and under one warp. In successive rows the floats are offset to create a brick-like appearance. This style of inlay produces designs on only one side of the weaving. The colors are less prominent on the backside. In the example shown at left, the transparent areas create borders between inlaid geometric motifs, much as in Märta Måås-Fjetterström's designs.

Kuultokudos

Between 1940 and the mid-1970s, the weaving of sheer, translucent textiles called kuultokudos became quite popular in Finland. The Finnish textile design studio Helmi Vuorelma was influential in creating a popular market for this style of home textiles, which were used as room dividers as well as lightweight curtains for windows and doors, and later as a form of decorative art. The move toward this style was perhaps born of necessity: During and after World War II, there was a scarcity of the materials needed for making clothing; for a while, making interior textiles from cotton and wool was not permitted.[3] The availability of homegrown linen helped fuel the popularity of kuultokudos.

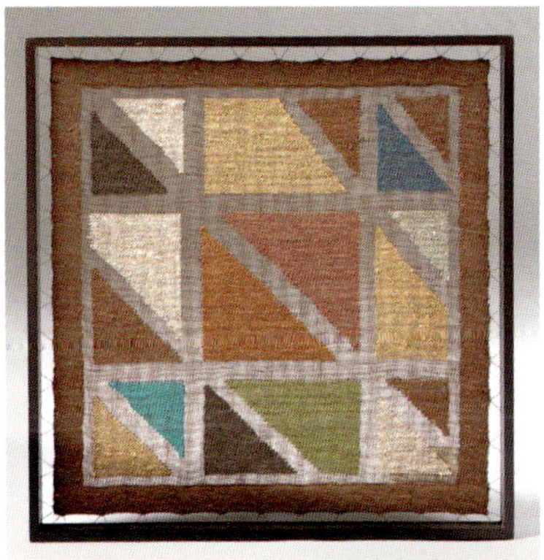

Sirpaleita designed by Maija Kolsi-Mäkelä for Helmi Vuorelma Oy, Finland, 1960s. Linen: 18.25 × 18.25 inches. Courtesy of Modernity Gallery, Stockholm.

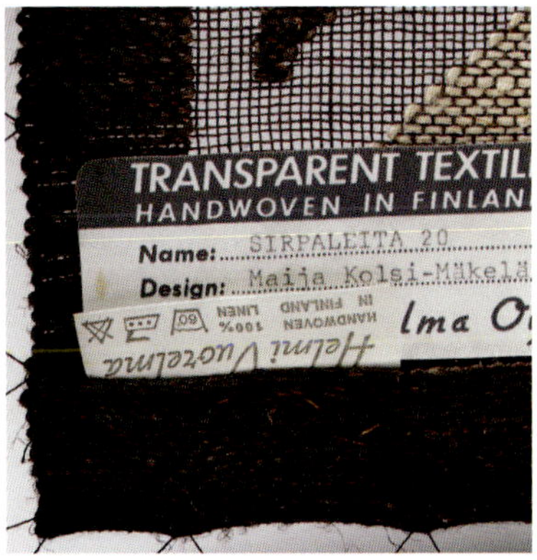

Detail of back of piece. Courtesy of Modernity Gallery, Stockholm.

The popularity of kuultokudos among Finnish weavers and decorators peaked in the late 1960s and early 1970s. Designs created at Helmi Vuorelma were made available to weavers throughout Finland in magazines and through a network of home industry advisory organizations and civic colleges that provided technical advice offering everyone the opportunity to make textiles suitable for their own home.[4] Designs became smaller and primarily featured geometric motifs, often based on historical patterns. Transparencies were woven for draperies or smaller window dressings that would distract passersby from *see*ing into homes. For display, the small weavings were often laced into frames so that light could be transmitted through the weaving.

Transparencies Come to America

It was into this milieu that American weaver Doramay Keasbey stepped when she visited Finland during the 1960s and first encountered kuultokudos in a Helsinki department store. When Keasbey returned to Finland in the 1970s, she found that this technique had become extremely popular, and she was able to learn the structure.

Behind the scenes, though, it was another Finnish weaver, Inger Harrison, who wielded the greater influence on the developing interest in transparency weaving in America. Harrison emigrated from Finland in 1970 and rapidly began building a business of weaving transparencies for sale. She soon found that the abstract designs that were favored in Finland did not appeal to the American audience, so she began to weave pictorial designs.[5]

WHAT'S IN A NAME?

The Finnish term *kuultokudos* can translate as either "transparent cloth" or "translucent cloth." Although "translucent" may be a better word to describe the effect created by this weaving style, Doramay Keasbey chose to use the word "transparent," and so that word has gained popular usage.

Why did Keasbey choose "transparent" over "translucent"? The answer may be traced to Inger Harrison's influence. Harrison was from Finland, true, but she was from a Swedish-speaking part of Finland. (Sweden colonized parts of coastal Finland in the thirteenth century; even today, Swedish is the first language of many people in the region.) Harrison learned about transparency weaving at the Swedish-speaking Borgå Kvinnliga Hemslöjds Skolan, a school in Borgå. The Swedish term used there for this style of weaving was *transparent* (imagine it pronounced with a Swedish accent). Harrison brought this term with her when she immigrated to America.

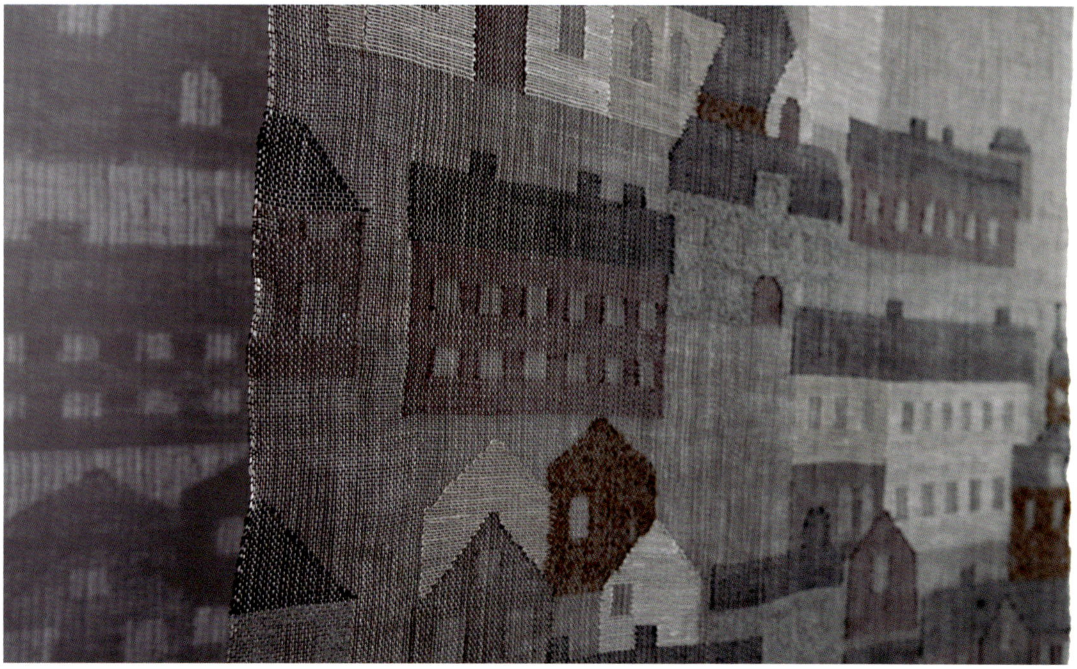

LEFT: Inger Harrison Seitz. *My Hometown*, 1978, detail showing shadows cast by the weaving.

RIGHT: Inger Harrison Seitz. *My Hometown*, 1978. Linen and wool: 35 × 55 inches.

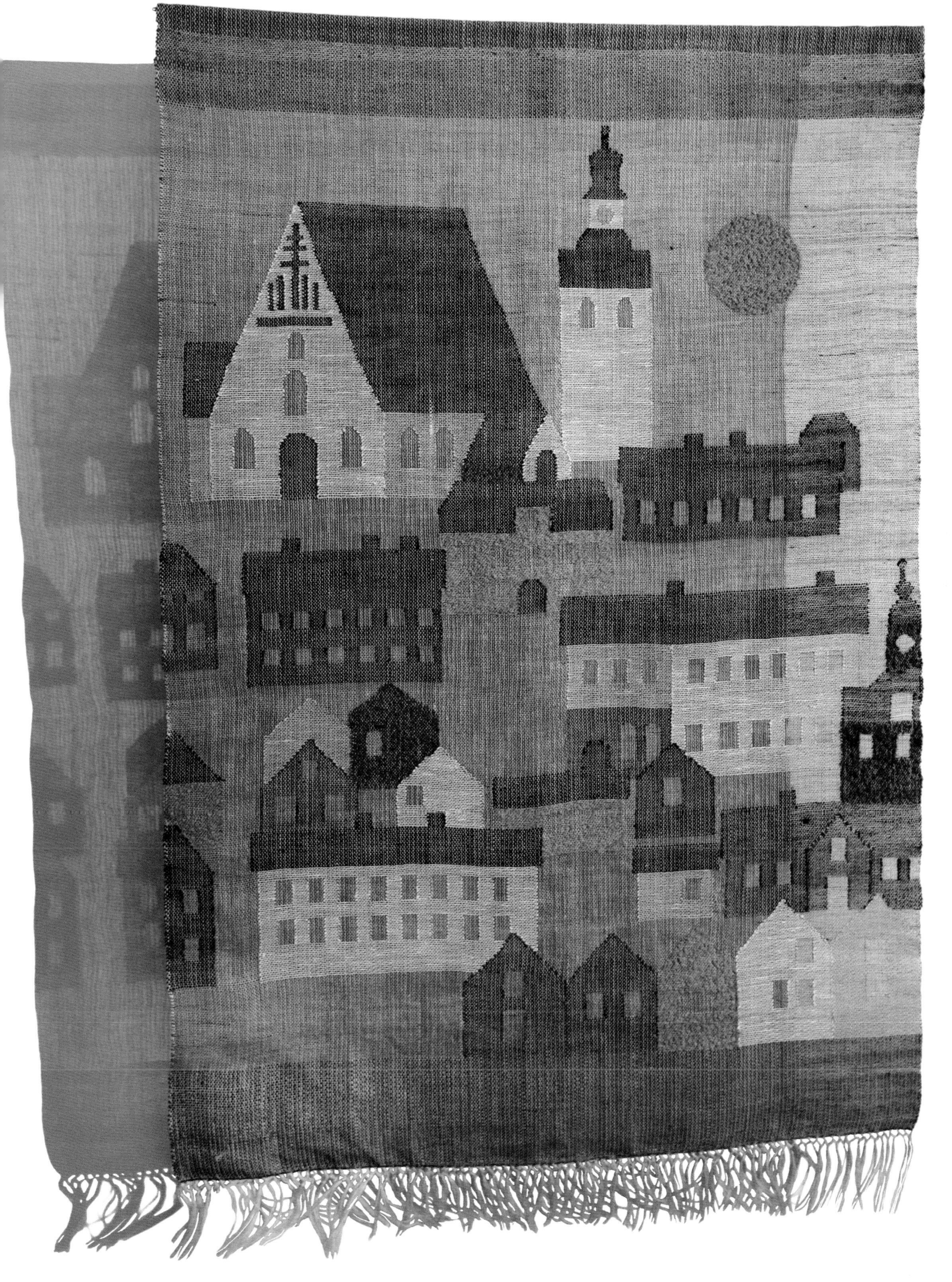

It was Harrison who suggested that Keasbey write a book about transparency weaving. Published in 1990, *Sheer Delight: Handwoven Transparencies* quickly became the definitive source for American audiences for information about this beautiful weave style. Many of the weavers whose works are featured were Harrison's students. The selection of works has a clear slant toward pictorial designs over abstract or geometric designs, propelling this style of design to the forefront of American weavers' interest in transparency weaving.

RELATED TECHNIQUES

Frida Hansen

In the late 1890s, Norwegian tapestry weaver Frida Hansen devised a technique to leave open spaces of unwoven warp in her tapestries to allow light to pass through. Hansen called this transparentteknikk or, in English, transparent technique.

The Frida Hansen technique is often confused with transparency weaving due to their shared reference to the concept of transparent weaving. While both produce transparent effects, their weave structures are different. In the Hansen technique there is no ground weave to hold the designs in place on their open warp. Woven areas of weft-faced tapestry are separated by areas of open warp. To avoid issues with slippage or sagging of the densely woven design areas, Hansen devised a technique that uses the friction created between coarse wool warps spun with a z-twist, and equally coarse wool weft spun with an s-twist. The friction created between the warp and weft allows the weft to cling to the warp to prevent slippage.

The innovative weaving styles that emerged among Scandinavian weavers during the twentieth century were the tip of a much-larger iceberg. The mid-twentieth century was a period of massive innovation in the world of fiber art. It is a period that is referred to as the Fiber Revolution. Transparent textiles appeared in the work of weavers of this time, introducing new ideas about pursuing weaving as an art form.

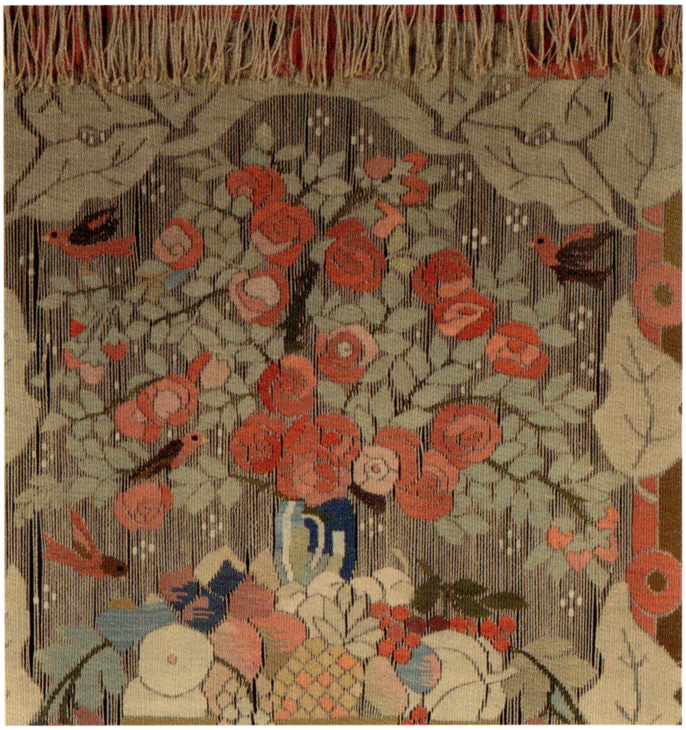

Detail of Frida Hansen's *Hoisommer* (High Summer), 1921. Wool: 38 × 87 inches full piece. Stavanger Kunstmuseum, Photographer: Dag Myrestrand.

Theo Moorman

In fact, *Weaving as an Art Form* is the title that British weaver Theo Moorman selected for her book that introduces what was to become the Theo Moorman technique.[6] In the 1950s, Moorman began experimenting with weave structures that would allow her to express artistic concepts through weaving. Her prime motivation was to find a technique that would be faster and less laborious to weave than traditional tapestry. She felt that "traditional inlay techniques" did not yield the density and richness of color and texture that she desired.[7]

Moorman formulated her technique to meet two requirements:

- The ground weave should lie at the back of the inlay design, forming a solid cloth background that did not break into the design areas.
- The inlaid design areas would be held in place by tie-down warps that would be finer than the background warp so as to be barely visible.[8]

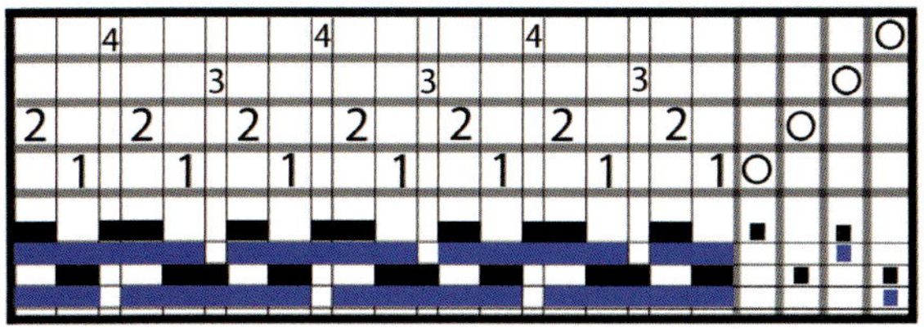

Theo Moorman technique: inlay shown in blue.

The ground weft is woven on shafts 1 and 2, and the finer tie-down warps alternate between shafts 3 and 4. Each row of inlay floats over five warps before coming to the next tie-down warp. This gives the inlay a much more pronounced presence on the surface of the weaving. The inlay is visible only on the front of the weaving; the ground weave forms a solid cloth behind it.

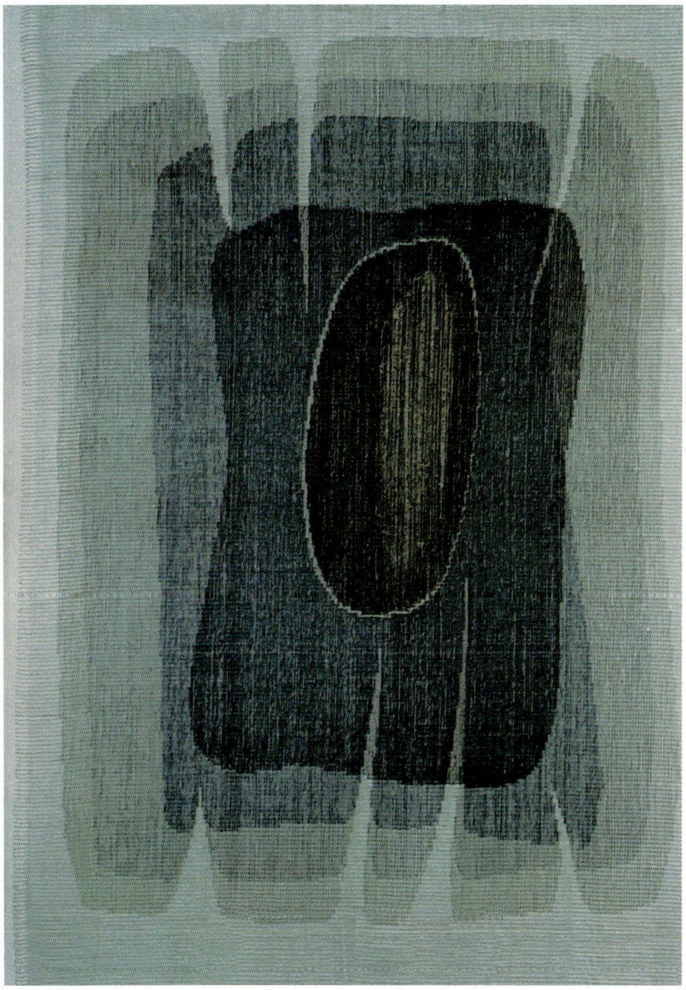

Theo Moorman. *Dark Form on Blue*. Unknown; circa early 1970s? Linen and cotton: 30 × 38 inches. Courtesy of Schiffer Publishing.

Moorman did not intend that her weaving would be transparent. The dense sett she employed was intended to produce solid cloth. Moorman relates in her book how she was pleasantly surprised when she saw the backside of one of her commissions hanging mid-room "that the inlay showed plainly through the nonopaque cloth as a monochrome design."[9]

Even though the weaving itself was not transparent, Theo Moorman was an expert at creating an illusion of transparency in her designs. She did this by overlapping pattern areas, varying the color and thickness of the various pattern wefts, so that the lighter areas look see-through compared to the darker areas. These same effects can be created in transparency weaving and are explored in chapter 7.

Lenore Tawney

At the same time, across the pond, American fiber art pioneer Lenore Tawney began to weave what she termed "open warp" wall hangings.[10] Tawney's work from this period was a definitive break with traditional, structure-driven weaving. Her contribution to transparency weaving was to open a path to a free-form style of weaving that allowed the yarn to trace its own path to create shapes within the design.

In 1954, Tawney spent seven weeks studying at Penland School of Crafts under the tutelage of a Finnish tapestry weaver, Martta Taipale.[11] Although Taipale's tapestries were not transparent, she was a major figure in the Finnish weaving world at mid-century, when the weaving of *kuultokudos* was gaining popularity. Tawney began weaving open-warp tapestries the year after her studies with Taipale, from whom she had seen "the potential of woven cloth to be a filter of light."[12]

Birds and Flower, woven in 1955, was one of her first pieces in this style. In this piece, we can see Tawney experimenting with various degrees of transparency. Assorted colors of ground weft create an almost patchwork appearance. The birds are woven with inlay, but the flower is formed by the opposite effect, omitting even the ground weft to leave an area of unwoven warp.

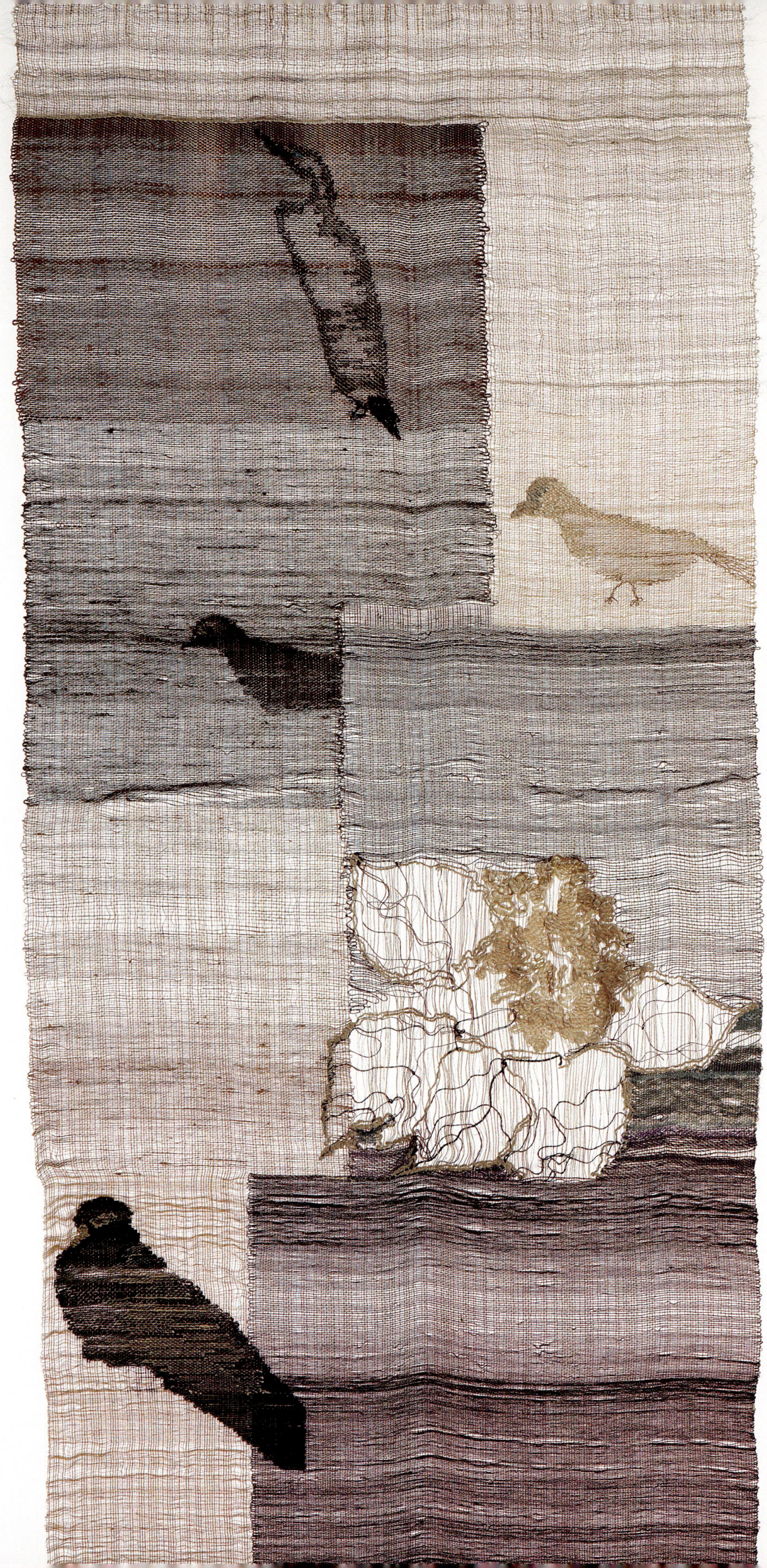

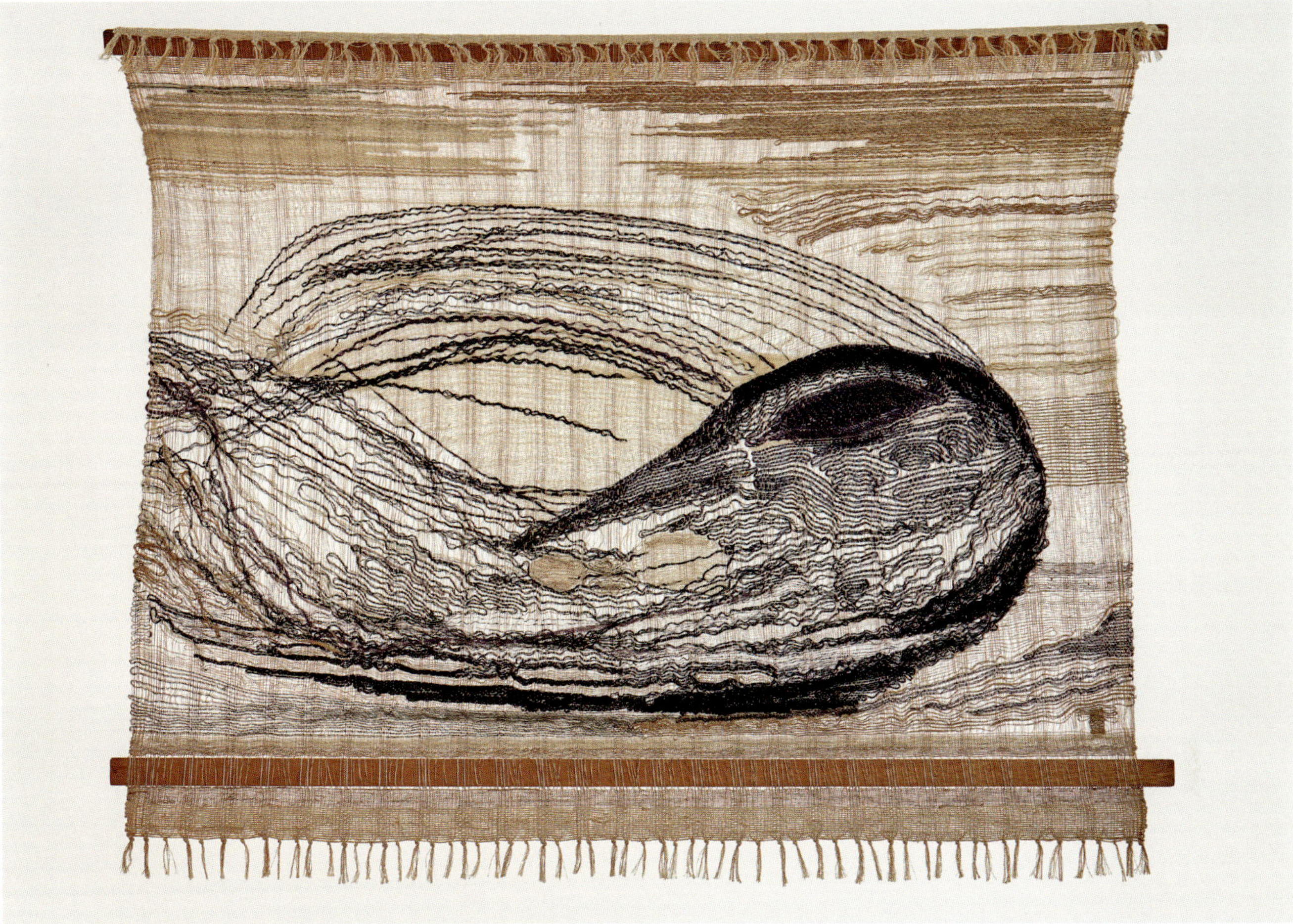

Lenore Tawney. *Lost and Proud*, 1957. Linen, silk, and wool: 51½ × 43 inches. Collection of the Lenore G. Tawney Foundation, New York. Photo: Rich Maciejewski, 2018, courtesy of John Michael Kohler Arts Center.

A more free-flowing style soon emerged in *Lost and Proud*, woven in 1957. In this piece, the weft travels at eccentric angles to the warp, and there is only a sporadic use of ground weft. The free-flowing spirit of Tawney's weaving and the abandonment of the traditional role of ground weft are the hallmarks of Tawney's open-warp style.

INTERPRETING TRANSPARENCY TODAY

Where does transparency weaving stand today? Its Finnish heyday of the 1960s and 1970s and the innovative ideas of the mid-twentieth-century fiber revolution are well in the past. What are the lasting influences that might still be found among contemporary weavers? We can look to the following artists' work to help us connect the threads between the old and the new, suggesting ways that transparency weaving might continue into the future.

LEFT: Lenore Tawney. *Birds and Flower*, 1955. Linen and wool: 24 × 57 inches. Collection of the Lenore G. Tawney Foundation, New York. Photo: Rich Maciejewski, 2018, courtesy of John Michael Kohler Arts Center.

Helena Vento (Finland)

The career of Helena Vento provides a bridge between the early years of transparency weaving in Finland and the more contemporary look of transparencies today. Between 1980 and 2016, Vento was an instructor of textile and weaving arts in both vocational and design schools, where she taught transparency weaving among other subjects. Transparency weaving in Finland lost popularity after 1980, and the school where she was teaching took the stance that weaving was old-fashioned, and began to decrease its offerings of weaving classes.

Vento wanted to show that modern textiles can be woven with the loom. In 2004, she undertook working toward a bachelor of fine arts with the aim of finding a new expression and technique for transparent weaving. She envisioned a multilayered effect where figures would appear to float over each other. After a period of experimentation with various weave structures—double weave with objects in pockets, combining plain weave and satin in the inlay, hanging multiple woven pieces together in layers—she finally tried weaving only plain weave, letting the figures weave over each other. In her words:

> This was a revolutionary experiment. Then something cleared in my brain. I went back to the beginning; I wanted to do something modern and simple. I abandoned colors and natural figures. Suddenly the designs came easily one after another, using only plain weave and varying the thickness of yarns.[13]

Encountering Vento's work on the internet provided the spark that led me to explore transparency weaving. Her technique for weaving shapes that float over one another, increasing the density where they intersect, became the basis of my understanding of how to create depth in transparencies.

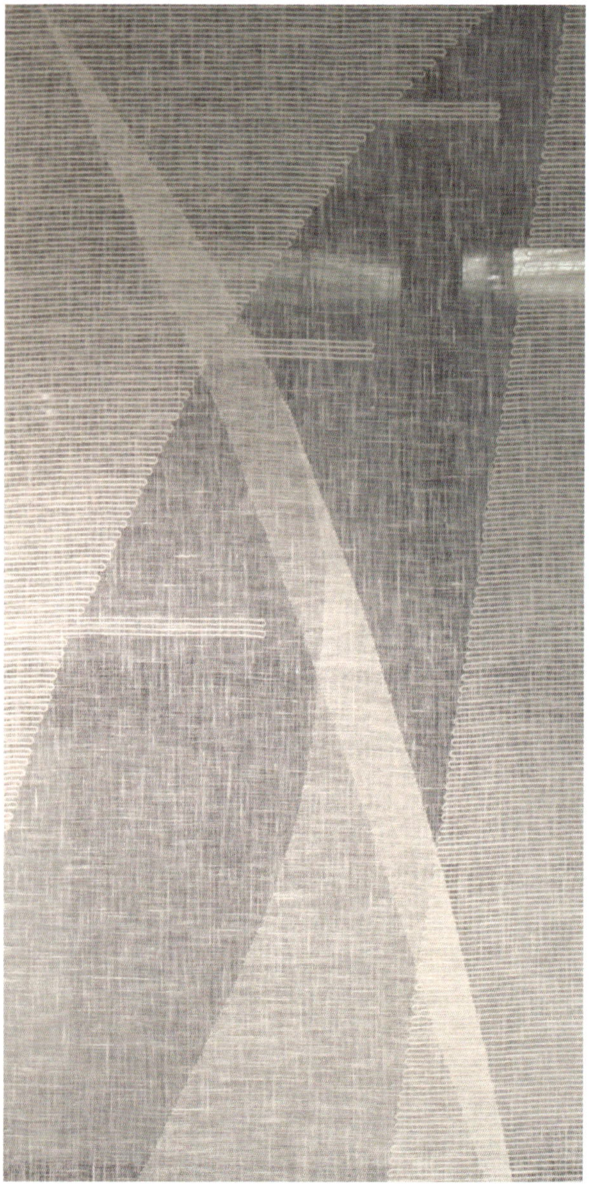

Helena Vento. *Sails*, 2010. Linen: 30 × 85 inches. Courtesy of the artist.

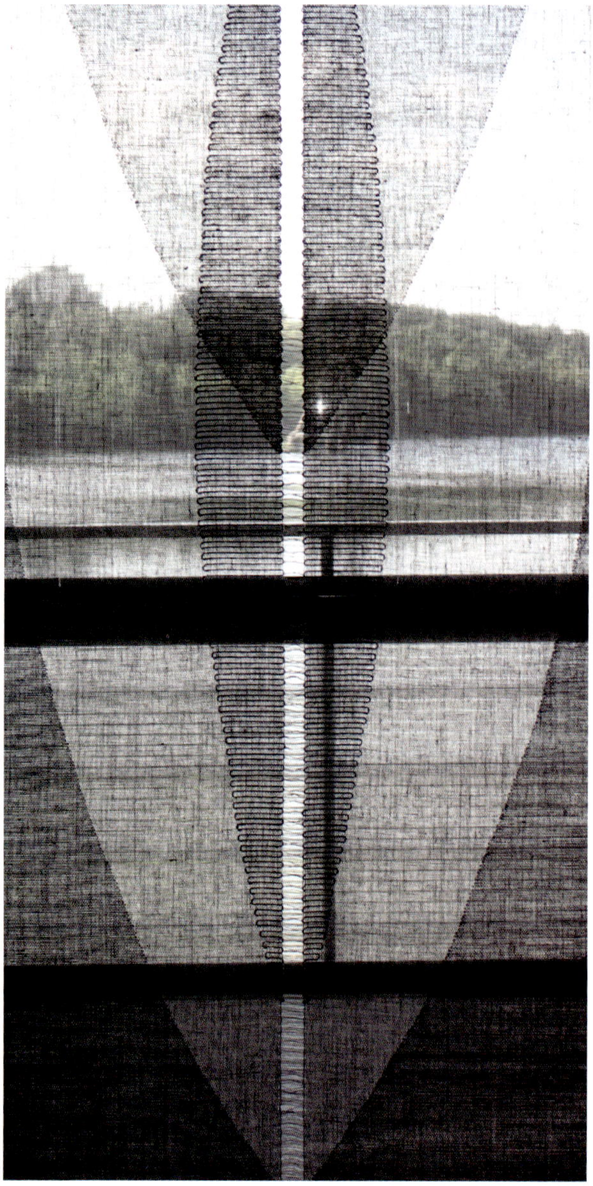

Helena Vento. *Bud*, 2010. Linen: 29 × 90 inches. Courtesy of the artist.

Muriel Beckett (Ireland)

Muriel Beckett's style for weaving transparencies stems from her training in Finland, where she studied at the Federika Westerhoff Craft School in 1974. At the Westerhoff school, various patterns for weft inlay were taught, most notably patterns such as satin weave that accentuated color through weft floats. In Finland, Beckett absorbed the principles of Scandinavian design, their clear lines and minimalist approach. These principles can be seen in her current work, of which she says,

> I focus mainly on color and a limited number of weave structures. I abstract aspects of landscape, taking inspiration from the colors, contours, and textures found in nature, especially around where I live. I often use photography and drawing in the initial development of ideas, or design directly with the yarns themselves, doing wrappings, blending, and mixing strands of linen or wool.[14]

Meticulously planned bundles of weft colors enable Beckett to interpret the landscapes of her coastal home in Ireland. The ground weft is often made up of more than one strand of fine linen, while the supplemental inlay may have up to six strands. Yarns are matched to an enlarged photo of the subject to capture the subtle

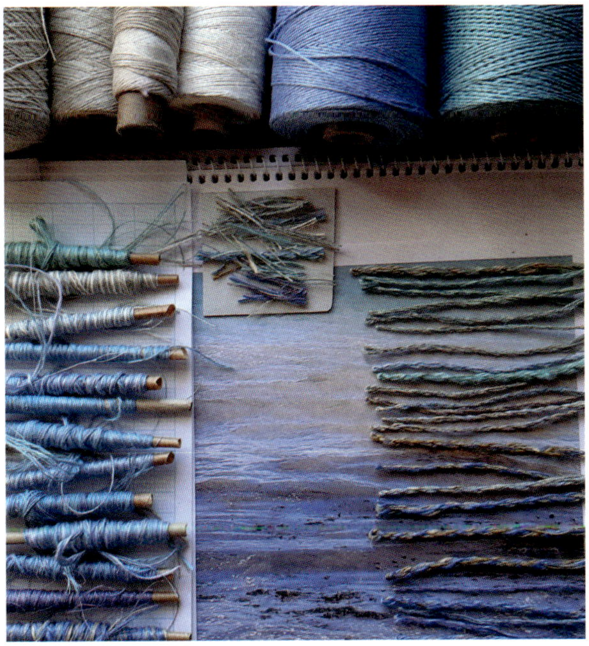

Muriel Beckett, planning for *Shimmer* series. Courtesy of the artist.

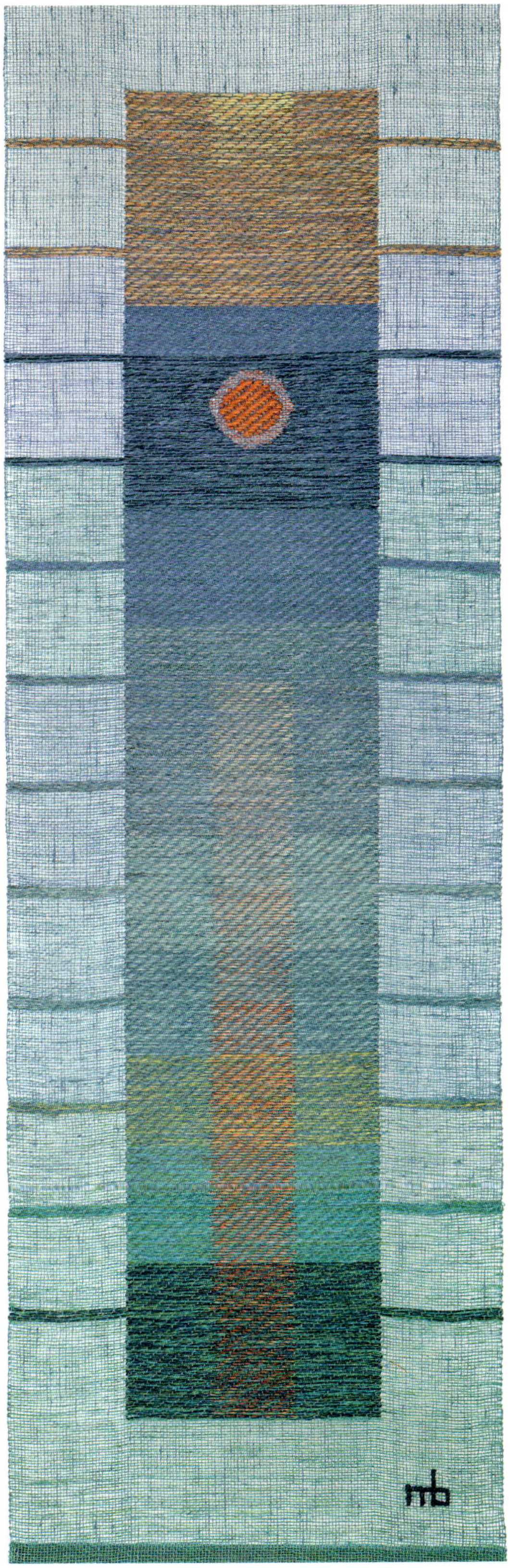

Muriel Beckett. *The sun rises in spite of everything*, 2024. Linen, wool: 19.5 × 59 inches. Photo: Andrew Miller Photography.

nuances of color. The detail image of *The sun rises in spite of everything* allows a glimpse into the color blending used in both the ground and inlay wefts.

Beckett employs both satin and twill weaves for her supplemental inlay. Both structures create floats on the surface of the cloth by weaving the inlay over-three, under-one warp, allowing Beckett to emphasize her subtle color manipulations.

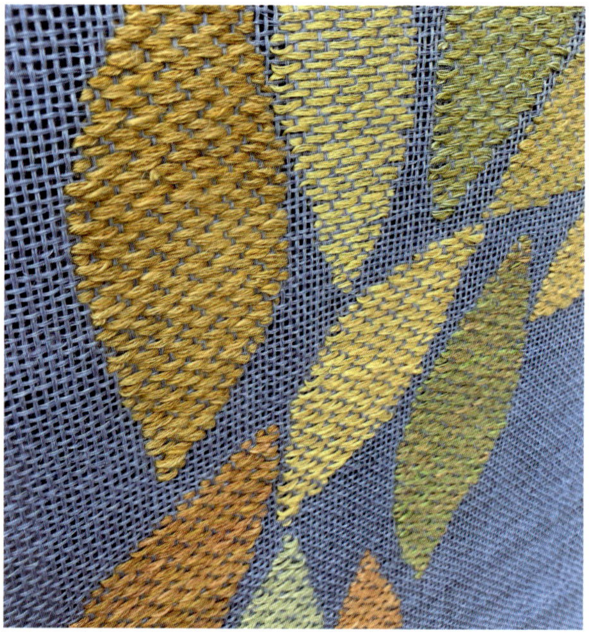

Detail of Muriel Beckett, *Falling leaves*, 2018. Linen, wool: 20 x 47 inches full piece. Courtesy of the artist. Inlay is satin weave.

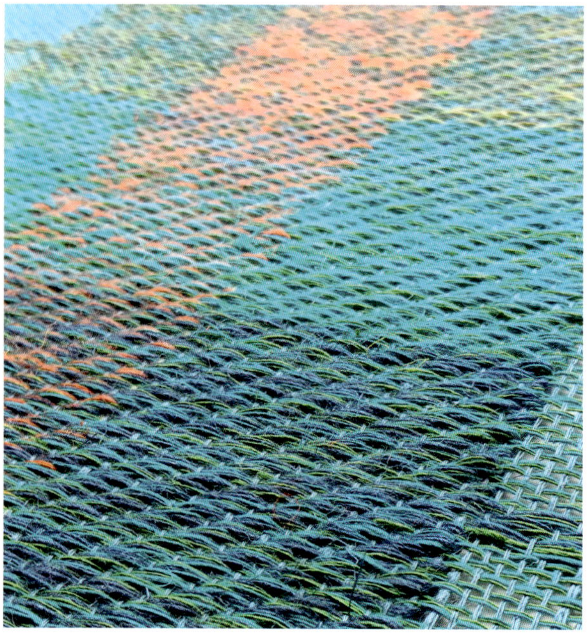

Detail of Muriel Beckett, *The sun rises in spite of everything*. Inlay is twill weave.

Satin weave is used for figurative work as seen in *Falling Leaves*, while twill is used for geometric designs since it is easier to control the edges of the geometric shapes. The warp is widely spaced (3 ends per cm, or roughly 7.5 warps per inch), and the ground weft is beaten for the same number of picks per inch, allowing ample room for the multistrand inlay weft without displacing the rows of ground weft. The result is a sharp contrast between the openness of the ground weave and the denser surface of the inlay.

Boisali Biswas (USA)

Boisali Biswas takes her inspiration from jamdani, a traditional weaving style in her home country of India. Jamdani is woven on a two-shaft loom and is characterized by a ground weave with hand-manipulated inlay. The technique has traditionally been employed to weave saris, using threads so fine that, despite being woven as a solid cloth, they appear to be translucent. The hand-manipulated inlay is woven into the same shed as the ground weave in intricate geometric and floral patterns.

Biswas has adapted the jamdani weaving style to a coarser cloth structure suitable for contemporary woven art. Using a four-shaft loom, Biswas threads her warp in a rosepath threading to allow her to weave the inlay in patterns other than plain weave. Her piece *Asemic Letter to Myself* employs the rosepath pattern to symbolize asemic writing, a type of writing that has no specific semantic meaning. Boisali describes this piece:

As an immigrant fiber artist from India, my work is constantly informed by my existence between the two cultures, woven by the threads of transcending memories, nostalgia, and cultural identity. Most often, I find myself drawn to my roots, exploring the complexity of migration, belonging, and emotions that emerge from those feelings. A lot of times the interpretations remain deeply personal and ambiguous. This piece felt like weaving a page from one of my most intimate journals.[15]

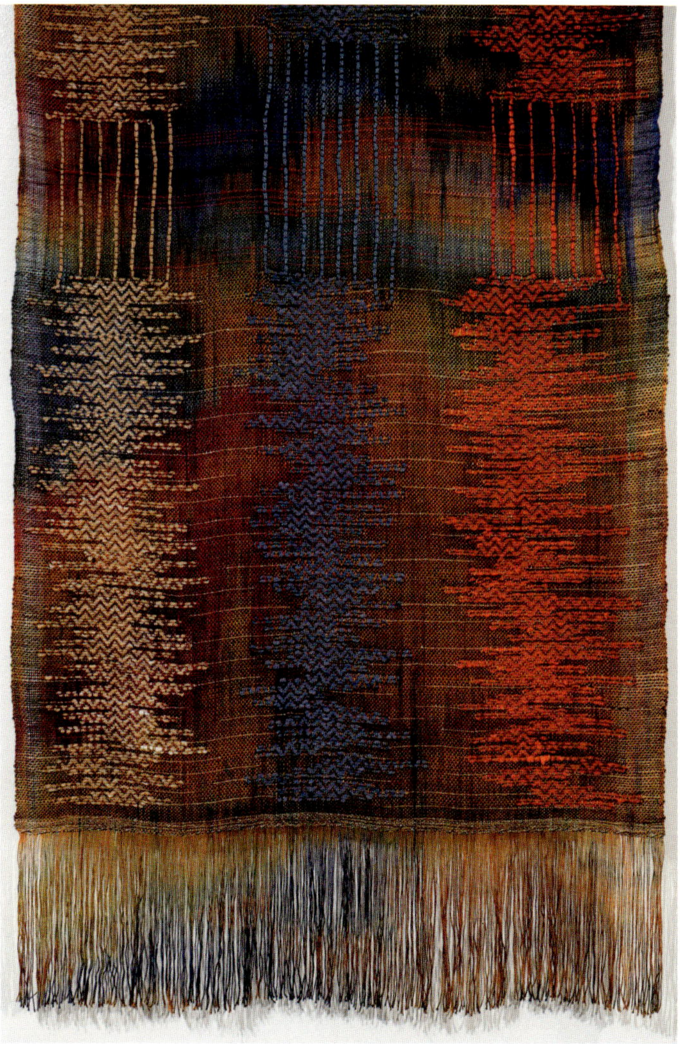

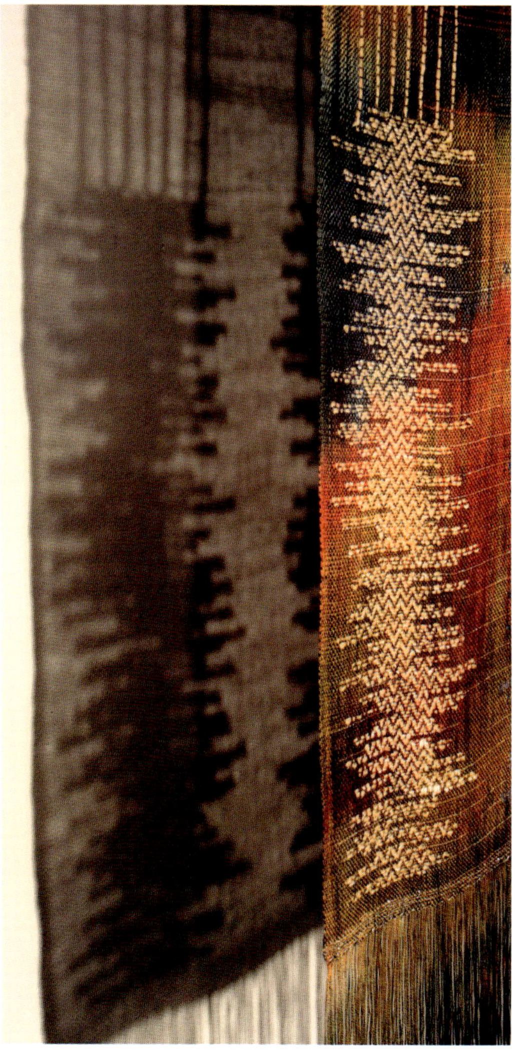

Boisali Biswas. *Asemic Letter to Myself*, 2024. Linen, wool, cotton: 22 × 34 inches. Detail shows shadows cast by transparent weave. Courtesy of the artist.

Biswas often uses layering of multiple pieces that interact with each other. Shadows are important—indeed, crucial—to what she seeks to express. In The Wait, the various pieces create a vignette or story of a time and a place from her memory. The pieces are movable and changeable, so each installation of this piece is unique from what it was before and what it will be in the future. This is perhaps a metaphor for how she feels about her life, which straddles two completely distinct cultures.

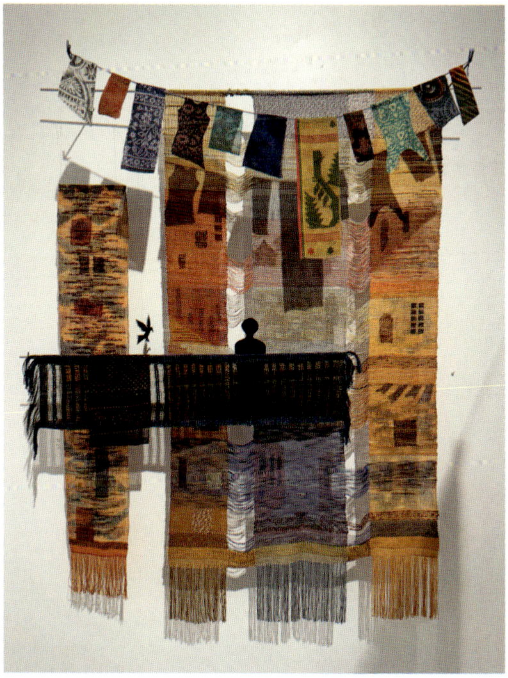

RIGHT: Boisali Biswas. *The Wait*, 2023. Linen, wool, commercial fabrics: 41 × 52 inches. Photo: Buckham Gallery

Kathleen Morris (Canada)

The words "transparency" and "transparent" are not synonymous in the textile world. There are many textiles that share the quality of being see-through without being woven in the "transparency" style. These alternative weaving techniques can be used to complement the sheer look of transparency weaving. The mixing of styles has a contemporary feel to it that makes the work exciting.

Such is the case with Kathleen Morris's weavings that combine lace weaves with freeform weft and the insertion of natural materials as weft. In Morris's large-scale works, natural materials appear to float in space. Different lighting, however, reveals that there are three levels of opacity/transparency in the work. Open lace weaving frames more opaque areas of densely woven ground weft, which themselves frame the completely opaque natural materials (see detail view of *imbibe like roots*).

Morris finds that the slow pace of weaving finger-manipulated lace allows her to take a more thoughtful approach to her work. Working with ancient techniques such as leno makes her feel grounded in tradition, while utilizing natural materials allows her to feel like she is in dialogue with her environment. She is meticulous in documenting the plant materials used in each piece, since they provide a connection, both literal and metaphorical, to her sense of place.

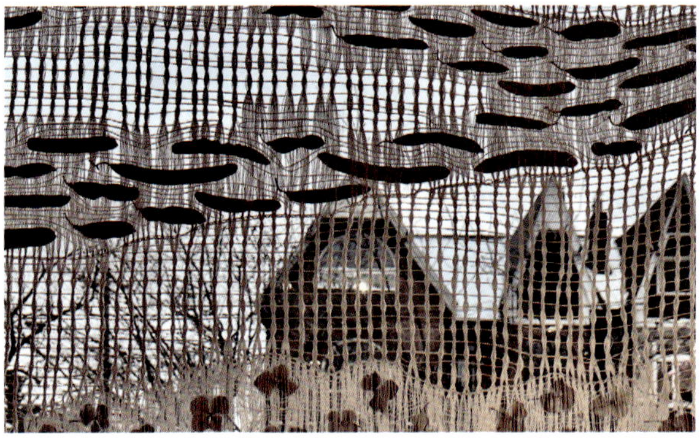

Kathleen Morris. *imbibe like roots*, 2023, detail. Hemp, paper threads, eastern redbud pods, hydrangea blossoms, linden and euonymous leaves: 28 × 60 inches per panel (two panel work). (Morris used this title twice, for a two-panel series in 2023 and for a three-panel series in 2024.) Courtesy of the artist.

Morris's work brings together free-form weaving, leno lace, and the introduction of materials other than yarn, which are three of the innovative ideas that will be explored in chapter 8.

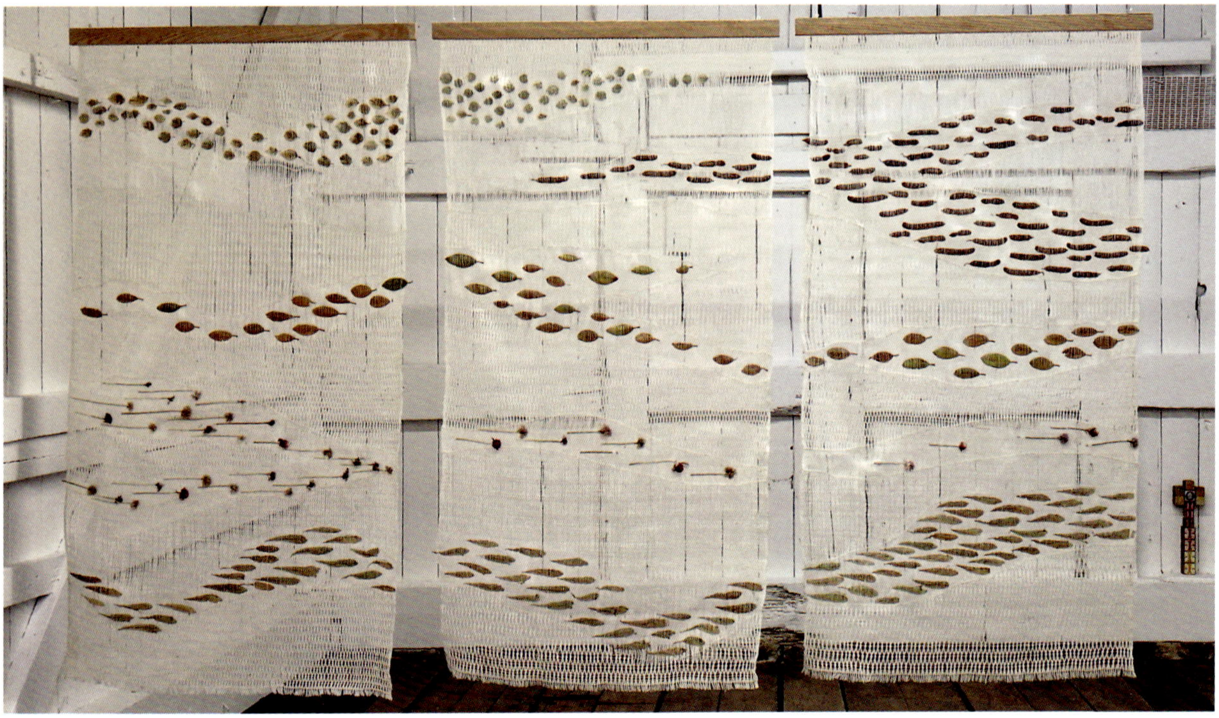

Kathleen Morris. *imbibe like roots*, 2024. Hemp, paper threads, linden, euonymus, eastern redbud, and rhododendron: 31 × 60 inches per panel (three panel work). Photo: Kelsie Conley.

Morgan Clifford (USA)

At the opposite end of the spectrum of transparent weave style from Kathleen Morris is the work of Morgan Clifford. Clifford was initially inspired by pre-Columbian gauze weaving that she saw in an exhibit at the Textile Museum in Washington, DC, in the 1980s. Gauze is a hand-manipulated, openwork weaving technique that today is better known as leno lace.[16] It planted a seed that eventually led her away from the warp-faced ikat rugs she had been weaving and toward an open-weave style. She still uses the term "gauze" for her work even though she has stopped using leno lace in favor of an open-warp plain-weave structure.

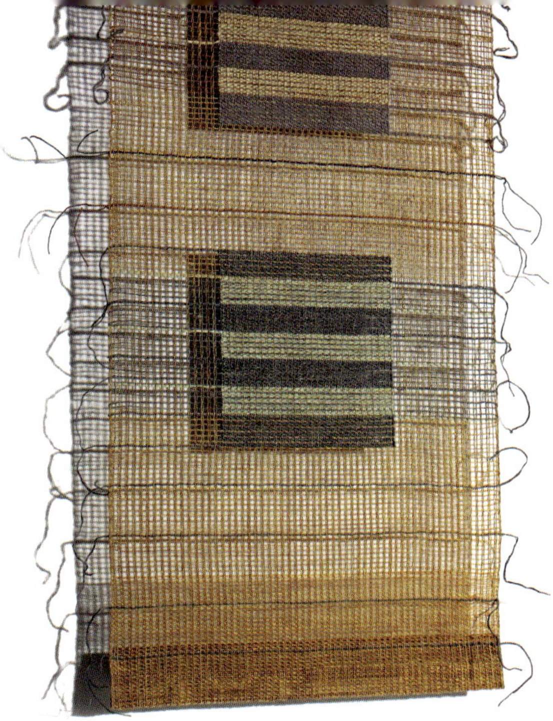

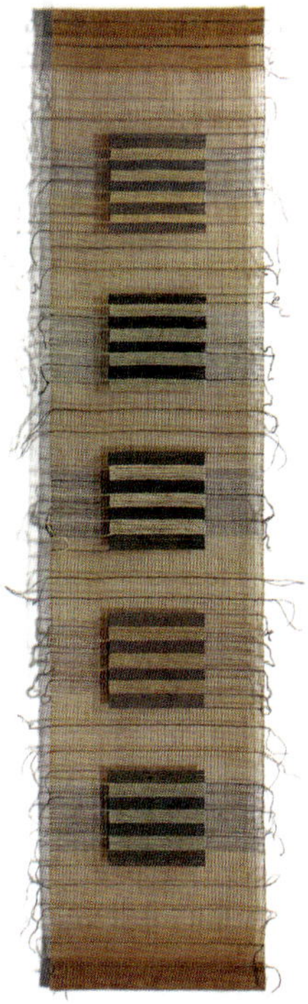

TOP & BOTTOM: Morgan Clifford. Window runner, 2015. Linen, silk: 12 × 54 inches. Photos by the artist.

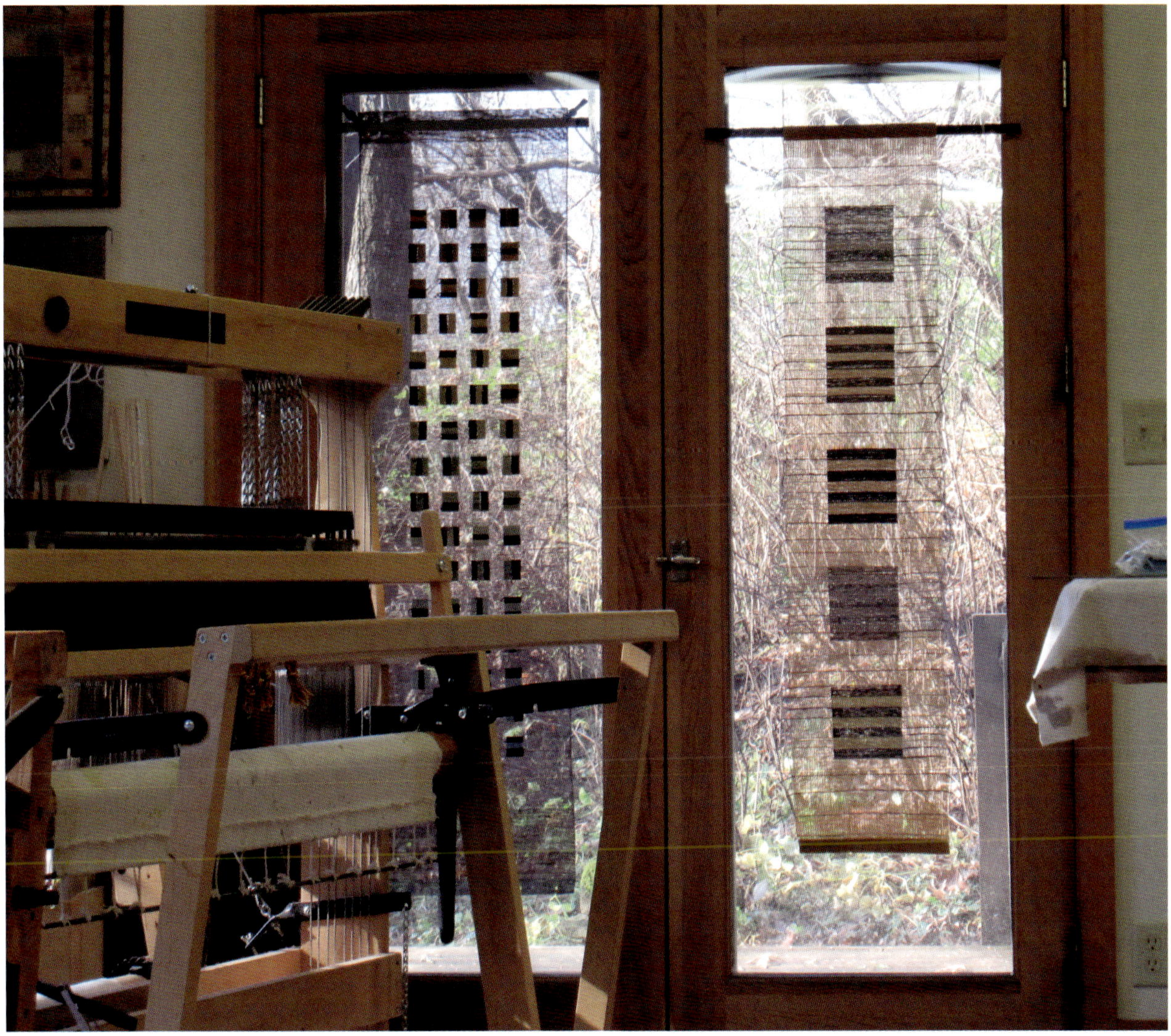

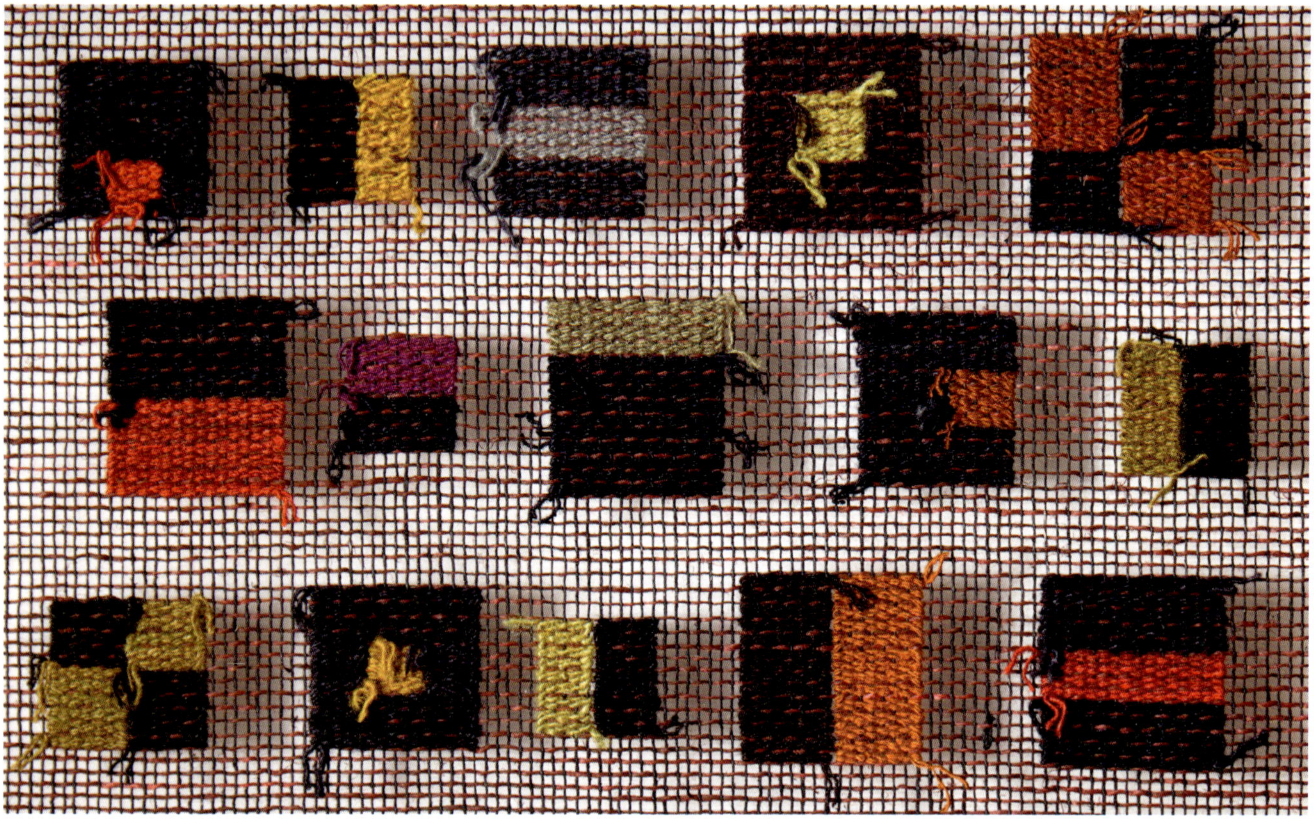

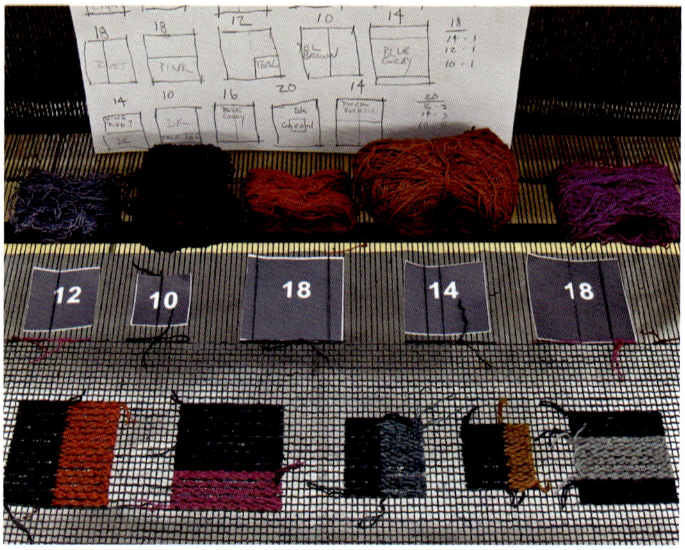

TOP: Morgan Clifford, *30 Little Squares*, detail of completed work.
RIGHT: Work in progress.

Clifford's work is characterized by an exacting geometric inlay woven into a coarsely sett ground weave. The material for the warp and ground weft is 8/1 linen, while the inlay is throwster silk. Throwster silk is a smooth, silky yarn that is spun from curly pieces of silk fiber waste. She sometimes uses synthetic metallic yarn for the inlay. Metallic inlay is especially dramatic for her series of window runners. During the day, the runners sparkle in the sunshine, while at night they catch the artificial light. Clifford states,

> They are the "gauziest" of my pieces. When the sun is strong, they almost disappear and at night they become opaque and colorful. I find that fascinating. It's like getting two different pieces in one.[17]

Acute attention to detail makes these pieces appear straightforward, but they are anything but simple. Clifford plans the overall composition ahead of time and then plays with colors and details on the loom. All the materials are hand dyed, and extremely careful records are kept along with samples of color recipes, setts, media type, and mounting techniques. A detailed look at Clifford's mounting technique is given in chapter 9.

The most surprising element of these carefully planned and executed designs is the little weft tails that are left on the surface. Perhaps these are an inside joke, a little wink that says don't take things too seriously.

Cyndy Barbone (USA)

The meticulous portraits woven by Cyndy Barbone are a unique addition to the field of transparency weaving. Barbone's work is most closely related to that of Helena Vento in her use of a monochrome palette that uses woven density rather than color to achieve their artistic effect. Barbone's approach to transparency weaving evolved through a creative trajectory that began at the California College of the Arts, where she studied with Lia Cook and learned to weave inlay in a double-weave framework. In the 2010s, Barbone was influenced by the increasing water shortages in many parts of the world and made a commitment to weave only with undyed yarn to conserve water.

Barbone's woven portraits were made in series, each series arising out of personal or world events. About this work, Barbone states,

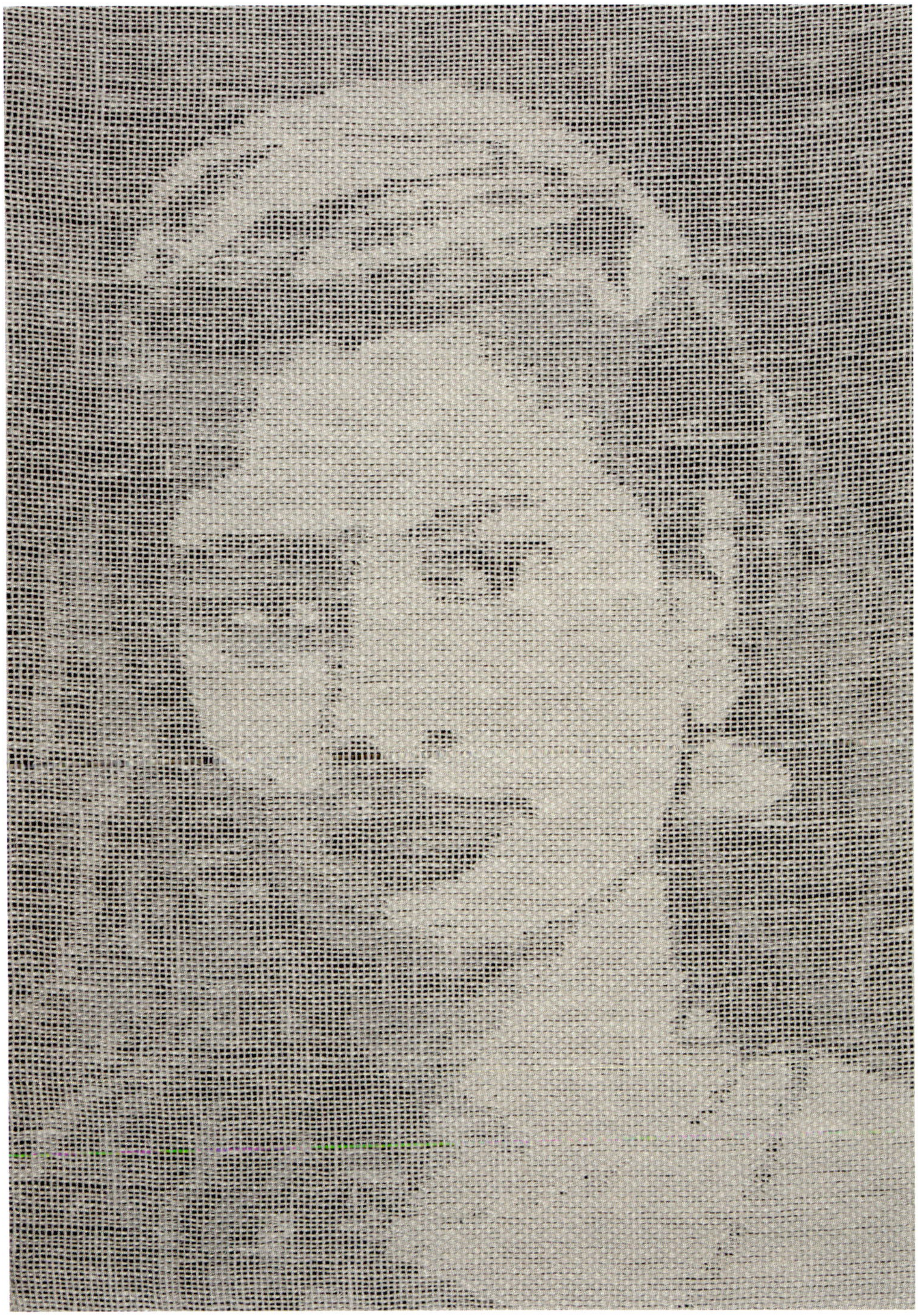

Cyndy Barbone. *Surabi*, 2020. Half-bleached linen; 12 × 17 inches. Photo: Barry Lobdell.

In my most recent series of work, I am weaving portraits of women I know whose stories parallel the broader issues facing women today. Using this ancient craft, largely associated with women's work, I am weaving portraits in a loose, open structure that is fragile, yet strong, as a way of describing a new energy of women's voices rising up around the globe.[18]

Working from black-and-white photos, Barbone reduces the detail to a limited set of densities or values. These values are translated to weaving by using varied sizes of inlay weft. The portraits are woven to be displayed against a dark background to allow the contrasting densities to stand out. A more in-depth study of Barbone's technique is included in the discussion on weaving density and monochromatic design in chapter 7.

The history of transparency weaving over the past one hundred years might be summarized as an awakening to the artistic potential of this weaving form. From its early roots as functional textiles that feature traditional geometric motifs, the technique became a medium for artistic expression that more often featured pictorial and abstract subject matter. Experimental approaches to weaving in an open-warp format, and the introduction of nontraditional materials for weft, have set the stage for further innovation in the weaving of transparent textiles.

What types of transparencies will you weave? By studying this book, you will gain the knowledge needed to weave the full spectrum of transparency styles, from geometric and pictorial to abstract and innovative. Your creations will set the stage for the future of transparency weaving. Enjoy the journey!

Rebecca Smith. *It Comes in Waves Trilogy*, 2024. Linen, mixed fibers: 12 × 60 inches; 19 × 72 inches, 10 × 60 inches.

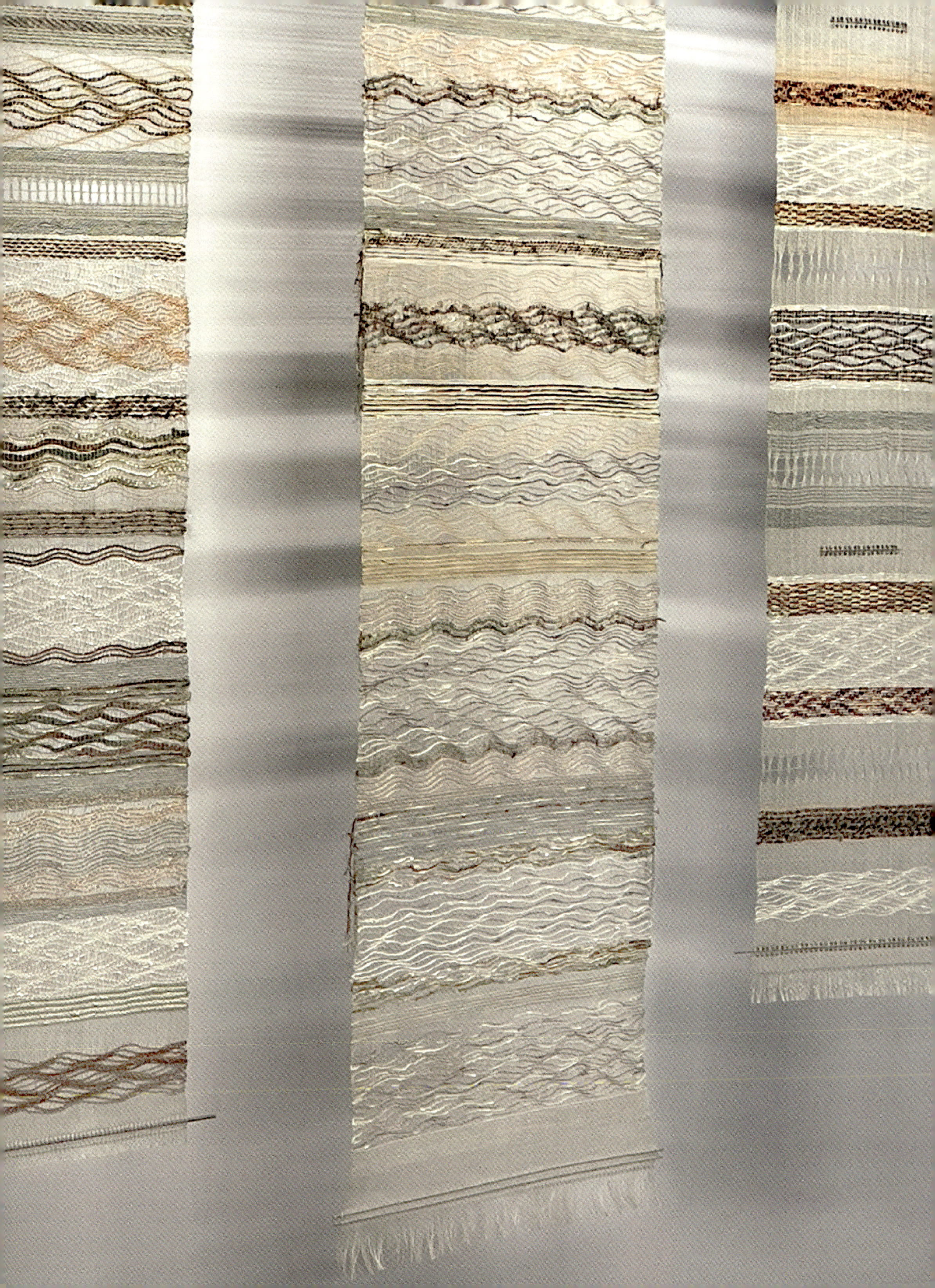

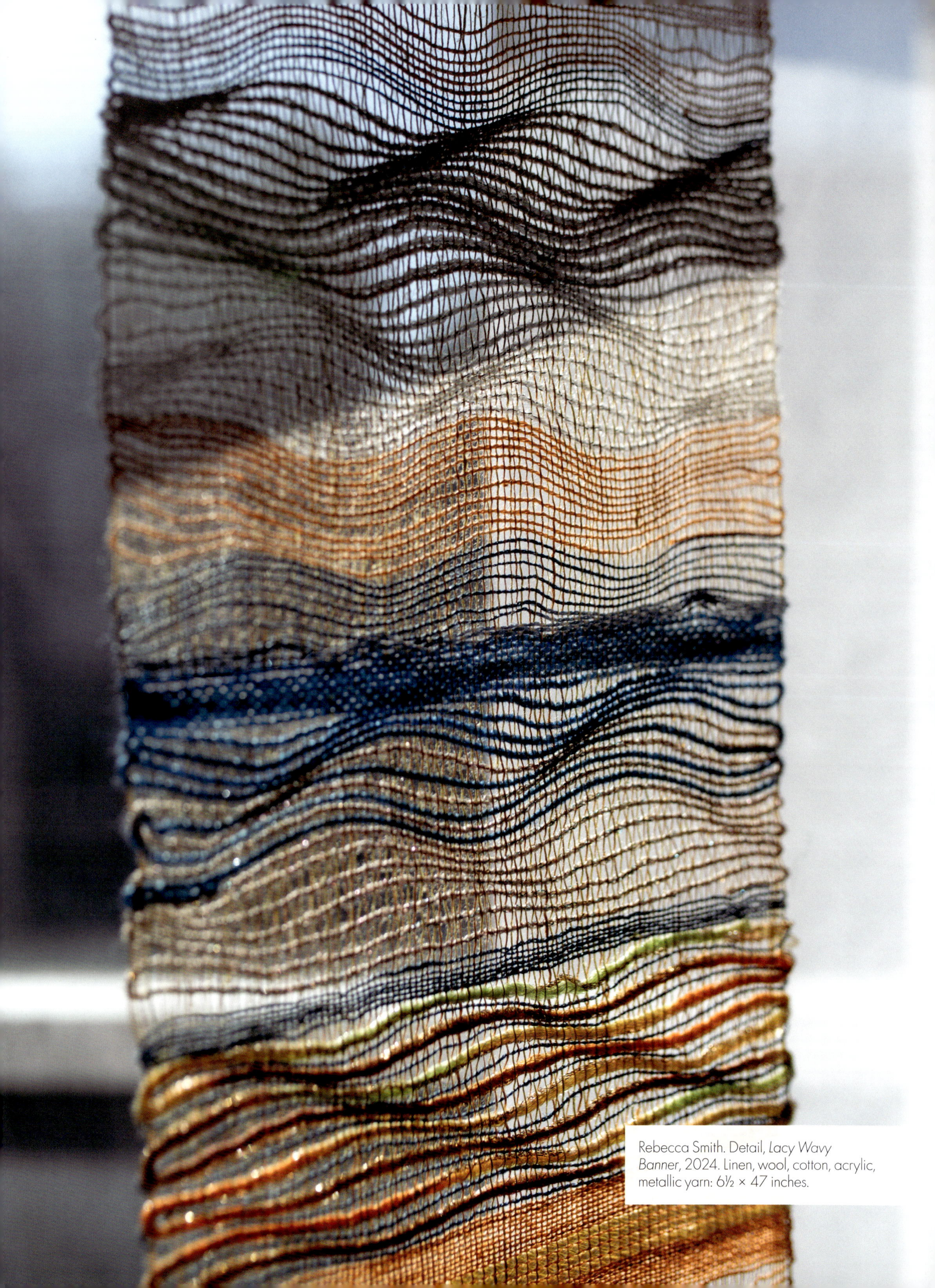

Rebecca Smith. Detail, *Lacy Wavy Banner*, 2024. Linen, wool, cotton, acrylic, metallic yarn: 6½ × 47 inches.

Chapter 2

SETTING UP: LOOMS, TOOLS, AND MATERIALS

LOOMS

Transparency weaving is a simple weave structure that does not require any specialized equipment. The basic structure of transparency weaving relies on a balanced plain weave. Plain weave can be woven on as few as two shafts (harnesses). Additional shafts beyond two open possibilities for including twill weaves and other pattern structures in both the ground weave and inlay. A four-shaft loom will enable you to weave all the techniques presented in this book.

Floor looms and table looms are ideal choices. The two qualities that make these the best choices are as follows:

- They hold warp tension well. Transparencies are woven under high tension. The braking system on the loom must be up to the task of keeping the tension tight.
- They have a reed and beater. The reed assists in maintaining even spacing between the warps, while the beater makes it possible to weave straight, evenly spaced rows of ground weave.

Looms that are less than ideal but still possible choices include tapestry looms and rigid heddle looms. Let's look at why these types of looms are less than ideal, and how they might be adapted to work better for transparency weaving.

Rigid Heddle Looms

Rigid heddle looms are possible to use but can present tension problems when weaving under high tension. Transparencies are usually woven with a linen warp.

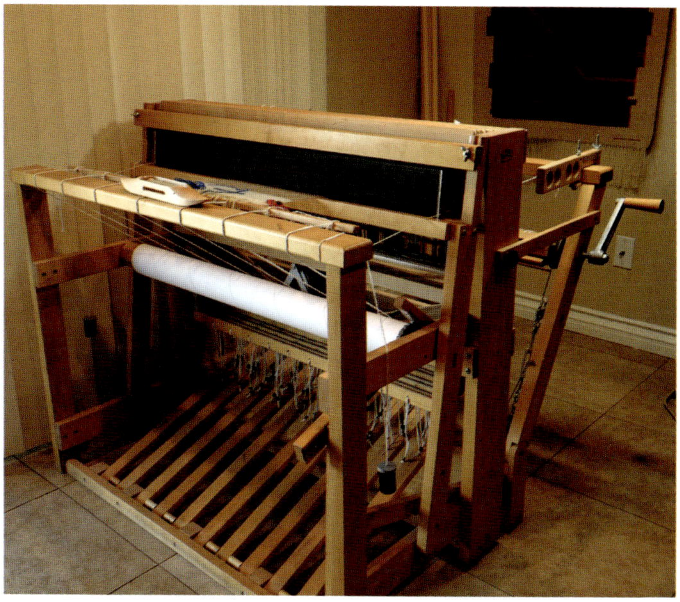

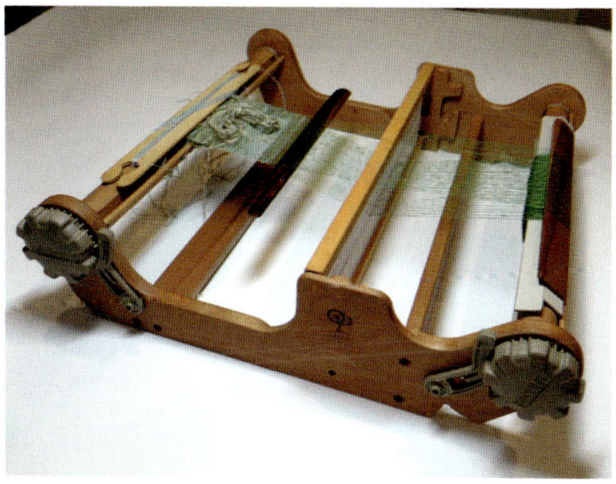

ABOVE: Standard floor loom

LEFT: Rigid heddle loom with adaptations: tensioning stick placed under warp at back, and shed stick used for beater.

Because linen is a nonstretchy fiber, the warps in the slots tend to go slack when the heddle is raised or lowered. Try this adaptation to weave transparencies on a rigid heddle loom:

- With the heddle in the lowered position, place a tensioning stick under the raised warps and move the stick so that it rests on the back beam. Leave this in place throughout the weaving.

- Don't use the heddle for beating the weft into place. Instead, place the heddle in the neutral position and insert a shed stick with a tapered edge to press the weft into place.

While these adjustments make it possible to weave transparencies on a rigid heddle loom, I would advise anyone hoping to weave transparencies on a rigid heddle loom to experiment with this method to see if it works for your loom. The solution may be different for various brands of rigid heddle looms. My research into weaving transparencies on a rigid heddle loom was done using an Ashford rigid heddle loom. Schacht Spindle Co. offers a similar solution for their Flip and Cricket looms.

Tapestry Looms

Tapestry looms equipped with a shedding device operate like a two-shaft loom. Tension issues should not arise if the loom has been warped properly. Because tapestry looms lack a built-in beater, tapestry weavers use a tapestry fork or comb to press the weft into place. Using these tools for transparency weaving, it is difficult to control the spacing between weft rows to achieve a uniform ground weft. Using a wider comb such as a haircomb helps control the placement of the weft. Free-form transparency weaving, presented in chapter 8, might work better since it doesn't require weaving a uniformly spaced ground weft.

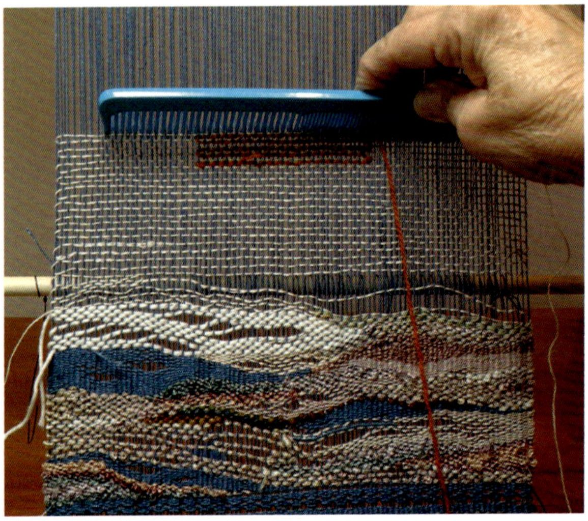

(*Top*) Hair comb helps to control placement of the weft. (*Bottom*) Freeform weaving works well on a tapestry loom.

TOOLS

Only a few tools are required to begin weaving transparencies. Here are some recommended items:

- ***Reed:*** It is important to use the proper reed for your sett. The reed determines the *ends per inch* (epi), a term used by weavers to refer to the density of the warp sett. Uneven denting—for instance alternating one warp end per dent with two warp ends per dent in order to fit twelve warp ends per inch using an eight-dent reed—will hamper your ability to weave geometric and pictorial designs. In addition, since transparencies will not be wet finished, inconsistencies in warp spacing will remain in the finished cloth.

MAKING BUTTERFLIES

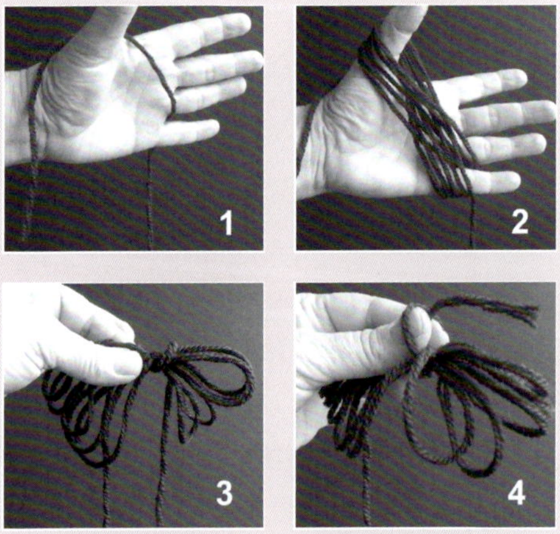

Wrap inlay weft into a butterfly.

To keep your inlay weft more manageable, tie it into neat little bundles called butterflies. These are figure-8s created by wrapping yarn around your fingers.

1. Lay the yarn across the palm of your hand.
2. With the long end, wrap figure-8s across the palm of your hand. Be careful to stack each figure-8 on top of the previous one without overlap.
3. Grab the butterfly at its middle and wrap the last of the yarn around it several times.
4. On the last wrap, pass the yarn over your thumb and index finger to create a loop. Pass the loose end through the loop and pull snug.

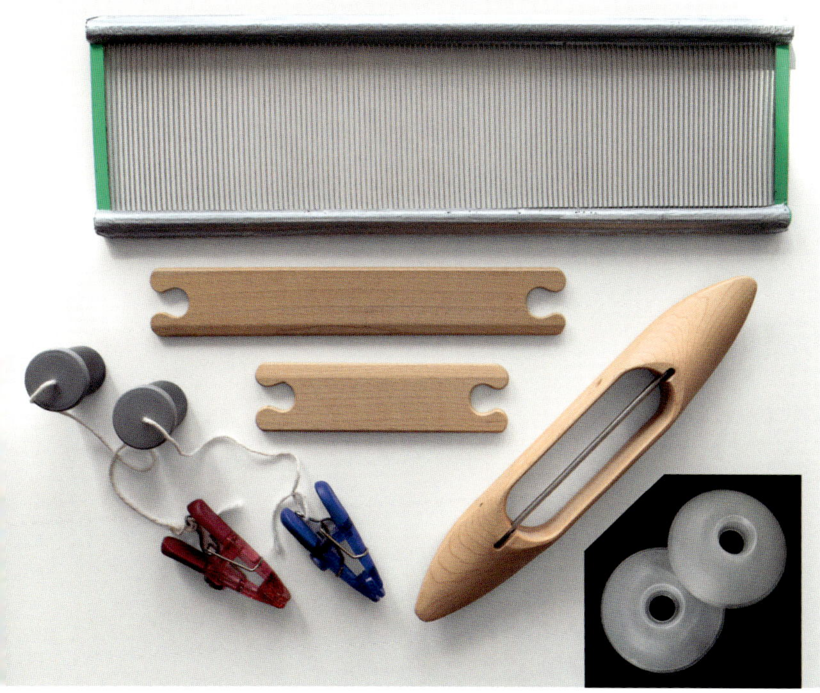

Tools (*clockwise from left*): reed, stick shuttles, boat shuttle, weights with chip clips; inset shows kumihimo bobbins.

- ***Boat shuttle and bobbin:*** The ground weft weaves from selvedge to selvedge, so it is best to use a boat shuttle for this weft.
- ***Stick shuttle or bobbins:*** The inlay weft covers only portions of the weaving area. Inlay wefts are best managed by using short stick shuttles or small bobbins such as round plastic kumihimo bobbins or tapestry bobbins. Alternatively, you can wrap your inlay weft into a butterfly.
- ***Temple/weights:*** Some weavers use a temple to maintain width during the weaving. But a temple can leave unsightly holes and gaps in the delicate edges of a transparency. Instead, use weights hung from a chip clip that is clipped to the weaving's outer edges. I use film canisters or pill bottles filled with quarters. Each weighs about 3 ounces.

  To use weights, tie a taut string at each side of the loom from the front beam to the back beam. Connect each weight to a chip clip with a long string. Attach the clips to the outer edges of the weaving and drape the weight over the string that you tied at each side of the loom (*see* floor loom on page 33).

MATERIALS

Warp Yarn

Linen is the most common choice for the warp in transparency weaving. Linen's beneficial qualities include the following:

- Linen is strong, which helps minimize warp breakage during weaving.
- Linen is a bit coarse compared to other fibers such as cotton. The yarn's roughness helps prevent the weft from moving about in the open-weave structure, both during weaving and after the piece is taken off the loom.
- Linen is a bit stiff, making it easier to leave spaces between rows of ground weft.

Line linen is preferable to tow linen, although both are usable. Line linen is spun from longer fibers and is smoother and more lustrous than tow linen. Tow linen is spun from short fibers and has many more slubs that are visible in the transparency fabric.

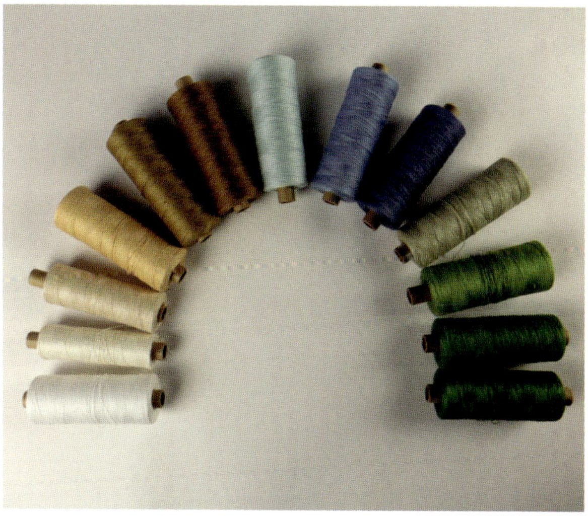

These are just a few of the many colors of line linen that are available (*see* "Resources," page 154).

Linen sizes 16/1 and 16/2 are most commonly used in traditional transparency weaving. Size 16/1 is woven at a denser sett (15–16 epi) than 16/2 (12 epi). For both sizes, the sett is more open than it would be for weaving regular cloth. This open sett allows for spaces between the warps. Coupled with a very light

Recommended linen sizes *from finest at top to heaviest at bottom.*

Yarn size	Yards per pound	Plain weave sett	Transparency sett
16/1 line linen	4800	24epi	15–16 epi
16/2 line linen	2400	20 epi	12 epi
10/2 line linen	1500	15 epi	8 epi
4/1 tow linen	1448	15 epi	8 epi

beat to create a balanced weave, the ground weave will have gaps both between the rows of ground weft and between the warps. These gaps will either get filled by inlay weft or be left open to create the transparency effect.

Heavier linen warp is suitable for some situations. Geometric designs work well at wider setts, especially when coupled with an unbalanced inlay pattern, where the longer floats of inlay will help cover the heavier warp. The wider sett for 10/2 line linen and 4/1 tow linen make these unsuitable for designs with lots of detail such as pictorial designs.

QUICK TESTS FOR WEFT YARN THICKNESS

One quick method to test the suitability for weft yarn at a given sett is to wrap the warp yarn around a ruler, spacing it to match your chosen epi. Place a strand of weft yarn between two warps and look at how it fits. In this example, the orange weft fits nicely between the warps; the brown weft is thinner and leaves gaps where the blue ruler can be seen.

A second method is to hold a strand of weft yarn between two warps on a warped loom. Visually check how much space is left between the weft and the warps.

From both tests you will see that some yarns are thinner than the space they are meant to fill (A). Yarns that are too fine to fill the space between rows of ground weft can be used in bundles of two or more strands.

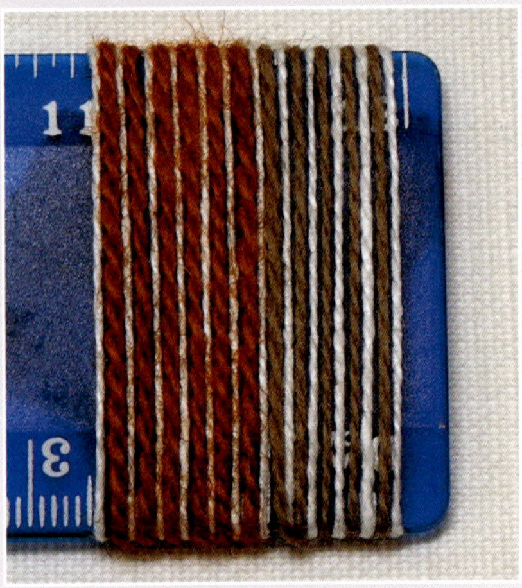

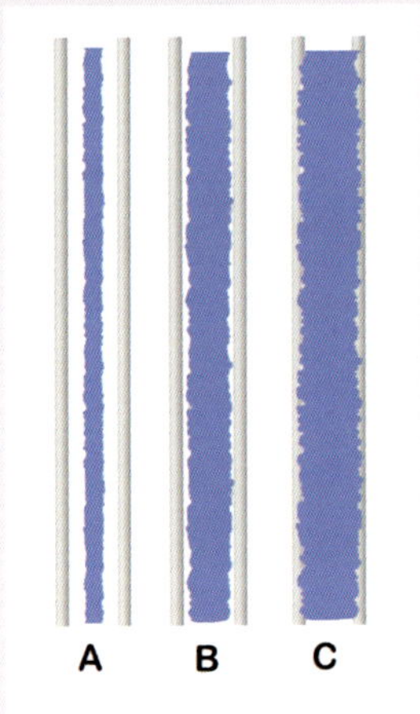

Thicker yarn weights overlap the warp threads (C). Thick inlay weft may force the rows of ground weft to become distorted. Using thick inlay weft over a large pattern area could cause uneven tension and buckling when the weaving is removed from the loom.

Ground Weft

Linen is typically also used for the ground weft. For a true balanced weave, the ground weft should be the same size of linen as the warp. Differences in the color and size of the ground weft open possibilities for design variations.

Inlay Weft

Almost any type of fiber can be used for inlay weft. Wool is always a good choice: It will "bloom" to fill the spaces between the ground weft, especially when the piece is finished with heat and moisture. Cotton, linen, and Tencel will not bloom, so what you *see* is what you get as far as how well it fills the space. But each of these will lend a subtle but beautiful sheen to pattern areas. Novelty yarns with nubs or metallic threads can add unusual effects.

The thickness of the yarn will determine how much light is blocked by the inlay weft. For simple plain-weave inlay, the ideal yarn is one that will fit perfectly in the space made by the loosely beaten ground weft. It meets two crucial criteria:

- It blocks all the light.
- It matches the picks per inch of the ground weft without pushing the ground weft out of its horizontal rows.

Inlay yarns that just fill the space between rows of ground weft are perfect to use for simple plain-weave inlay. But there are many reasons to keep a variety of yarn weights on hand. In the coming chapters, you will learn ways to take advantage of wefts of varying thickness.

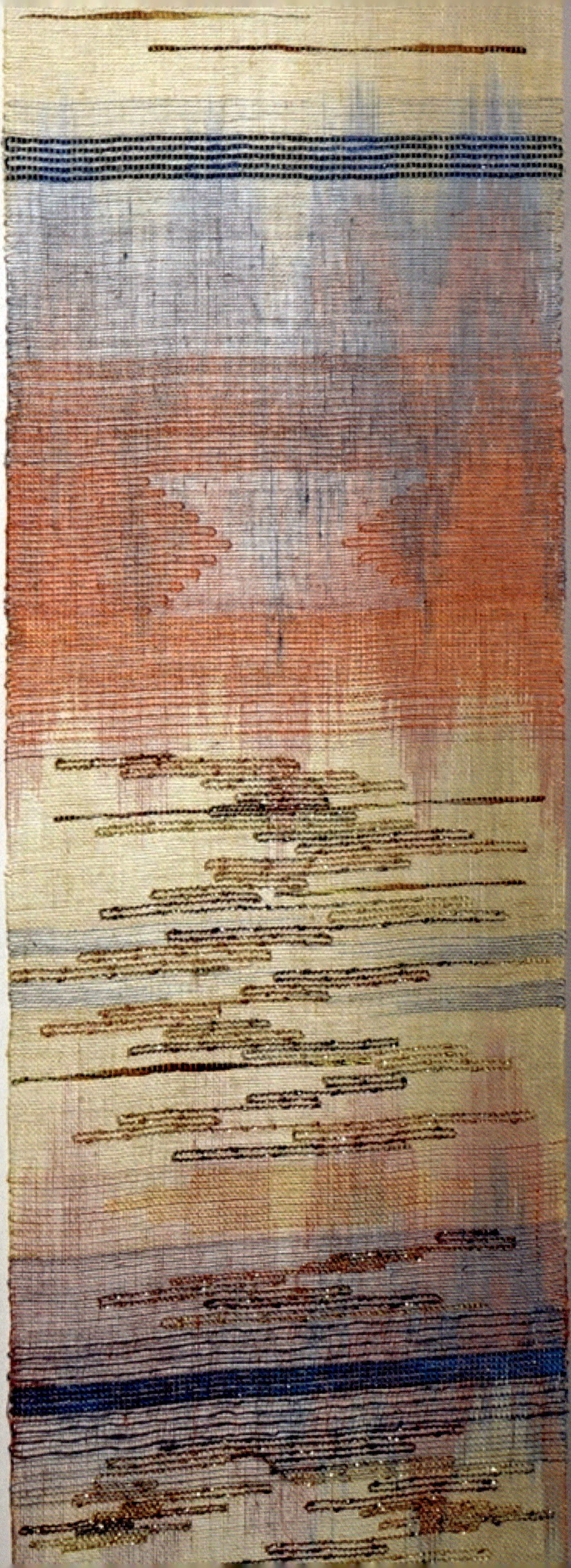

Rebecca Smith. *Amber Waves*, 2024. Linen, cotton, wool, metallic: 12 × 48 inches.

Chapter 3

WARPING AND WEAVING: TIPS FOR SUCCESS

WARPING A FOUR-SHAFT LOOM

Warping a loom to weave transparencies is easy and straightforward. My preferred method is to warp front to back. This approach serves me well for controlling the tension as I wind the warp onto the beam. It is also a useful method when warping for certain effects, such as offsetting warps for the faux ikat method described in chapter 8.

There are multiple resources available to guide you through warping from front to back. As I experimented, I took many pointers from Daryl Lancaster's digital monograph (*see* the bibliography) and added a few adjustments that work for me. Keep in mind while you are warping the loom that transparencies benefit from tight, even tension, and lack of draw-in. Expect the weaving width to be about ½ inch narrower than the width in the reed.

Choose a Weaving Draft to Match Your Loom

In traditional transparency weaving, a straight draw of 1-2-3-4 is most common. The treadle tie-up for floor looms will depend on the number of treadles available on your loom. The six-treadle tie-up shown is suitable for plain weave as well as other balanced weave patterns that will be introduced in chapter 7. Looms with only four treadles will use a direct tie-up. Table looms generally rely on direct tie-up connecting the levers to their respective shafts.

The weaving draft shows treadling only for the inlay weft. Ground weft is woven in plain weave between each row of inlay.

Winding the Warp

Winding a warp for transparency weaving is no different than winding warps for other types of projects. It isn't necessary to use a floating selvedge, since the ground weft is woven in plain weave.

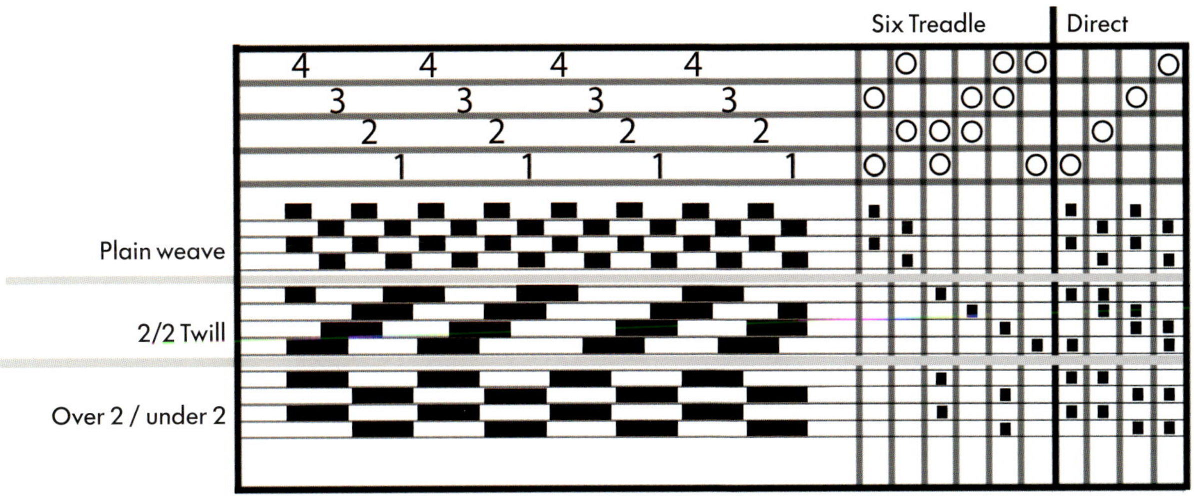

An odd number of warp ends is an advantage for a couple of reasons:

- A geometric design can be centered on an uneven number of warps.
- Both selvedges are up or down at the same time, giving a neater look to the edges.

It will be easier to maintain even tension if you wind several smaller warps instead of one big warp. Consider adding a few extra warp ends to compensate for an anticipated draw-in of ½ inch.

Before removing the warp bundle from the warping board or reel, tie a very tight choke around the warp: Measure the distance on your loom between the front beam and the back beam and tie the choke at this distance from the beginning of the warp. Don't forget to insert ties into the cross!

Sleying and Threading

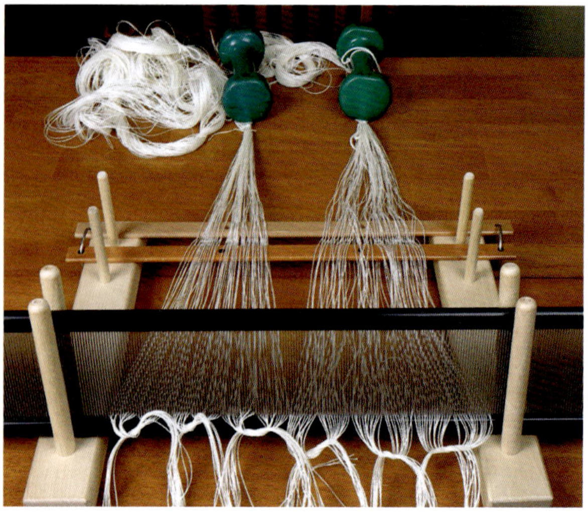

I find it easiest to remove the reed from the loom and prop it on a table. Place lease sticks into the crosses so that you can spread the warp ends a little. With the warp lying behind the reed, thread the warp ends through the dents. Once threaded, replace the reed in the beater with the cut ends of the warp facing the back of the loom.

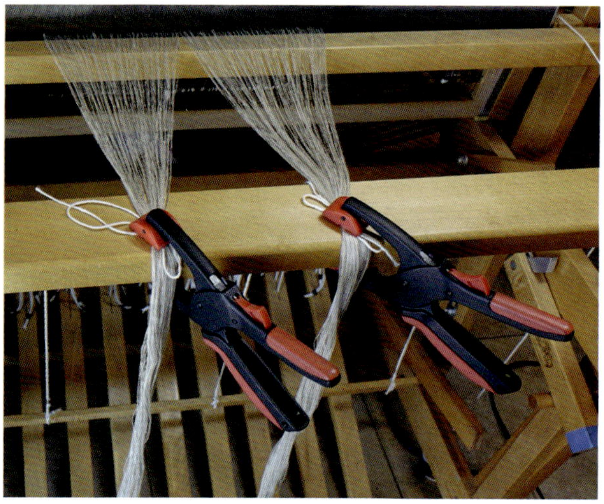

Clamps help maintain tension on the warps while threading.

Use large clamps to secure the warp segments to the front beam at the choke tie. The clamps will remain in place until after the warp is tied to the back apron rod (bar). Proceed with threading the heddles.

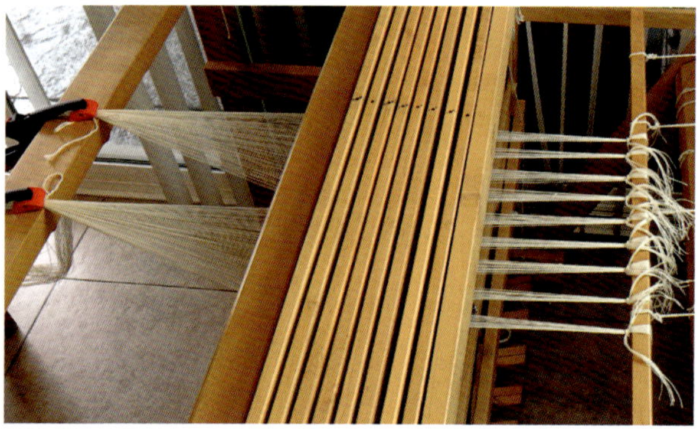

Tie the warp ends in 1-inch bundles to the back apron rod. With the clamps still in place, there should be just enough slack in the warp to reach the back apron rod and tie the knots. If there is too little warp to reach this distance, or too much, carefully adjust the position of the chokes at the front beam by sliding them forward or back, then reposition the clamps.

Beaming the Warp

Be sure to maintain consistent tension on all the warp ends while beaming the warp. One method is to insert wooden dowels into the warp sheds just in front of the back beam. The dowels work as a tensioner as the warp moves over and under them during beaming.

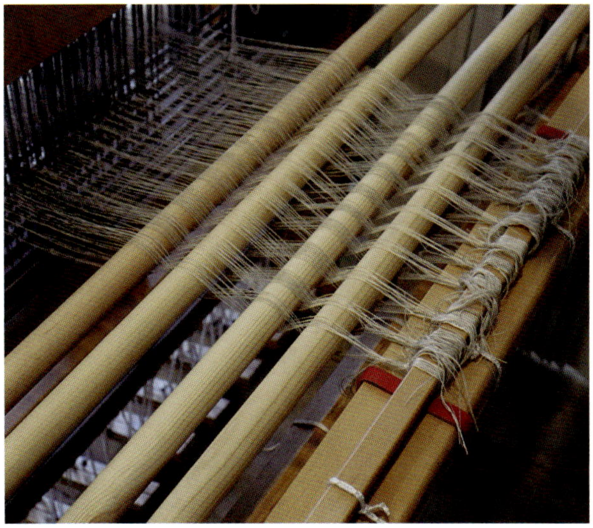

Dowels help keep the warp under even tension while winding onto the beam.

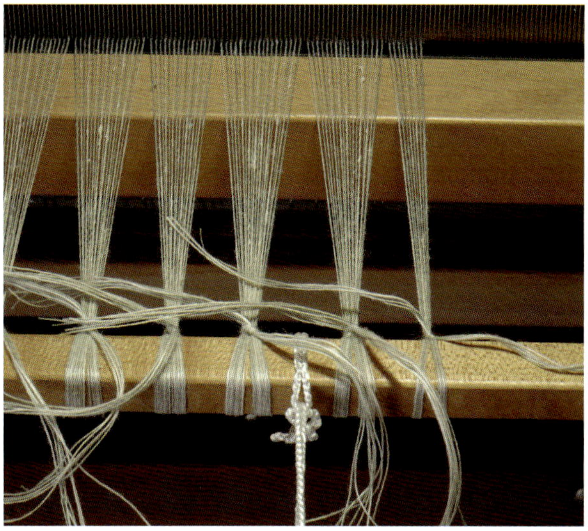

Use a small bundle at the edges when tying on to the front apron.

Wind the warp onto the beam, using the crank-and-yank technique: After each turn of the warp beam, go to the front of the loom and sharply pull bundles of warp to tighten the warp and remove any inconsistencies.

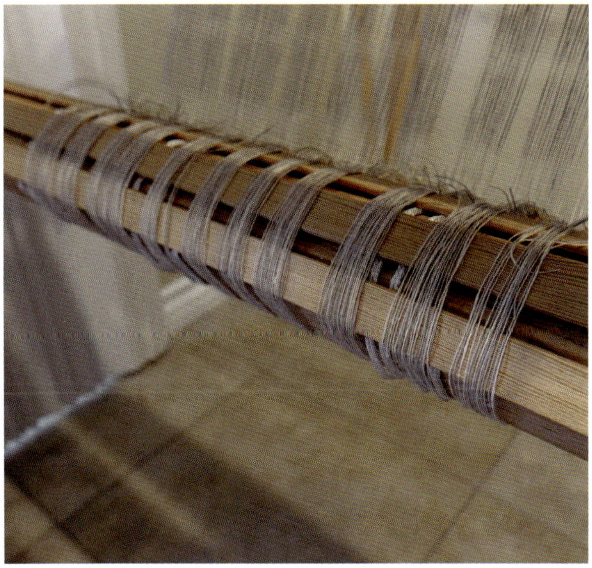

Warp sticks in place

As soon as the warp begins to wind around the beam, insert warp sticks between the beam and the warp to create an even surface. Continue inserting warp sticks as you wind to prevent the layers of fine warp from slipping down between previous layers.

USING DOWELS FOR WARP TENSION

A device called "angel wings" will hold the dowels in place while tensioning the warp (see "Resources," page 154). The same thing can be achieved by tying a double cord from the front to the back of the loom. Twist the cords to secure the dowels, as shown. Starting at the back of the loom, place one dowel at a time into alternating sheds. After inserting each dowel, straighten the warps to remove any twists.

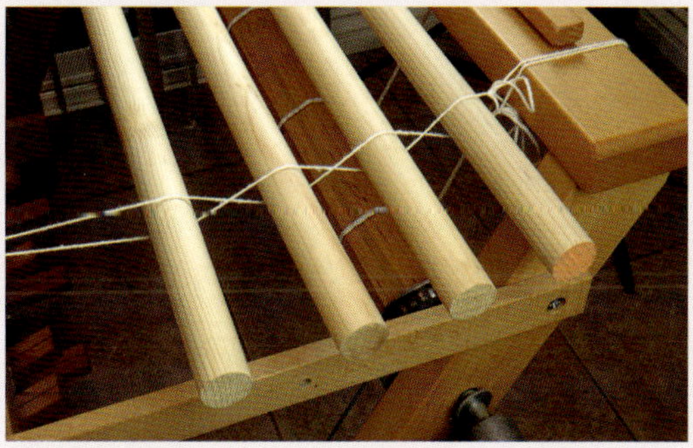

Tying to the Front Beam

Draw-in can be the weaver's bane. Many weavers create draw-in right from the get-go in their warping technique by using wide bouts when attaching the warp to the front apron rod. Ideally, the warp ends should be tied or lashed to the apron rod directly in front of their placement in the reed. Using a small bundle (no more than a half-inch worth of warps) at each edge should help maintain a straight line from the reed using either lashing or direct tie-on.

TERMINOLOGY

Shots, picks, passes, and rows: What are they, and how do they differ? Weaving terminology can be confusing. Sometimes several words are used to mean the same thing. Such is the case with shot and pick. Both refer to the weft traveling through the warp one time, either left to right or right to left. A substitute term for this is row.

Passes are different: A pass is two picks. To weave a pass, the weft travels through the warp in one direction (a pick), the shed is changed, and the weft travels through the warp in the other direction.

TRANSPARENCY-WEAVING BASICS

Spreading the Warps

Your first few picks of weft serve two functions: They spread the warps evenly, and they establish the weaving width. It is crucial to avoid causing draw-in when weaving these first picks.

- Using a yarn the same size or slightly larger than your ground weft, throw one pick, make a hill in the middle, and change the shed without beating.
- Throw a second pick, then make a hill on top of the first hill. Close the shed and gently pull the beater toward you. Do this two or three times until the gaps between the warp bundles have closed.

Some weavers weave three picks between each beat. The stiffness of the linen yarn can make it hard to beat three picks at once, but two seem to get the job done. After three repeats of two picks each (six picks total), the warp should be evenly spread.

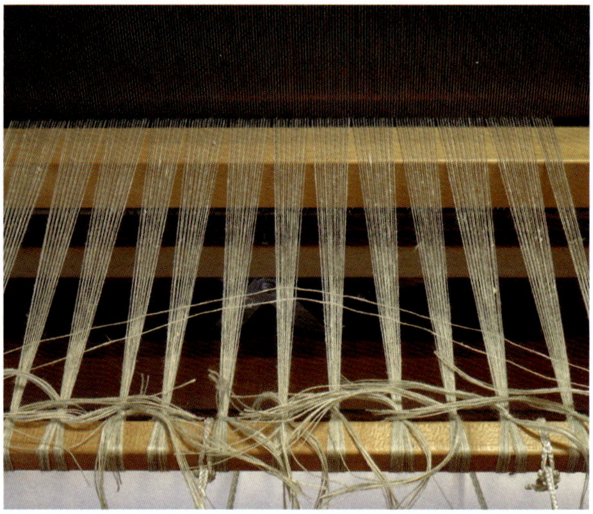

Spreading the warps to establish weaving width.

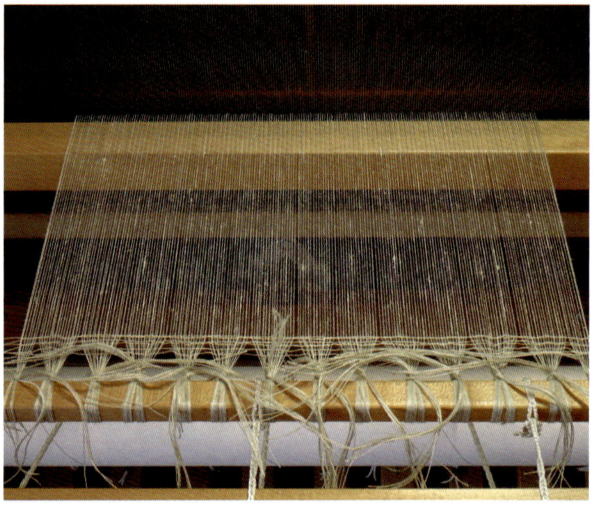

Warps are evenly spread with no draw-in after six picks.

If the outer warp bundles look like they're buckling, correct this by taking the weft around the end of the apron rod between each pick.

Weave a Header

A header is usually 1 to 2 inches of regular weaving that serves to lock in the weaving width before you begin the actual transparency. Use weft that is similar to the ground weft for your transparency.

It is especially important when weaving transparencies to have all the warp ends evenly spaced. This means avoiding drawing in as much as possible. Draw-in can occur when the weft is pulled too tight, causing the warp ends at the selvedges to move closer together. This will cause the width of the weaving to become increasingly narrower. Draw-in will be quite noticeable, and once it begins, it is hard if not impossible to reverse.

To avoid draw-in, I recommend beating on an open shed with absolutely no pressure put on the weft as you beat. Beating on an open shed allows the reed to naturally draw the weft out to where it should be. Change the shed while the beater is resting against the weaving. This locks the weft into place.

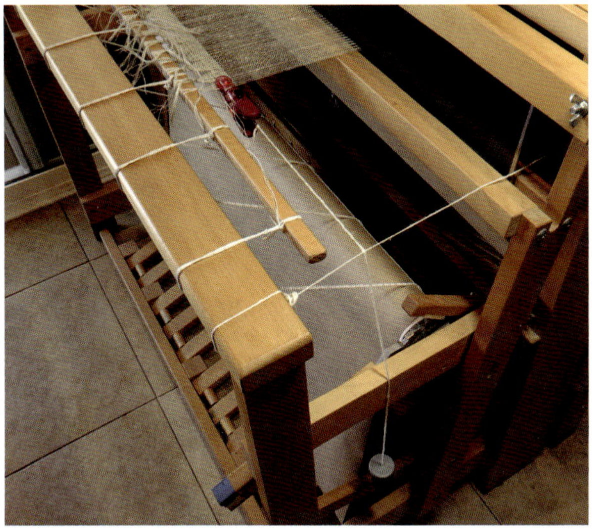

Install the side weights to avoid draw-in.

Even after following the method above, your warp may be a tad narrower than intended, perhaps by ½ inch. This is acceptable as long as you avoid further draw-in during the weaving. To help avoid draw-in, place the side weights in position. Tie a cord from the front beam to the back beam on each side of the loom, pass the string holding the weight over the cord, and let it hang down at the side of the loom. Moving the position of the weight is a lot easier than repositioning a temple, and it doesn't leave any holes.

Weaving Ground Weft

The ground weft weaves from selvedge to selvedge. Use a boat shuttle to place the weft into the shed. Since the warps are set unusually wide apart, the weft must be lightly beaten to leave spaces between the rows, creating little open squares that will either be filled with inlay or be left open to create the transparency effect. The goal is to achieve a balanced weave with the same number of picks per inch as warps per inch. I use the word "press" to describe the action of the beater, rather than "beat." After pressing the weft into place with an open shed, change the shed and tap the weft again with the beater. This serves to settle the weft into a straight line.

Use the side weights to help maintain the desired width throughout the weaving process.

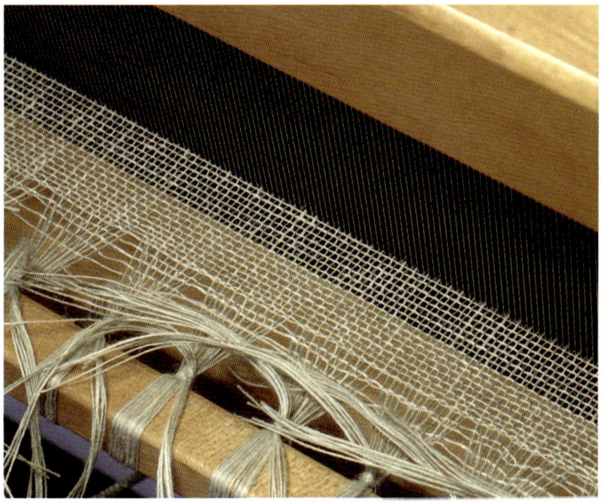

The beater presses gently against the weaving, leaving space between the rows of weft.

Weaving Inlay Weft

The inlay weft weaves over small portions of the weaving surface, following the shapes of your design. These small areas of inlay need to enter and exit the weaving surface between warps. There are several ways to keep inlay wefts manageable and tangle-free: Wrap them in butterflies, use short shuttle sticks or netting shuttles, or use tapestry or kumihimo bobbins. Tapestry bobbins tend to roll around and even fall off the weaving surface, so I prefer to use kumihimo bobbins.

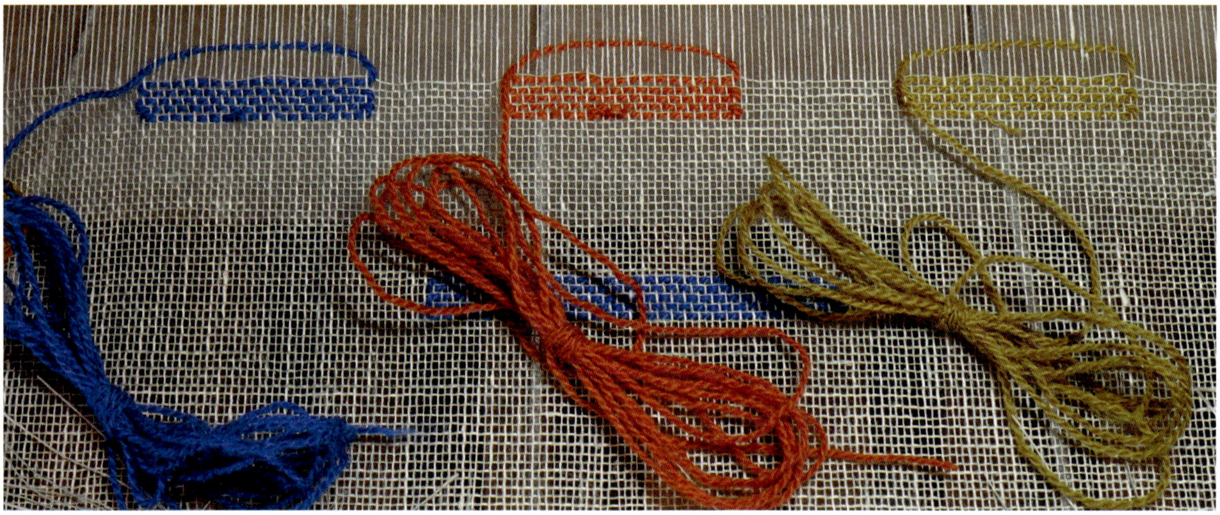

Bubbling the inlay weft will help avoid pulling warps out of alignment.

The inlay weft may need to be bubbled as it is laid into the shed, to avoid pulling the warps at the edge of the inlay shape out of alignment. It is particularly important to bubble the inlay weft if it is a stretchy yarn—for example, wool, which tends to stretch when you lay it in the shed and then—guess what—it draws in when you beat. A small bubble, depending on the size of the pattern area, will suffice. The wider the inlay shape, the bigger the bubble should be. But never make the bubble so big that the weft buckles when pressed into place.

Hiding Weft Ends

It's important to conceal where weft segments begin and end. Any disparities in weft thickness tend to be visible in the sheer weave structure of a transparency. As much as possible, try to maintain a uniform width where two weft ends meet. This can be done by thinning the weft and overlapping the ends.

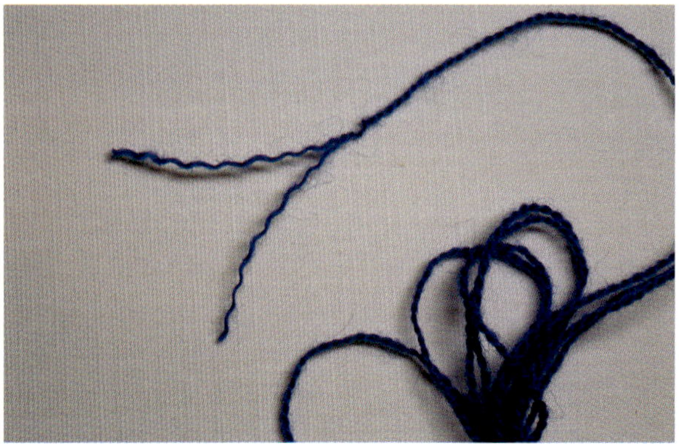

Two-ply weft unplied.

Thinning the weft refers to reducing its thickness. Thin the last 2 inches of a weft as follows:

- If your weft is a single yarn with two or more plies, unply the yarn by twisting it in the opposite direction.
- If your weft is a single-ply yarn, reduce the thickness by pulling off some of the fibers to feather the ends.
- If your weft is a bundle of two or more strands, divide the bundle in half.

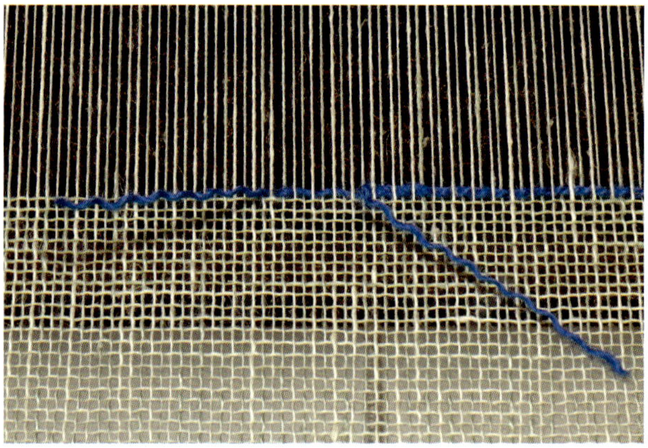

Beginning an area of inlay.

To overlap the thinned ends at the beginning or end of an area of inlay:

- Drop out one-half of the weft several warps before the edge of the shape. Weave to the edge of the shape with the other half of the weft.
- Turn around the appropriate warp and weave back in the same shed to where the other half emerges; overlap the two ends by one warp.

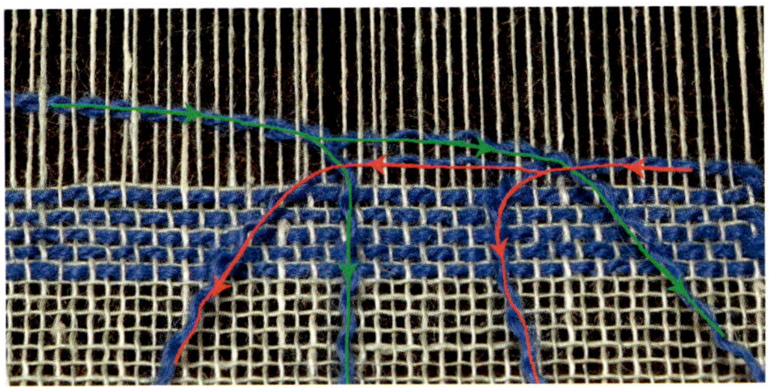

Adding new weft in the middle of a shape.

To add more weft in the middle of a shape:

- Drop out one-half of the old weft segment several warps before the join; weave another ½ inch with the other half.
- Insert the new weft into the shed: Each half should emerge from under the same warp as the respective halves of the old weft; they will overlap by one warp only.
- Leave the weft ends hanging out for now; they will be trimmed as part of the finishing process.

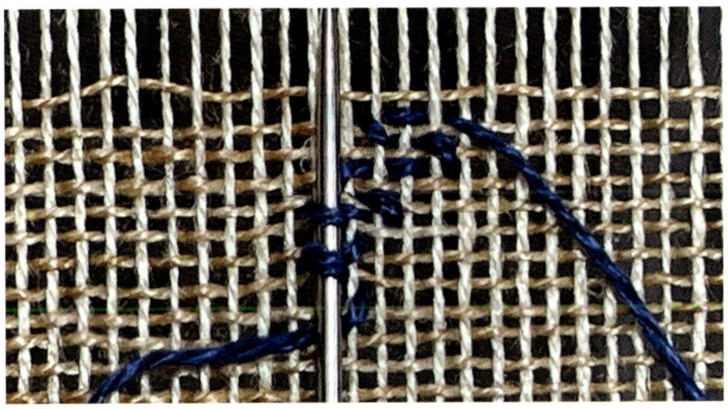

Beginning an inlay on just one warp for a diamond shape.

Sometimes a design demands that a weft begin or end on a single warp; for instance, the tip of a diamond. Since there is no room for overlapping ends, the simplest solution is to leave a tail at the beginning of the shape. After weaving a few rows, use a needle to draw the tail under two or three weft turns.

Weaving Row by Row

Like most forms of weaving, transparencies are woven row by row. Each row of inlay is followed by a row of ground weft in the same shed. Some weavers opt to weave the inlay before the ground weft in each shed. It really doesn't matter whether you weave the inlay before or after the ground weft. My personal preference is to get all the inlay in place, then weave the ground weft to finish off the row.

EXERCISE 1: WEAVE A BLOCK OF INLAY

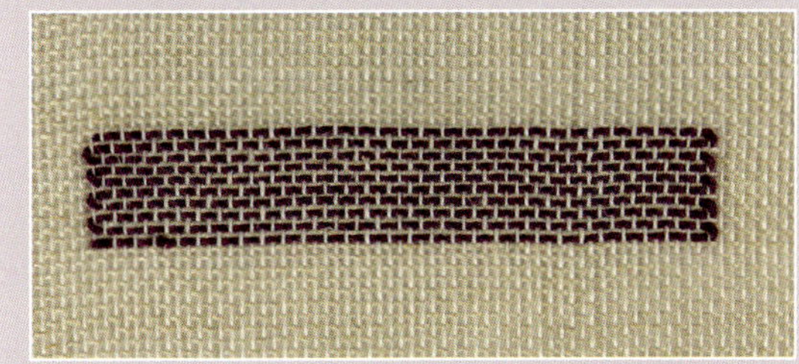

Weave a rectangular block of inlay like the one shown here. Practice each of the following:

- Hide the weft tails.
- Bubble the inlay weft.
- Weave row by row, weaving the inlay followed by the ground weft in the same shed.
- Beat on an open shed.

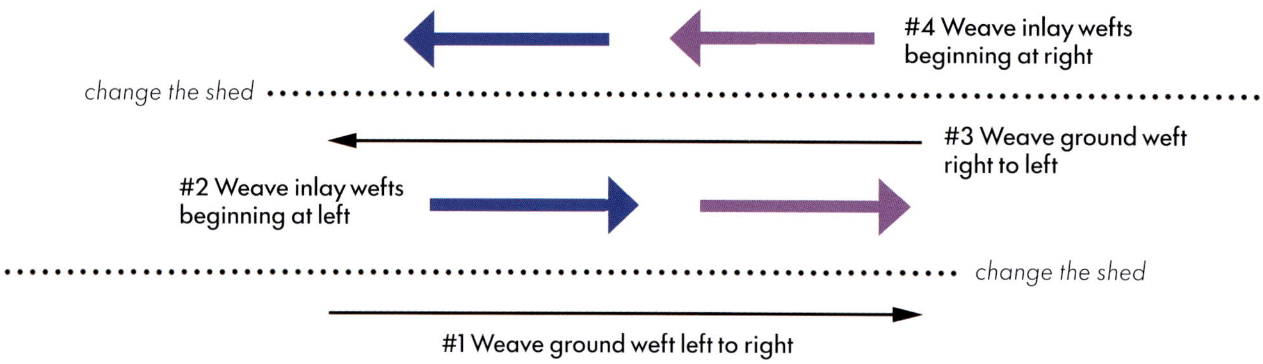

Order of weaving ground weft and inlay weft row by row.

Managing Multiple Inlay Wefts

Many times you will weave several inlay wefts in each row of weaving. It's important to weave them in a consistent order and to make sure each one gets woven in each row. I use a system to meet both of these goals. Here are the steps:

1. Weave a shot of ground weft from left to right.
2. Change the shed. Beginning at the left side, weave each inlay weft over its respective area. Press the inlay wefts into place with a light beat of the beater.
3. Without changing the shed, weave a shot of ground weft from right to left. Press it into place with the beater.
4. Change the shed. Beginning at the right side, weave each inlay weft.

Besides maintaining a consistent order and ensuring that each inlay weft gets woven, this method achieves a third objective: It helps minimize the amount of unweaving that is needed if (when) you find an error in the previous row!

Weft Direction

Should multiple inlay wefts all be woven in the same direction? The answer: It depends. In tapestry weaving, multiple wefts in the same shed must travel in opposite directions (meet and separate) so that they can easily weave over one another without both weaving in the same shed. The same holds true for transparency weaving, sometimes.

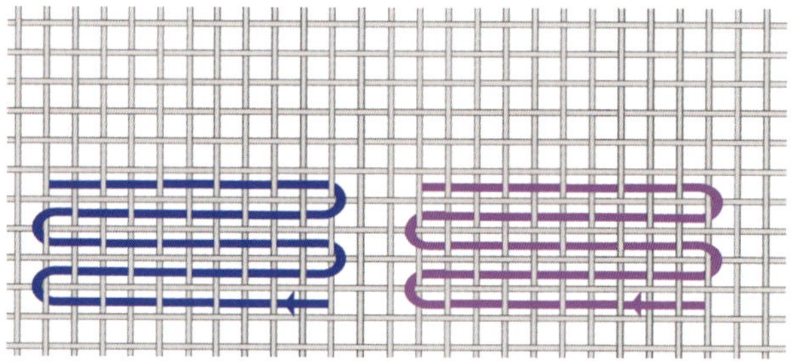

Inlay areas separated by ground weft

Multiple isolated inlay sections that all are separated by ground weft can be woven without regard to the direction that the inlay wefts weave. It is sometimes easier to keep track of which weft to weave next when they all move in the same direction.

EXERCISE 2: WEAVE MORE THAN ONE INLAY WEFT IN EACH ROW

Weave two blocks of inlay side by side, separated by ground weft, as shown in the diagram above. Be mindful of the direction of travel and the order in which the wefts are woven. Try to develop a consistent pattern so that no wefts are forgotten.

When two shapes share a common border, it's better to weave each pair of adjoining wefts in the opposite direction to one another. The two wefts "meet and separate" at adjacent warps. There is no need to overlap or interlock the two wefts.

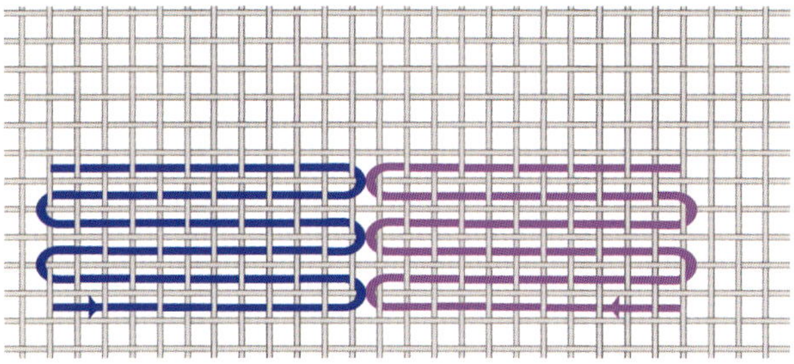

Inlay areas that share a common border

Weaving the wefts in opposing directions anticipates that the meeting place between the two wefts will move as the shapes develop. One shape "increases" by weaving over more warps, while the other shape "decreases" by weaving over fewer warps. The overlapping of one shape over the other will happen more easily if the two wefts travel in opposite directions in the shed. This prevents them from overlapping in the same shed.

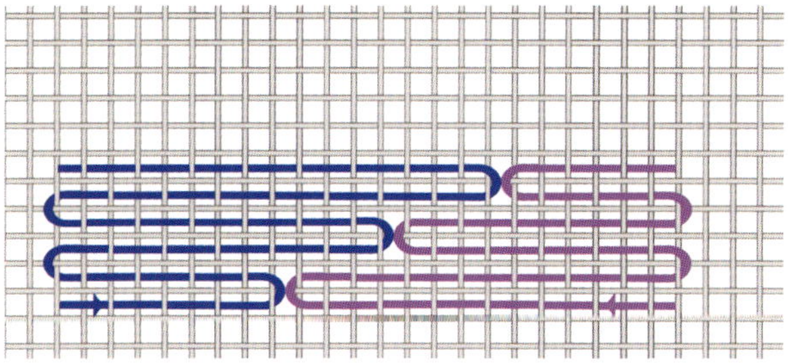

Inlay weft advancing over an adjoining shape

EXERCISE 3: WEAVE AN ADVANCING SHAPE

Weave two colors where the shapes share a common edge. Weave the two wefts in "meet and separate" fashion. Make one weft advance over the other weft, as shown in the left column's bottom diagram.

Shapes that share edges are far less common in transparency weaving than in tapestry weaving. This is because areas of inlay are most often surrounded by areas of open ground weft in order to take advantage of the transparency effect.

Maintaining Even Warp Tension

Even tension is of paramount importance for weaving transparencies. Strategies for achieving even tension while warping were discussed earlier (see page 40). Tension problems can arise during the weaving. Often just a single warp will become too loose for some mysterious reason. This can easily be fixed by attaching a weight to the problem warp and hanging the weight behind the back beam.

Other tension issues might result from take-up. *Take-up* refers to the shortening of the warp as it interlaces with the weft. Uneven take-up can result when there are more pattern wefts in some areas of the weaving than to others. A design woven in the center of the warp can cause warps at the edges to become looser over the course of the weaving. Several solutions can address this problem:

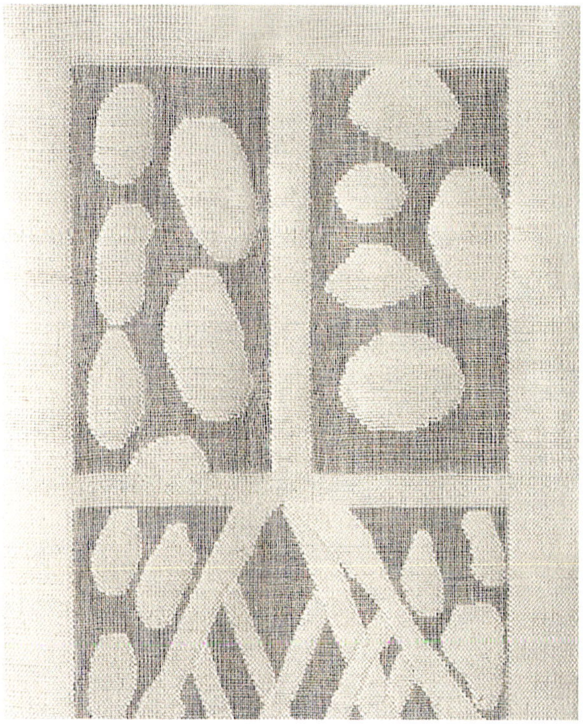

Woven border. Laura Viada. *Confessions*, 2007. Detail. Photo: Mike McCormick.

- Weave a border of inlay weft along both edges. Combined with weaving a border at the top and bottom, this provides a nice framing effect for the design (see Laura Viada's *Confessions*, previous page).

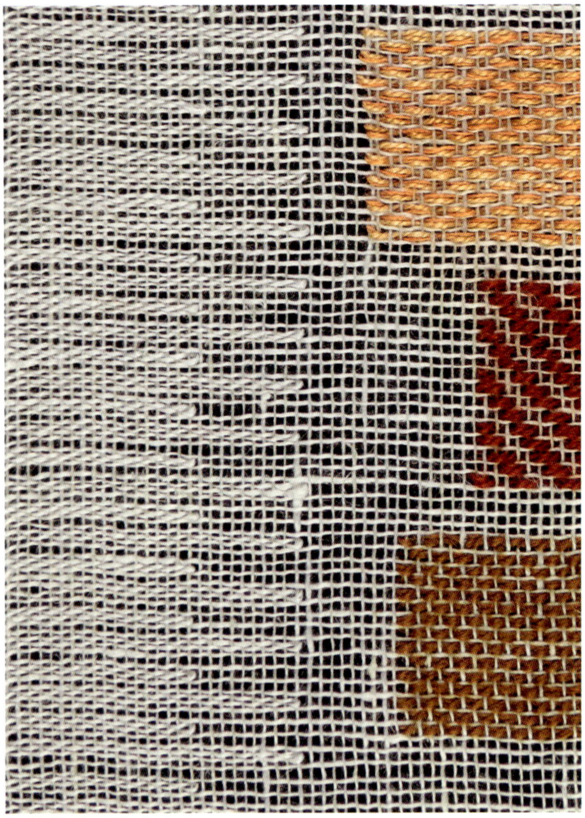

Border woven with ground weft. See Project 3.

- Use the ground weft to form a border: weave the ground weft 1 or 2 inches in from the edge, change the shed and weave back to the edge, then weave the entire row of ground weft.

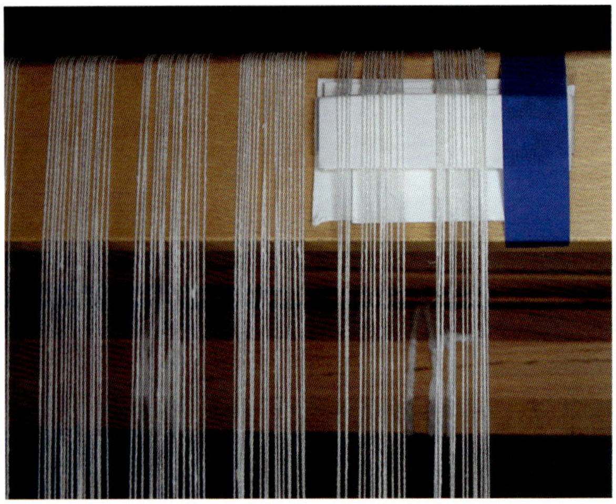

Shims placed under warp at back beam.

- Place "shims" underneath the outer warps where they lie on top of the back beam. Cardboard, mat board, or thin strips of wood make suitable shims for adding a slight increase to the tension of the outer warps. Tape the shims to keep them in place when the warp is advanced.

A smile may appear when the woven piece is cut from the loom.

When the weaving is taken off the loom, you may notice that the fabric curves at the end, resembling a smile. This is evidence that the warps were looser at the edges. The smile can be fixed by blocking the fabric during the finishing process (see page 119).

Cloth Beam Protection

Just as you inserted warp sticks while winding on the warp to smooth out the surface of the warp beam, you should insert sticks or heavy paper over the cloth beam as the woven transparency begins to wind around it. Cords that attach the beam to the tie-on rod can make indentations in the woven cloth. Since this is linen, those indentations can be quite stubborn to get out. Protection is needed only for the first rotation of the cloth around the beam.

RIGHT: Rebecca Smith. Detail, *Plain Geometry*, 2021. Linen, Tencel: 15 × 41 inches.

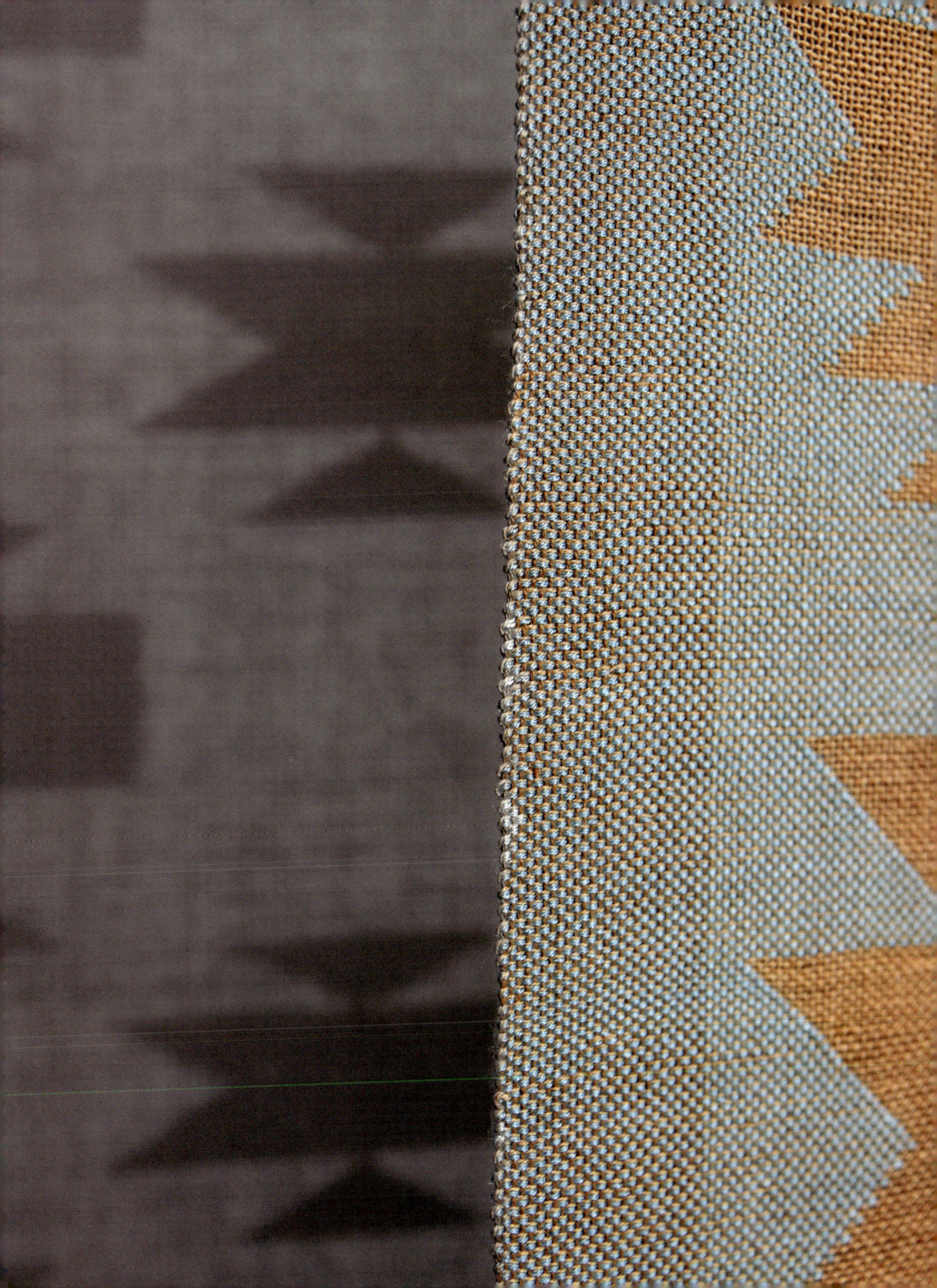

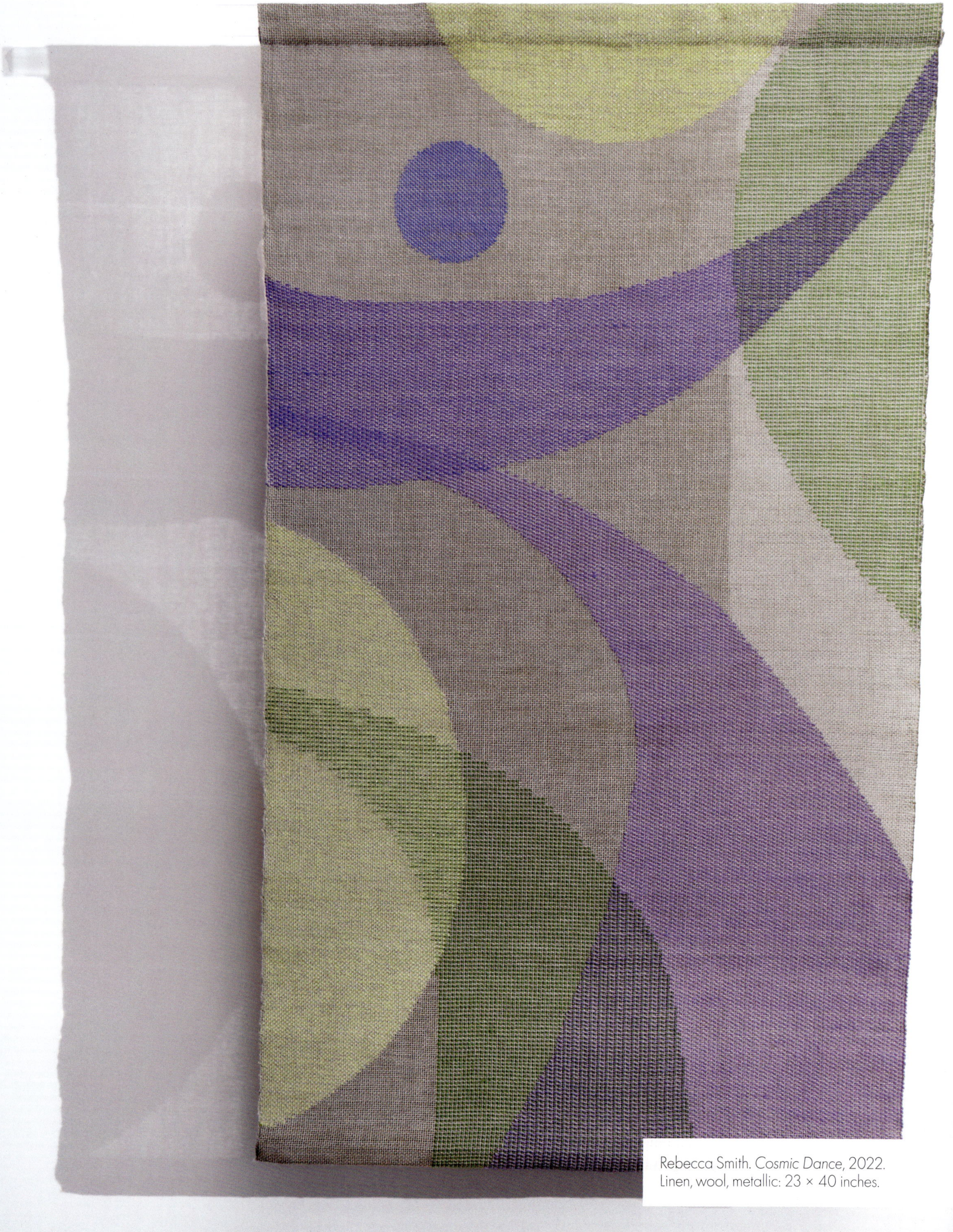

Rebecca Smith. *Cosmic Dance*, 2022.
Linen, wool, metallic: 23 × 40 inches.

Chapter 4

DESIGNING YOUR TRANSPARENCY

"There's no failure. You eat your mistakes and move on."

—JACQUES PEPIN

DESIGN DECISIONS

At the beginning of the design process, you must make some decisions. These decisions will clarify the subject or content of your design, the size of the finished piece, and how it will be displayed.

Content

What is the subject matter or content of the piece you plan to weave? You might have in mind a straightforward design such as flowers, or you might have a scene from a photo you took that you want to weave. Your interpretation of these subjects could be realistic—a viewer would undoubtedly recognize what the subject is—or they can be more abstract, using colors and shapes that don't attempt to represent objective reality.

Geometric shapes can be another source of inspiration. Geometric designs form a subcategory of abstract design in which the subject matter is portrayed by precise shapes such as rectangles, squares, and circles. Motifs from weaving traditions such as Navajo rugs, Turkish kilims, and traditional Scandinavian designs can provide lots of ideas for coming up with your own geometric design.

Formalism describes an approach to art that focuses on the visual and material qualities of a work, rather than a specific subject matter. A focus on the materials used, and how they are used, has inspired much contemporary fiber art. You might consider the ground weave of transparency as a blank canvas on which you can be as realistic or abstract as you want, or just revel in the colors and textures of your materials.

Format

What size will your transparency be? What are the dimensions: Is it square or rectangular? If you have a specific location where you will display the piece, the size and dimensions will be determined by the display site. Give some thought to whether your design should be woven bottom to top or side to side. Some designs lend themselves better to being turned 90 degrees and woven from the side rather than from bottom to top. Designs that have a lot of vertical elements, whether straight-edged or curved, are often easier to weave from the side. A horizontal line is easier to weave than a vertical line. A long, gradual curve will look less jagged if the curve is woven from the side.

If you decide your design might be easier to weave from the side, you will need to rethink the dimensions: What was the length is now the width, and vice versa. This may change the number of warp ends and the length of the warp.

Scale

The scale of the work and the number of warp ends per inch (epi) will determine how much detail you can include in the design. A sett of 12 epi will allow less detail than a sett of 15 or 16 epi. It may not sound like a significant difference, but those extra three or four warp ends will make it possible to refine your shapes.

The larger the format, the more detail that can be woven at a given sett. By comparing your full-size cartoon to the graph paper in the appendix, you can determine if your sett is dense enough to weave the shapes in your design.

GALLERY OF STUDENT WORK

"Transparency weaving is really easy." These words of encouragement were spoken by a past workshop student to a group of weavers who were unfamiliar with the technique. The transparencies here, woven by students during or immediately after taking my workshop, attest to the ease of learning the basic techniques required for weaving your first transparency.

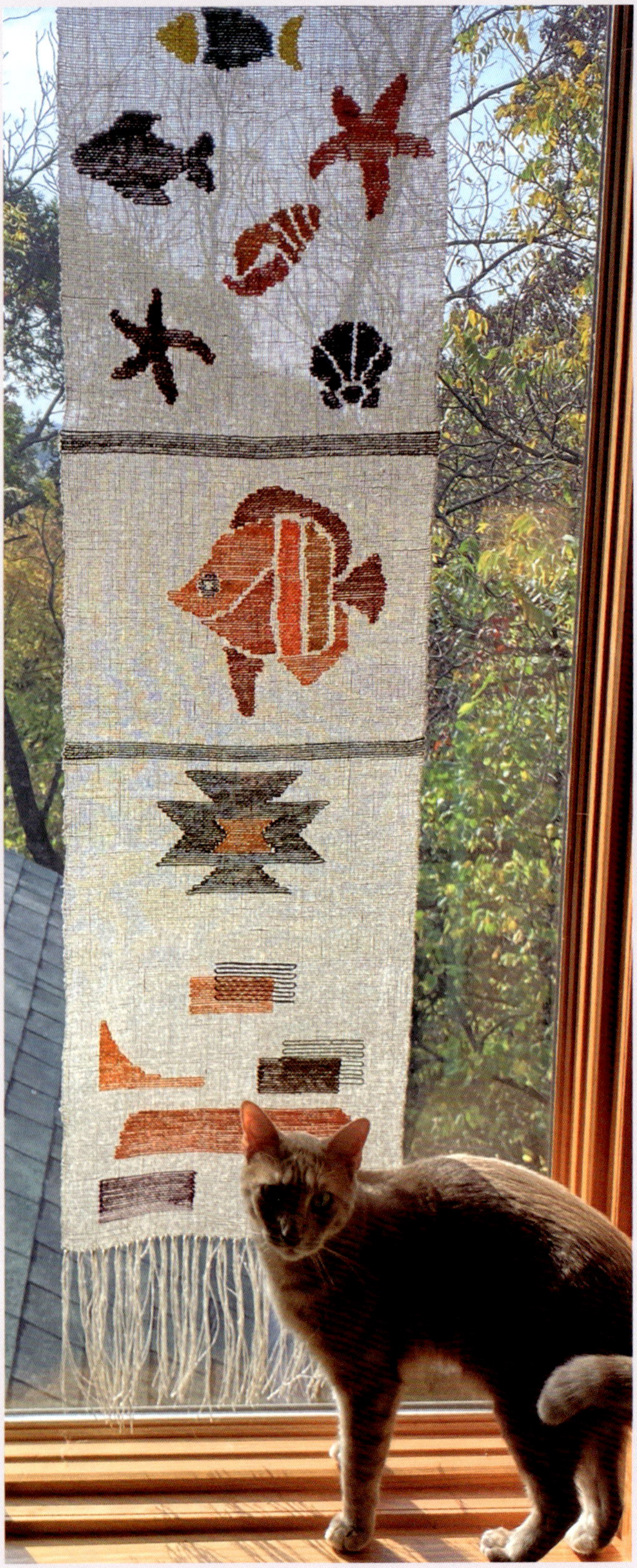

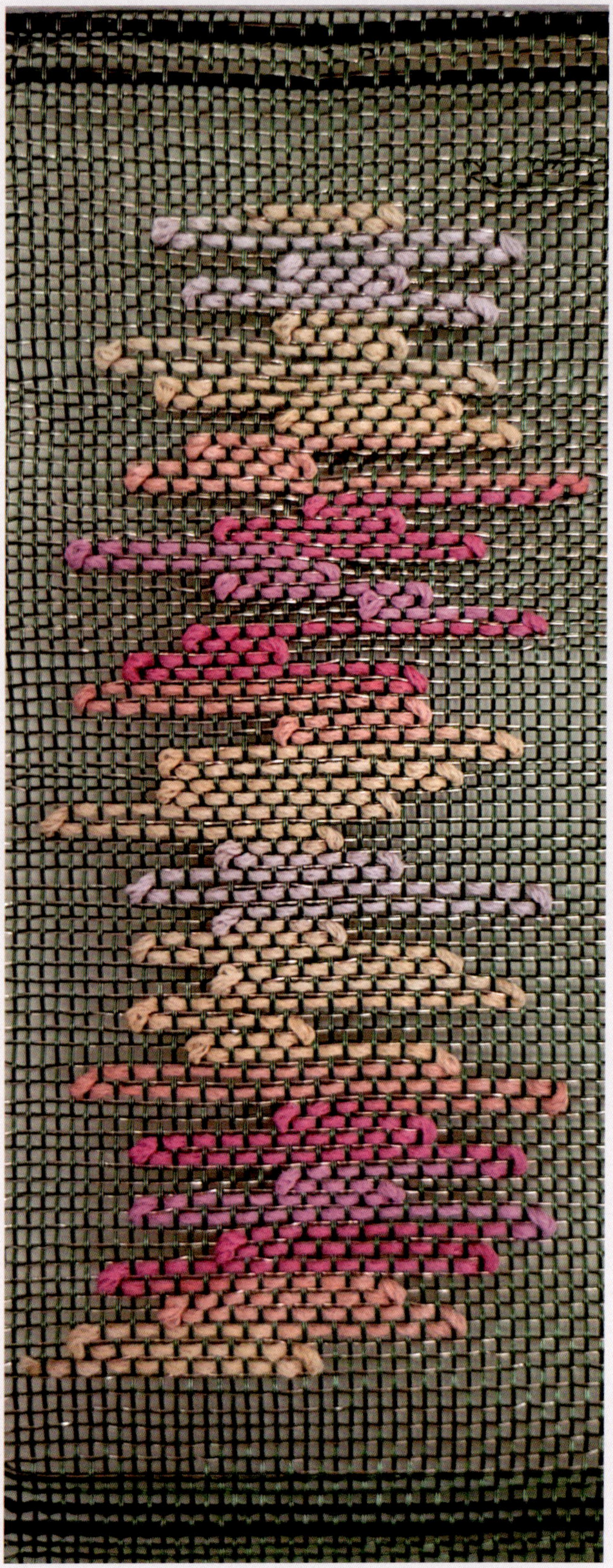

OPPOSITE PAGE, LEFT: Becky Gaskill, untitled (shown with Arlo the cat), 13½ × 46½ inches.

OPPOSITE PAGE, RIGHT: Ellen Richard, untitled, 4 × 8½ inches, woven with 28-gauge wire warp.

THIS PAGE, CLOCKWISE FROM TOP: Alison Levy, untitled, 14 x 14 inches. Christine Williamson, untitled. Ruth Ronan, *Cool Dude*, 13 × 17 inches. All photos courtesy of the artists.

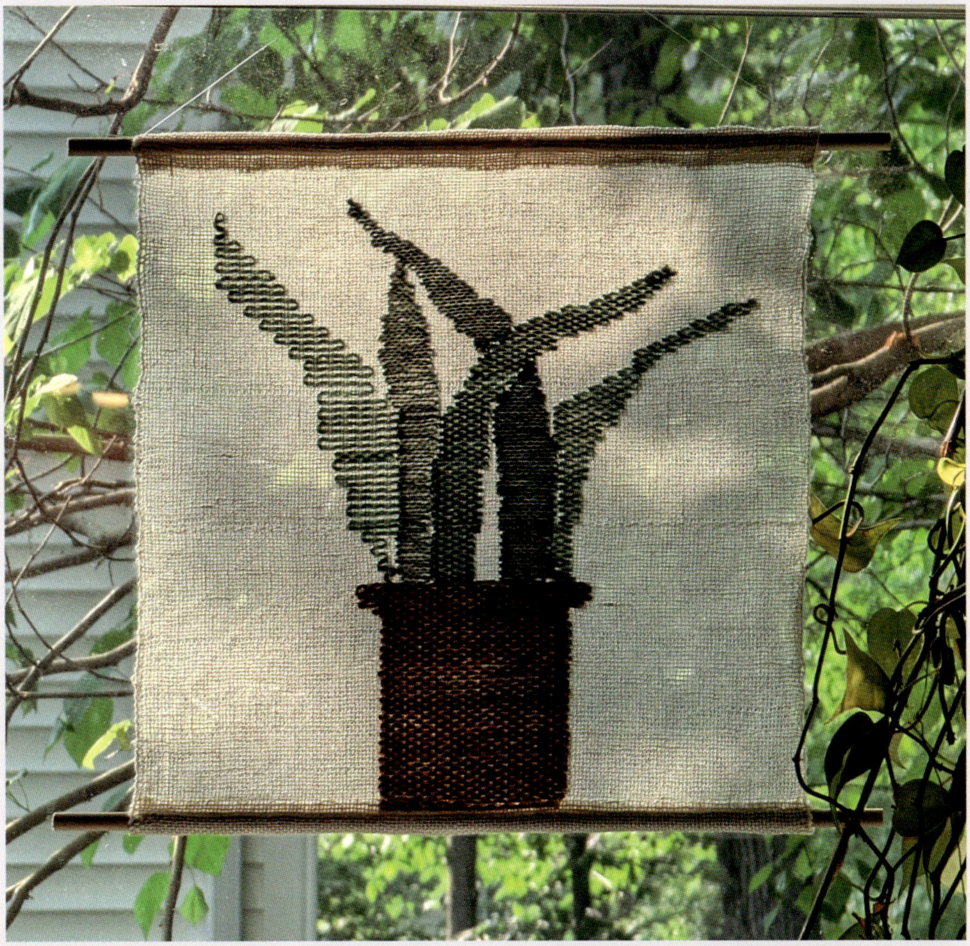

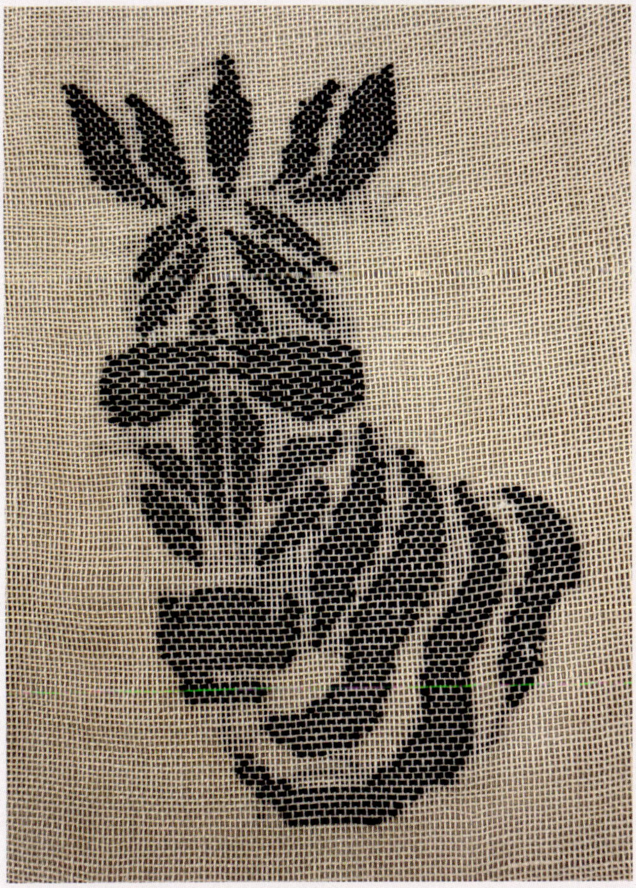

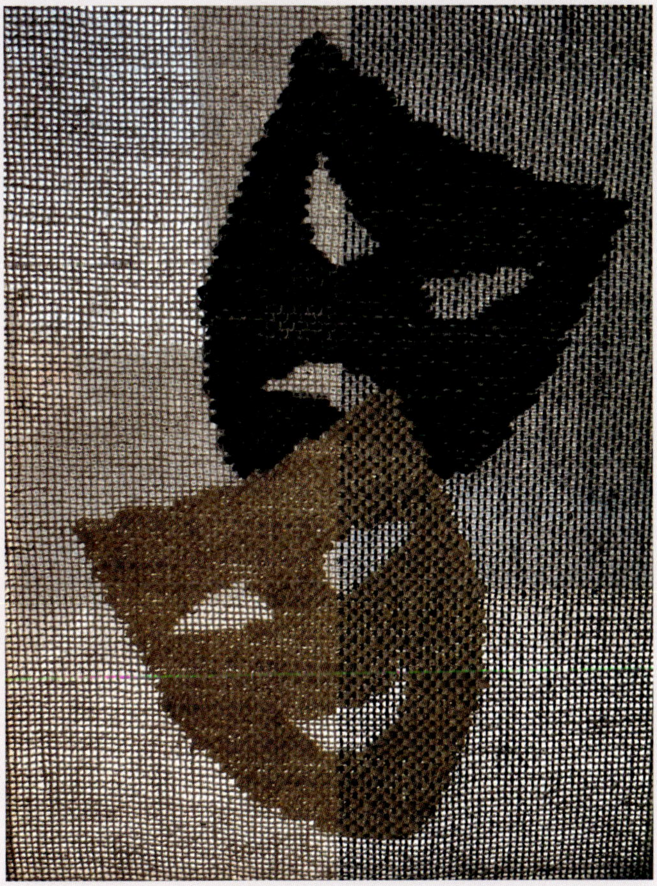

HOW MUCH DETAIL IS IT POSSIBLE TO WEAVE?

It is often not possible to perfectly translate the shape from the cartoon in the weaving. There are only so many warps where the weft can turn, and the turns do not always fall exactly on the line of the cartoon. Accuracy depends on the relationship between the sett of the warp and the size of the shape. At a given sett, the bigger the shape, the more accurately it can be woven. For instance, at 16 ends per inch, a leaf that measures 2½ inches from side to side has less opportunity for detail than if the leaf is woven at 3½ inches at the same sett.

Before you commit to weaving your design at a given size and sett, compare the design to the graph paper provided in the appendix. Draw at least a portion of the design on the graph paper for your sett to see if the shapes can be adequately interpreted at that combination of size and sett.

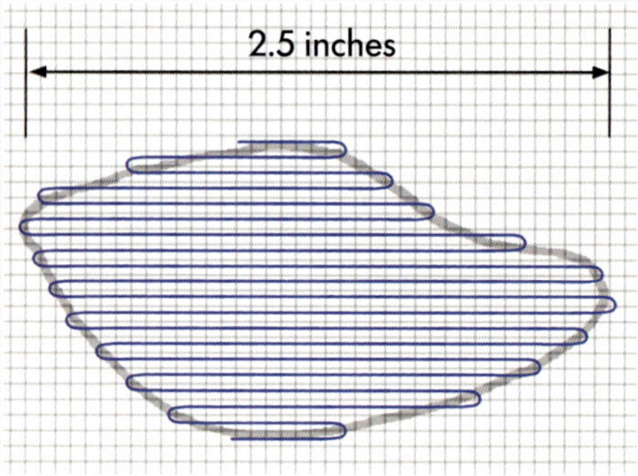

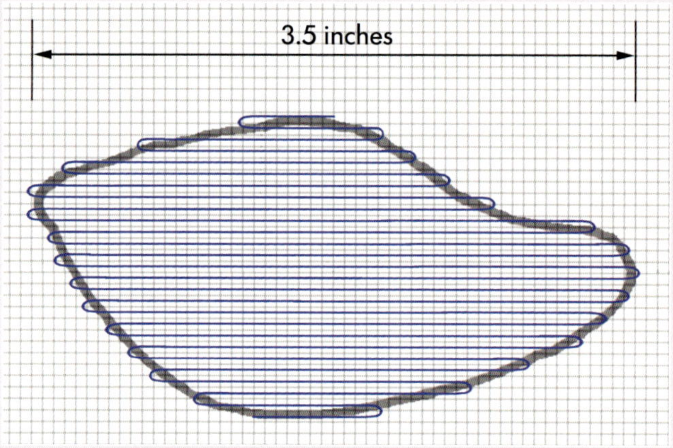

CREATING A CARTOON

Pictorial and geometric designs are usually planned out in advance. A full-scale drawing of a design is called a "cartoon," which is the English equivalent of the Italian word cartone, which has been used for centuries to describe large-scale designs made by artists to guide tapestry weavers.

The purpose of the cartoon is to help you weave the shapes in your design in their proper place. If your design is a geometric figure, you will want to weave your straight-edged shapes to match the shapes on your cartoon. If your design is figurative, the cartoon will guide you to weave curved edges that mimic the shapes in the design.

Many designs can be woven without the aid of a cartoon: Geometric designs can be worked out on graph paper; free-form designs can be worked out as you weave. But if your design relies on specific imagery, you will probably want to create a cartoon to guide the weaving so that the various parts of the image end up in the right place!

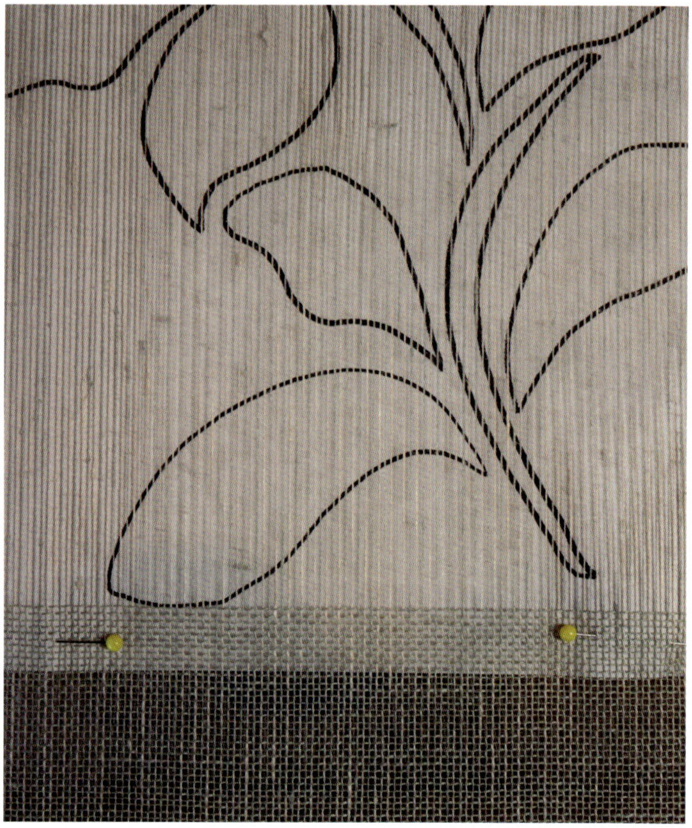

A cartoon can be attached behind the warp to guide you while weaving.

Putting Your Idea on Paper

Cartoons can be anything from a simple line drawing to a full-color depiction of the design. If you are good at freehand drawing, then you are a step ahead of many of the rest of us. Use your drawing skills to put down on paper the imagery that you want to weave. You might start with a small-scale rendering of the overall design before blowing it up to full scale. Remain cognizant of the amount of detail you will or won't be able to weave at your chosen sett and size (review the discussion of scale on page 51).

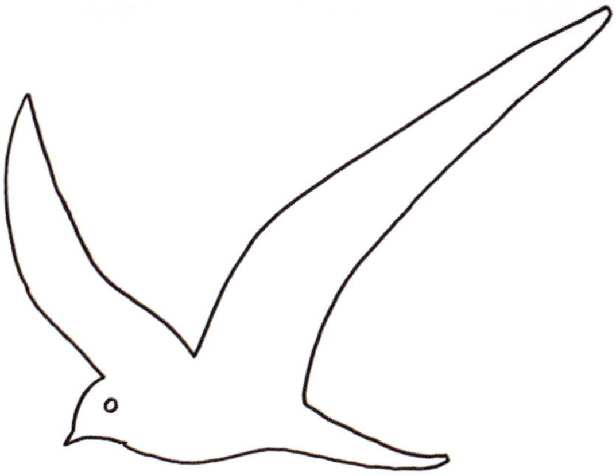

Simple drawing of a bird shows the recommended degree of detail that it is possible to weave. Image is based on a silhouette design found on the internet.

I am not good at freehand drawing, so I depend on other aids for my design process. I often find imagery on the internet that I can use. Searching for "silhouette" or "stencil" for almost any object will yield simple images that have minimal details. If there are subtle details that you won't be able to weave, simply smooth out the edges to remove unnecessary details.

Steps to Developing a Cartoon

WHICH SIDE IS THE FRONT AND WHICH IS THE BACK?

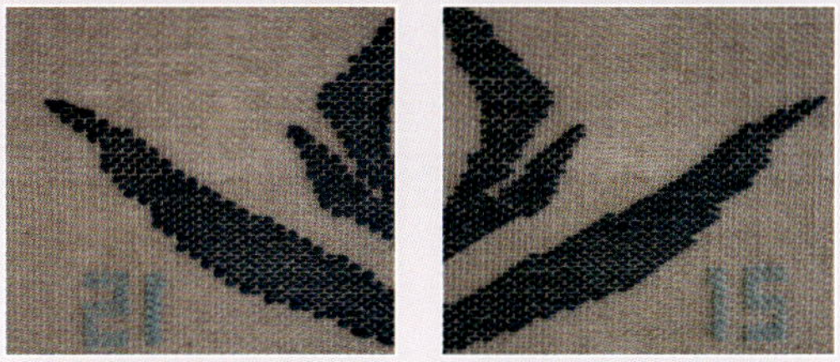

Left: working side. Right: front side.

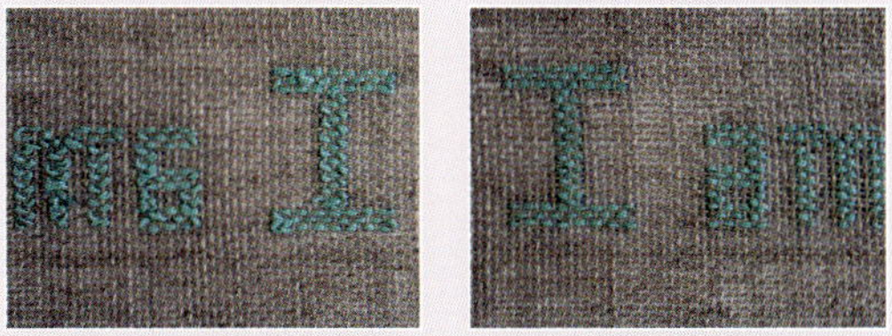

Text is woven backward (on left) so that it reads correctly on front side of transparency (on right).

The side facing up as you weave is called the working side and is generally considered the back of the transparency. On this side you can see the small floats that are created when the inlay weft makes a turn. On the other side, those turns are not visible and the surface is much smoother.

Does your design include text? If so, you may need to reverse the direction of the text so that it reads backward on the cartoon. Your cartoon is really a mirror image of the way the transparency will look, so elements such as text need to be woven in reverse.

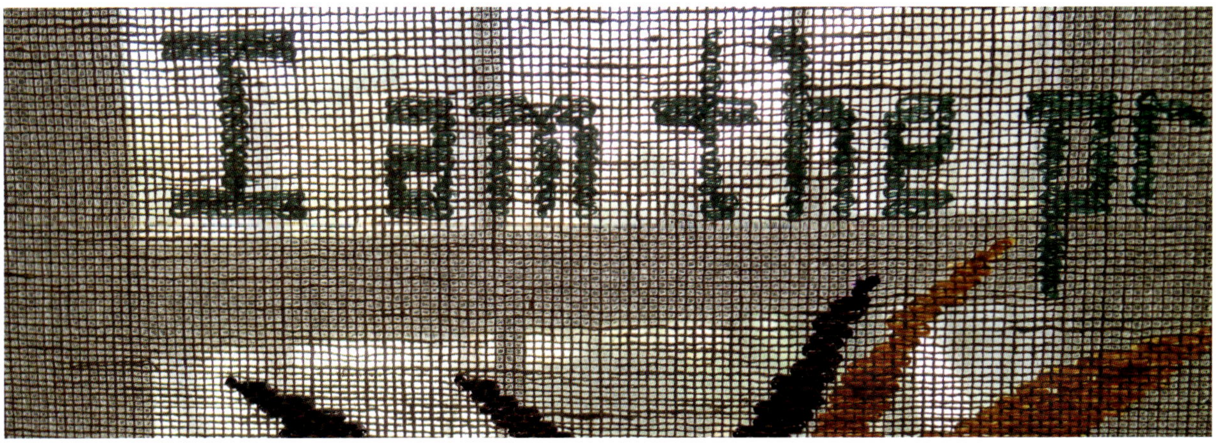

Enlarging the Design

How do you go about enlarging a design to full scale for a large weaving? Here are two options that I've used.

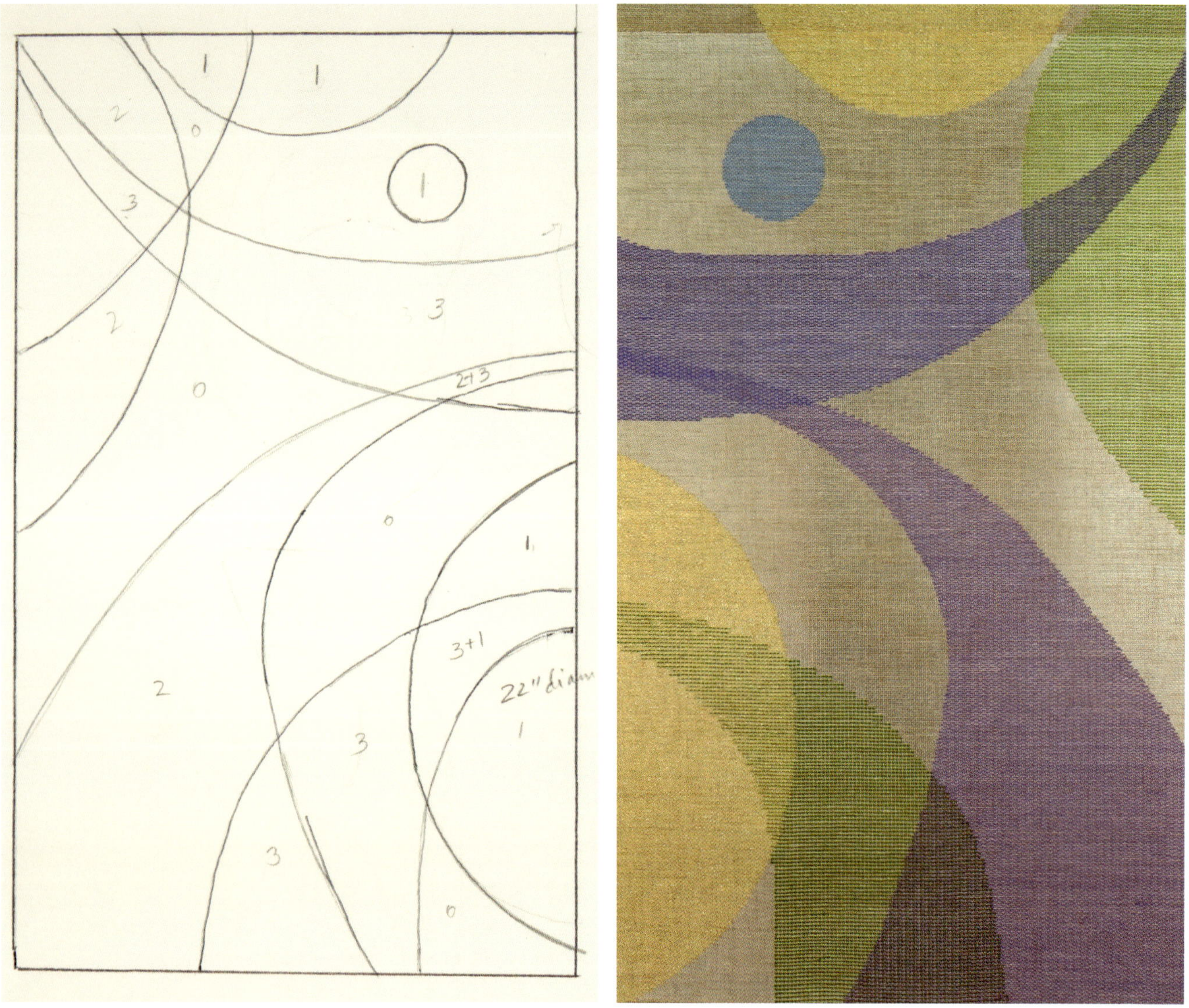

Rebecca Smith. *Cosmic Dance*, 2022. Linen, wool: 23 × 40 inches. Shown with cartoon.

For my piece *Cosmic Dance*, my concept was to show overlapping shapes that form arcs to convey objects orbiting in space. At the top, the bottom edge of the sun hovers just above the "pale blue dot," Carl Sagan's famous description of planet Earth seen from deep space by Voyager II. I drew a rectangle to establish the dimensions of the piece, then added the arcing lines and the circle. The numbers indicate levels of density created by overlapping shapes (inlay density is introduced in chapter 7). I took the drawing to an office store and printed it out at the full size, 23 inches wide by 40 inches long.

I used a slightly different method to enlarge the cartoon for *Flight*. I drew all the elements of the design at a small scale on graph paper. I scanned the drawing and enlarged it in Photoshop to the scale at which I wanted to weave it. Using Photoshop, I cropped the image into 8-by-10-inch overlapping segments, printed each segment, then taped the segments together to make a full-size cartoon.

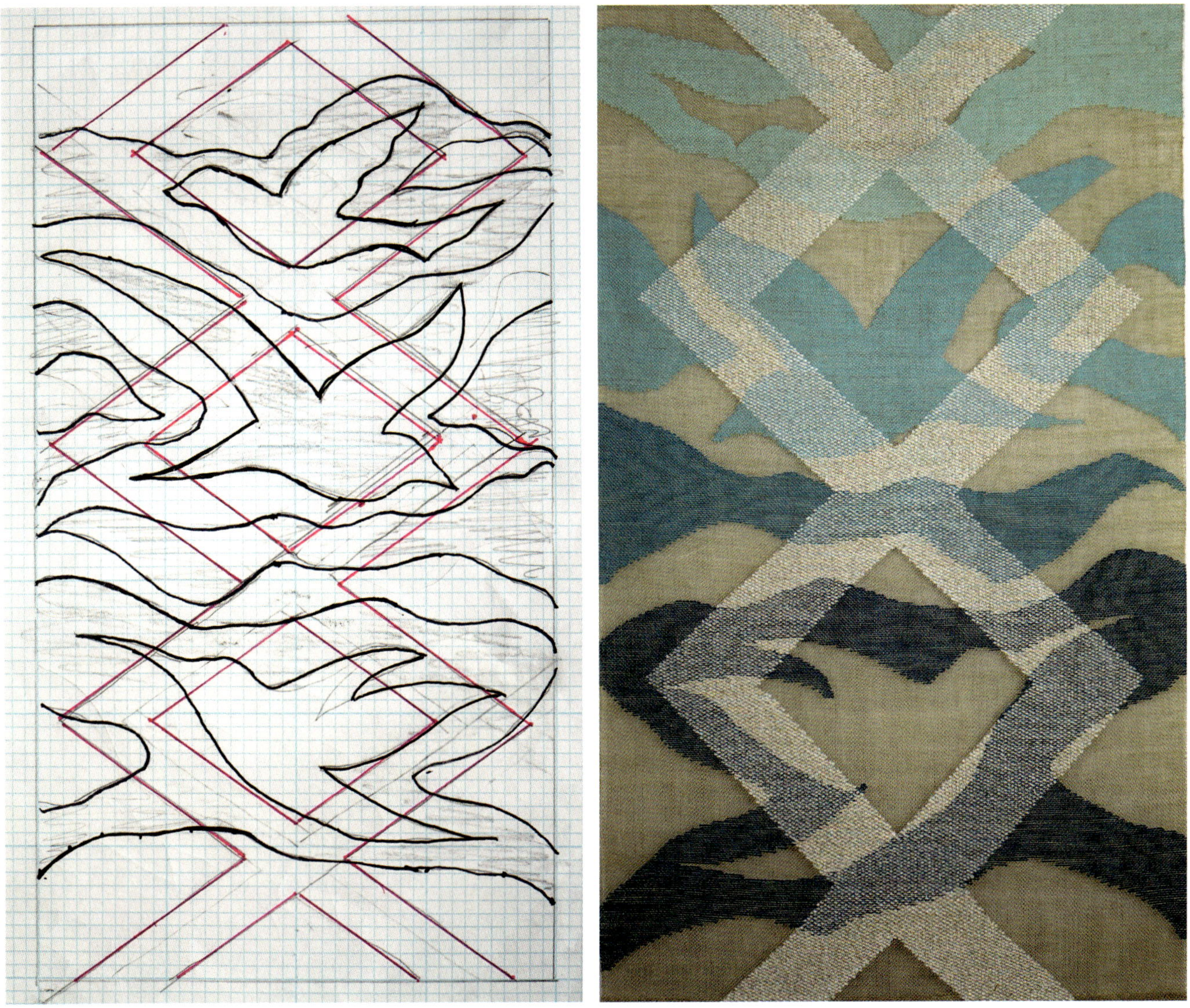

Rebecca Smith. *Flight*, 2022. Linen, wool, acrylic: 21 × 37 inches. Shown with cartoon.

Following the Cartoon

Be sure to leave a border at the bottom of the cartoon to attach it to the warp. Align the bottom of the image with the fell line and attach the bottom border of the cartoon to the weaving, using straight pins, magnets, or sewing thread. I use a combination of pins and magnets. You cannot mark the design on the warps as tapestry weavers sometimes do. The marks will show!

As you weave, reach under the cartoon and hold it up against the back of the warp to get an accurate sense of where to make your turns. When you are ready to advance the warp, first move the pins or magnets closer to the fell line, then advance the warp. Don't let the used portion of the cartoon advance over the beam along with the weaving. This can cause the cartoon to be pushed out of alignment. Instead, let it hang loose or roll it up.

GRAPHING GEOMETRIC MOTIFS

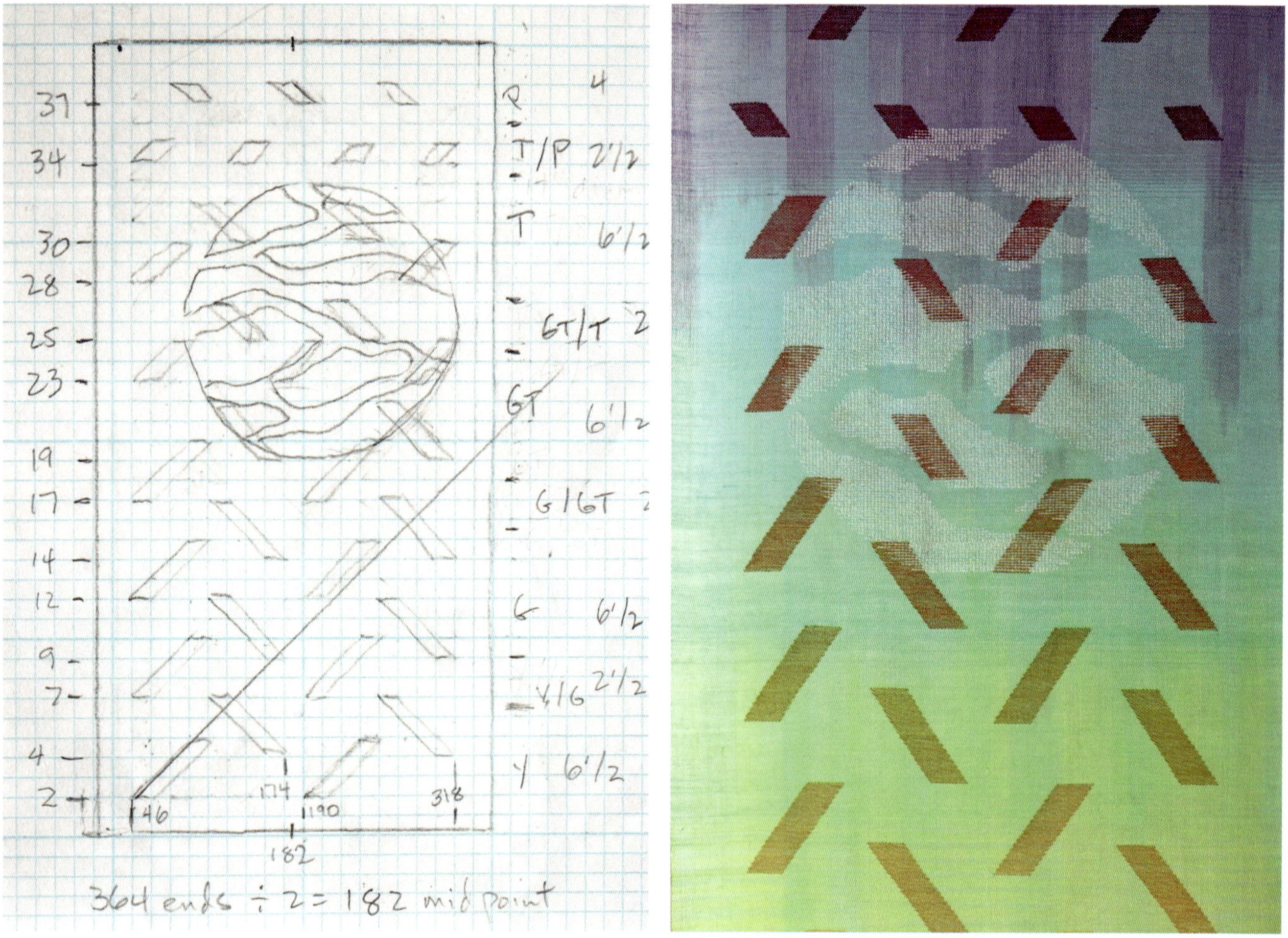

Rebecca Smith. *Fractured Orb,* 2020. Linen, wool, acrylic: 21 × 39½ inches. Shown with graphed design.

If a design is mostly geometric shapes, it's possible to work it out on graph paper without needing to blow it up to the size of the weaving. I designed *Fractured Orb* in this way. My small rendering on graph paper is filled with notations to guide the weaving. On the left side, I marked the positions for the diagonal shapes. On the right side, I marked where the ground weft would change colors to match the color gradient in the hand-dyed warp. The circular shape was drawn separately on graph paper at full scale, following the method introduced on pages 80–83.

Did you notice the diagonal line that starts at the lower left? This is not part of the design: I drew the line to calculate the turns per warp that are needed to weave the diagonal shapes (see page 69). All the shapes have the same angle, so I needed to calculate only once.

Working from graph paper requires constant measurements to be taken as you weave. It's the equivalent of holding the cartoon up to the back of the warp to make sure you are staying true to the design. The more often you take these readings, the more accurately you will transform the cartoon into a weaving.

GETTING READY TO WEAVE

ORDER OF WEAVING

A transparency has several parts that must be woven in the correct order:

- Warp the loom
- Weave a header
- Hem/hemstitch/border
- Weave the design
- Repeat hem/hemstitch/border
- Repeat header

Warping and Header

Now that you have your design and know the dimensions of your piece, you are ready to warp the loom and get weaving! The amount of detail in the design will help you decide whether you should weave at a fine sett or a slightly coarser sett. The most common choices are to use a warp of 16/1 linen at 15 or 16 epi, or 16/2 linen at 12 epi (see page 36). Knowing the sett will allow you to calculate the number of ends to wind in your warp. Add an extra ½ inch to the width of your warp to allow for a small amount of draw-in. The length of your warp is determined by the length of your designed piece plus extra for loom waste and take-up. The amount of loom waste will vary by type of loom. Take-up is minimal, usually about 3%–5%.

Detailed instructions for warping for transparency weaving are given in chapter 3. Follow the instructions given there for spreading the warps and weaving a header of about 2 inches.

Hemming, Hemstitched Edges, and Borders

While it may seem too early to be concerned with how the piece will be displayed, you really need to plan for it right up front. Various methods of display (covered in chapter 9) require that steps be taken during the weaving process to accommodate the display. Those steps are the first thing you must consider when you begin weaving your piece. Here are some options:

Hemmed Edge

A hemmed edge is used when the piece is to be suspended from a rod. Weave an extra 2 inches of ground weft to use for sewing the hem. Hanging instructions for using a rod are given in chapter 9. Remember to also weave a hem at the other end of the weaving: A rod at the bottom provides weight to help the piece hang straight.

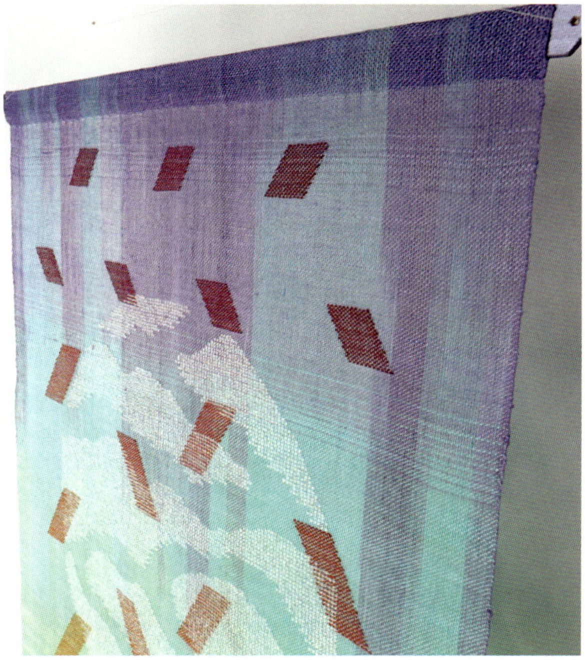

Weave a hem if you plan to suspend the transparency from a rod.

Hemstitched Edge

Hemstitching is an edge treatment intended to prevent the warp from unraveling. Use this method if you want to leave a fringe at the top and bottom of the piece. Hemstitching itself does not provide support for hanging the finished transparency. To provide hanging support, one option is to weave in a rod near the top of the transparency. It's a good idea to drill holes in the rod before weaving it in (see chapter 9). A rod woven in near the bottom of the transparency will provide stabilizing weight. Other options for ways to hang a hemstitched transparency are discussed in chapter 9.

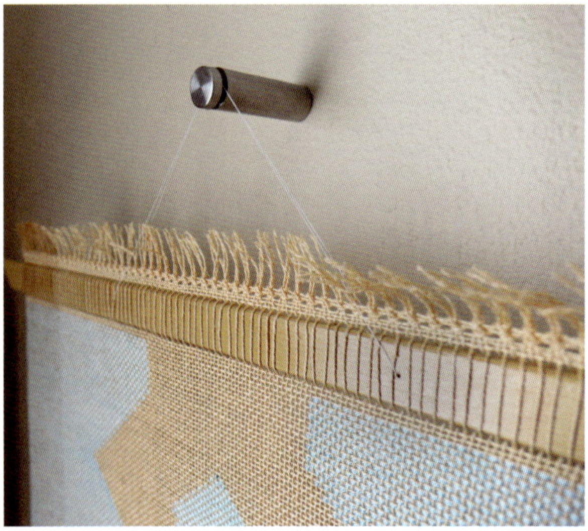

Hemstitched edge with wooden rod woven in, holes predrilled

Border

A border woven with ground weft at the top and bottom will provide a separation between the design and the hem or hanger. Weave at least 1 inch of border at the top so that the hanging mechanism does not interfere with the inlay design. Weave a matching border at the bottom to balance the design.

A border is needed on all four sides if the piece is to be framed under mat board or stretched on stretcher bars. If it is to be stretched, plan for a border wide enough to wrap around the edge of the substrate the piece will be mounted on. A border is optional if the piece is framed to float on mat board or between pieces of glass or acrylic (see page 125 for suggestions on using a float frame).

The next five chapters will introduce a variety of techniques and effects that can be incorporated into the open-warp format of transparency weaving. The techniques range from the simplest and most traditional—using plain-weave inlay to weave geometric and pictorial designs—to adding more complexity to the designs with pattern and density variations, and finally to innovative techniques that provide a stepping-off point for future exploration of the technique.

This array of techniques provides options for you to think about as you prepare to design and weave your first transparency. It is unlikely, and not really recommended, that you will use all the methods in one transparency. Think of it as a supermarket, where you can pick the items that appeal to you today, and save the rest for another shopping trip.

Rebecca Smith. Detail, *Entwined*, 2020. Linen, wool, rayon: 20 × 36 inches.

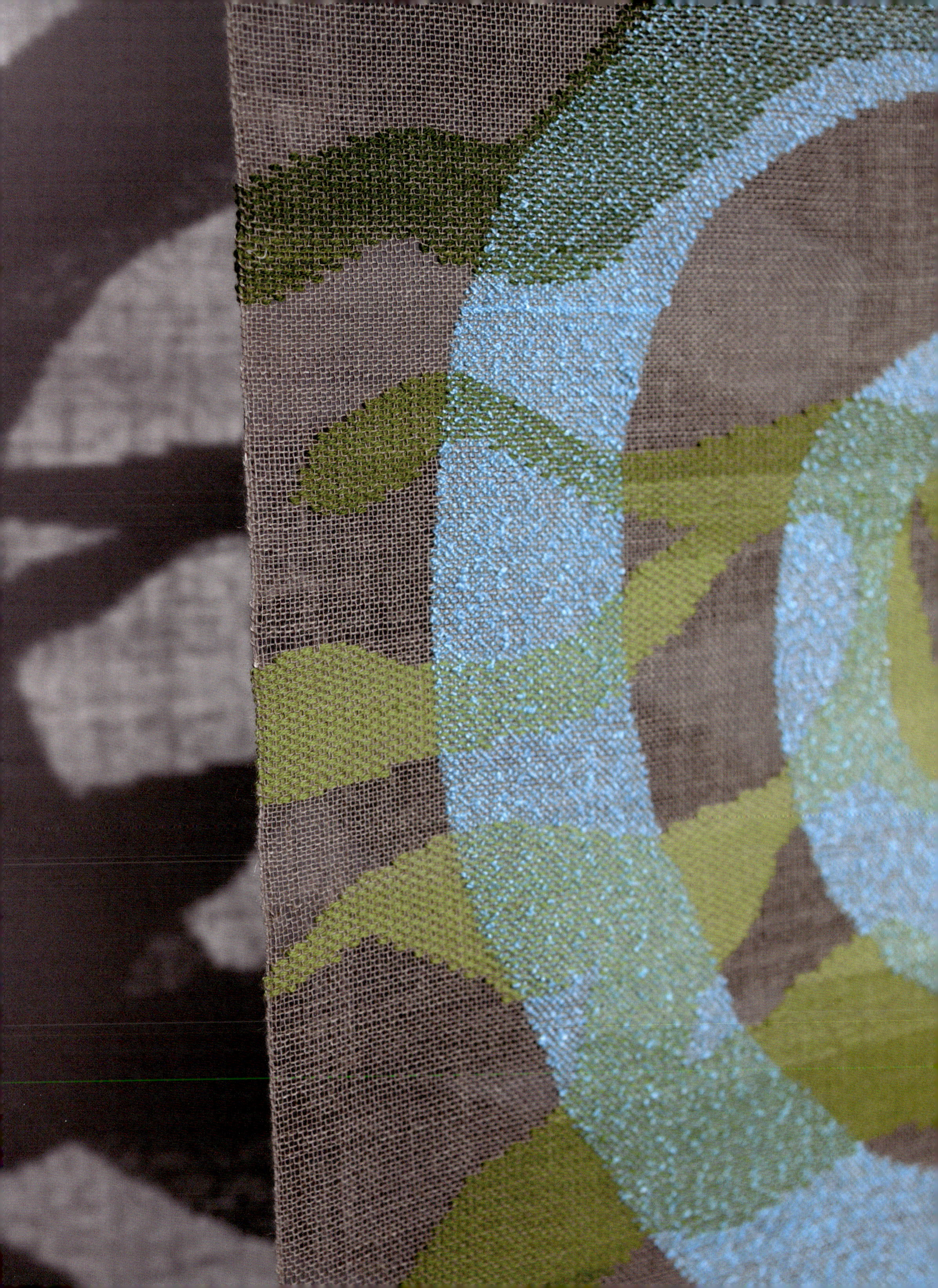

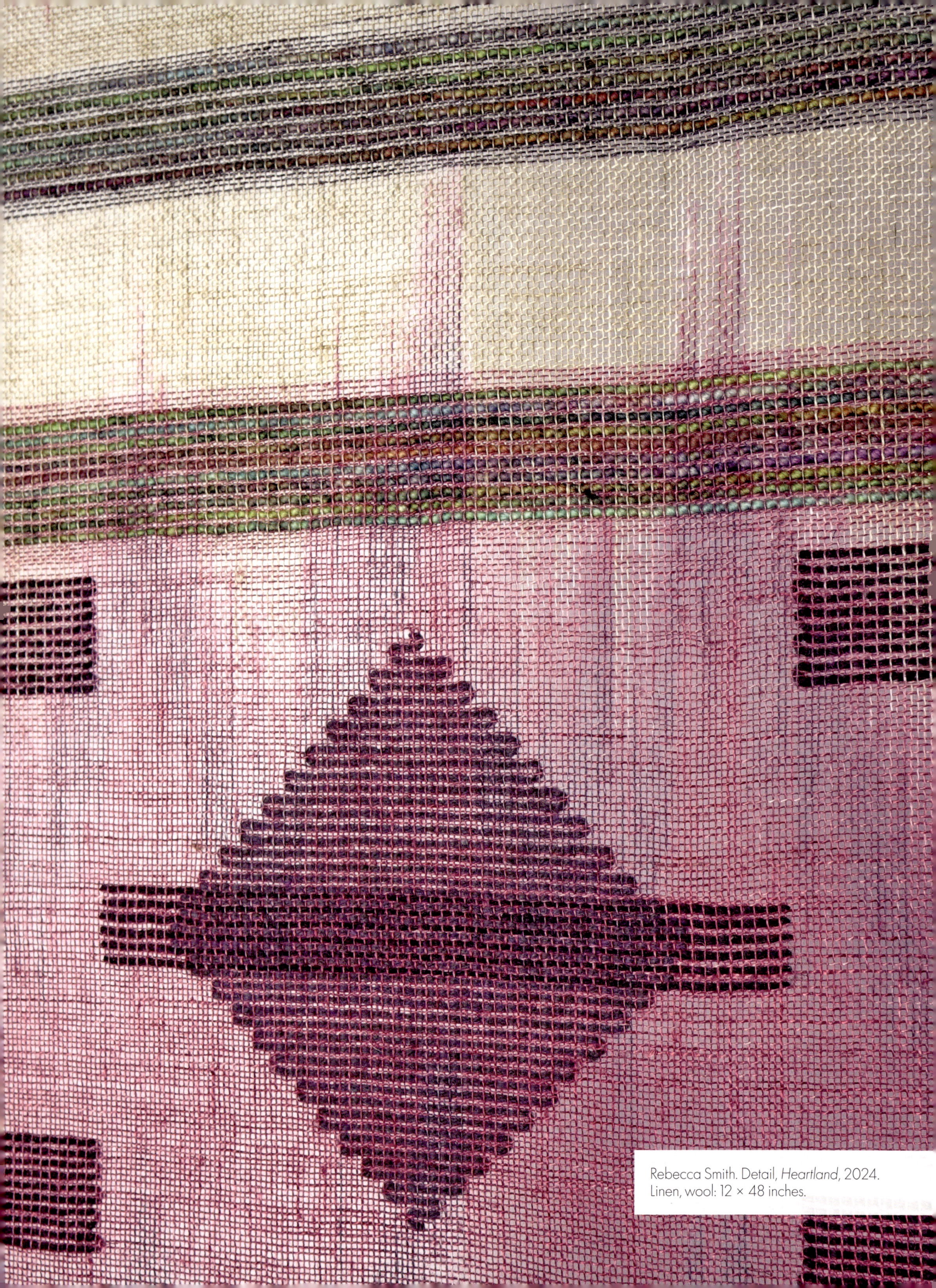

Rebecca Smith. Detail, *Heartland*, 2024.
Linen, wool: 12 × 48 inches.

Chapter 5

WEAVING GEOMETRIC DESIGNS

The primary use of the transparency technique historically has been to weave geometric or pictorial designs. In this chapter and the next, we will look at the basic building blocks for weaving these kinds of designs.

A straightforward way to think about both geometric and pictorial designs is that they are an assortment of shapes. The edges of shapes are lines that are either straight or curved, or both. If we focus on weaving the lines, it makes weaving shapes much more straightforward.

Weaving figures for transparencies is similar to weaving a tapestry. The design is woven using discontinuous inlay weft that covers only a portion of the weaving surface. A big departure from tapestry weaving is that the background—the space between the shapes—has no inlay weft. It is wide-open ground weft only. So, the rules are slightly different for weaving transparency designs.

STRAIGHT EDGES

Geometric designs are composed of shapes with straight edges. Straight edges can be horizontal, vertical, or diagonal. A horizontal edge is simply the bottom row of inlay that is woven to begin a shape. A vertical edge is created by turning the weft around the same warp for several passes. Weave the inlay weft to the same point each time and turn around the same warp end each time.

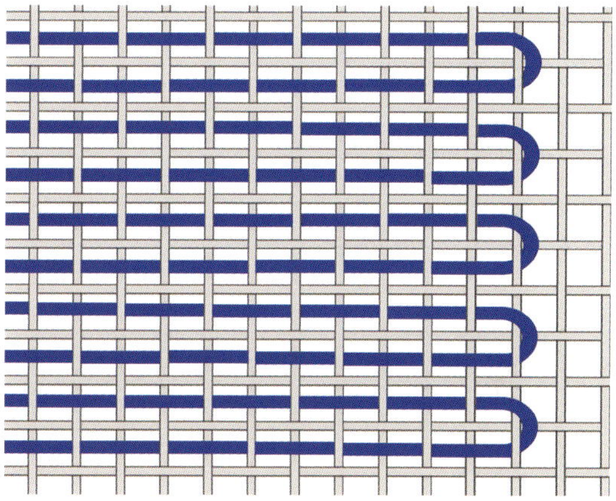

Horizontal and vertical straight edges.

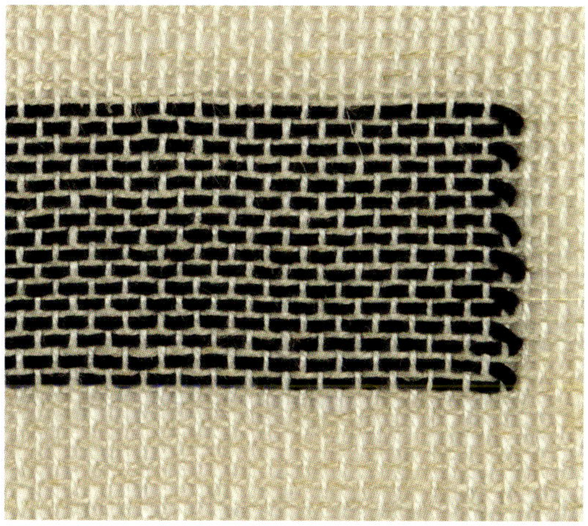

As woven (working side).

A TIP

Try not to get too bogged down by the technical details in the following sections. They are intended to anticipate questions that may arise as your skills as a transparency weaver develop beyond the basics. For now, you can simply read the beginning of each section to get the gist of it and skim the rest, or wait until later to come back to it. Your first transparency project may not be perfect, but it should be fun!

DIAGONAL EDGES

Any straight edge that is not either horizontal or vertical is a diagonal edge. Diagonal edges can be broken down into two types: steep and shallow. Steep diagonals require that the weft turn at least once around every warp. Turning the same number of times at each warp results in a straight line with no lumps or bumps. The first illustration shows the weft turning once on each warp to match the desired angle.

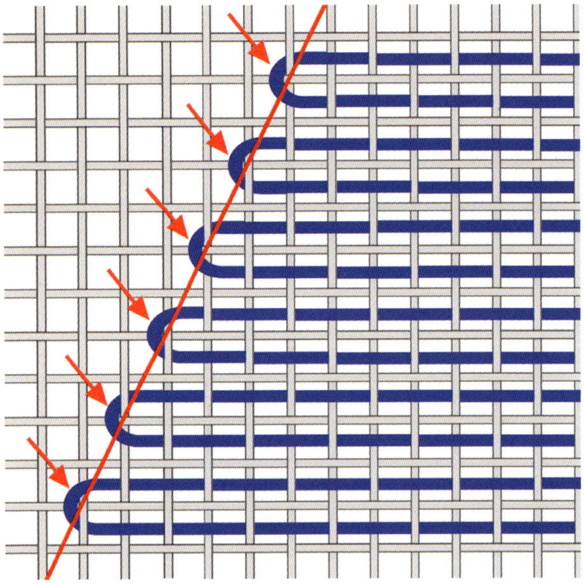

Steep diagonal edges have at least one turn at each warp. This diagonal turns once at each warp.

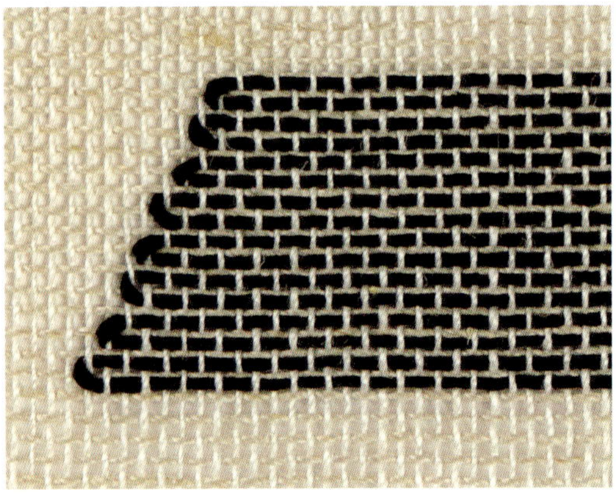

Woven example, seen from working side.

The steeper the diagonal, the more times the weft must turn at each warp. The second illustration shows the weft turning twice at each warp before moving to the next warp. Angles that require multiple turns at each warp appear a little jagged, more like a terraced hillside than a smooth slope. When seen from a distance or against backlighting, the eye tends to interpret the angle of the steps rather than the individual rows that make it up.

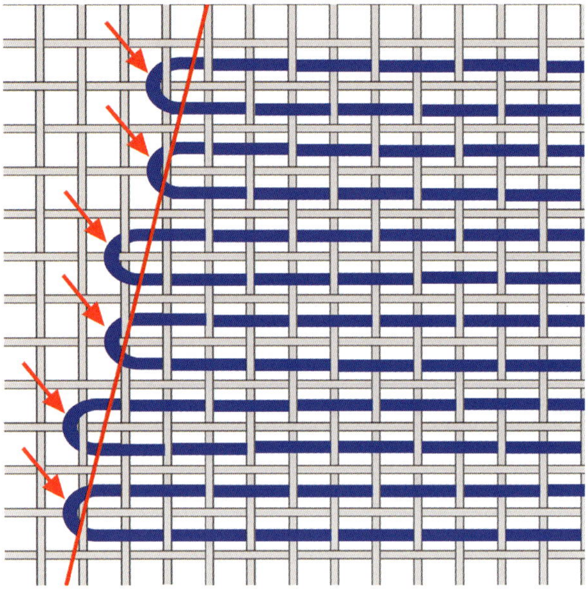

Steeper diagonal edges have multiple turns at each warp. This diagonal turns twice at each warp.

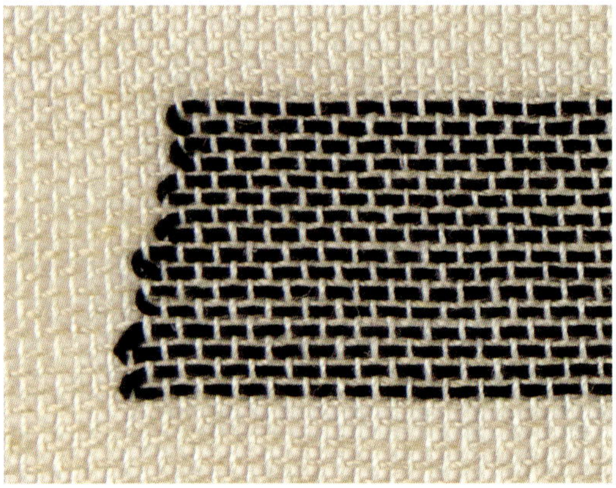

Woven example, seen from working side.

Many times, the angle of the diagonal is too shallow to turn even once around each warp. In these cases, you will skip warps to weave the desired angle. The shallower the diagonal, the more warps are skipped. The third illustration shows a shallow diagonal where the weft turns on every second warp, skipping one warp between each turn. Skipping the same number of warps for each turn ensures that the diagonal will be smooth.

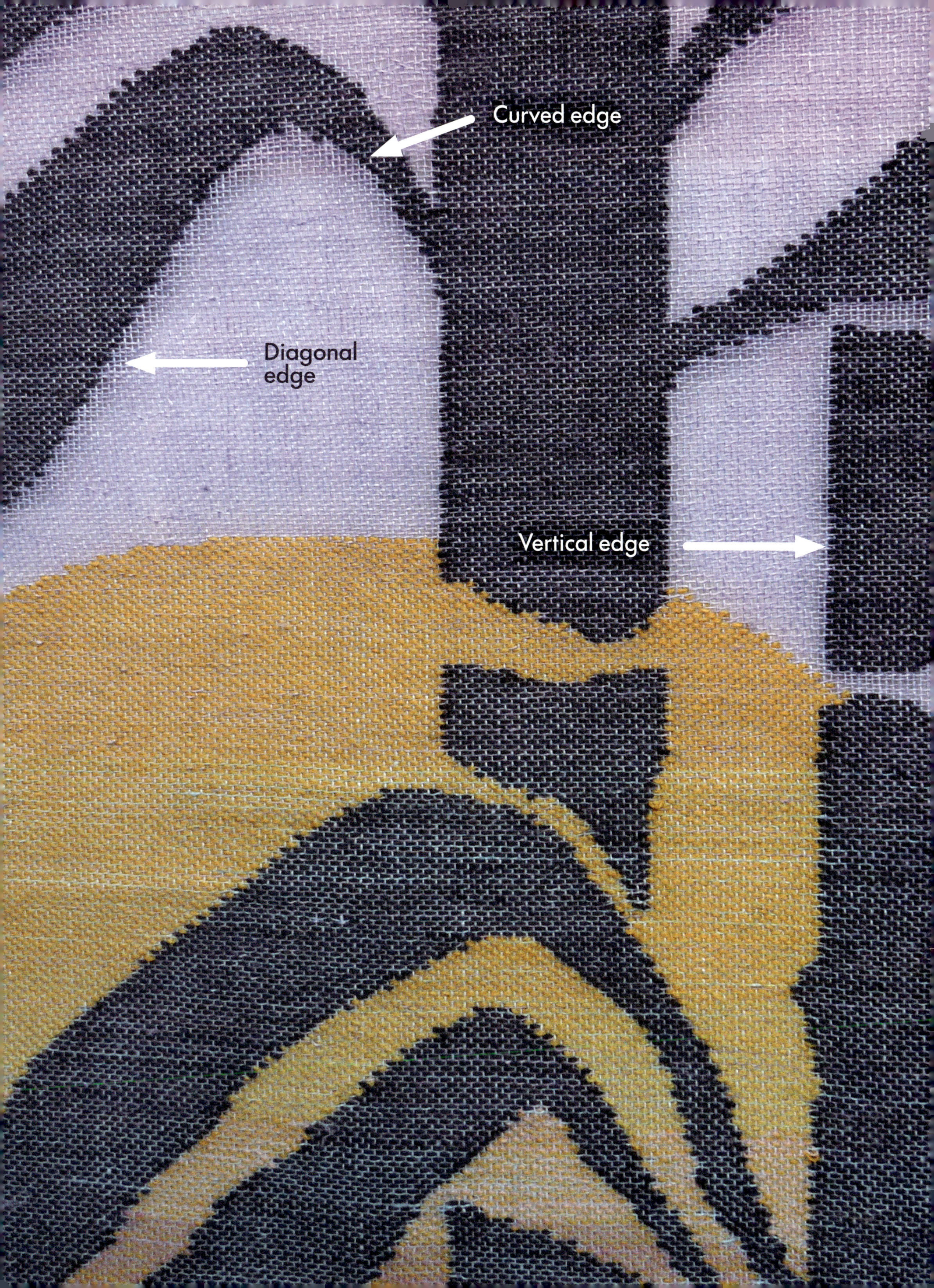

Curved edge
Diagonal edge
Vertical edge

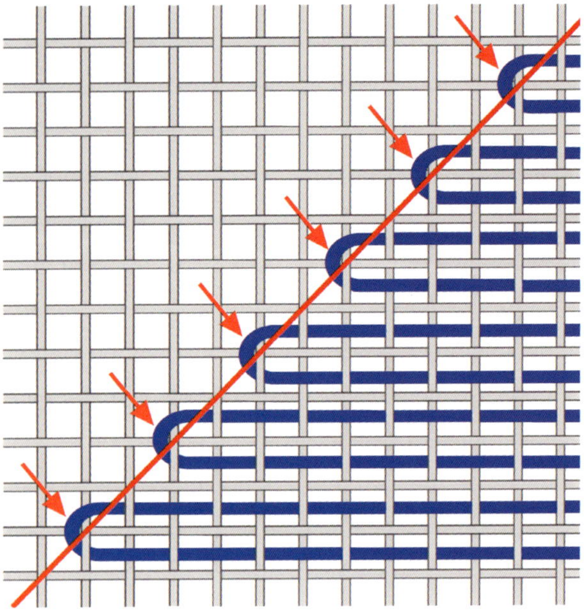

Shallow diagonal edges skip warps between turns. This diagonal turns at every second warp.

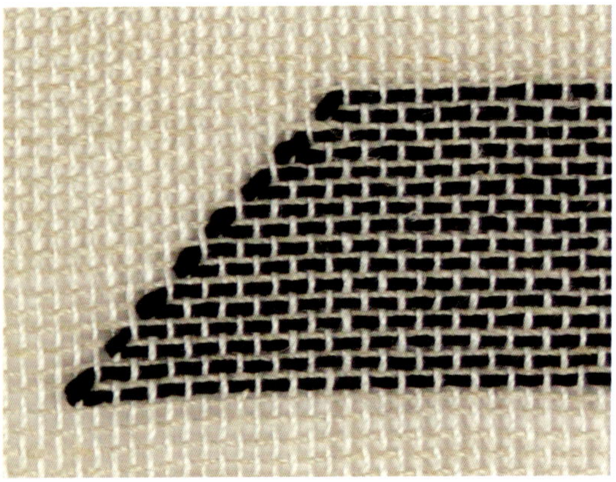

Woven example, seen from working side.

These are just three possible angles that can be woven with inlay. The angle of a diagonal edge may be so steep that it requires more than two turns per warp, and there really is no limit. The same goes for extremely shallow diagonal edges. Any number of warps can be skipped between turns. The essential rule to remember is to be consistent. If your angle requires one turn per warp, always turn once per warp.

EXERCISE 4: WEAVE DIAGONAL EDGES

Practice weaving the three diagonal edges discussed here:

- A steep diagonal that turns once on every warp
- A steeper diagonal that turns twice on every warp
- A shallow diagonal that turns on every second warp

FINDING THE CORRECT ANGLE FOR A DIAGONAL EDGE

What happens if the slope of the diagonal edge you want to weave is steeper than one turn per warp, but not as steep as two turns per warp? The slope can be fine-tuned by alternating between one turn and two turns per warp. This breaks the rule of always turning the same number of times at each warp, but it does not break an even more important rule: Be consistent. If the angle demands that you alternate turning once and then twice, be consistent in turning once and then twice.

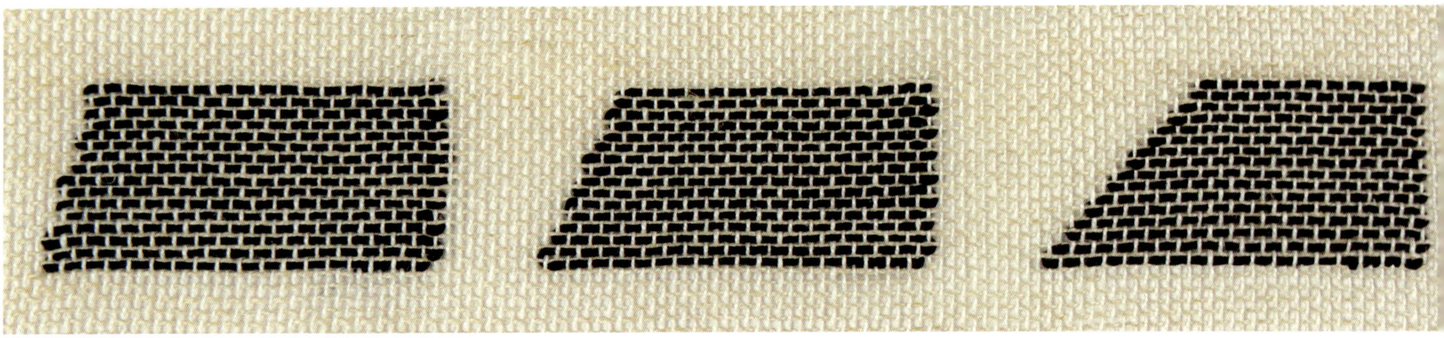

Three woven diagonal edges seen from the front. From left to right: two turns per warp, one turn per warp, two warps per turn.

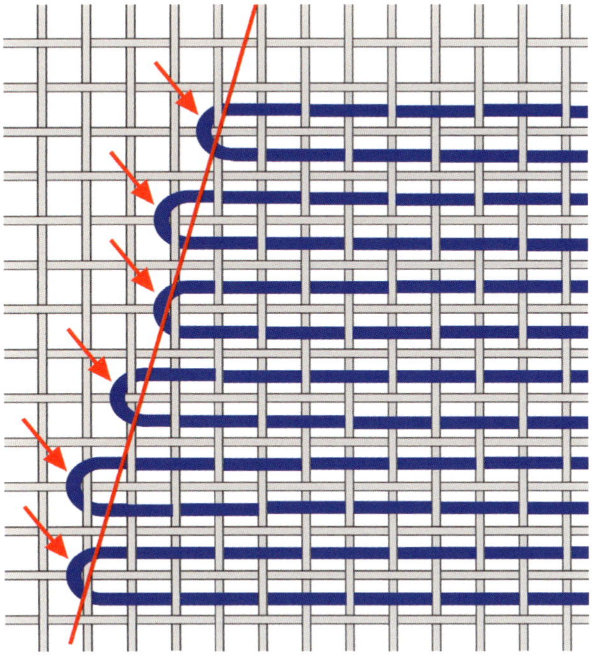

Fine-tuning the angle of the edge: This diagonal alternates between turning once and turning twice at each warp.

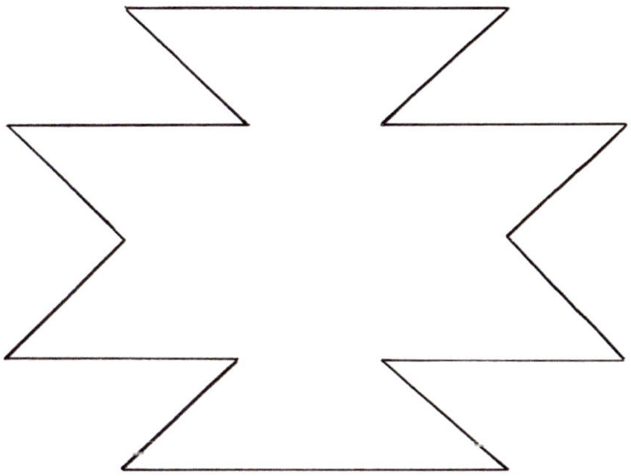

Geometric designs often have precise angles that must be woven accurately.

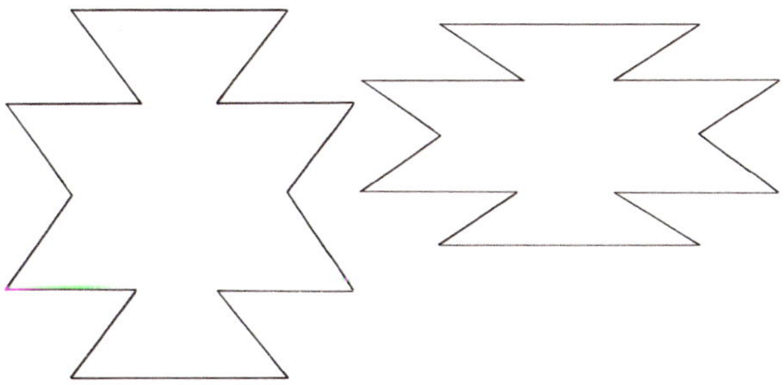

Consequences of weaving the angle too steep *(left)* or too shallow *(right)*.

The challenge when weaving diagonal edges is matching the woven angle to the angle in your design. Consider the geometric figure that you will weave in Project 1. The diagonal edges must be woven at precise angles in order to replicate the drawing on the cartoon. If the angles are too steep, the design will be elongated. If woven too shallow, the squash blossom will appear, well, squashed.

You may find yourself unweaving your work if after a few rows you see that the line you are weaving is too steep or too flat compared to the design. Never try to "correct" the angle by jumping out of sequence. Any departures will create unwanted bumps in the diagonal edge.

There are three approaches to determining how to weave the correct angle:

- Wing it
- Graph it
- Calculate it

Wing It

The simplest approach is to just jump in and weave the diagonal, keeping your turns as close as possible to the line on your cartoon. As you strive to turn the same number of times at each warp, you may find your woven diagonal becoming either too steep or too flat compared to the cartoon. This could result in having to unweave and try again. Personally, I hate unweaving, so I rarely use this approach.

Graph It

When weaving geometric shapes, graph paper can be a huge help. The appendix has graph paper for 12 epi, 15 epi, and 16 epi. Scan and print these pages to use for determining how to weave your angle.

Copy the diagonal line from your cartoon or design to the graph paper. Draw it at whatever length you want, but make sure it has the correct slant.

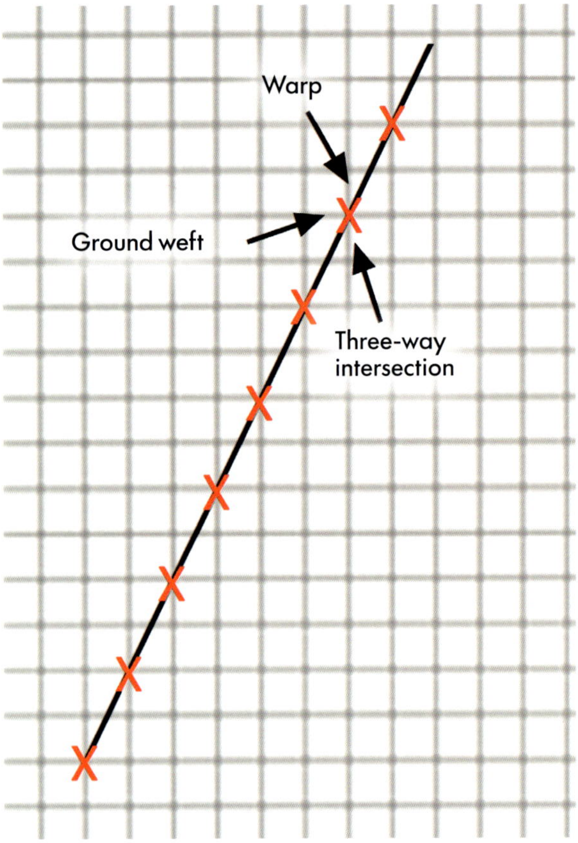

Find the points where the diagonal intersects with the warp and ground weft.

Assume that the vertical lines on the graph paper represent warps and the horizontal lines represent rows of ground weft.

Make a mark at each point where three lines intersect: the diagonal line, the warp line, and the ground weft line. These are your potential turning points. Now mark the inlay weft, which weaves between rows of ground weft. The inlay weaves toward the diagonal edge, turns, and weaves away from the turning point.

In the bottom left diagram, the diagonal line meets an intersection of warp and weft for every pass of weaving, indicating that the weft should turn once on each warp. The middle diagram shows a steeper diagonal that meets an intersection of warp and weft only every other pass of weaving. This indicates that the weft must turn twice on each warp in order to match the angle of the diagonal. The second of the two turns in each pair will be slightly above the diagonal line. You may think this is a mistake, but it is not. The third turn will line up once again with the diagonal line, and, as we saw above, the jagged edge will appear smooth.

On the right-hand diagram, the turning point moves over two warps for every pass of the inlay weft,

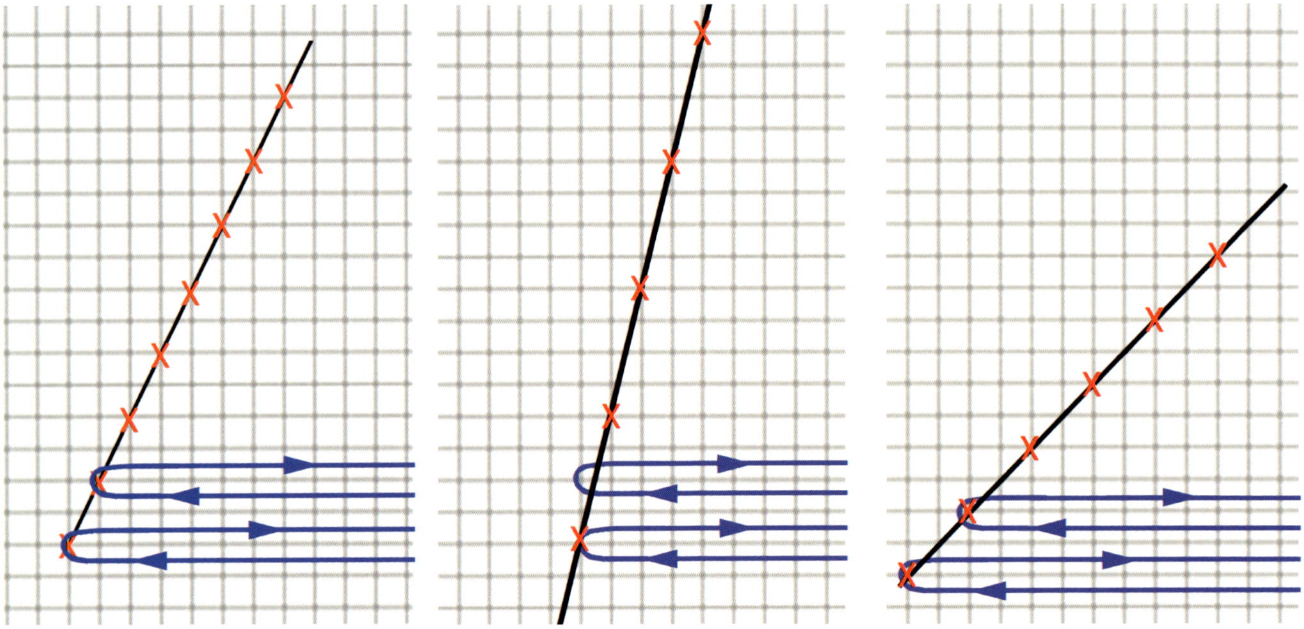

LEFT TO RIGHT: Graphing steep and shallow diagonals.

skipping a warp in between turns to weave a shallow diagonal edge.

Calculate It

What would you say if I told you that you could mathematically determine how to weave any given angle? If your eyes just glazed over, that's okay. But stay with me if you want to learn a simple formula that will save you a lot of unweaving.

After transposing the diagonal line from your cartoon or design to the graph paper, do the following:

- From bottom to top of your diagonal line, count the number of warps that are crossed.
- From bottom to top of your line, count the number of picks you would need to weave it.
- Divide that number in half to find the number of turns or passes that are needed.

The rest is a simple formula:

- # of passes ÷ # of warps = turns per warp

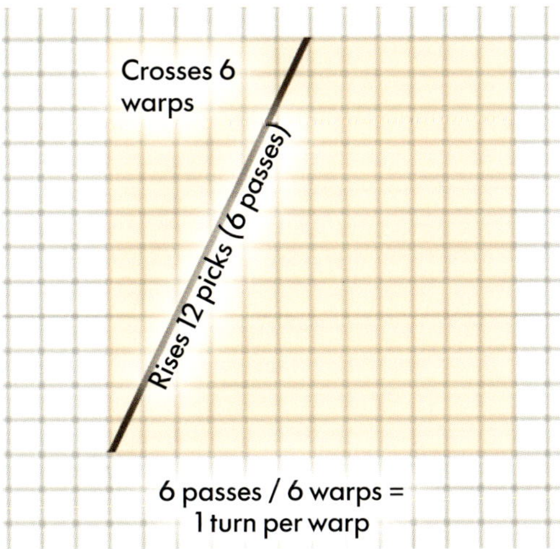

Let's look at the same diagonal lines we have been discussing. In the above illustration, the diagonal line crosses six warps from bottom to top. To weave from bottom to top will take 12 picks or 6 passes, using the formula:

- 6 passes ÷ 6 warps = 1 turn per warp

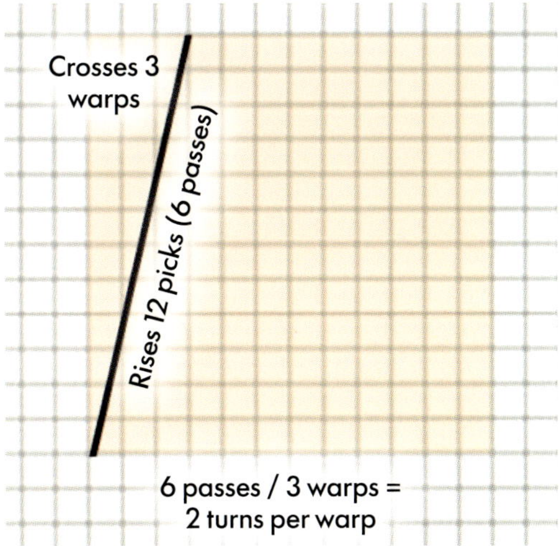

If the diagonal line crosses only three warps in the course of weaving six passes, as in the above illustration, then the formula would tell you to turn twice on each warp:

- 6 passes ÷ 3 warps = 2 turns per warp

Calculating Shallow Angles

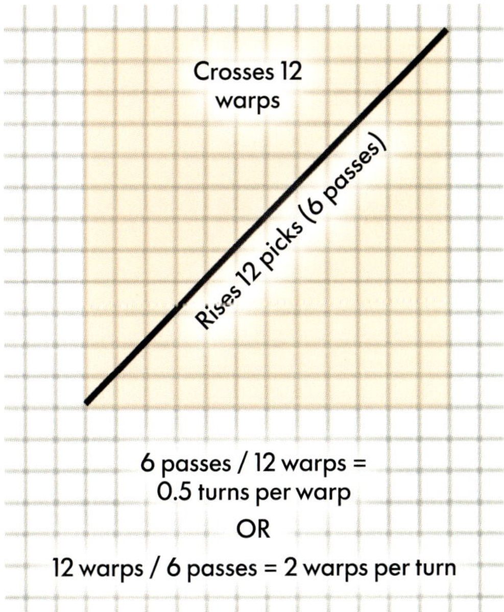

The calculation changes for shallower angles. In the bottom illustration, the diagonal line crosses 12 warps and takes 12 picks or 6 passes to weave. Employing the formula, we get the following:

- 6 passes ÷ 12 warps = 0.5 turns per warp

How do you weave 0.5 turns per warp? By turning on every other warp. One turn per two warps is a half turn per warp. To avoid working with fractions, for angles with less than one turn per warp, reverse the numerator and denominator in the equation:

- # of warps ÷ # of passes = warps per turn

Stating the formula this way gives this result:

- 12 warps ÷ 6 passes = 2 warps per turn

Note the difference between *turns per warp* for steep angles and *warps per turn* for shallow angles. *Turns per warp* indicates that every warp is turned on by one or more passes. *Warps per turn* indicates that warps are skipped between turns: *2 warps per turn* tells you to turn on every second warp.

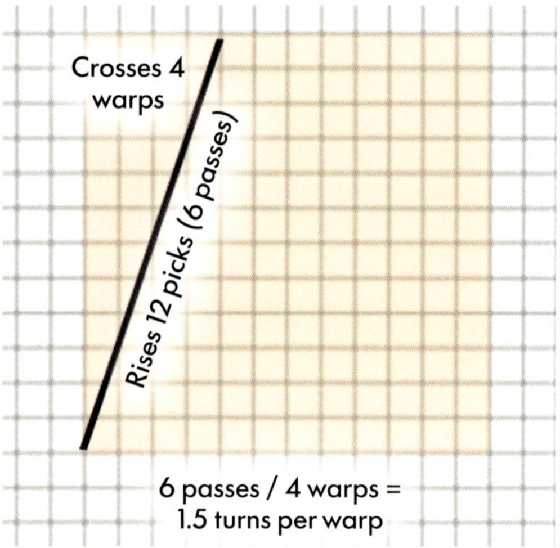

One benefit of using the calculation is that it accommodates fine-tuning the angle. In this illustration, the diagonal crosses only four warps, with six passes required to weave it. Putting these numbers into the formula:

- 6 passes ÷ 4 warps = 1.5 turns per warp

This diagonal would be woven by alternating turning once per warp with turning twice per warp.

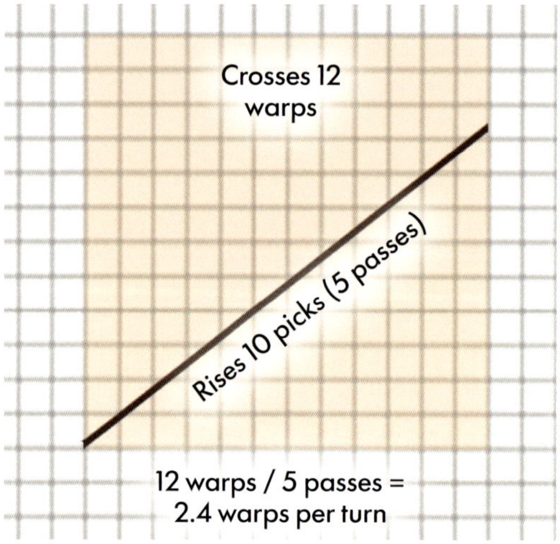

When applied to shallow angles, the formula may give a result that is not a whole number. The formula for this illustration would be as follows:

- 12 warps ÷ 5 passes = 2.4 warps per turn

At 2.4 turns per warp, this diagonal lies midway between turning at every second warp or turning at every third warp. The closest solution would be to alternate turning every two warps with turning every three warps.

When the formula yields a number that is closer to one whole number than the other—say it is 0.2 or 0.8—rounding up or down to the nearest whole number will get you close enough to the actual angle.

EXERCISE 5: CALCULATE THE ANGLE OF A DIAGONAL

Create a copy of the 12 epi graph paper in appendix 1. Using a ruler, draw a diagonal line approximately 2 inches long. Mark two points along the diagonal line where it coincides with an intersection of the horizontal and vertical lines of the graph. Mark these points as A and B. Count the number of warps (vertical lines) that are crossed to get from A to B (do not count A; that is your starting point). Count the number of wefts (horizontal lines) that are crossed to get from A to B (again, do not count A). Apply the formula to find the number of turns per warp needed to weave that angle. That was easy, wasn't it?

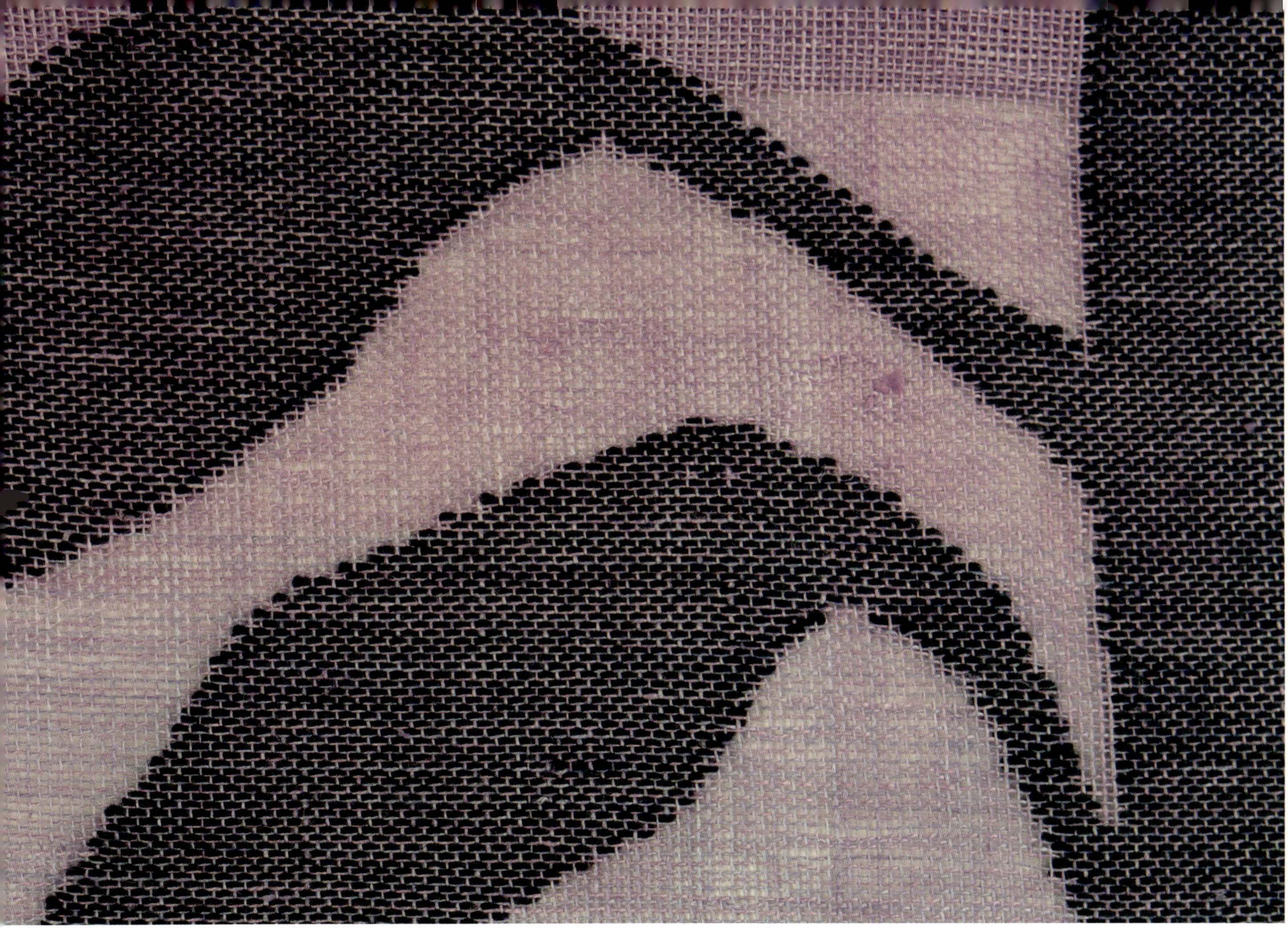

Jagged edges result from turning on the wrong warp.

AVOIDING JAGGED EDGES

Tapestry weavers place a lot of emphasis on how the weft turns around the warp. In transparency weaving, it's usually not such a big deal . . . except when it is. After weaving my first transparency, I discovered a curious effect on some of my diagonal edges. There were places where the inlay jutted out from the edge, creating a jagged line that looked kind of weird. I looked at how I had woven those areas, and a pattern emerged. Although it's not an essential make-or-break element to transparency weaving, this is an instance where I can share my hard-learned lessons so that your transparencies can be closer to perfect.

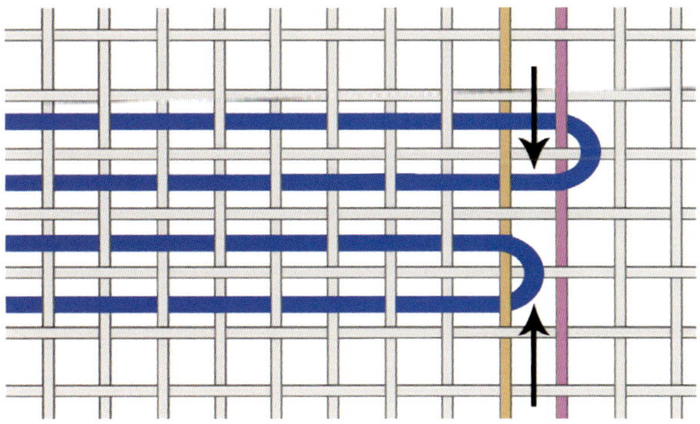

Both picks emerge between the gold and pink warps before turning.

The crux of the issue lies in which warp the inlay weft turns around when it changes direction. The illustration shows two passes of inlay weft. Each time the inlay weft reaches a turning point, it emerges between two warps, the first in the up position and the second in the down position. The arrows indicate that the first pick in each pass comes to the surface after passing under the raised gold warp. After changing the shed to weave the next pick, the gold warp will be lowered and the pink warp raised. Notice how the turns differ depending on which warp the weft turns around. The weft at the bottom turns back and weaves over the lowered gold warp. The weft at the top steps forward to turn back under the raised pink warp.

The decision about which warp to turn on is often determined by the cartoon: Which warp is closer to the line that you are following in the cartoon? When weaving a steep diagonal where one or more turns are made on each warp, the turns alternate between stepping back on one warp and stepping forward on the next warp, leaving you no choice about which warp to turn on. The one and only situation in which you'll want to pay attention is when weaving shallow diagonals that skip an even number of warps between turns. That's pretty specific, but it comes into play more often than you might expect.

Weft turns that produce the smoothest edges are shown in the illustration. At the top, the shape is decreasing. That is to say, it is covering fewer warps at each turn. Choosing to turn the weft back over the lowered warp will give a smooth edge. At the bottom, the shape is increasing. It is incorporating more warps into the shape. In this scenario, step forward to turn around the raised warp. To put it succinctly:

- Decreasing shape turns back.
- Increasing shape steps forward.

These rules work best when the shapes are increasing or decreasing in increments of an even number or warps. If you step forward on the first turn, you will step forward on all subsequent turns in that series. This rule of thumb will be familiar to tapestry weavers, since it mirrors the rules that apply in tapestry weaving when weaving with the back of the tapestry facing you.

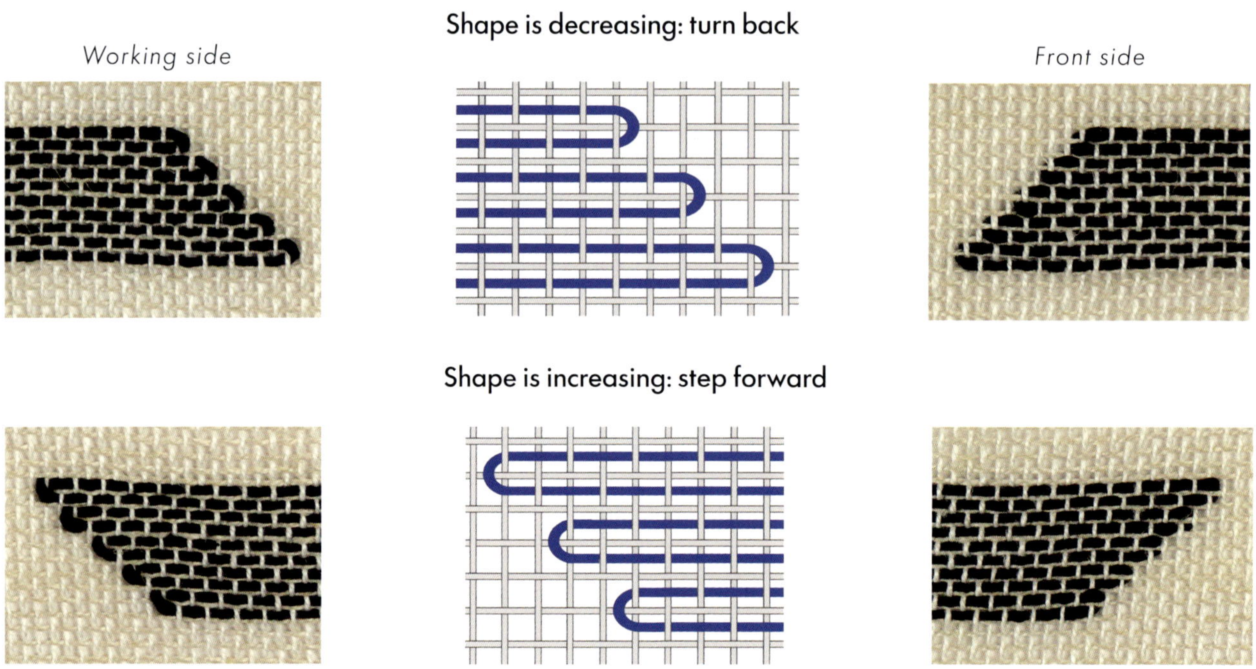

Weaving the smoothest edges for shallow diagonals.

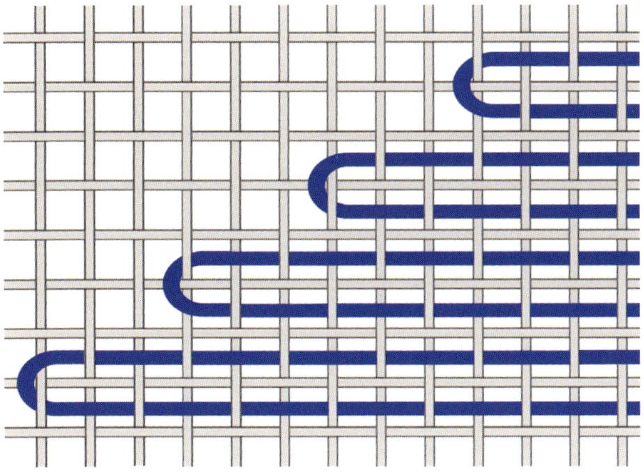

Diagonal edge where the turning point moves over three warps for each turn.

When the slope of the diagonal edge crosses three warps at each turn, the turns will be forced to alternate between stepping forward and turning back. This will create some unevenness at the edge of the shape, which is unavoidable if this is the slope required by the design.

Fortunately, any amount of backlighting will tend to minimize the impact of the unevenness caused by the choice of which warp to turn on. This is because the two picks of weft leading toward and away from the turn are visible through the ground cloth, making the shape appear as a cohesive whole.

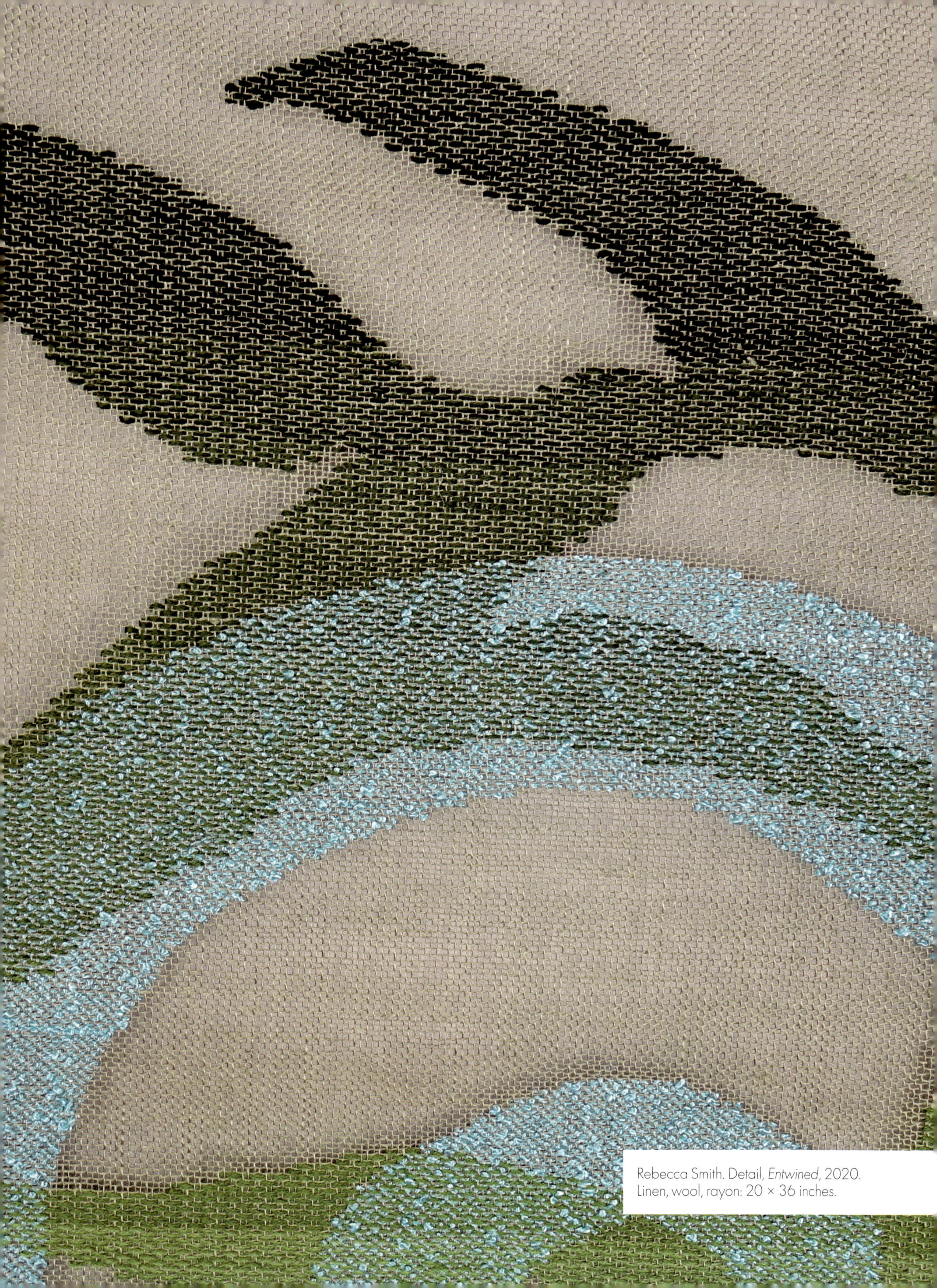

Rebecca Smith. Detail, *Entwined*, 2020.
Linen, wool, rayon: 20 × 36 inches.

Chapter 6

WEAVING PICTORIAL DESIGNS

Suppose you are weaving a flower design. Your cartoon will tell you the shape of the various flower parts and where they appear. Weaving the flower shapes is a matter of following the edges of each shape. This section will teach you to weave curves so that you can follow a planned design.

SIMPLE CURVES

In its simplest form, a curve is really a diagonal that gets progressively steeper or flatter. Like diagonals, curves can be steep or shallow. In fact, the same curve can have both steep and shallow parts (see examples below). These curves have a steep section where there are multiple turns per warp, and a shallow section where some warps have no turns.

For a curve to get steeper (turn up), steadily increase the number of turns. The bottom portion of the curve is a shallow curve that is slowly getting steeper. It is woven by moving the turns gradually closer together (i.e., progressively skipping fewer warps between each turn). This will allow the shape to curve up. The steep section begins when there is at least one turn on every warp. A steady increase in the number of turns per warp causes the curve to continue to turn up.

For a curve to get less steep, steadily decrease the number of turns per warp. In the steep part of this curve, there are progressively fewer turns at each warp. In the shallow section, each turn is a little farther away from the previous turn.

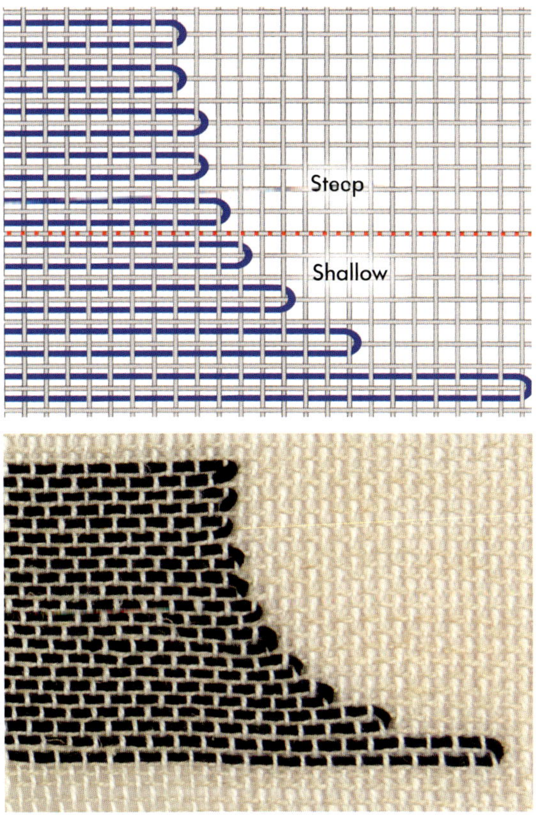

Curve that gets steeper

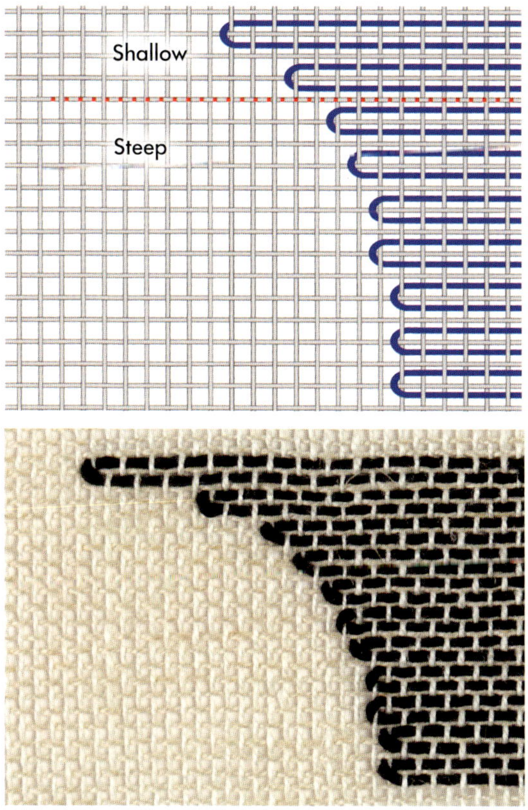

Curve that gets less steep.

COMPLEX CURVES

Most curved shapes do not adhere to the orderly set of steps shown above. Curved shapes can be quite complex. Depending on the size of the curve, the steps may need to be repeated or skipped in order to weave the desired shape. There may be parts of the curve that are getting steeper, and parts that are getting flatter. Nestled between the two extremes is a section of the curve that is really a diagonal line, because there is the same number of turns at each warp. These components are diagrammed here for two classic complex curves: the S-curve, and the Bell curve.

A typical shape in a transparency design will contain a variety of curves. A leaf is a good example. There are parts of the leaf that are getting steeper and parts that are getting flatter.

The bottom side of the leaf shown here has two different curves, each getting gradually steeper but at different rates. For each curve, the turns at the bottom of the leaf should be farther apart than the turns higher up the sides. This will ensure that the shape curves up.

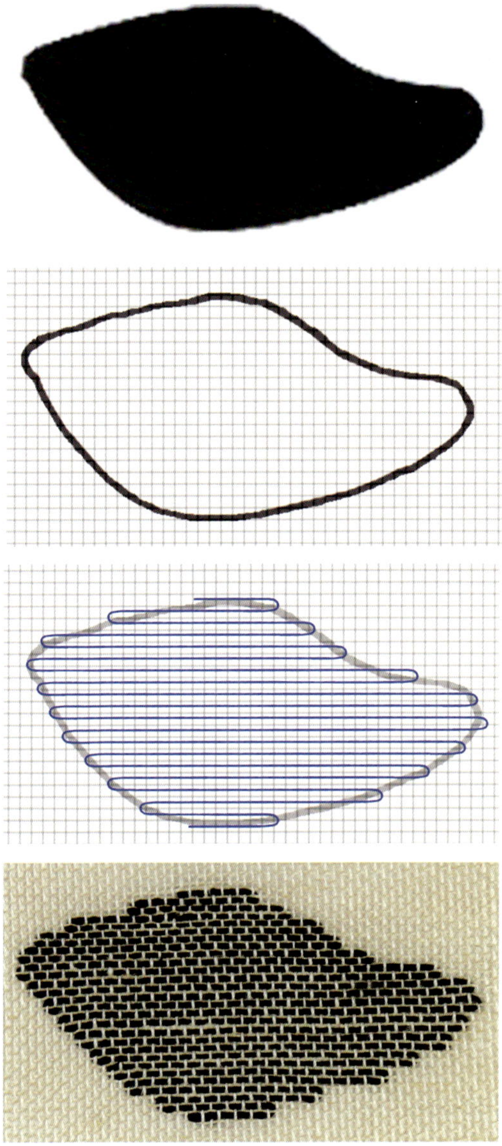

TOP TO BOTTOM: Steps for weaving a leaf shape: Draw the shape to scale on graph paper; map out the turns for the inlay weft; weave it.

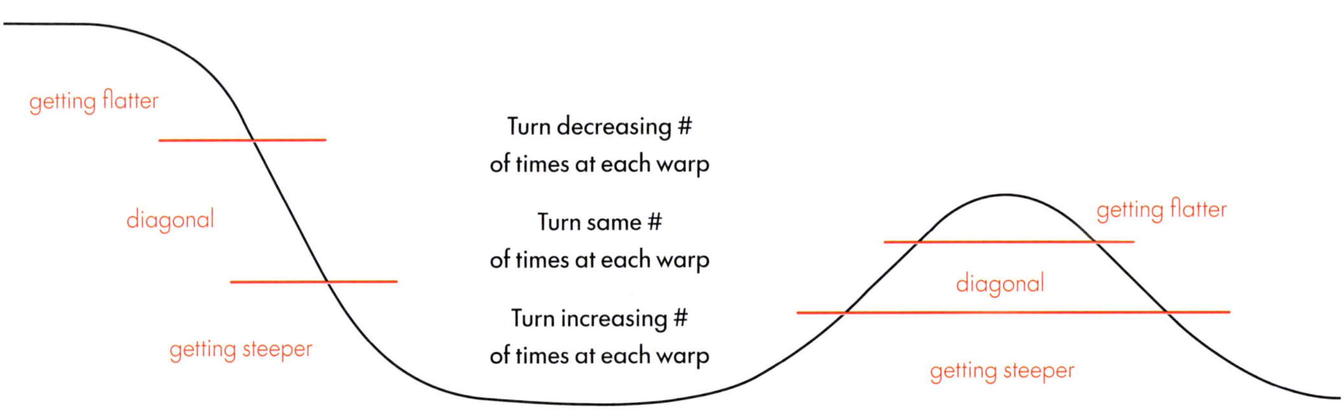

Classic S-curve and Bell curve are examples of complex curves that bend both up and down and even have portions that are diagonal lines.

The most complex part of the leaf is the upper side, where, starting from the right, the curve shifts from relatively flat to steeper and then back to flatter. It's similar to a classic S-curve.

Graphing Curves

It is relatively easy to weave a curve just by following the cartoon. Each pick weaves to where the edge of the shape meets the fell line of the weaving: This is where you would make the turn. Graph paper can be a helpful aid in mapping out the turns prior to weaving and may help improve accuracy in the woven shape. Draw the shape at the scale you will weave it on graph paper that matches your sett. The vertical lines on the graph indicate warps, and the horizontal lines correspond to picks of ground weft.

Choose a starting point at the bottom of the leaf and begin drawing lines for the weft as it travels from side to side. Turn the weft where the line on the cartoon meets a vertical line on the graph. It is okay if the turn is at times slightly inside or outside the line.

EXERCISE 6: WEAVE THE LEAF

Create a cartoon of the leaf design examined above. If you wish, use graph paper to map out the turns. Attach the cartoon behind the warp and weave the shape of the leaf by following the lines on the design. Pay attention to the description given above for weaving the various leaf parts.

WORKING WITH COMPLEX CURVES

Joining Two Shapes into One

Often, the bottom edge of a curved shape begins on two different rows of weaving: One part of the shape is lower than another part, with a gap in between that has no inlay. Organic shapes, such as seen in *A Memory of Trees* shown here, have lots of curves that typically fit this scenario.

Let's look at the area highlighted by the white rectangle. The left lobe of the shape begins three picks before the right lobe. Eventually the two sections join and only one weft is needed.

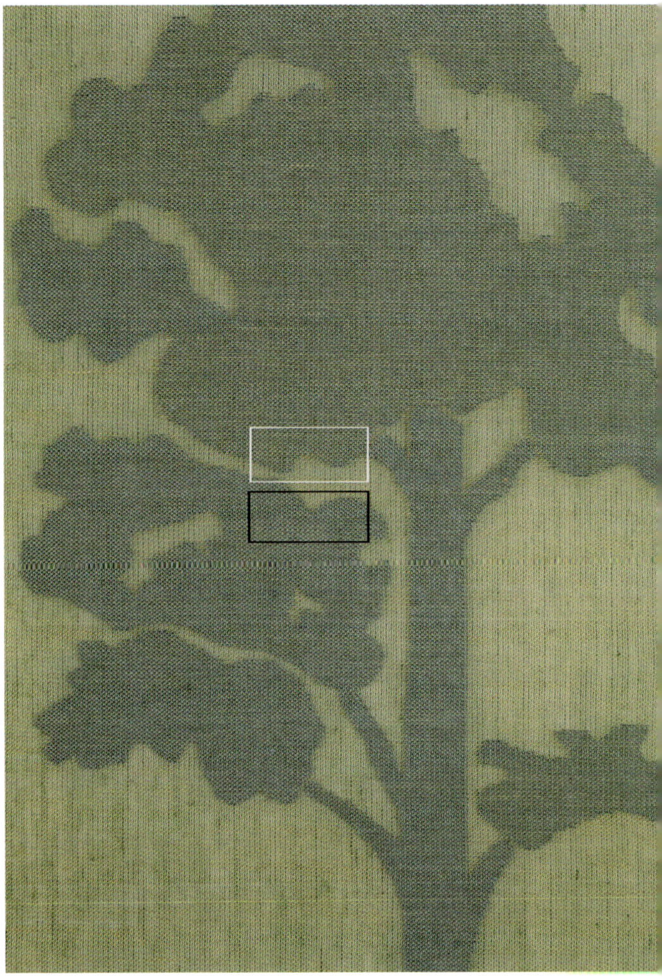

Rebecca Smith. *A Memory of Trees*, 2021. Linen, Tencel: two panels, each 18 × 30 inches.

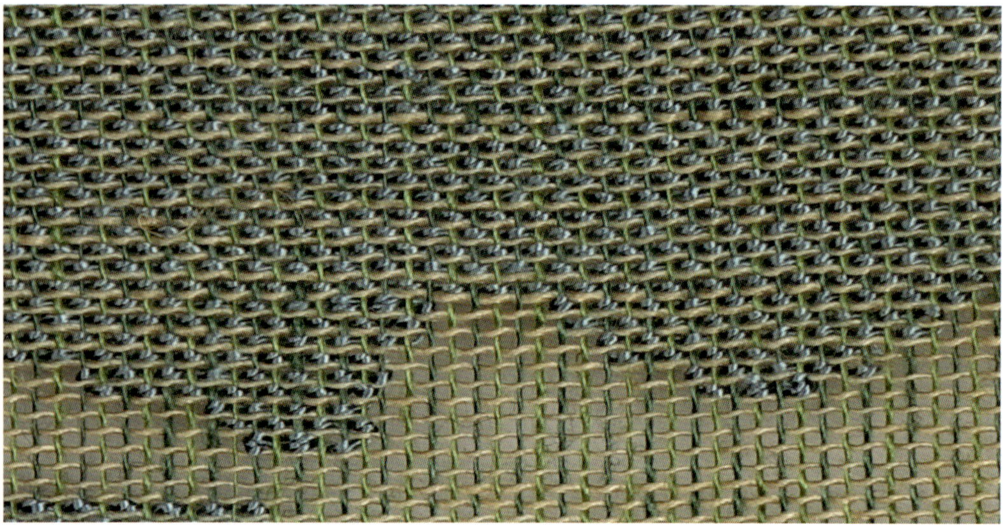

Two shapes converge into one shape.

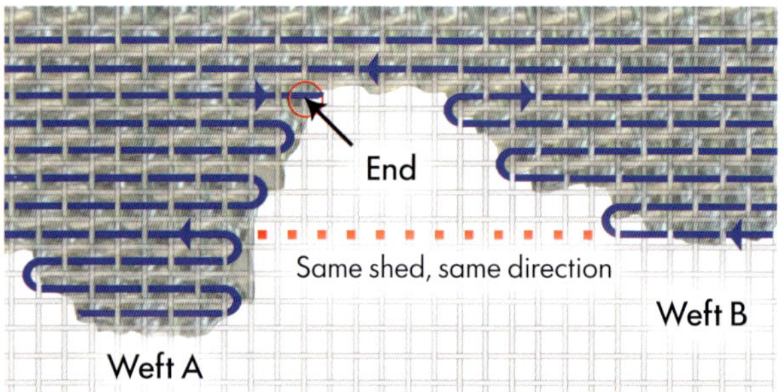

Example with weft A and weft B weaving in the same direction in each shed.

Now let's examine how the shape was woven. When weft B starts, it weaves in the same direction as weft A in the same shed, as indicated by the dashed red line. When the point is reached where the two shapes merge into one, one of the wefts is ended, in this case weft A. This makes it possible for the next pick of weft B to weave over weft A in the correct shed.

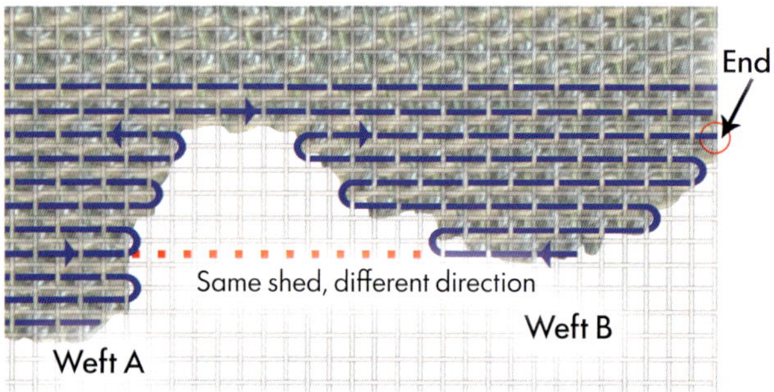

Example with weft A and weft B weaving in the opposite direction in each shed.

Is it necessary for the two wefts to weave in the same direction in each shed? Not at all. You may develop a preference for one or the other (I prefer to weave the two wefts in the same direction). If the two wefts are weaving in opposite directions in the same shed, the picture changes slightly. The weft that is ending will end at the opposite side (the outer edge) of the shape. The other weft will then weave in the correct shed as it continues to weave across the shape.

The rule of thumb is this:

- If two wefts are weaving in the same direction, end one when it is on the side closest to the other weft.
- If two wefts are weaving in opposing directions, end one when it is on the side farthest from the other weft.

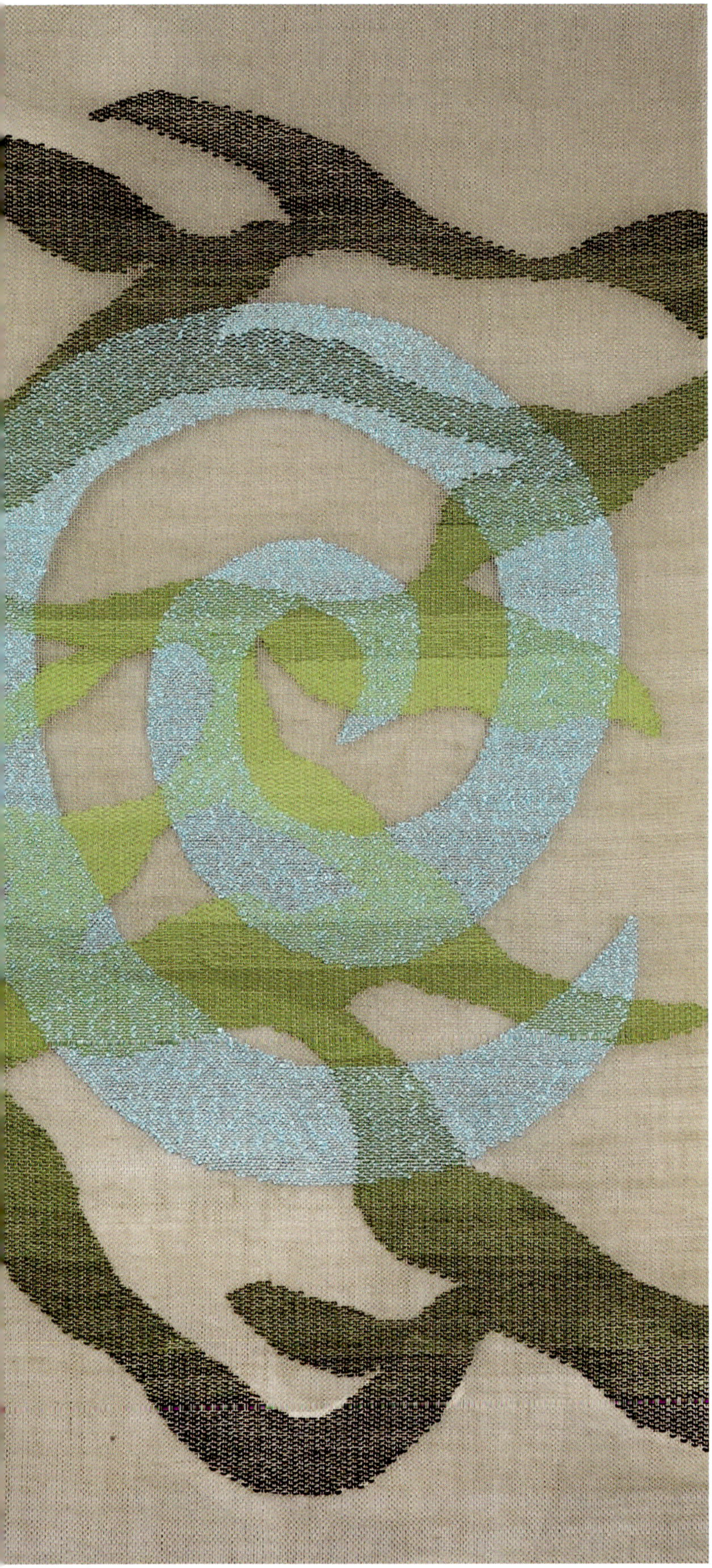

Rebecca Smith. *Entwined*, 2020. Linen, wool, rayon: 20 × 36 inches.

Separating One Shape into Two

At the top of a shape, the opposite scenario can occur: The shape splits into two sections with a gap between them. The black rectangle (page 77) marks an area like this. Where the two sections split, a new weft is started. The new weft can start on the side closest to the other weft and weave in the same direction, or it can start at the side farthest from the other weft and weave in the opposite direction.

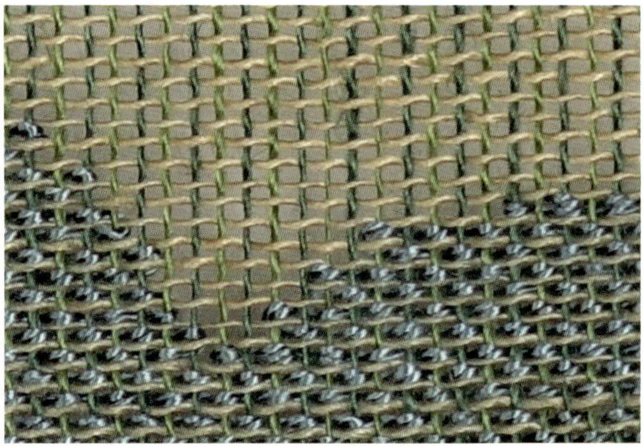

One shape splits into two sections.

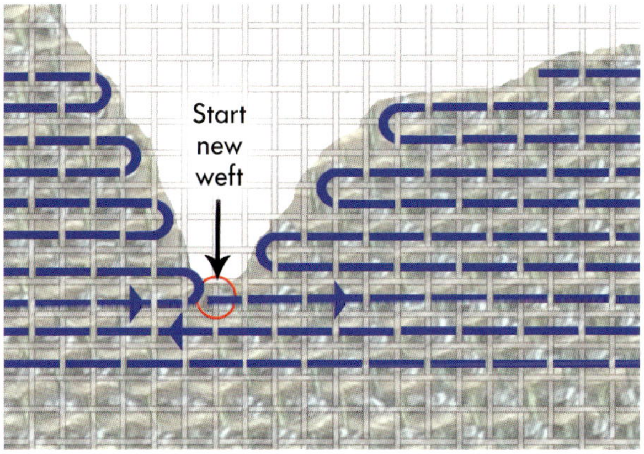

Both wefts weave in the same direction in each shed.

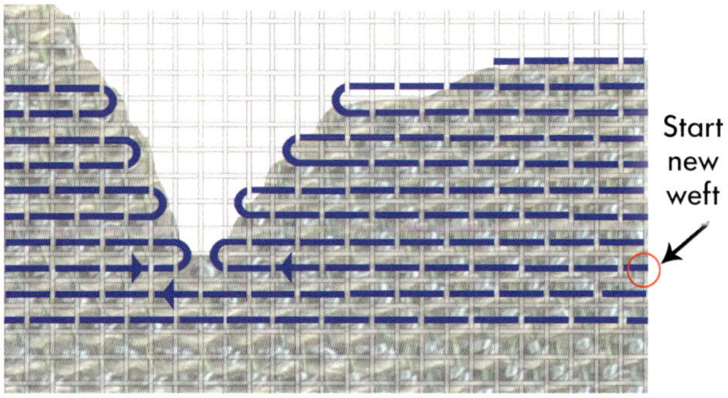

Wefts weave in opposing directions in each shed.

WEAVING A CIRCLE

Everyone wants to weave a circle. Even students in their first transparency workshop want to weave a circle. Why is that? I suppose it's the ultimate weaving challenge. And it certainly is a challenge. But I have found a solution that makes the challenge somewhat easier.

The solution involves using graph paper to plan the circle, similar to how graph paper was used in planning diagonal edges in the last chapter. A compass is the other requirement. Not the kind of compass that tells you which direction to head when you're lost in the forest; the kind of compass shown here.

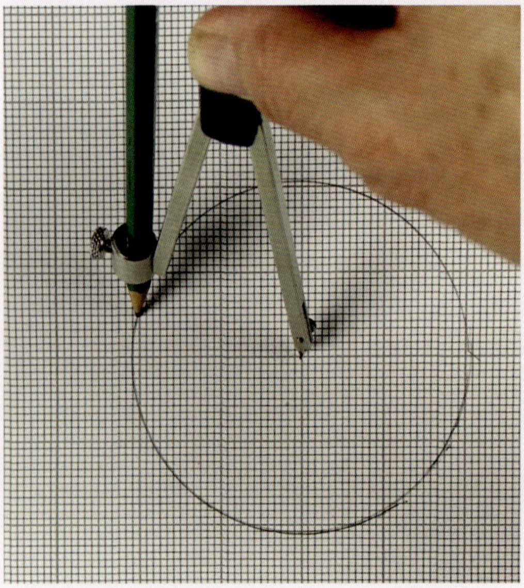

Use a compass to draw a circle on graph paper.

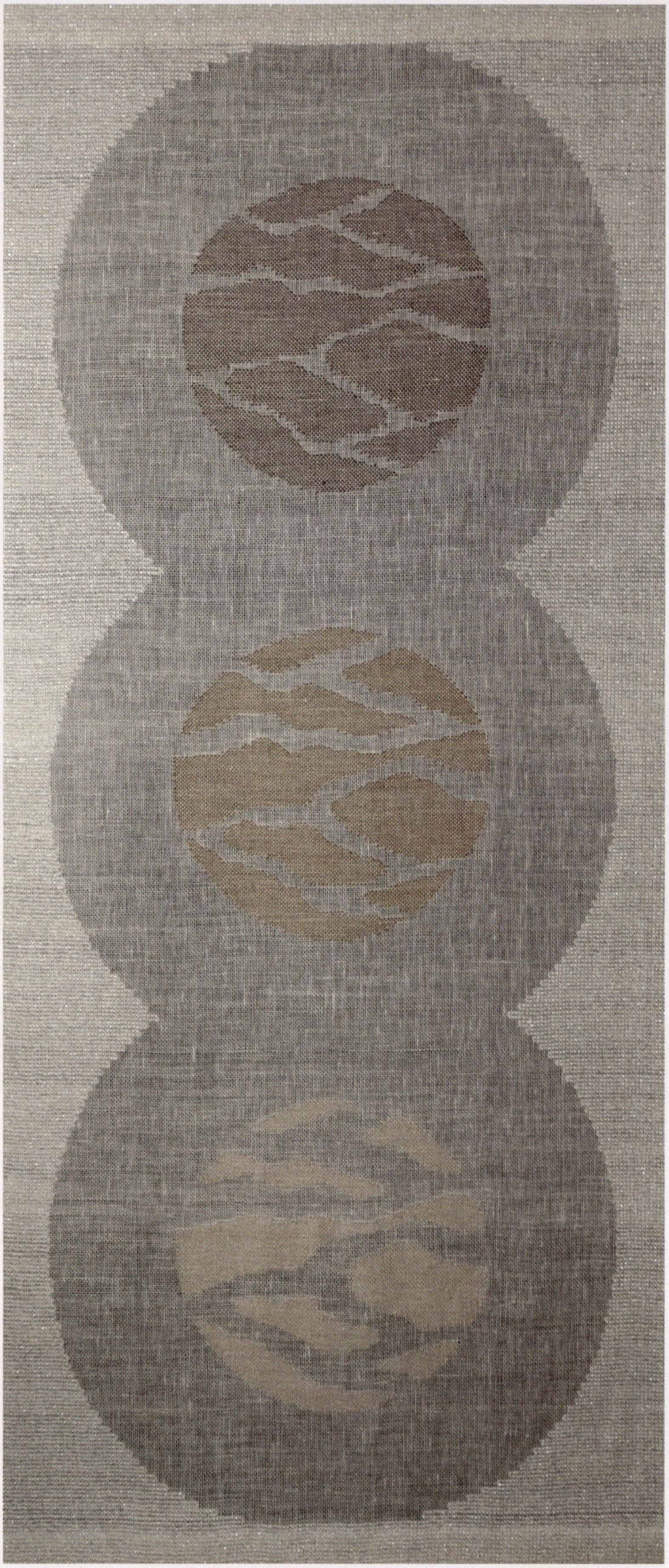

Rebecca Smith. *Carbon Crisis*, 2023. Linen, wool, rayon/metallic: 28 × 50 inches.

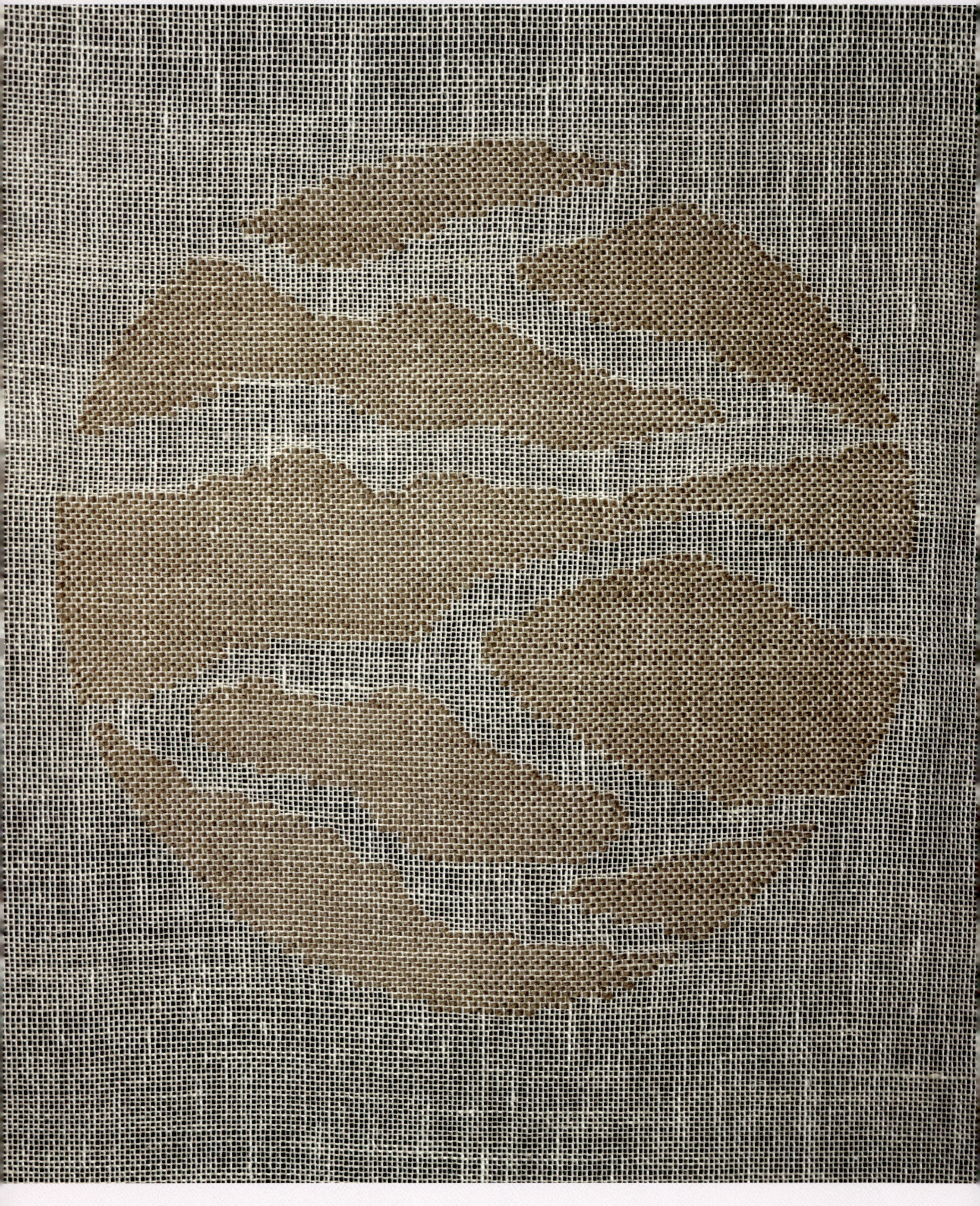

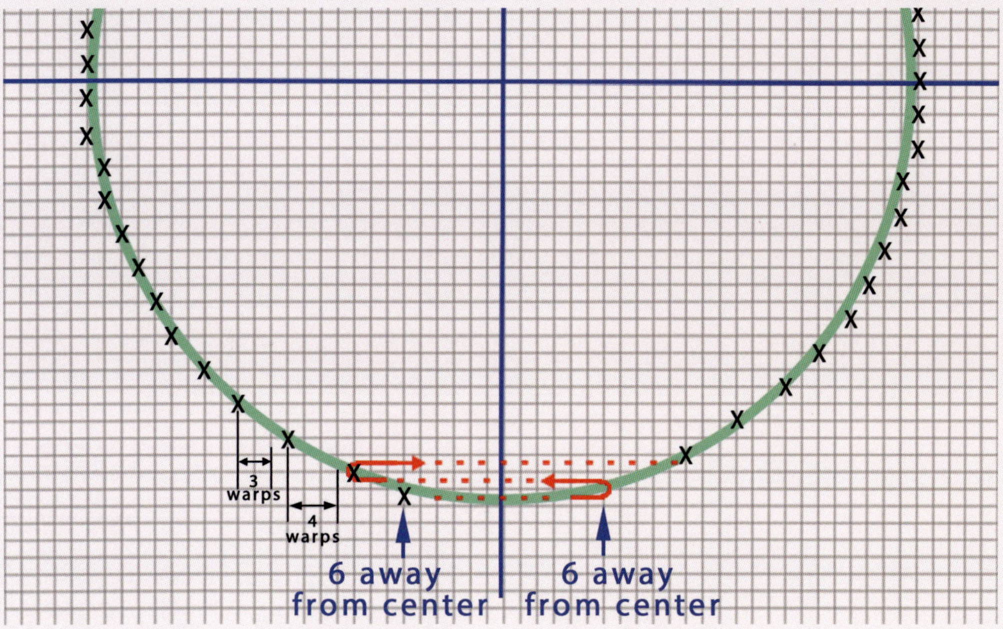

Mark turning points for weaving the circle.

Use the compass to draw a circle on the graph paper at the same size that you want to weave the circle. Try to position the bottom of the circle along a horizontal line on the graph paper, and the sides of the circle along vertical lines. It's helpful to mark the center of the circle in both directions. The horizontal lines represent ground weft, and the vertical lines represent warps.

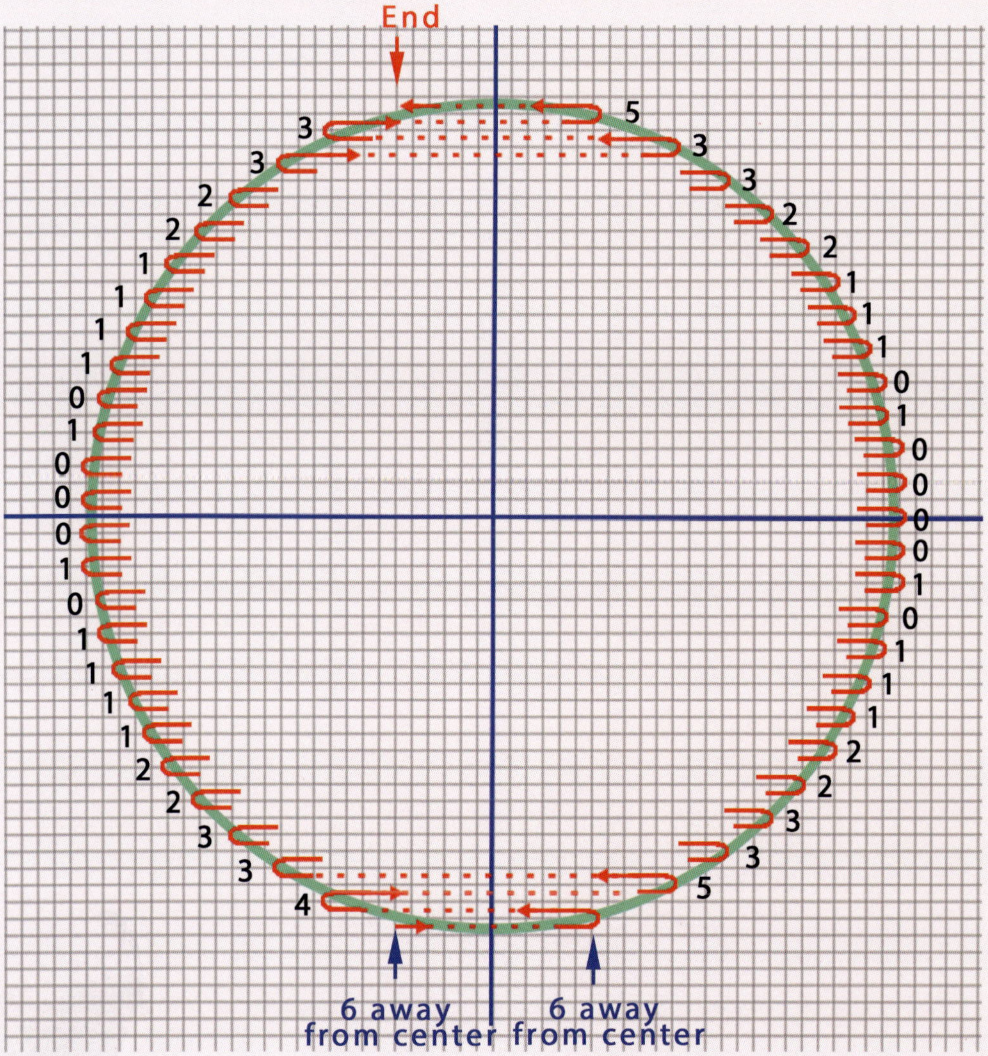

The bottom of the circle is several warps wide. Locate the point where the curve of the circle coincides with an intersection of warp and weft. That is your starting point for weaving. I've marked the point with a blue arrow. At the other side, locate the corresponding point where the curve of the circle falls at the intersection of a warp. This is your first turning point. The two points should be the same number of warps away from the center of the circle. The length of this first pick will be between 20 and 25 percent of the circle's diameter.

6 from center	6 from center
4	5
3	3
3	3
2	2
2	2
1	1
1	1
1	1
1	0
0	1
1	0
0	0
0	0
0	0
1	1
0	0
1	1
1	1
1	1
1	2
2	2
2	3
3	3
3	5
4 (end)	

From here, it is just a matter of moving from side to side to find the points where the intersections of warp and ground weft (vertical and horizontal lines) coincide with the edge of the circle. Mark the path of your inlay weft (shown with red dashed line) to find the correct intersecting points. Next, mark with an X all the intersecting points up through the midpoint of the circle. Count the number of warps between the turns and mark it on the graph. Note that you don't count the warp that you turned on, just the warps up to the next intersection. When two turns are made on the same warp, mark zero, indicating that there are no warps between the turns.

The top half of the circle can be graphed by using a straightedge to find the corresponding warp that you turned on in the bottom half. This ensures that the circle will be symmetrical.

When you are finished, you will have all the information needed to weave the circle. For large circles, I go one step further. I list the turns for both the left and right sides. As I weave, I follow the list instead of following the cartoon, checking off each turn as I go so that I don't lose track of where I am. This has proved invaluable in reducing the number of mistakes I make!

I used this approach to weave the six circles, some of them concentric circles, for my piece *Carbon Crisis*, shown on page 80.

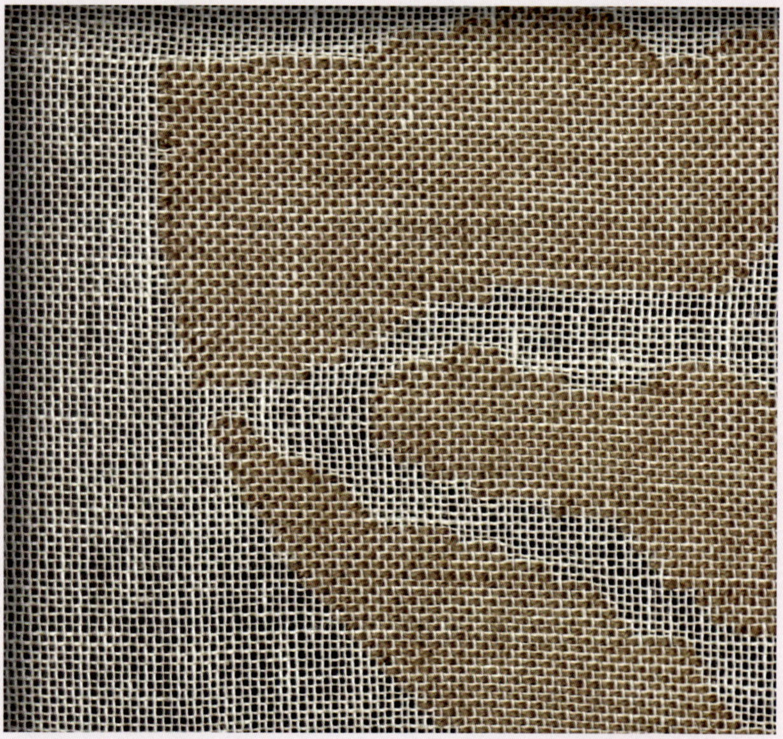

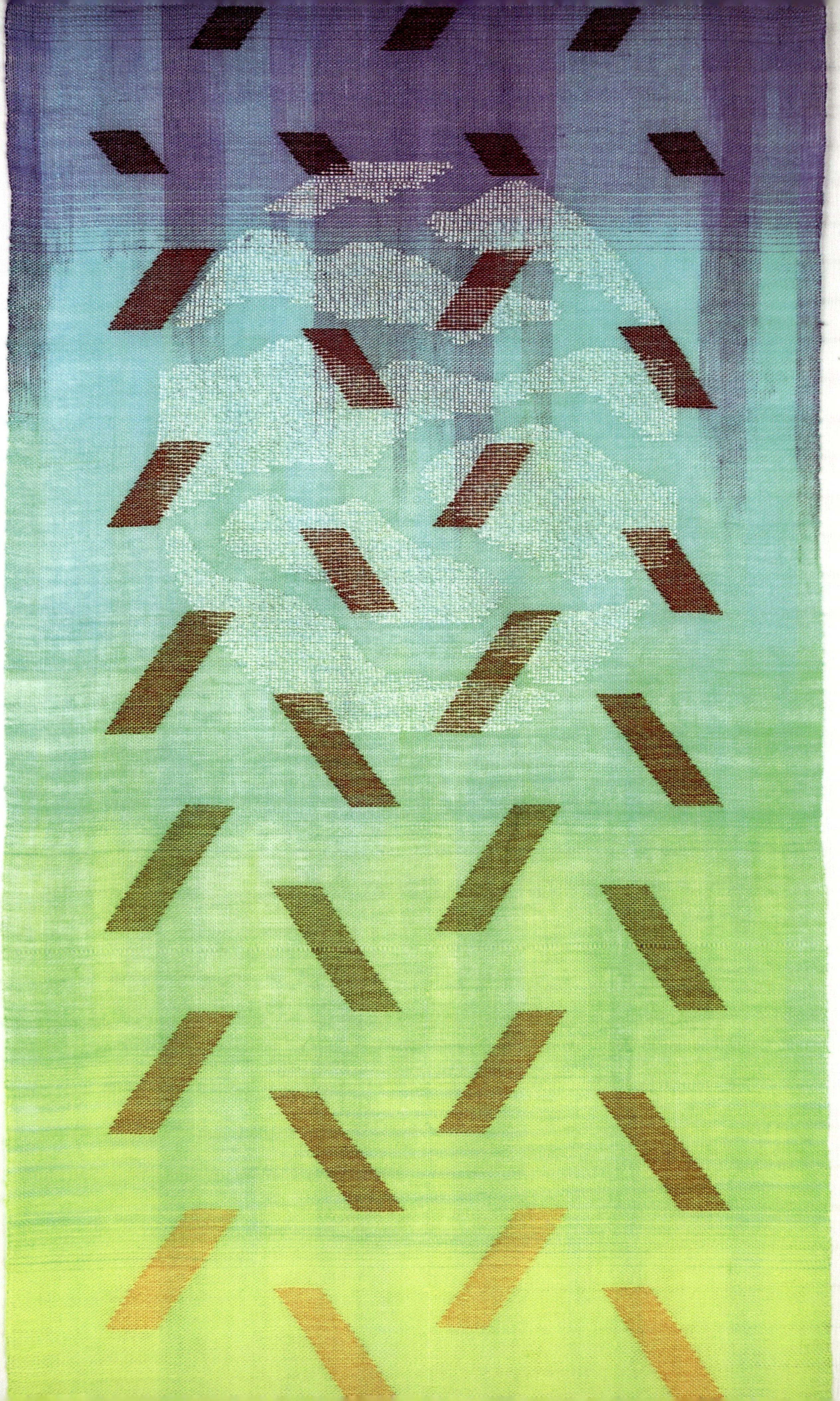

Chapter 7

DESIGN ELEMENTS: PATTERN, DENSITY, AND COLOR

The shapes you learned to weave in chapters 5 and 6 form the backbone for your journey into transparency weaving. If you can translate a shape from a cartoon to a woven cloth, you are ready to start incorporating more elements into your design. In this chapter, we will look at three design elements that add interest and visual complexity to your transparencies. These elements are inlay pattern, inlay density, and color.

INLAY PATTERNS

Inlay weft does not always have to be woven in the same plain-weave structure as the ground weft. Other weave patterns can be added to transparency weaving, for a variety of reasons. The patterns themselves add visual interest. Some patterns make the inlay weft appear more dominant. Inlay patterns that skip rows can be used to create variety of effects, from extending the range of density effects to aiding in color blending.

While there are probably limitless possibilities for using patterned inlay, the focus here is on four-shaft patterns that have most commonly or historically been used for transparency weaving. The alternative weaving patterns suitable for inlay can be categorized into two types: balanced and unbalanced patterns.

Balanced Patterns

Balanced pattern weaves go over and under a balanced number of warps. These are the only patterns that will appear the same on both the front and back of the weaving. Six balanced inlay patterns are illustrated on page 86.

Plain weave (**A**) is the ultimate balanced pattern, repeating an over-one, under-one pattern.

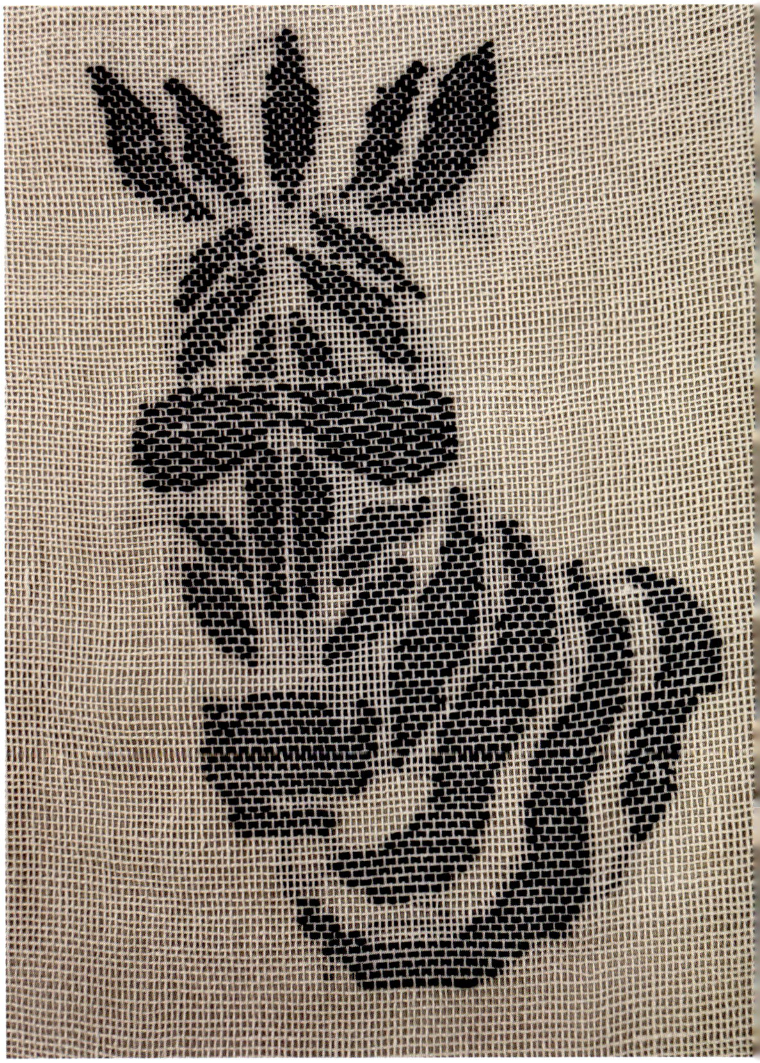

Ruth Ronan. *Cool Dude*, 2024. Linen, wool: 13 × 17 inches. Courtesy of the artist.

LEFT: Rebecca Smith. *Fractured Orb*, 2020. Linen, wool, cotton/metallic: 21 × 39½ inches.

Balanced Inlay Patterns

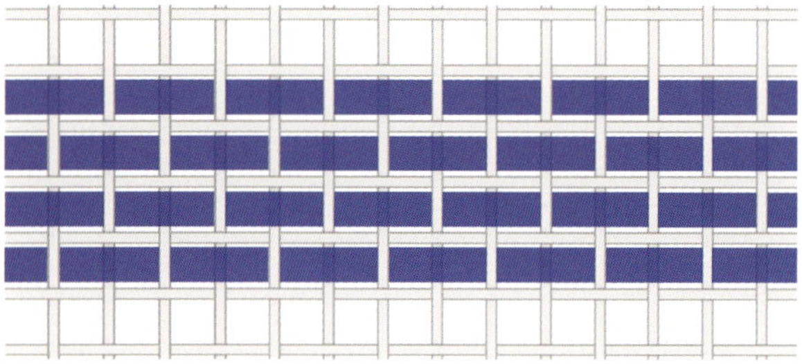

A

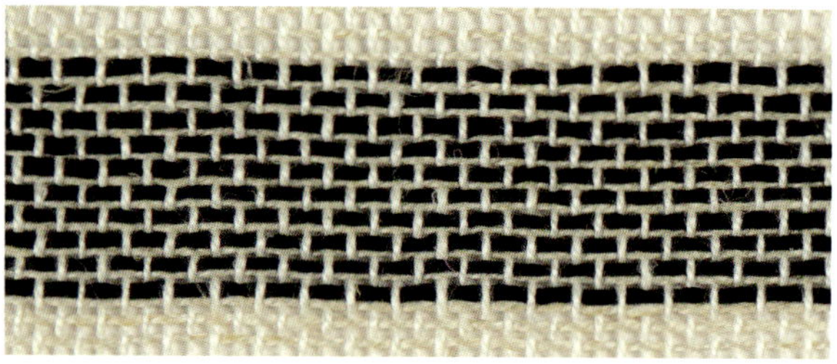

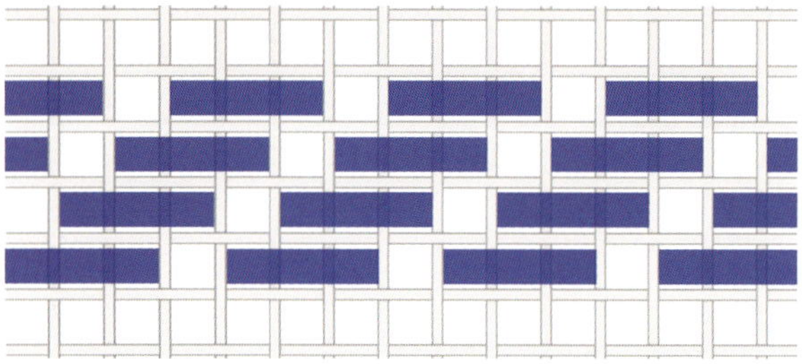

B

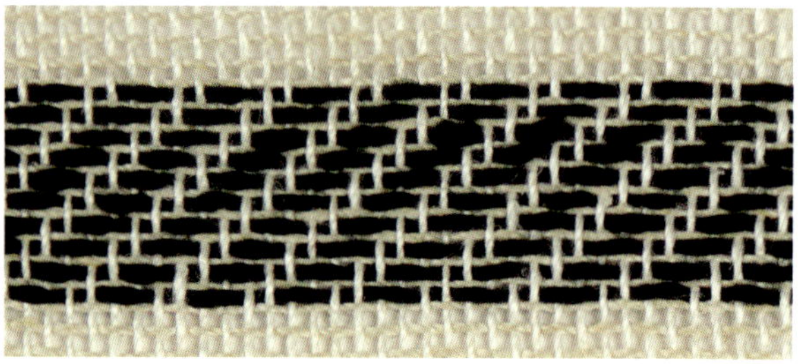

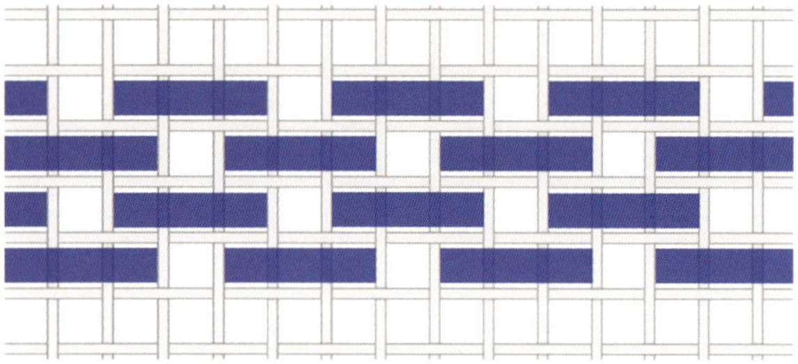

C

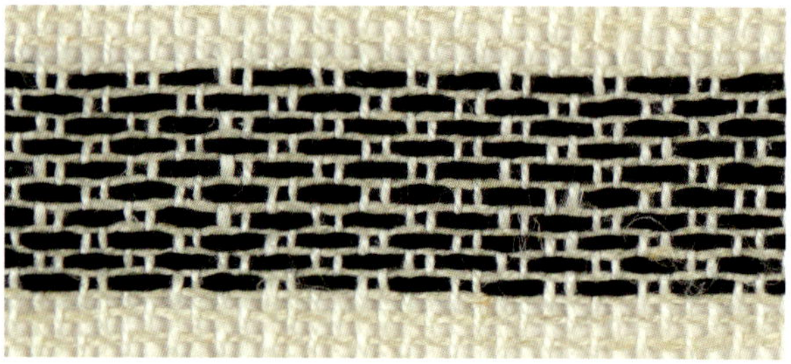

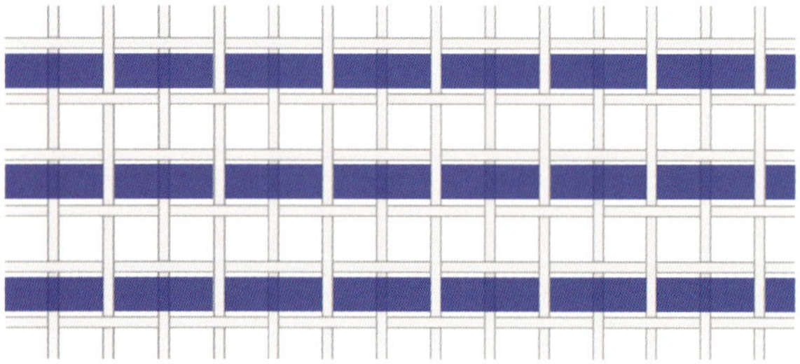

D

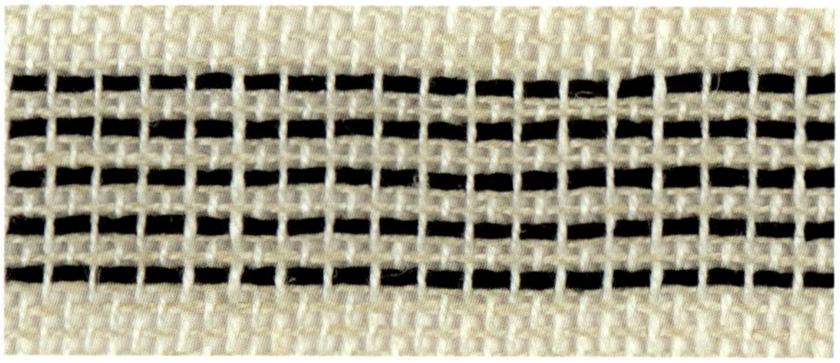

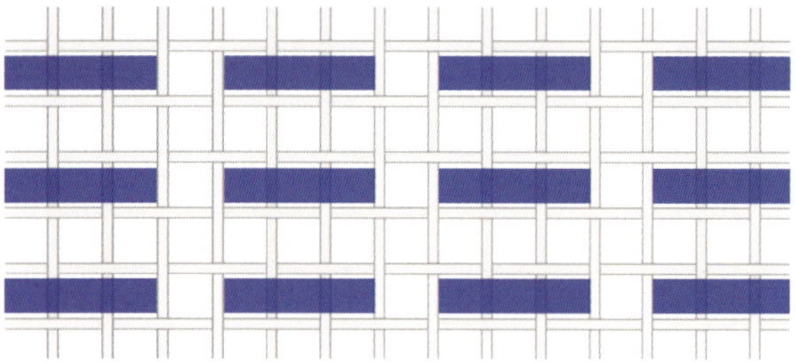

E

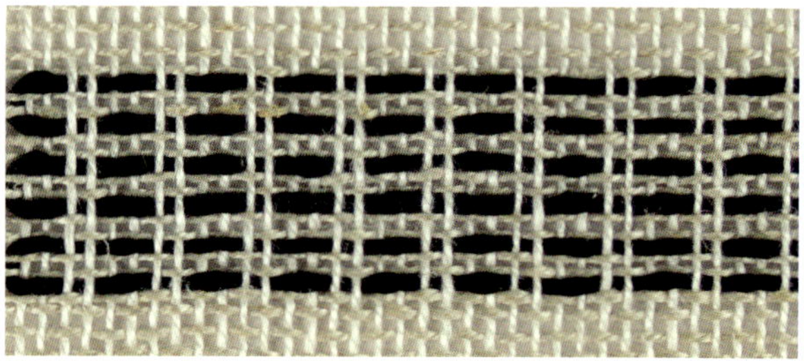

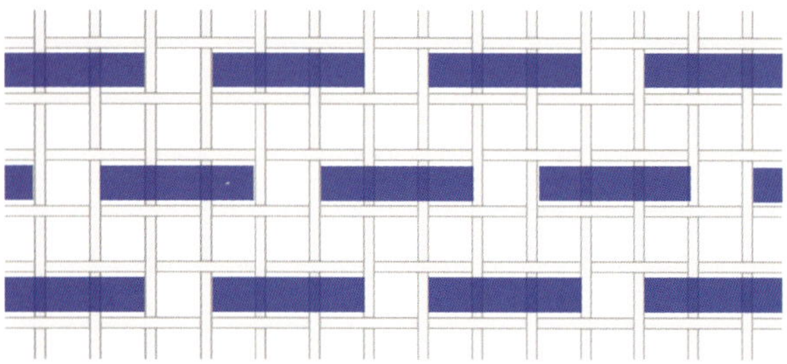

F

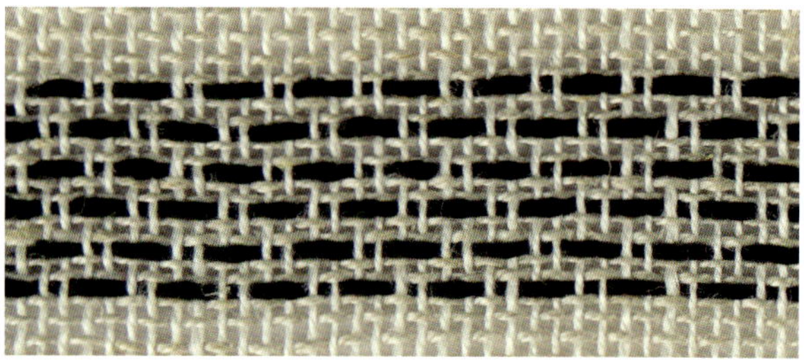

(**A**) Plain weave: this structure matches the ground weave; (**B**) 2/2 twill: goes over two and under two warps in an advancing pattern; (**C**) 12/34 repeat: creates a brick pattern; (**D**) Plain weave every other row: weft will be in vertical lines if inlay woven in same shed each row; (**E**) 12/34: every other row in same shed: similar to (D) but with longer floats; (**F**) 12/34: every other row in alternate sheds: creates extended brick pattern.

When weaving on four shafts, the only other balanced patterns are ones that repeat an over-two, under-two pattern. Variations depend on how successive rows are aligned: 2/2 twill (**B**) advances by one warp each row to form a diagonal pattern, whereas 12/34 (**C**) offsets pairs of floats in successive rows to form a brick-like appearance. Both 2/2 twill and 12/34 offset pairs will accentuate the boldness of the inlay because there are fewer warps crossing the weft. Notice the visual impact of using 12/34 offset pattern pairs to accentuate the sunglasses in Ruth Ronan's *Cool Dude* shown on the previous page.

Plain weave woven every second row will result in vertically aligned columns of inlay if the inlay is always woven in the same shed (**D**). See the detail of *Time Framed* for an example of this effect. This effect reduces the density of the inlay weft and can be used to lessen its visual impact.

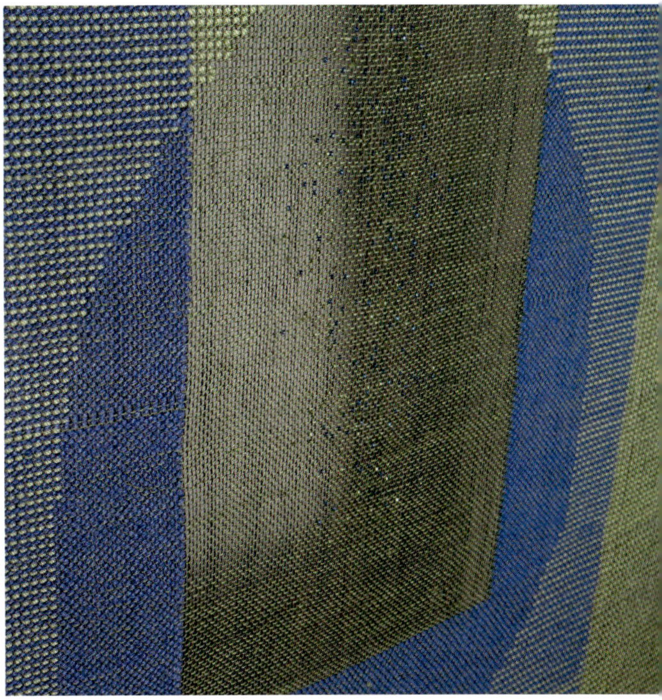

Rebecca Smith. *Time Framed* (detail), 2021. Linen, cotton, wool, seed beads: 20 × 29½ inches.

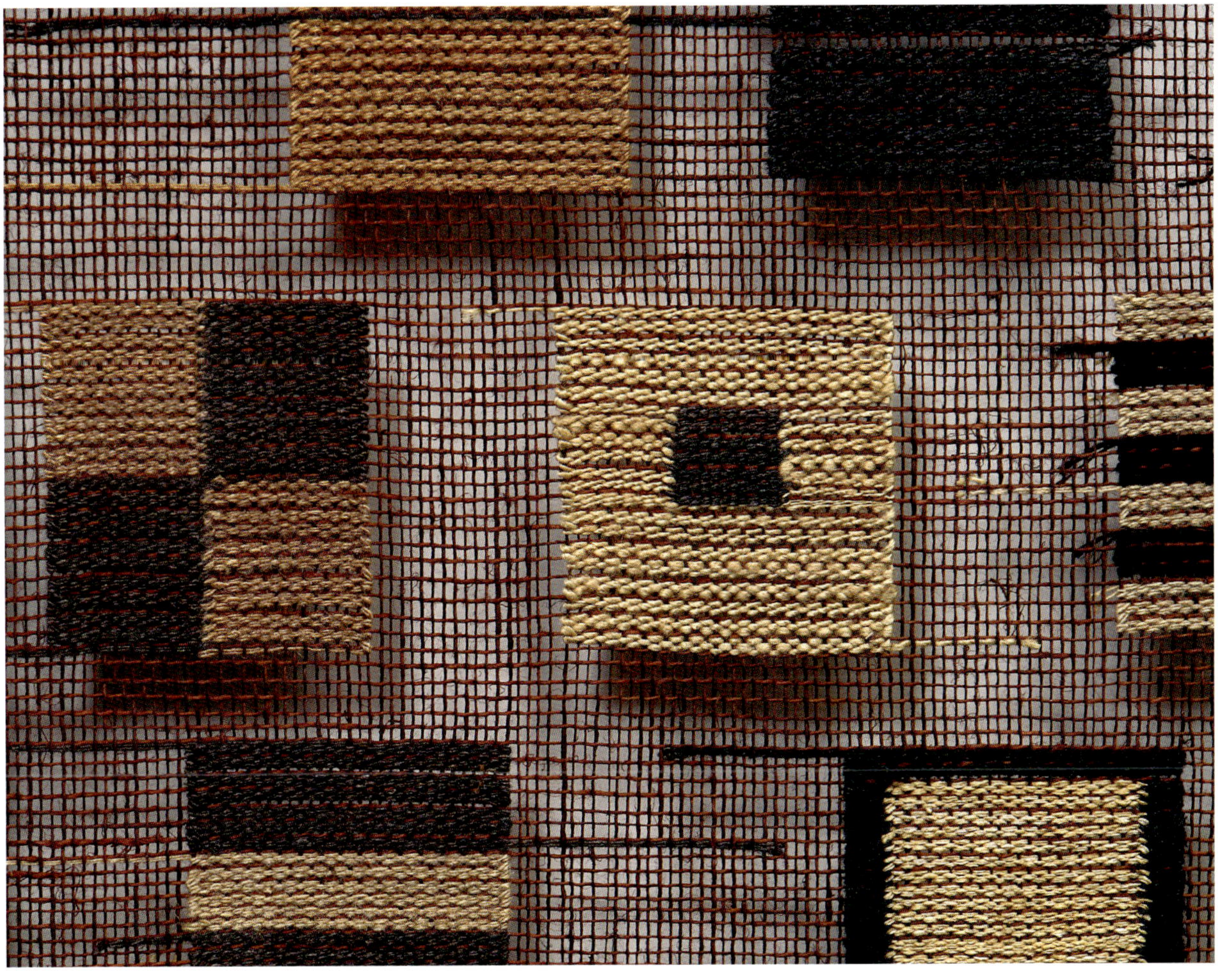

Morgan Clifford. *Tapestry Gauze 2* (detail), 2008. Photo courtesy of the artist. Warp is 8/1 linen sett at 10 epi.

The over-two, under-two pattern of 12/34 can also be extended by skipping a row between each inlay pick. Vertically aligned columns will form if the same pair of shafts is lifted each time (**E**). Note that an extended brick pattern forms when the pairs alternate in the usual pattern of alternating 12 and 34. Either way, the floats will be longer than plain weave, which helps accentuate the inlay.

Another balanced inlay effect is to "cram" multiple rows of inlay between ground wefts. In *Tapestry Gauze 2* (page 87), Morgan Clifford wove three rows of plain weave inlay between each row of ground weft. A coarsely sett warp can accommodate multiple inlay wefts without distortion.

EXERCISE 7: BALANCED INLAY PATTERNS

Weave a small sample of each of the balanced inlay patterns:

- (A) Plain weave
- (B) 2/2 twill
- (C) 12/34 repeat
- (D) Plain weave every other row
- (E) 12/34 every other row in same shed
- (F) 12/34 every other row in alternate sheds

Unbalanced Patterns

Unbalanced patterns appear on either the front or the back, but not on both sides of the weaving. Typically, unbalanced inlay patterns have been used to create bold designs woven with thick wefts on widely spaced warps. In a four-shaft weave, unbalanced patterns are limited to variations of raising three shafts while lowering one (3/1), or raising one shaft while lowering three (1/3).

Five unbalanced inlay patterns are illustrated at right. At the top, the weft floats over three warps and under one in a 1/3 twill (**G**). A diagonal pattern is created by advancing one warp at a time. This pattern results in long floats on the working side, but only spots of color on the reverse.

If you choose to make the reverse side the front of the weaving, you need to reverse the pattern of shaft lifts. For example, a 1/3 twill becomes a 3/1 twill in which the weft goes over one warp and under three warps (**H**). This puts the twill floats on the bottom or reverse side of the weaving. You might choose this approach if

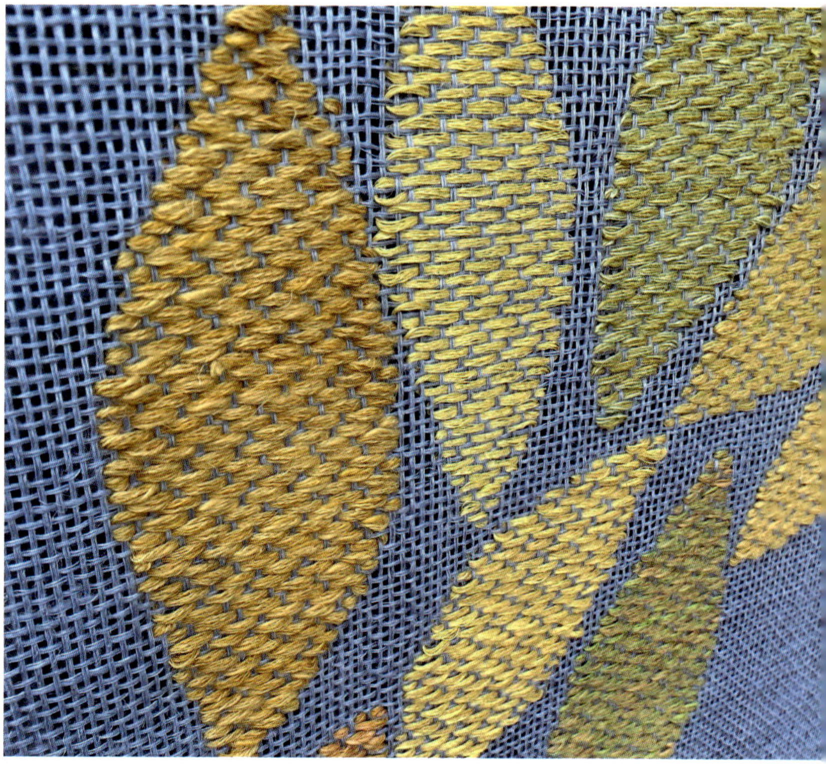

Muriel Beckett. *Falling Leaves* (detail), 2018. Linen and wool: 20 × 47 inches. Example of using satin weave for transparency inlay. Photo courtesy of the artist.

Unbalanced Inlay Patterns

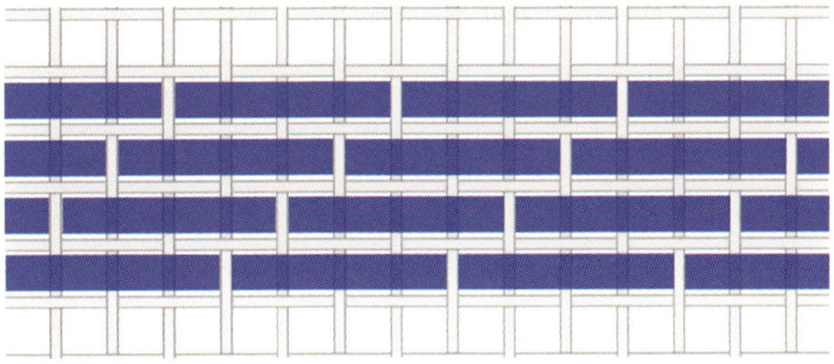

G

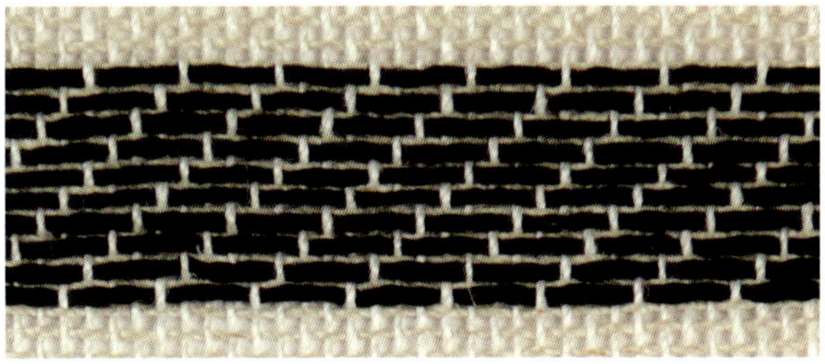

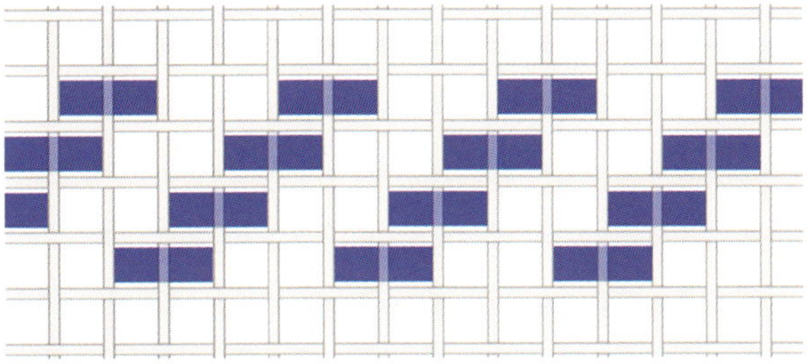

H

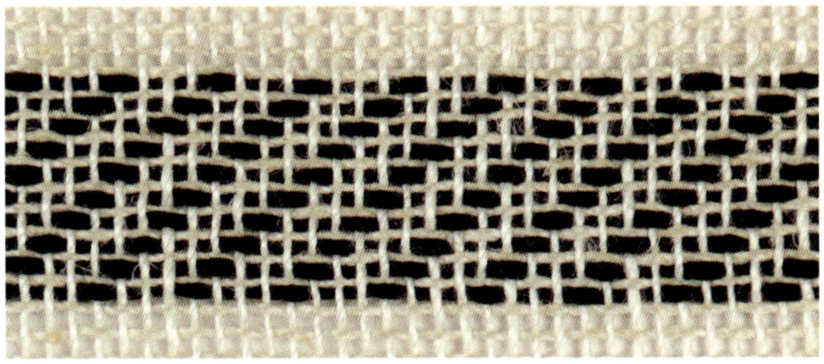

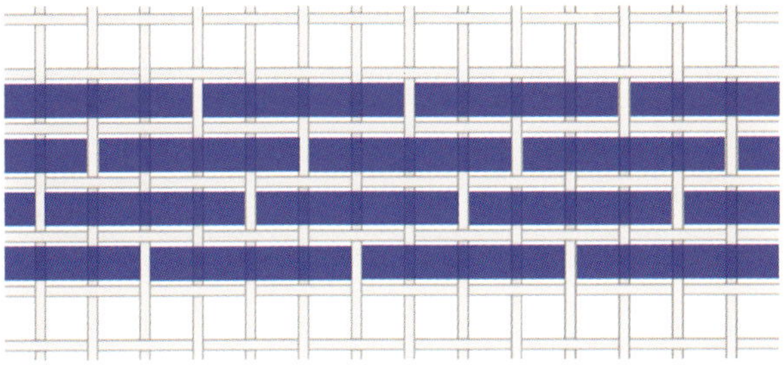

I

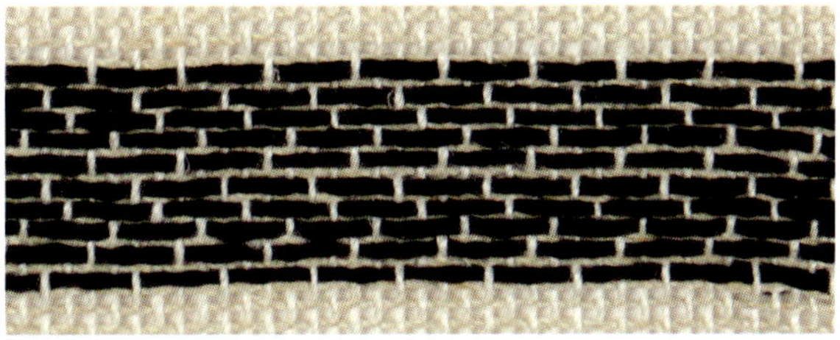

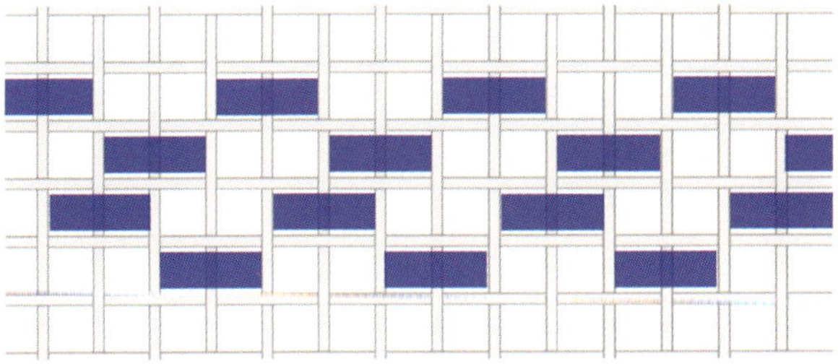

J

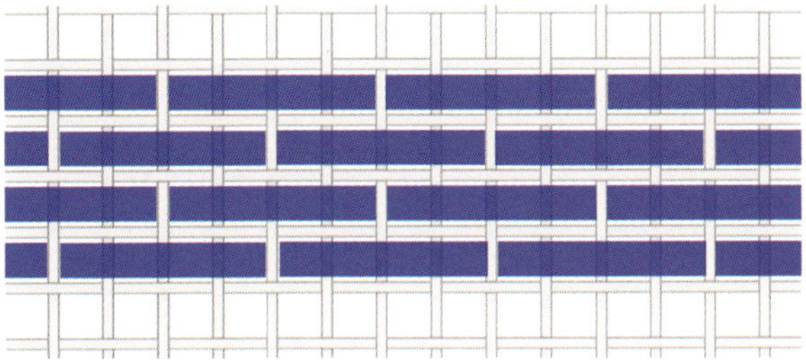

K

(**G**) 1/3 twill: goes over three warps and under one in an advancing pattern; (**H**) 3/1 twill: floats are on reverse side; (**I**) satin weave: over-three, under-one pattern with randomized placement of floats; (**J**) reverse satin: over-one, under-three pattern with randomized placement of floats; (**K**) ryssväv: raising shaft 1 and shaft 3 in alternating rows gives brick-like pattern.

you don't want the weft turns at the edges of shapes to show on the front of your work.

Four-shaft satin weave is another unbalanced pattern used for inlay (**I**). This pattern was popular in Finland during the latter half of the twentieth century. Four-shaft satin is often classified as "false satin" since true satin requires five shafts. This structure is similar to twill but uses a different treadling sequence to avoid forming a diagonal pattern. For this reason, it is sometimes referred to as "broken twill."

A good example of an unbalanced pattern weave is Muriel Beckett's *Falling Leaves* (see page 88). This piece is woven using four-shaft satin, with a warp of heavy tow linen spaced at 7.5 ends per inch. The weft is multiple strands of wool. Since the piece is woven with the back facing up, Beckett uses a reverse satin (**J**) tie-up and treadling (see "Satin on the reverse side" on the drawdown below).

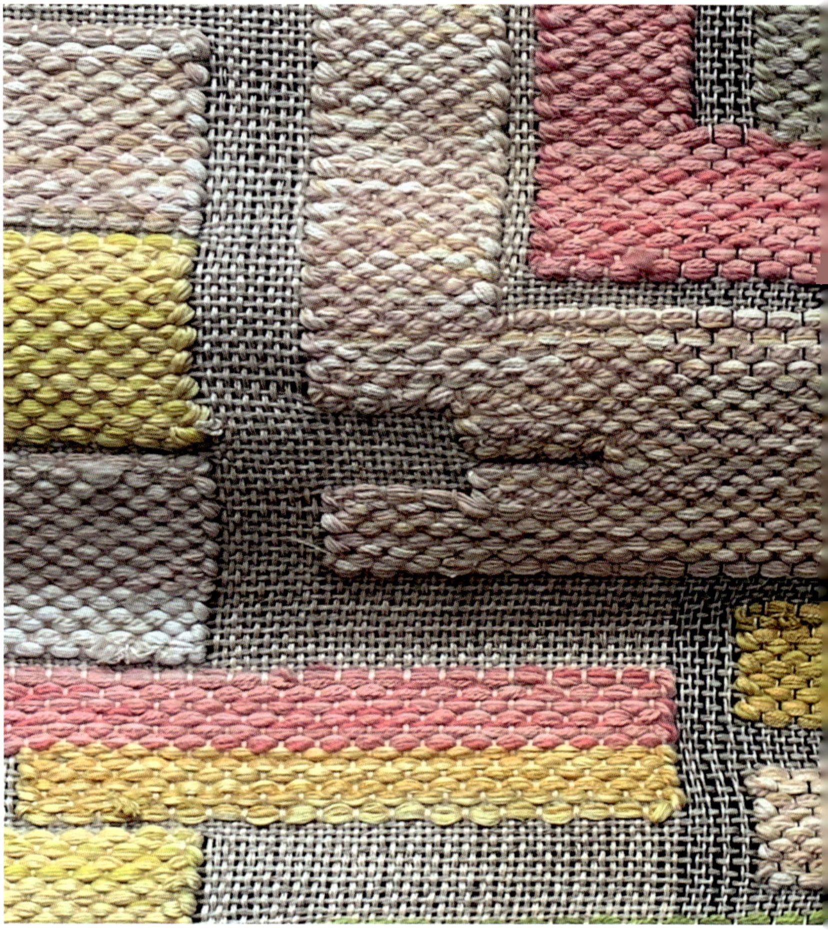

Detail of drapery by Agda Österberg. Rotated 90 degrees to show direction of weaving. Courtesy of Anne Whidden.

A pattern similar to four-shaft satin weave is ryssväv (**K**). We saw an example of ryssväv in the work of Agda Österberg in chapter 1. The pattern for ryssväv alternates between raising shaft 1 and shaft 3 in successive rows. This forms a brick-like pattern of floats on the working side. It is equally possible to weave ryssväv by alternately raising shafts 2 and 4 instead of shafts 1 and 3. In fact, the best practice would be to include areas woven both ways, to avoid developing tension issues due

BELOW: Weaving draft for unbalanced patterns

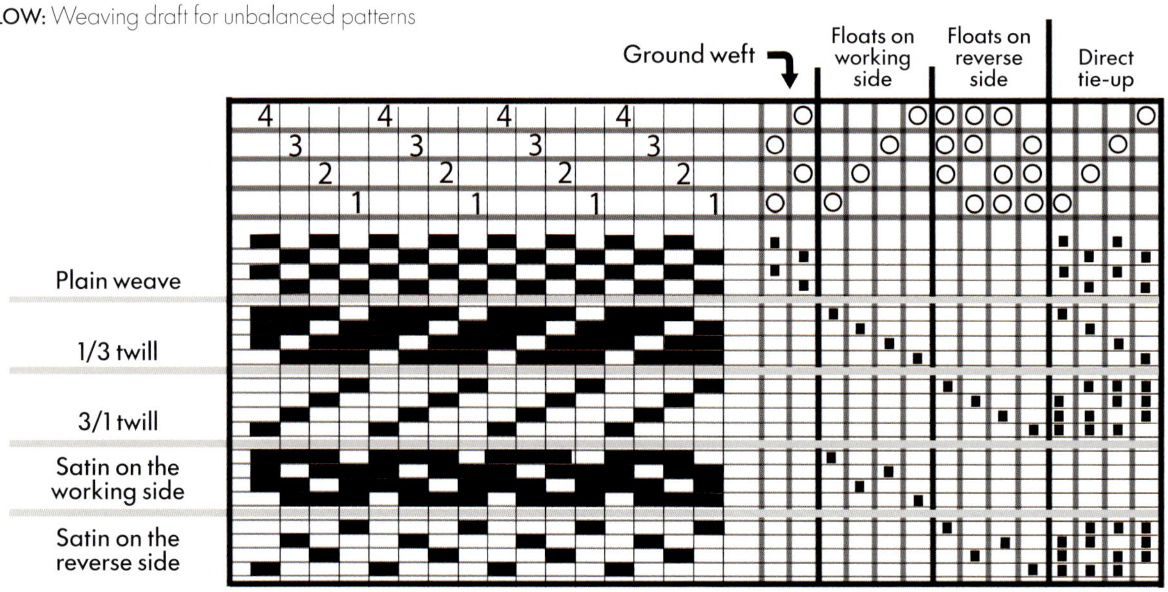

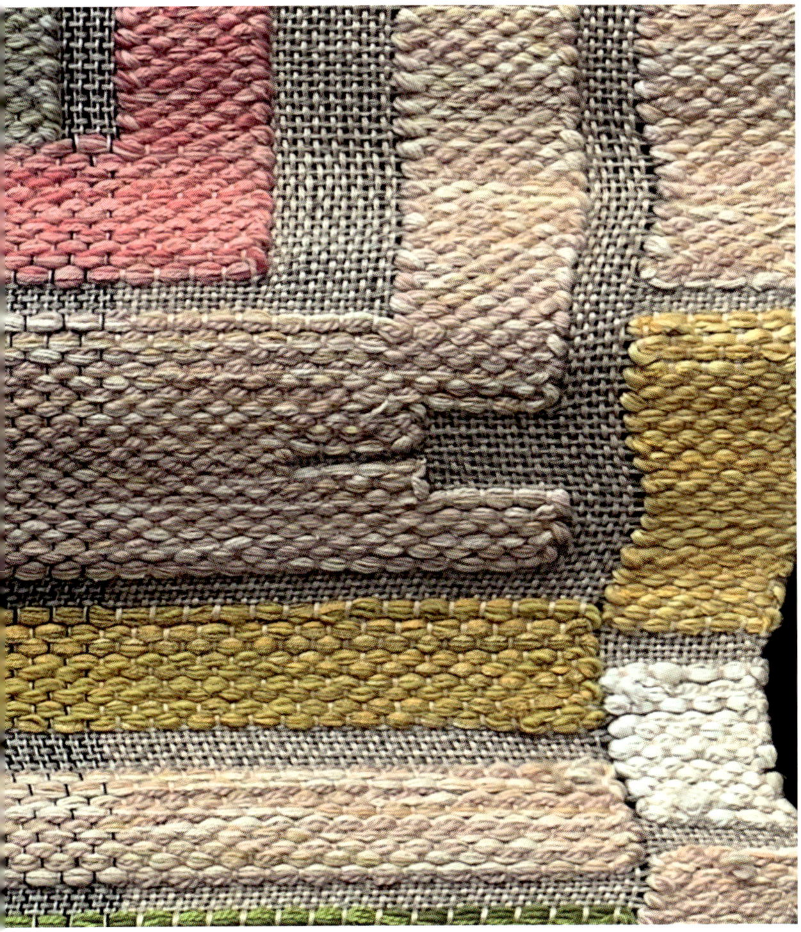

to uneven take-up. To weave ryssväv so that the floats appear on the reverse side, raise all shafts except shaft 1 or shaft 3 in successive rows.

Unbalanced patterns use a different tie-up depending on whether the floats are meant to appear on the working side or the reverse side. When the floats are woven on the working side, the warps on a single shaft are raised, allowing the weft to float over the warps on the other three shafts. To weave the floats on the reverse side, lift three shafts. The draft shows both options, as well as the lifts for a direct tie-up. The drawdown does not show the ground weft, only the pattern wefts.

Unbalanced patterns can be woven with thicker inlay weft without distorting the ground weave. The warps of only one shaft cover the inlay in each row, so there are fewer intersections between warp and weft. Thicker weft will spread out to completely cover the ground weft, giving greater prominence to the inlay. The examples shown above of Muriel Beckett's *Falling Leaves* and Agda Österberg's drapery use multiple wool strands in the inlay weft.

There are undoubtedly many more weave structures that can be adapted to weaving inlay weft. Those discussed here are just the most-often-used options. The common factor to remember is that the ground weft is always woven in plain weave no matter how the inlay weft is woven. Remember to change the shed between picks of ground weft and inlay weft.

Similarly, there are many more options available when the number of shafts is expanded beyond four. Six or eight shafts will allow you to weave longer floats and create even more patterns of twill, offset, or satin weaves. Greater emphasis can be placed on the inlay weft, diminishing the effect of the warps that cover the inlay.

EXERCISE 8: UNBALANCED INLAY PATTERNS

Weave a small sample of each of the unbalanced inlay patterns (Note: you may have to change your tie-up in order to weave the floats on the reverse side):

- (G) 1/3 twill
- (H) 3/1 twill
- (I) Satin weave
- (J) Reverse satin
- (K) Ryssväv

INLAY DENSITY

One of the most beautiful characteristics of transparency weaving is the ability to create a sense of depth by manipulating the density of the inlay weft. Density variation can be used to create the visual illusion that one part of the image is floating above or receding behind another part. Varying density can also simulate shadows, adding a three-dimensional effect to the weaving.

There are many ways to manipulate inlay density when weaving transparencies. In this section, we will look at two techniques that, individually or combined, allow you to control density variations. The two techniques are weft overlap and weft thickness.

Overlapping Shapes

My first introduction to working with inlay density in transparency weaving was when I ran across the work of Finnish weaver Helena Vento on the internet (read more about Helena Vento in chapter 1). In her transparencies, she created the illusion that one sheer fabric was floating in space over another.

Vento's piece Sails serves as a good model for examining the layering of shapes. The least dense areas (marked "0") have no inlay. They block the least amount of light and allow the darker background to show through. Areas marked "1" are plain-weave inlay. Where two areas of plain weave overlap ("1+1"), more light is blocked.

Vento used only plain weave for inlay. She created density variations by overlapping two shapes. The cumulative effect of two inlay wefts woven in the

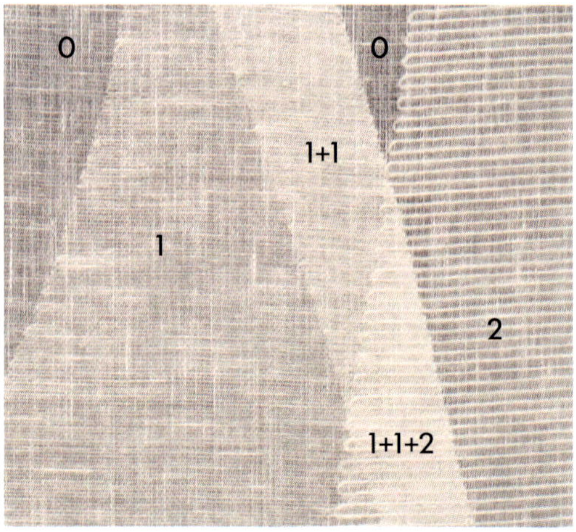

0 = ground weave only
1 = thin inlay weft every row
2= thick inlay weft every 4th row

A simple hierarchy of density levels based on Helena Vento's *Sails*

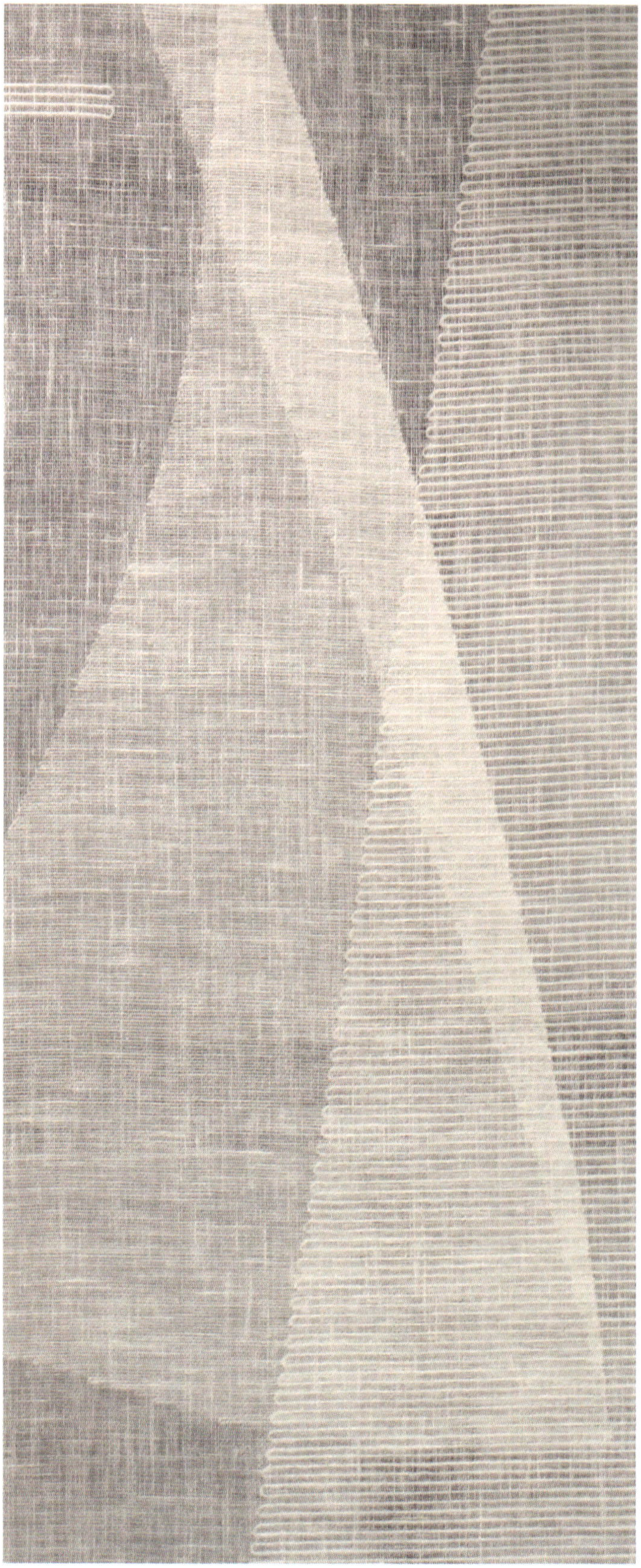

Helena Vento. *Sails*, 2010. Linen: 30 × 85 inches. Courtesy of the artist.

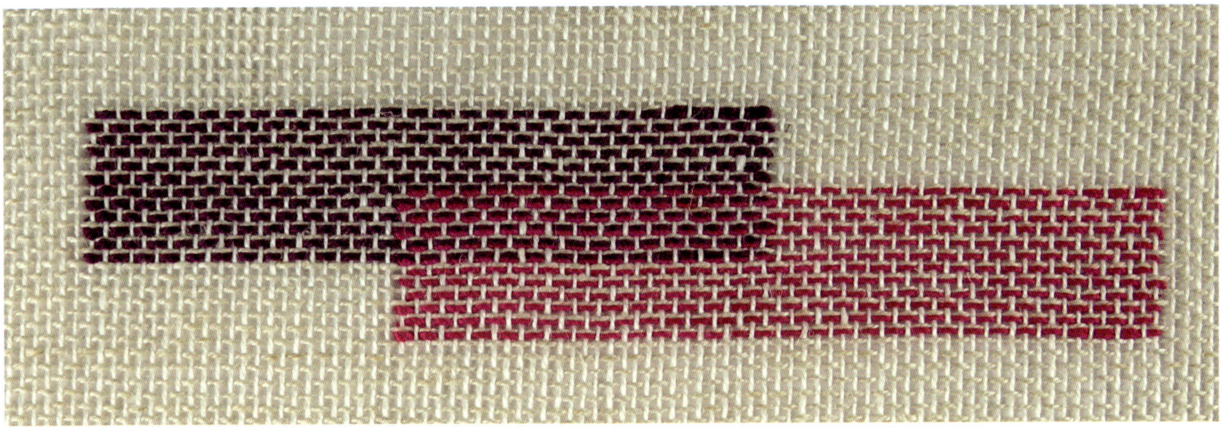

A simple example of overlapping shapes.

same shed is to make the overlapped area appear denser. Areas with denser inlay allow less light to pass through, making these areas appear darker.

Vento also used the thickness of the weft as a factor in creating density. In fact, increasing the weft thickness has a visually stronger effect than weaving rows of inlay closer together. The area marked "2" has inlay only every fourth row but is woven using a thicker weft. The effects are cumulative: The weaving is most dense where all three shapes intersect (1+1+2), completely blocking light from passing through the weaving.

You can plan for overlapping shapes in developing your design. The example above shows the simplest type of overlap: two rectangles that share a portion of their space. Each shape is woven as it normally would be, following the contours of its outline on the cartoon. To weave rows where the two shapes overlap, the most important thing to remember is to weave the wefts in the same order on each row. This keeps the colors in a uniform sequence and helps eliminate any visual inconsistencies that might draw the eye.

The diagram below illustrates the order of weaving two overlapping inlay wefts along with a ground weft. Both inlay wefts weave in the same shed, followed by the ground weft also in the same shed. *Then* change the shed to proceed to the next row.

It doesn't matter in which direction the two inlay wefts are woven. No matter which direction the wefts travel, there will be a small float where the weft

Order of weaving for two overlapping shapes.

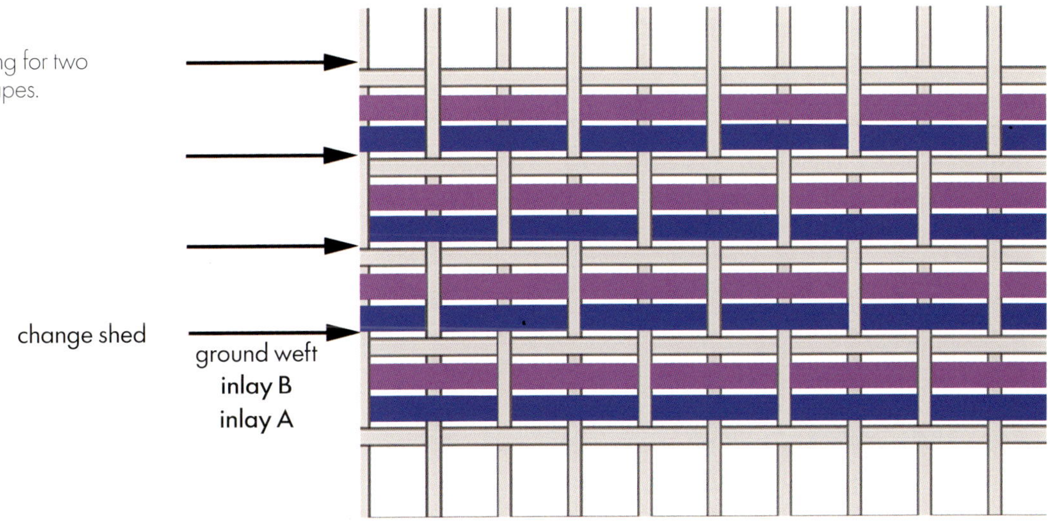

of one shape turns back over the weft of the other shape. Rather than focusing on the *direction* of the weft, be consistent with the *order* in which the wefts are woven, to make these floats as uniform as possible.

EXERCISE 9: WEAVE TWO OVERLAPPING SHAPES

Draw a simple design that has two shapes that overlap. Following the weaving order shown in the diagram, weave the design by using two distinct colors.

Varying Weft Thickness

In chapter 2, you learned that there is a "best" inlay weft thickness for simple plain-weave inlay (see page 36). But there are many ways that using weft yarns of varying thicknesses can work to your advantage. Let's look at how you can use weft thickness to add density and dimensionality to your design.

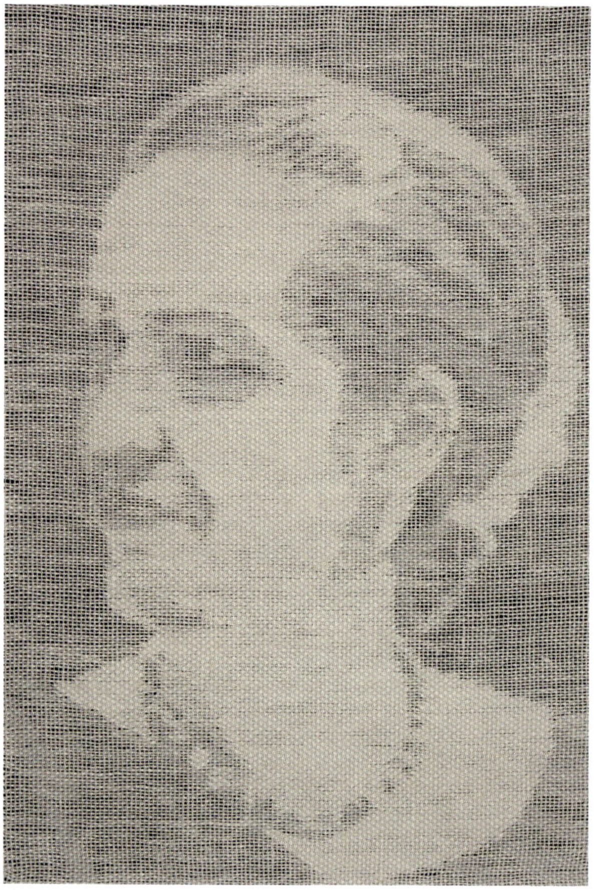

Cyndy Barbone. *Melanie*, 2020. Half-bleached linen: 12 × 17 inches. Photo: Barry Lobdell.

An excellent source to study the use of this attribute of transparency weaving to create depth or dimensionality is the work of Cyndy Barbone (read more about Cyndy Barbone in chapter 1). Rather than overlapping shapes to increase density, Barbone's work focuses purely on the thickness of the inlay weft. Working with a 16/2 linen warp and a sett of 12 ends per inch, Barbone creates a pattern of values by using different thicknesses of linen weft yarn all in the same color as the warp and ground weft. These monochromatic designs generally consist of no more than four values. The yarns may be different thicknesses, or the same yarn woven using multiple strands, or a combination of these options. For instance, using only 16/2 and 40/2 linen, a third value is created by combining a strand of each yarn.

Barbone's work creates a photo-negative effect: Shown against a dark background, the areas of finer inlay appear darker, while thicker inlay is used for the lighter areas. If the intent is to display the work against a light background, the opposite rules would apply: use a thinner inlay weft for areas that will

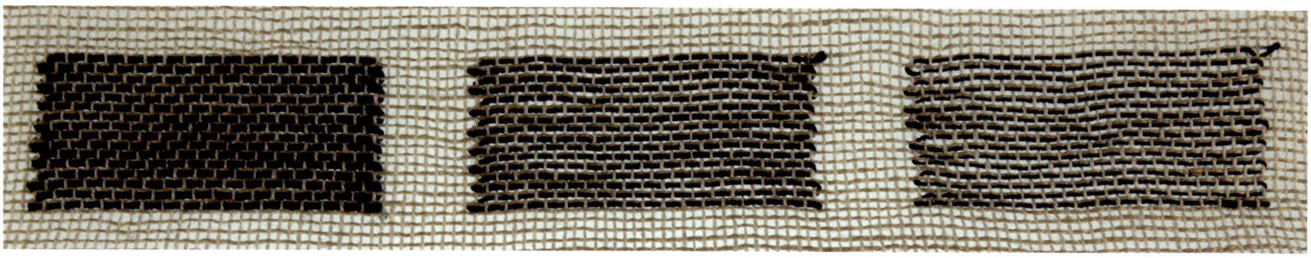

Three weights of perle cotton woven at 12 epi. From left: 3/2, 5/2, 10/2.

appear light, and thicker inlay to block more light and create a darker effect. Three weights of perle cotton were used in the example shown here to illustrate the effects of density when the weaving is lit from behind.

While this weaving approach encourages you to try heavier wefts, use caution to avoid yarns, or combinations of overlapping yarns, that are too thick for the space between rows of ground weft. Weaving thick inlay weft every row may distort the ground weft or cause excessive take-up, creating tension issues.

EXERCISE 10: DESIGNING FOR WEFT DENSITY: COLOR VS. MONOCHROME

You may have noticed that the works of both Helena Vento and Cyndy Barbone are woven in a monochrome color scheme. In the absence of color, structure can take the center stage. What would happen if these elements, weft overlap and weft thickness, were incorporated alongside color in a design? Here is your opportunity to find out the answer!

Weave a sample of two weft yarns that match the ground weft but are of two different thicknesses. Next, weave a sample of two weft yarns of two different thicknesses and also two distinct colors. Which shows the effect of weft density better?

COMBINING PATTERN WITH DENSITY

Where two shapes overlap, the density increases, as was *seen* above. It's equally possible to overlap shapes that are woven using different inlay patterns. It is a little trickier than using only plain weave for inlay. In addition to remembering to change the shed for each inlay pattern, you must remember to weave the patterns in a consistent order and remember to return to the plain-weave shed for weaving the ground weft.

In this example, each shape is woven in a different weave pattern. The diagram on page 96 shows the weaving order that was used. Notice that the 12/34 inlay is woven first in each row, before the plain weave inlay. This helps minimize the frequency of shed changes since the plain-weave inlay will then weave in the same shed as the ground weft that follows it.

Weaving multiple shapes, some that might overlap and some that are woven in different patterns, raises the question of how to handle the direction and the

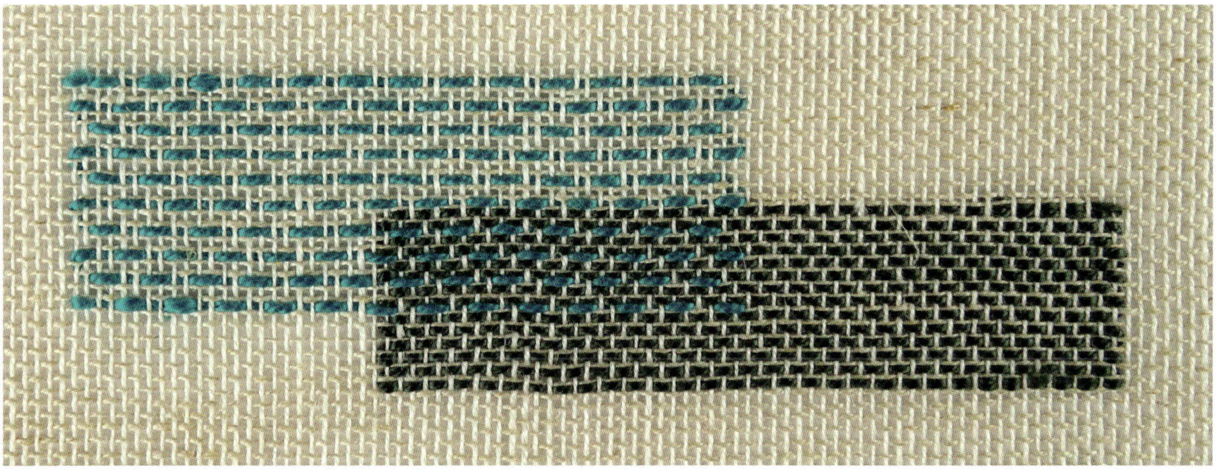

Overlapping shapes woven in two different pattern weaves. The lower rectangle is woven in plain weave; the upper rectangle is woven 12/34 offset pairs every second row.

Order of weaving showing shed changes. Inlay A (pink) weaves 12/34 every second row; inlay B (blue) weaves plain weave every row. Each arrow indicates where the shed must be changed.

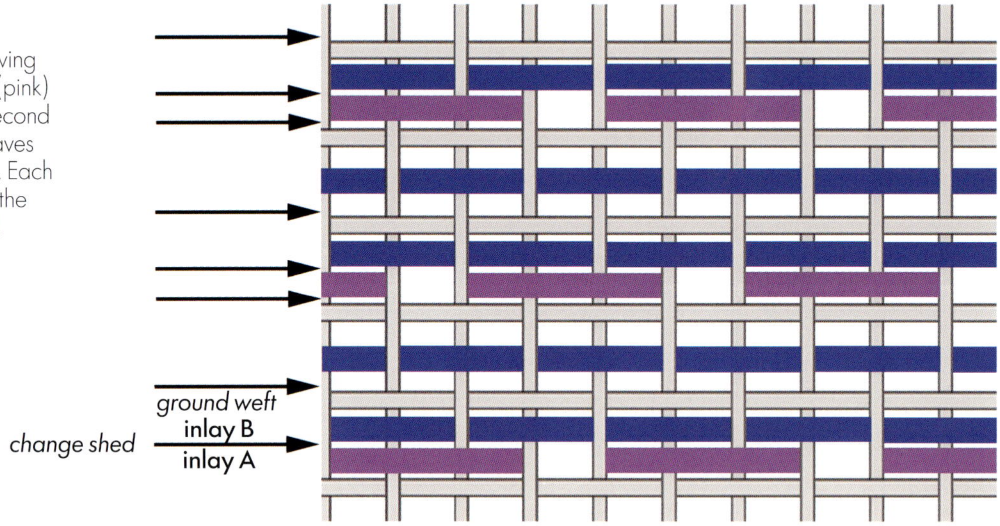

order in which the wefts are woven. Shapes will be varied sizes or have different contours. The borders of one shape may be inside another shape.

There is no fixed rule to govern the direction that wefts should weave in these situations. No matter which direction the wefts travel, there will be a small float on the working side where the weft of one shape turns back over the weft of the other shape, regardless of the direction or order that each weft is woven. Inlay patterns in which the weft is woven every second row will have longer floats at the turns, simply because the weft must jump over the unwoven row.

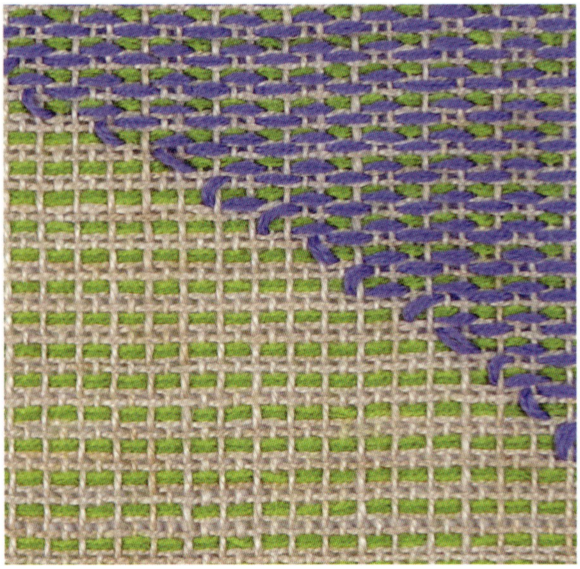

Small floats can be *seen* on the working side where one inlay weft turns back over another when the shapes overlap.

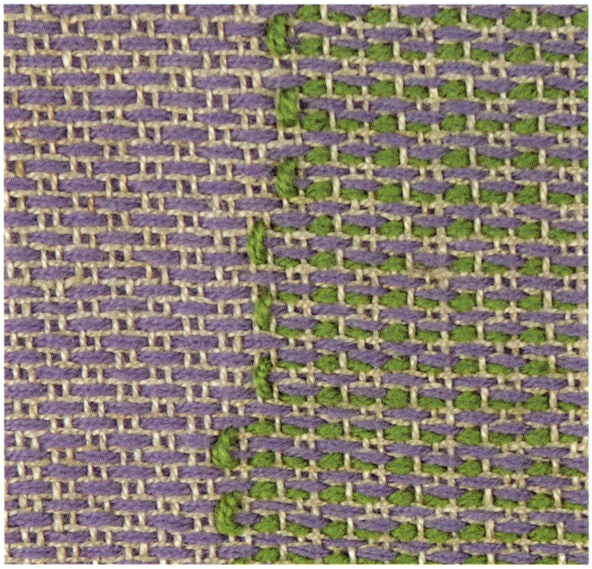

More noticeable floats occur when the weft is woven every second row.

PUTTING IT ALL TOGETHER: A DETAILED LOOK AT *TIME TO RISE*

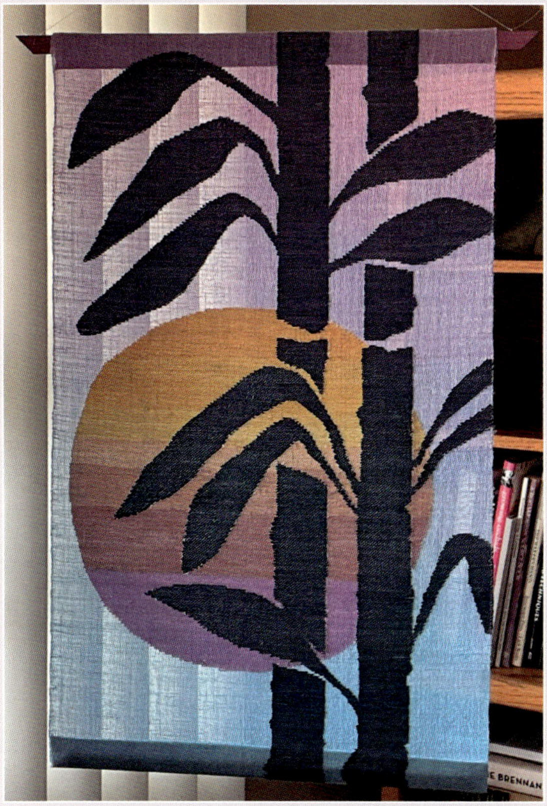

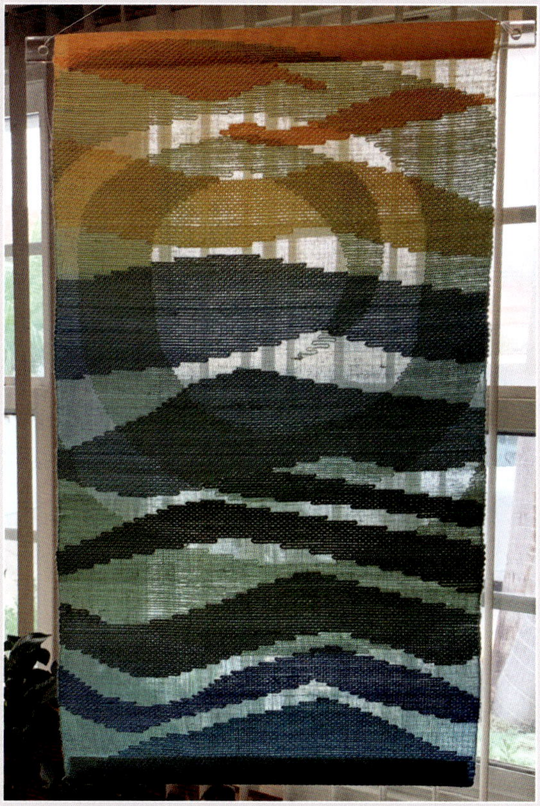

Two different transparency effects: *Quiet Time* (left) is woven tapestry style with discrete shapes; *Time to Rise* (right) is woven with patterned inlay and overlapping shapes.

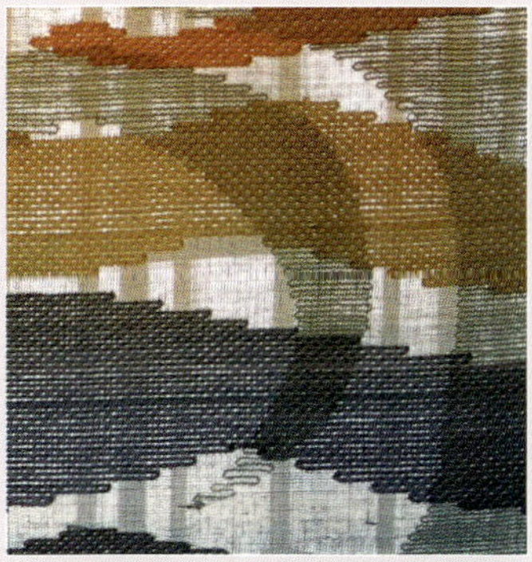

Let's compare two transparencies, woven in different styles. *Quiet Time* was woven as a single layer much like a tapestry: The shapes are discrete from one another. Edges of shapes "meet and separate" rather than crossing over one another. In contrast, *Time to Rise* illustrates layering: Shapes weave across each other. One shape is seen "through" another shape. For this design, I wanted the spiral to appear to float over the other shapes. Different inlay patterns, varied inlay weft thickness, and color variations helped create the illusion.

Here is a detailed look at how *Time to Rise* was woven. Compare the annotated version of the weaving with a transparent view that is backlit (the vertical stripes are window blinds behind the piece). Because the light is coming from behind the piece, the lightest areas are the ground weave without inlay; they are essentially the negative space that separates all the pattern areas. The spiral shape is woven with an inlay weft every other row. The blue mountains and yellow/gold clouds are woven over two / under two (12/34), using a thick weft. The view with backlighting fully illustrates the hierarchy of densities, with overlapping shapes creating the densest areas.

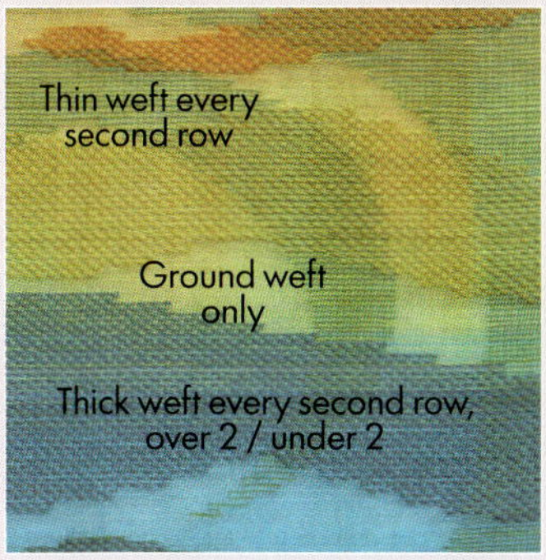

Variations in density created by using various inlay patterns. Effects are augmented when shapes overlap.

WORKING WITH COLOR

Is color important in transparency weaving? When a transparency is hung in front of a window or other source of backlighting, inlay density is the star of the show. The shapes formed by the inlay weft stand out against the lightly woven ground weft, while the ground weft itself all but disappears. At night, when there is no light behind the piece, color takes over as the primary player.

There are many excellent sources available for learning about the tenets of color theory, such as the color wheel, hue versus value, warm versus cool colors, and how to choose a pleasing color scheme. A good starting point would be Johannes Itten's *Elements of Color* (*see* the bibliography). In the end, choosing colors can be a very personal thing. There are very few "wrong" choices, even though there may be some choices that are better than others. Let's take a look at some of the ways that transparency weavers can employ color.

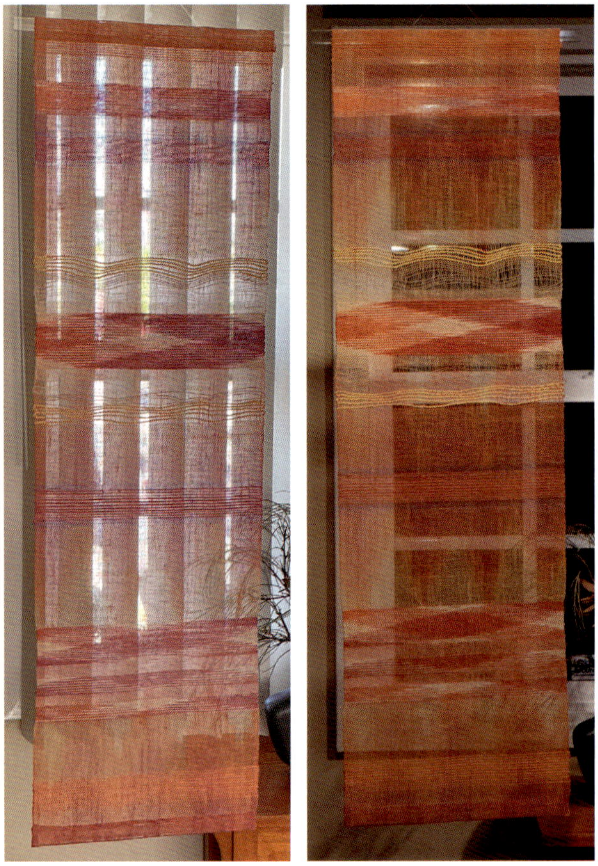

Rebecca Smith. *Faux Ikat Transparency*, 2023. Linen: 12 × 40 inches. Same piece photographed during the day and at night.

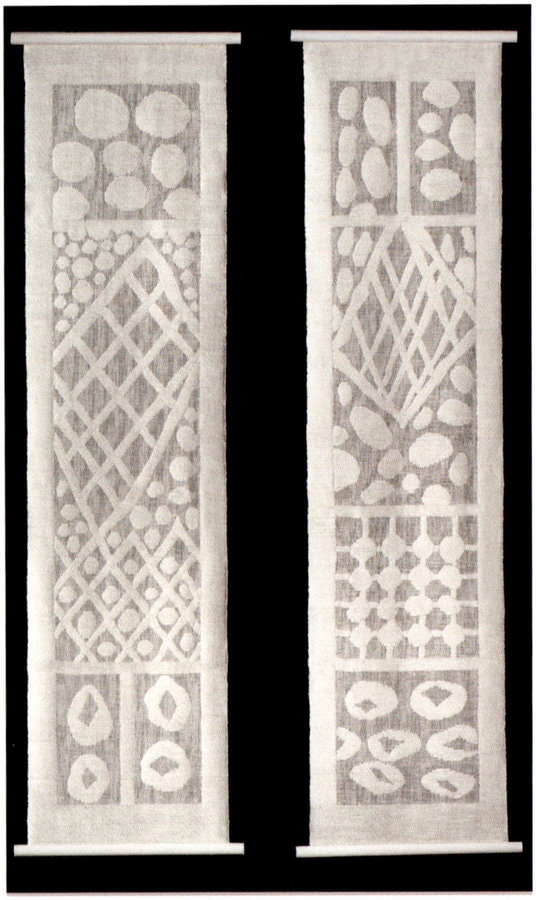

Laura Viada. *Confessions*, 2007. Linen: two panels, each panel 18 × 72 inches. Photo: Mike McCormick.

Monochrome Designs

Monochrome designs use a single color for both warp and weft. Traditional transparencies were commonly woven in this style and served a functional role as window coverings. In most cases, white, off-white, or natural are used. This color choice works well when placed in a window, since it stands out as well against strong backlight as against a dark background. Laura Viada's diptych *Confessions* illustrates well the impact that a dark background will have on a white or off-white transparency.

The monochrome format is a desirable choice for emphasizing structure and density, as illustrated above with work by Helena Vento and Cyndy Barbone. Their weavings may appear to contain various shades and tones of off-white, when in fact the effect is explained by varying densities of inlay weft.

A color scheme that is closely related to monochrome is one that uses two colors: one for the ground weave and one for the inlay. This color scheme suggests an array of possibilities, from two closely related colors (almost monochromatic) to two highly distinct colors; for example, white inlay on a black warp. A dichromatic color scheme could have the same benefits as a monochromatic scheme for placing the emphasis on structure and density of the inlay. Or it might be used to call attention to the dichotomy between foreground and background, positive and negative space, as I did in *Plain Geometry*, shown here. The background is inlay, while the subject of the piece is just ground weave (*see* more about reversing positive and negative space on page 103).

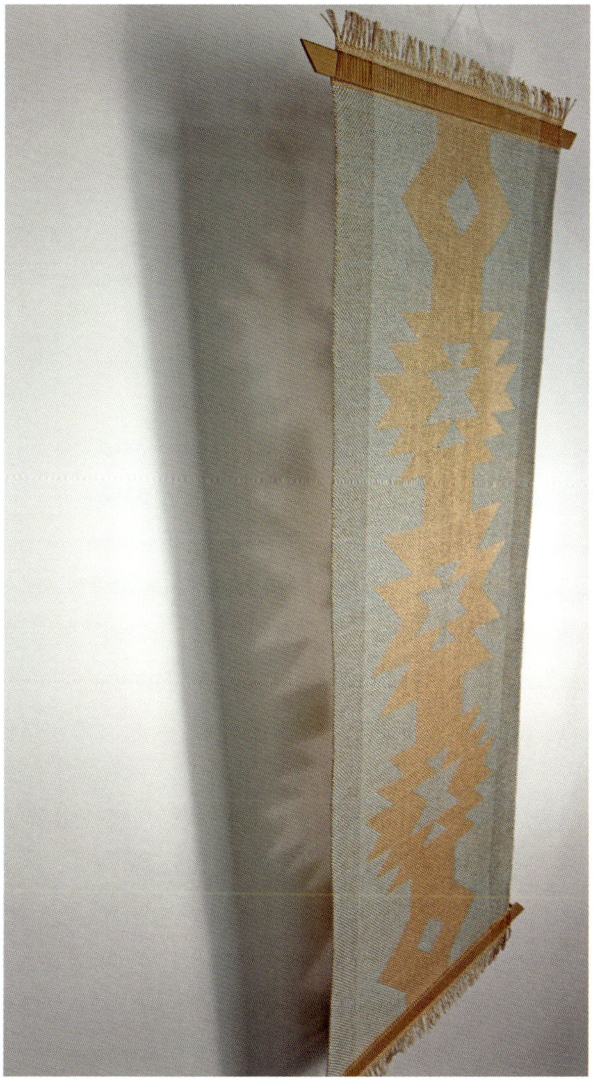

Rebecca Smith. *Plain Geometry*, 2021.
Linen, Tencel: 15 x 41 inches.

Color Effects

Transparency weavers can benefit from techniques commonly used in tapestry weaving to manipulate color and color interactions.

Hatching

Hatching involves blending two adjoining color areas by having the two colors take turns weaving into the zone between them. Hatching and hachure, a more formalized version of the technique, are used in tapestry weaving to blend colors. A second use of hatching is to create a sense of three-dimensionality by hatching muted tones of a color to simulate shadows.

Hatching can be used in transparency weaving to blend colors. The interplay of the two colors can sometimes create the illusion that a third color is present through optical blending. The closer the two colors are in hue and value, the more subtle the mixture of the two will be. When used for color blending, the effect can be random (top diagram) just to give a sense of shading between two colors. Or it can follow lines on the cartoon to form a specific shape between the two colors (bottom diagram). To make this work, it is important that

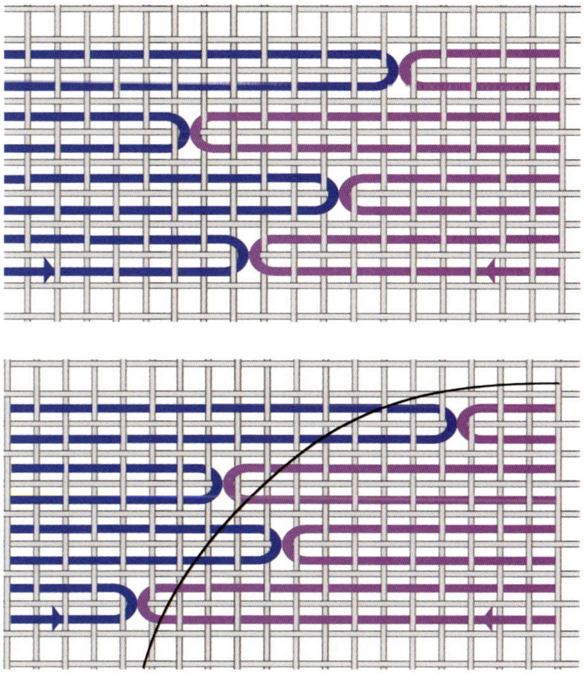

Hatching used to blend colors.

the two wefts travel in opposite directions in the same shed (meet and separate).

A second way to use hatching in transparency weaving involves a single shape whose edge is "hatched" into the surrounding ground weft. Instead of a hard edge, this use of hatching can give the shape a jagged or wispy edge. It is particularly useful when your aim is to suggest a faint or shadowy edge to a shape.

Both uses of hatching appear in *Sphere*. Random hatching was used for cloud shapes in the sky. Where the orb changes from bright light to shadow, gold and off-white are hatched to transition the color. The shadowy edge where the light transitions into shadow was woven using white weft hatched into the ground weft, weaving every other row.

An extension of this type of hatching would be to combine density variations with hatching. Utilizing thinner yarns to hatch into the ground weft will augment the subtle shift from opaque to transparent.

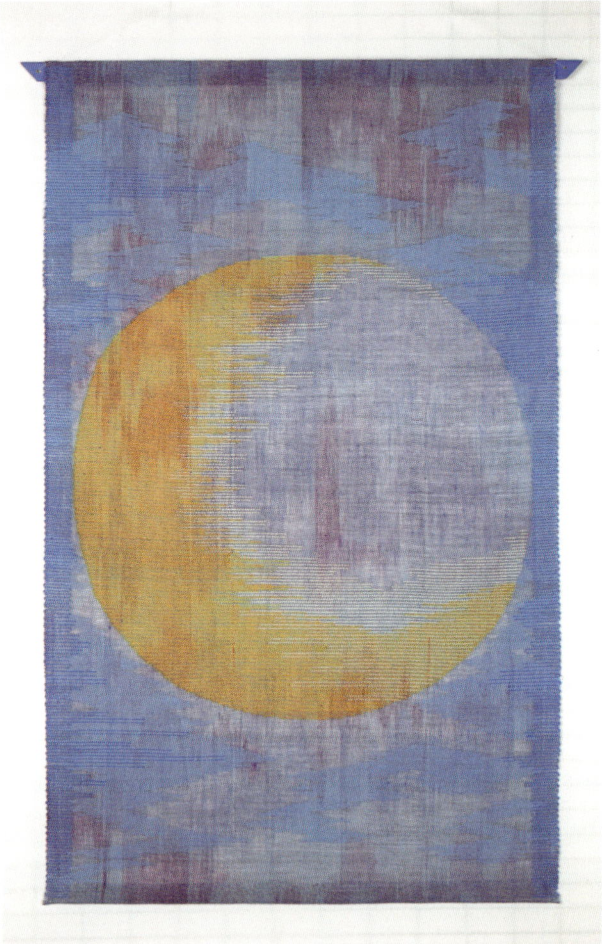

Rebecca Smith. *Sphere*, 2020. Linen, wool: 21 × 34 inches. Hatching used to soften colors and shapes.

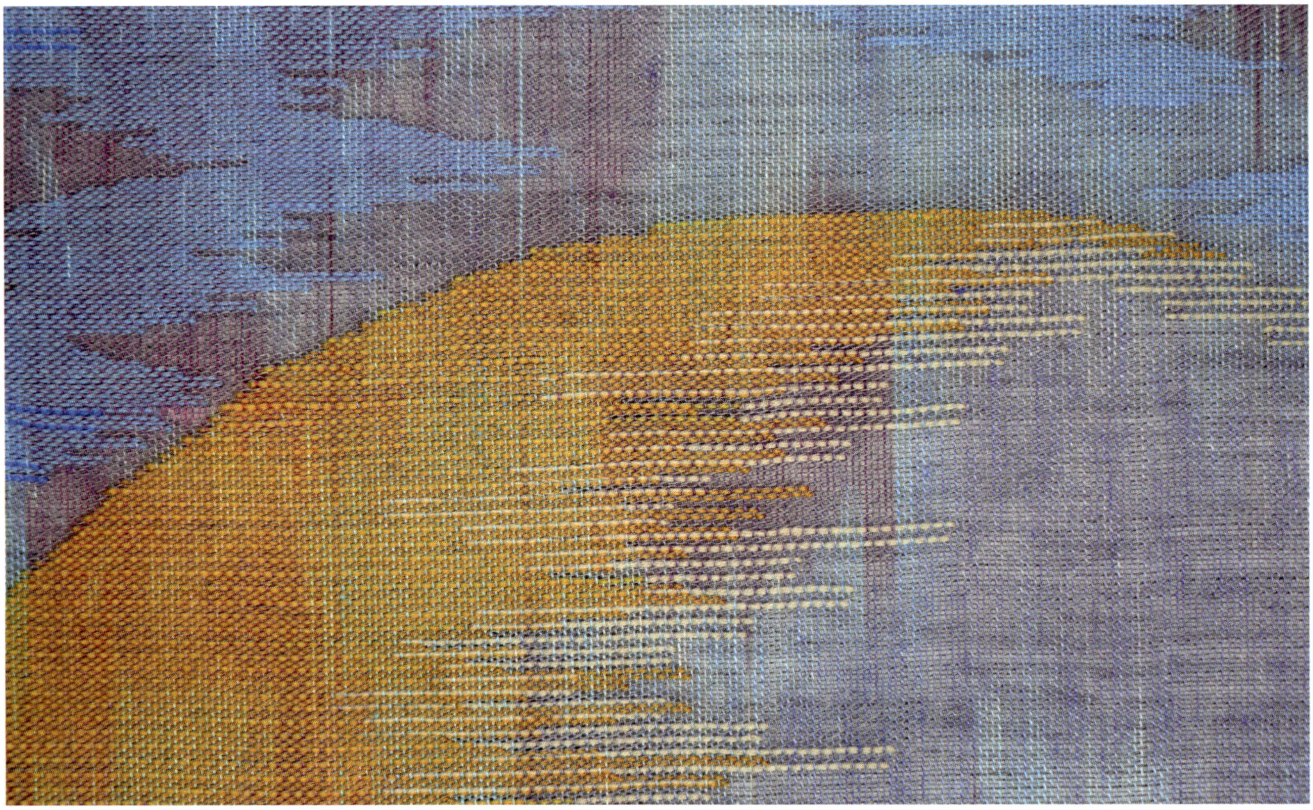

Optical Blending

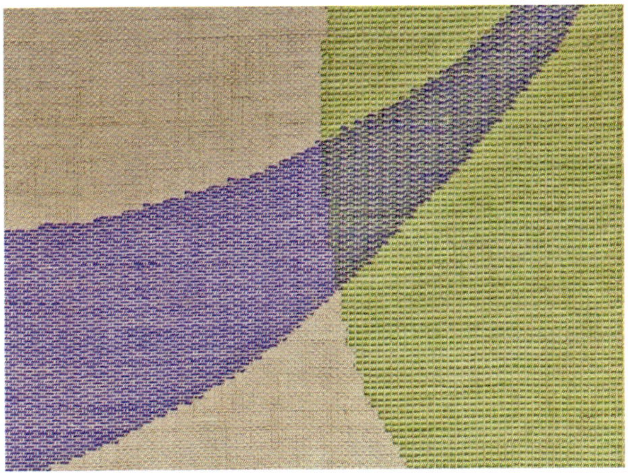

Rebecca Smith. *Cosmic Dance* (detail). When overlapped with yellow green, the violet shape appears bluer.

Overlapping shapes can create optical blending of colors. When shapes overlap, two colors are woven in the same shed. The colors will interact and may create the sense of a third color. Much depends on the hue, value, and temperature of the colors that are being used. Experimenting or studying color theory is the path to creating successful color illusions.

Color sequencing, gradually adding in a second color as a way to transition from one color to the next, is another way to work with color. A typical color transition for two colors A and B might look like this:

- 3 rows of color A → 1 row of color B → 2 rows of color A → 1 row of color B → 1 row of color A → 1 row of color B → 1 row of color A → 2 rows of color B → 1 row of color A → 3 rows of color B

While following this sequence will yield a gradual transition from one color to another, the outcome may not be as subtle as you might like. The intervening rows of ground weft between rows of inlay can disrupt the optical blending. Careful planning of which colors to use is important: Colors close in value will blend better than colors that are distinctly different in value. The same goes for hue: Colors close to each other on the color wheel will transition more easily than contrasting colors.

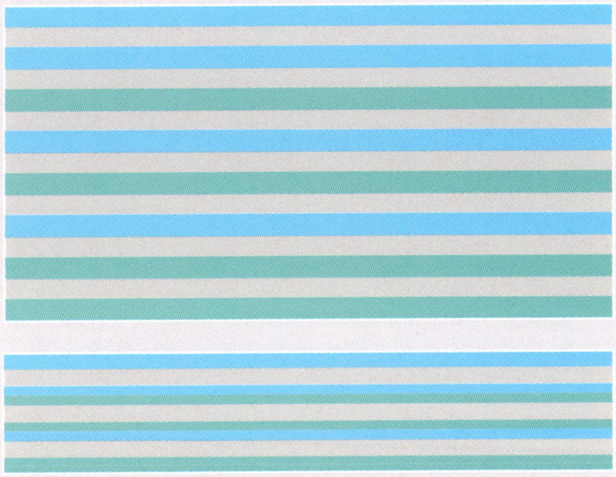

Top: Colors transition row by row.
Bottom: Colors transition in the weft bundle.

These two images were digitally generated by using the same two colors. The intervening rows of ground weft disrupt the clarity of the colors more in the row-by-row transition than in the blended weft bundle.

Finally, a darker warp and ground weft may help to reduce the "noise" caused by the intervening rows of ground weft.

Color sequencing can also be accomplished by mixing the colors in the weft bundle. The same sequence would be followed, substituting the word *strand* for the word *row*. Colors intermingled in a weft bundle are more likely to produce optical blending than colors in contiguous rows separated by ground weft.

- 2 strands of color A → 1 strand of color A + 1 strand of color B → 1 strand of color B + 1 strand of color A → 2 strands of color B

The transition could be made even more subtle by using three strands in the weft bundle instead of two. The closer the colors are in hue and value, the more subtle the interaction will be. The challenge is to find weft yarns that are fine enough to bundle without being too thick for the space between rows of ground weft.

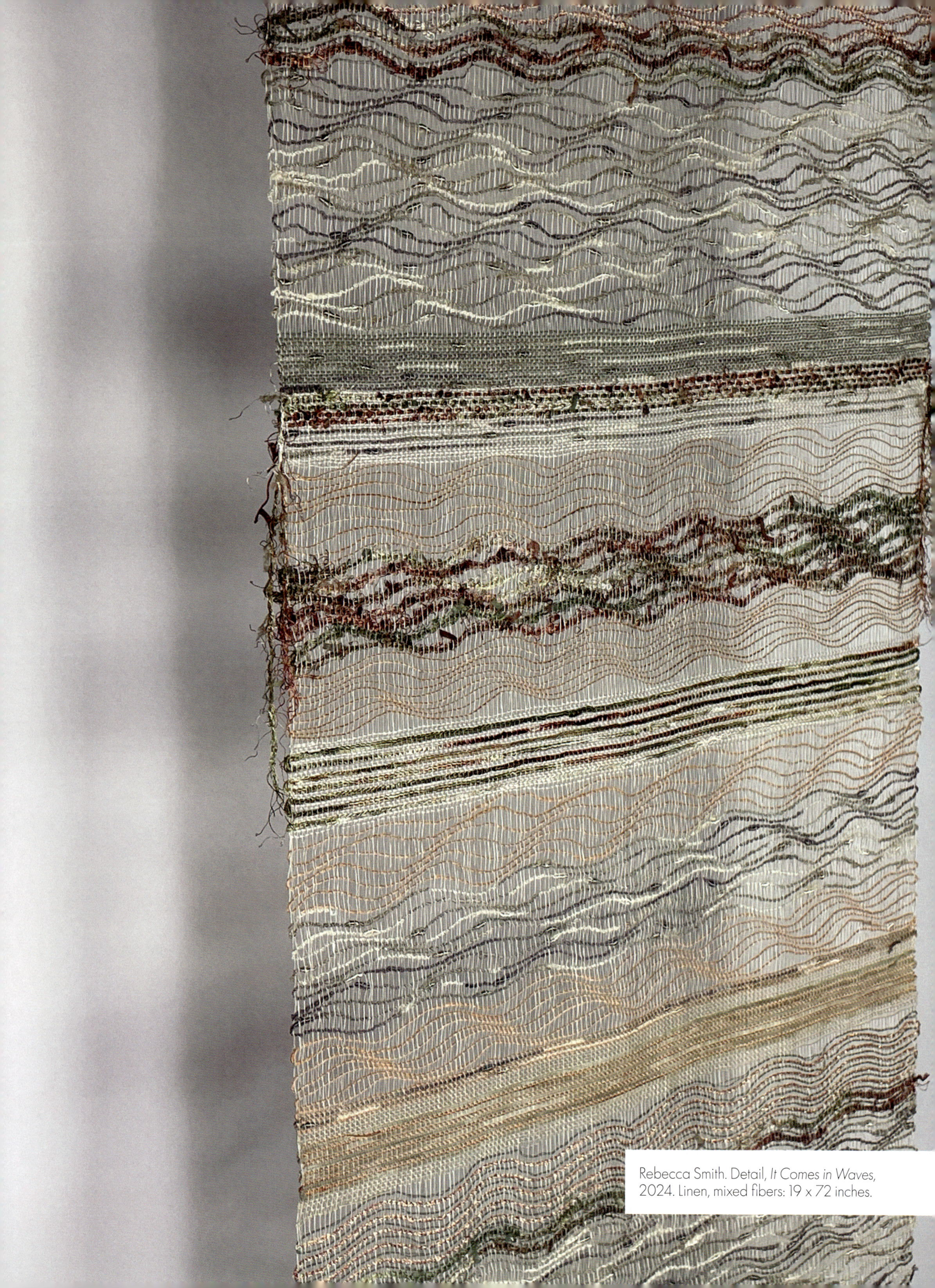

Rebecca Smith. Detail, *It Comes in Waves*, 2024. Linen, mixed fibers: 19 x 72 inches.

Chapter 8

INNOVATIVE TRANSPARENT EFFECTS

> *"Things take shape in material and in the process of working it, and no imagination is great enough to know before the works are done what they will be like."*
>
> —**ANNI ALBERS**, *We Need the Crafts for their Contact with Materials*, 1944

There are many different directions in which you can explore transparency in weaving once you have adopted the open-warp weave plan. In the words of Doramay Keasbey, transparency weaving is characterized by inlay patterns consisting of "additional decorative threads or other flexible material incorporated into a backing of fairly open plain-weave fabric."[1] Think of all the ways to expand upon that definition! The main focus is on the contrast between the sheer background and the heavier inlay. Chapter 7 introduced some inspiring examples of variations in the use of an open-warp framework. This chapter will look at ways to manipulate both warp and weft to achieve additional effects that can be explored in transparency weaving.

WEFT VARIATIONS

Reversing Positive and Negative Space

We generally assume that the role of inlay weft is to weave shapes and designs. The inlay is the focus, or positive space, of the design, and the ground weft is the background or negative space that surrounds it.

What if we reverse this so that the inlay forms the background surrounding the shapes that make up the design? The transparent part of the design is then the object itself, with the inlay serving as an outline to define the design. The light doesn't shine around the object; it shines through the object. It's kind of like the difference between looking at a keyhole and looking through a keyhole.

The dichotomy of positive and negative was the focus of my piece *A Memory of Trees* (see next page). The same design was woven twice, first with the tree as inlay and then with the background as inlay. The viewer's experience of each is different, since in the one case you are looking at the tree, and in the second case you are looking through the tree.

This transformation of positive into negative space is quite easy to do in transparency weaving. As an example, let's return to the simple leaf design that was examined in chapter 6. The figure below shows the leaf with the positive and negative portions of the design reversed. To weave around the shape, the weft must

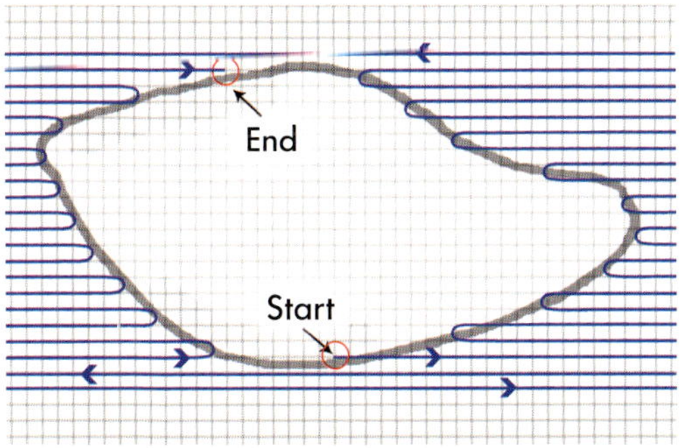

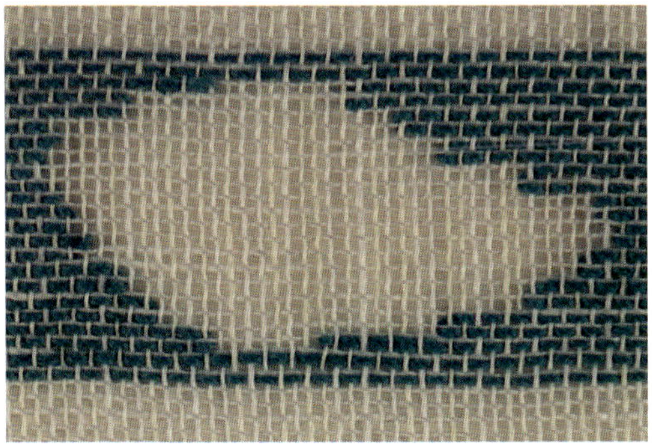

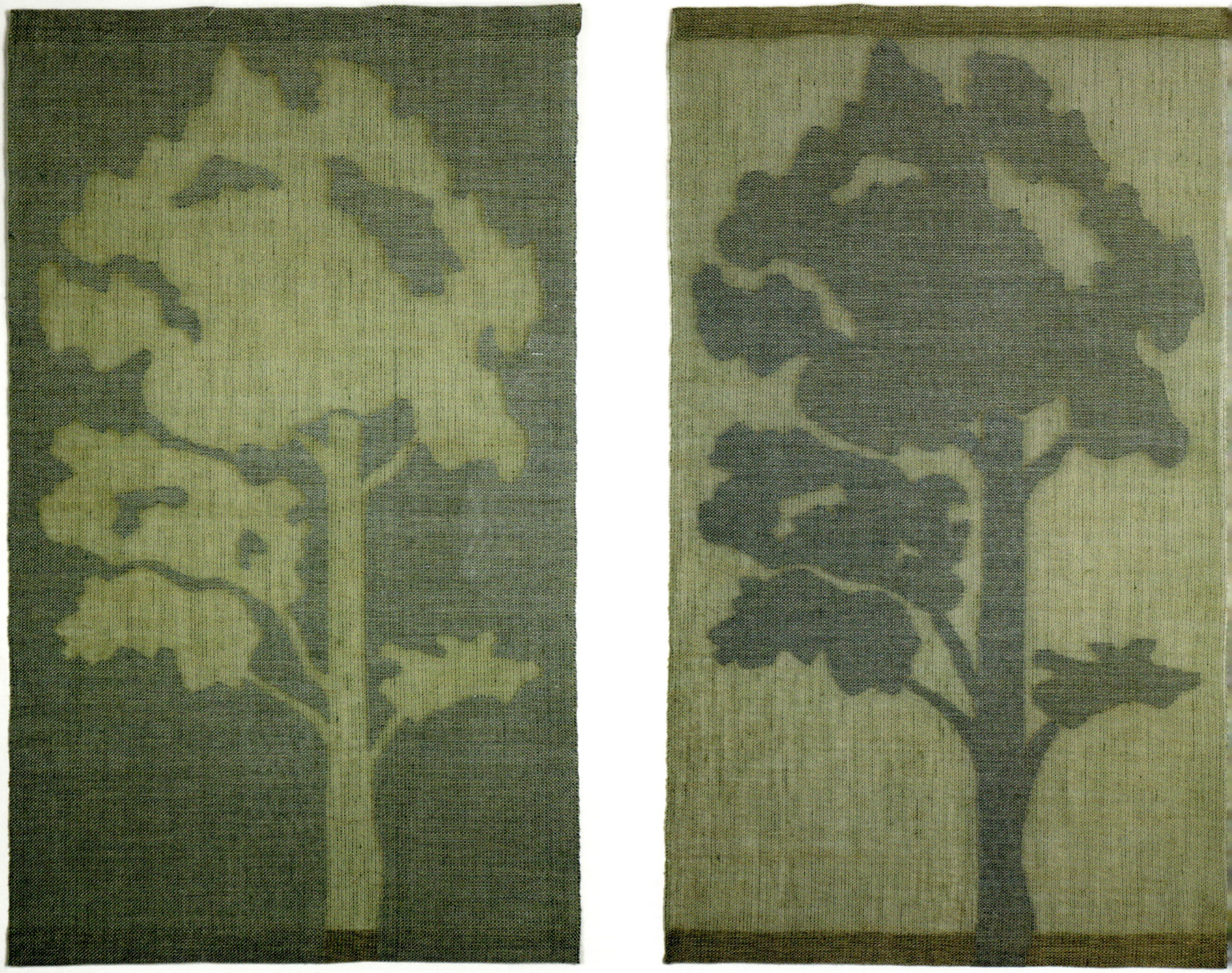

Rebecca Smith. *A Memory of Trees*, 2021. Linen, Tencel: two panels, each 18 × 30 inches.

split and become two wefts. The arrows indicate the direction of weaving and the points at which the wefts split and then where they come together again.

Wave Beater

The use of the loom's beater to form perfectly straight lines of ground weft creates an effect almost like a window screen. Other effects can be produced in open-warp weaving by omitting the use of the beater, and sometimes even omitting the ground weft.

A wave beater is similar to a "wave shuttle" except that it is not a shuttle. Its one and only job is to push the weft into place in a wave pattern. The wave beater can be used for either the ground weft or the inlay weft. You can choose to omit the ground weft and only weave inlay or even try alternating two different types of inlay weft. It is especially effective when using a heavy or textured weft.

You can make your own wave beater with a strip of mat board that is 2–3 inches high and several inches wider than your warp. See page 165 for a template for cutting the wave pattern into the mat board by using scissors. After cutting, mark ½-inch increments along the length of the beater.

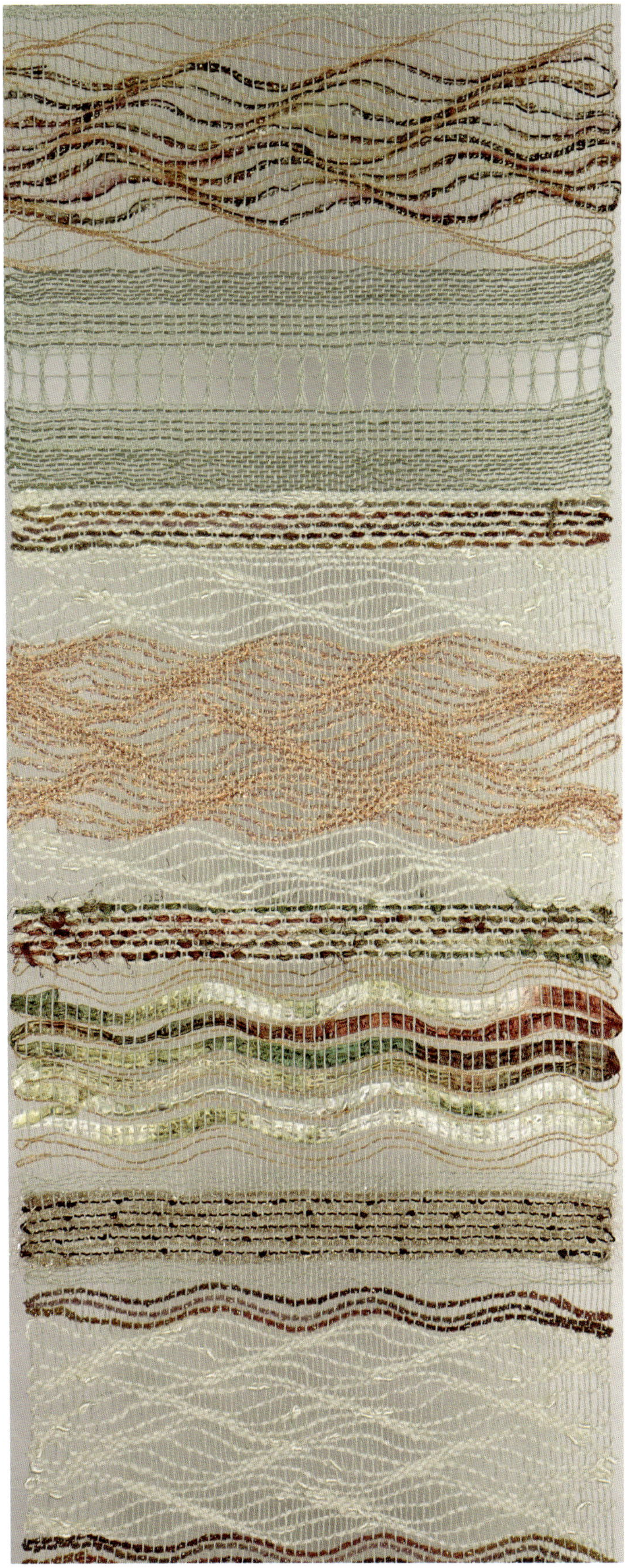

Rebecca Smith. *It Comes in Waves 2*, 2024. Linen, mixed fibers: 10 × 60 inches. Woven with a wave beater.

To weave with a wave beater, follow these steps:

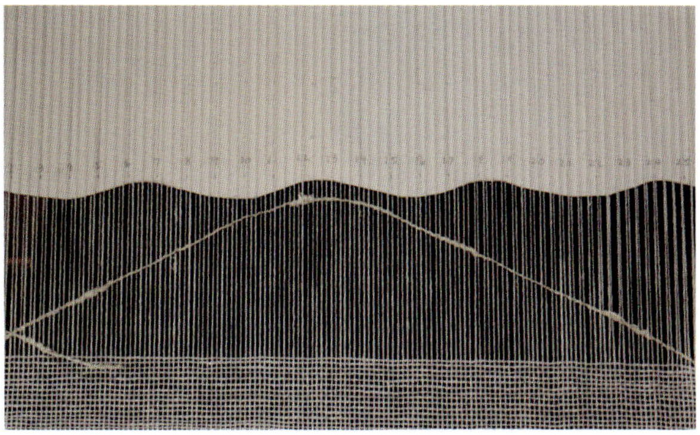

Insert the weft in the shed as usual. Arch the weft into a V shape in the middle. Insert the wave beater and close the shed.

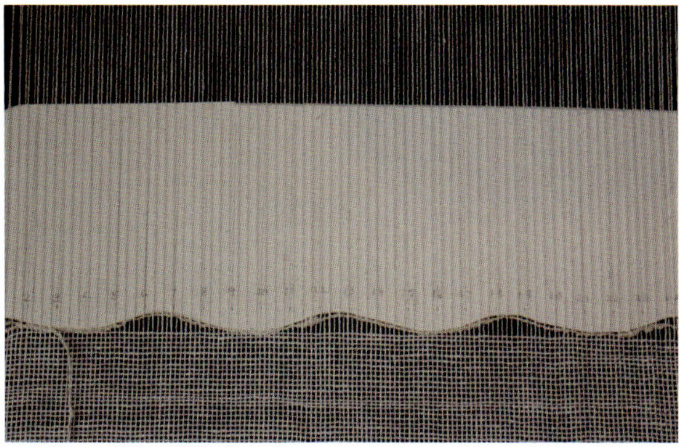

Carefully push the beater toward the fell, catching the weft as you go.

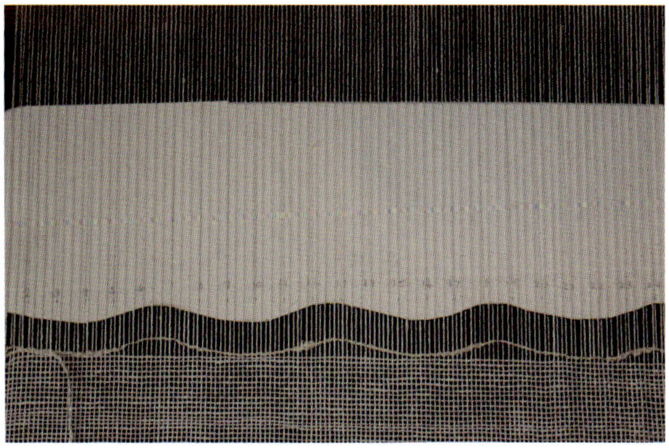

Note the wavy path of the weft.

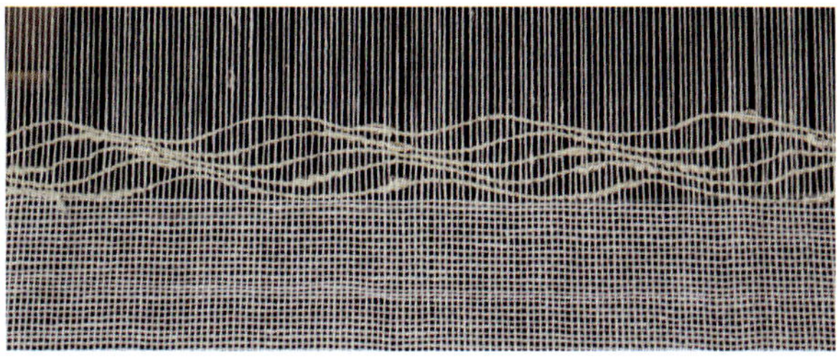

On each subsequent pick, move the beater ½ inch to the right or left. Continue moving the beater by ½-inch increments in one direction.

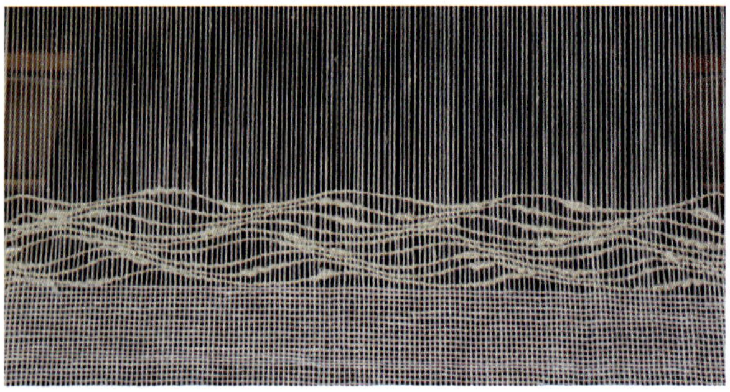

After a few rows, you can reverse the direction that the beater moves in order to create a pattern like the one seen here.

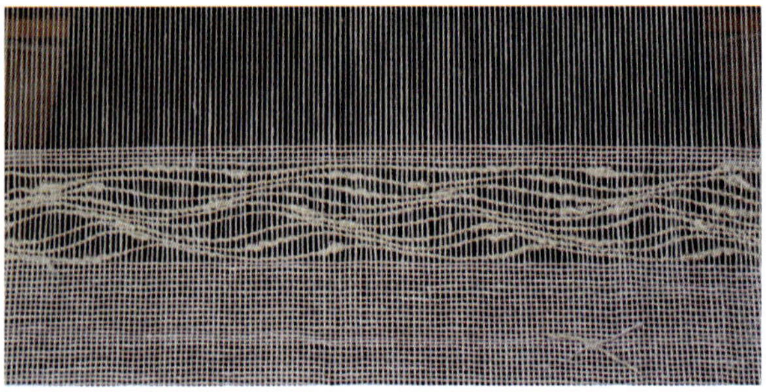

When you return to weaving straight rows with the loom's beater, press the weft gently into place to avoid flattening the waves.

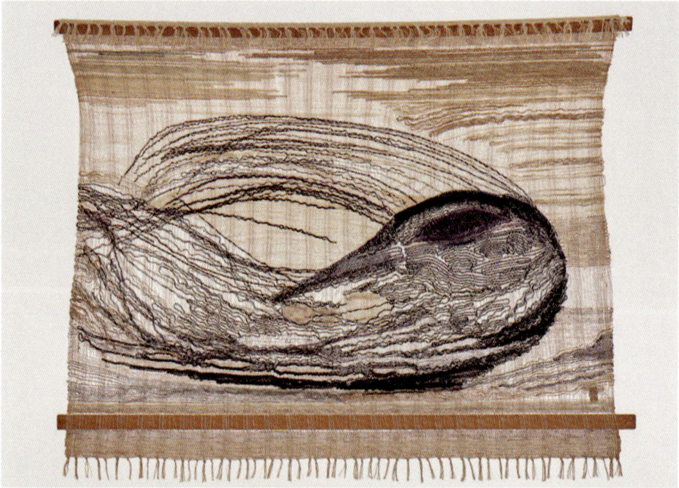

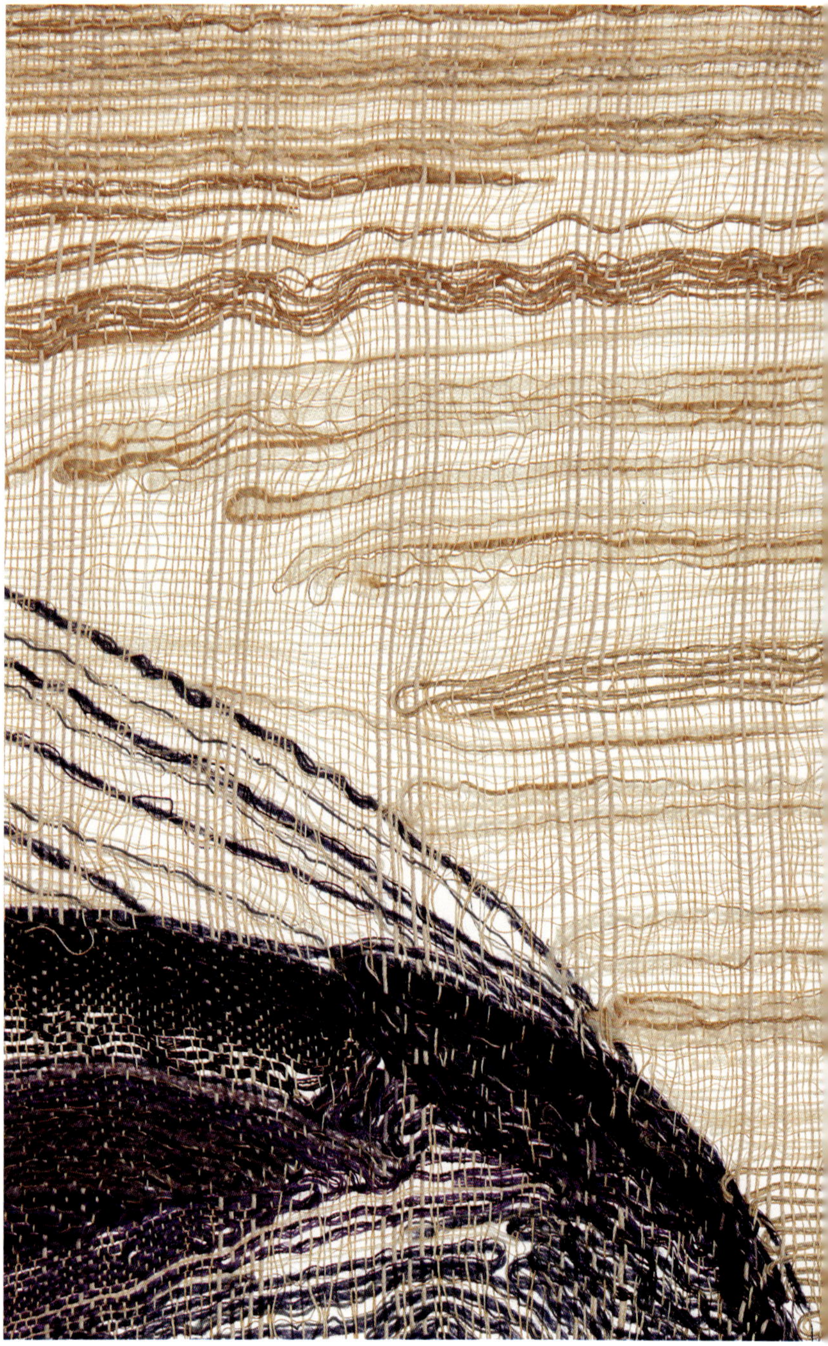

Make the V just big enough so that the weft fills all the contours of the beater as it presses the weft into place. Too much weft will buckle in unwanted curves, while too little weft will not be able to fill in the contours of the wave. Creating the V shape will also help avoid draw-in, which tends to occur when using a wave beater.

There are infinite options for ways to use the wave beater. See Project 6 for some ideas.

Free-Form Weft

Free-form weft is another way to let the weft travel its own path rather than woven in straight rows. The work of Lenore Tawney was groundbreaking in the development of free-form, open-warp weaving (read more about Lenore Tawney on page 19). Let's look at a detail of her piece titled *Lost and Proud*.

TOP & BOTTOM: Lenore Tawney. *Lost and Proud*, 1957. Linen, silk, wool; 43 × 51½ inches. Collection of the Lenore G. Tawney Foundation, New York. Photo: Rich Maciejewski, 2018, courtesy of John Michael Kohler Arts Center.

In her piece, curved rows of inlay defy the use of a beater while they define the contours of the bird. The relationship between ground weft and inlay is blurred. In some areas the ground weft weaves between rows of inlay. In other areas, thin weft and thick weft create variations in the density of the weave without overlapping each other. Weft is woven in rows that are close together or far apart, or even a mixture of the two, making it difficult to define one as ground and the other as inlay.

Free-form weft is woven without the use of a beater. Tools such as tapestry bobbins or combs are helpful to push the weft into place. Since the beater is not used, this form of transparency can be woven on a tapestry loom. Free-form weaving is especially useful for outlining focal points in a design, such as the bird in Tawney's piece.

There are a few cautions to be observed about free-form weft. The lack of a ground weave can diminish the stability of the weft. Ground weft is a stabilizing element that holds the inlay designs in place. Without ground weft, slick yarns such as silk and Tencel may slip out of place when the weaving is off the loom. These yarns don't grip the warp as well as other yarns such as linen and wool.

The density of the weaving will also have an impact on the stability of the weaving. Too few rows of weft, spread too far apart, can result in slippage of the weft when the piece is hung. Time and gravity are the enemies of a weaving that has too little structural strength. Many of Lenore Tawney's early open-warp weavings did not survive because they were simply too fragile.[2]

Textured Yarns and Nonyarn Materials

Thick or textured yarns and nonyarn materials can add visual and textural interest to a transparency. While they may be too thick to be used to weave an entire shape, a single row here and there will not displace the weft or cause tension issues.

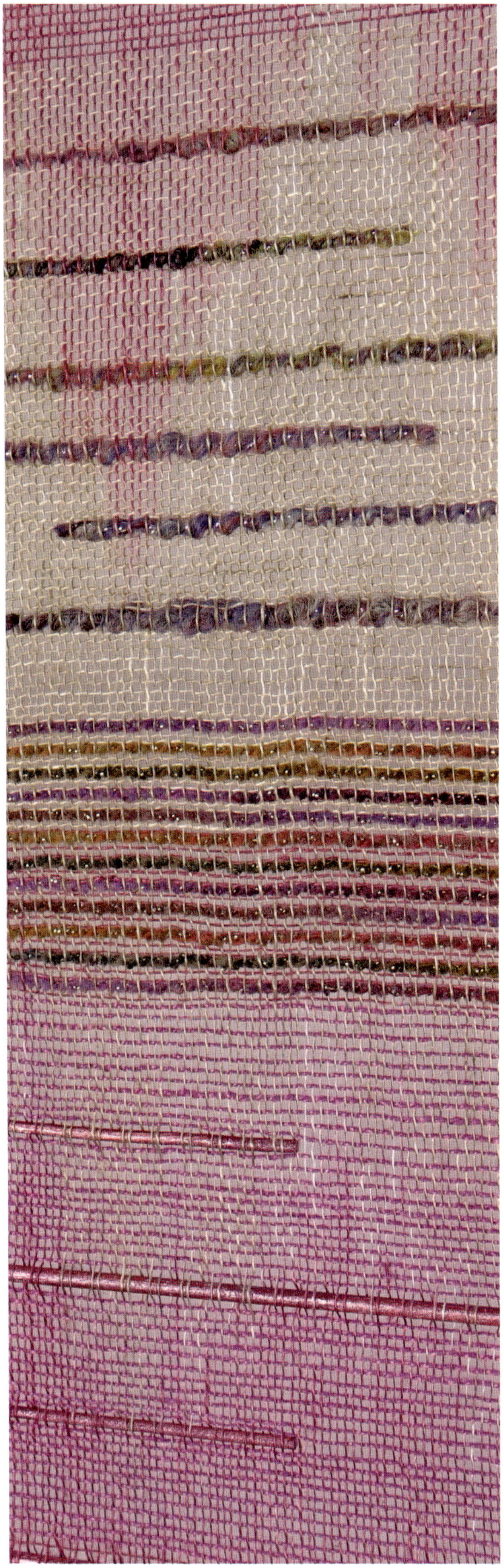

Rebecca Smith. *Rhythms*, 2024. Linen, mixed wefts, painted wood dowels, faux ikat: 12 × 48 inches. Detail.

Three different ways of incorporating thick materials are shown in the detail of *Rhythms*. At the top, individual rows of thick yarn add visual interest. Below that, another thick yarn is woven every second row. A row of ground weft separates each row of thick inlay weft. This allows some light to pass through the area, to make it appear less dense. At the bottom, painted wooden dowels were woven in. The paint protects the fiber from acids contained in the wood. Another option is to apply a polyurethane coating to the wood, which would preserve the natural color of the wood.

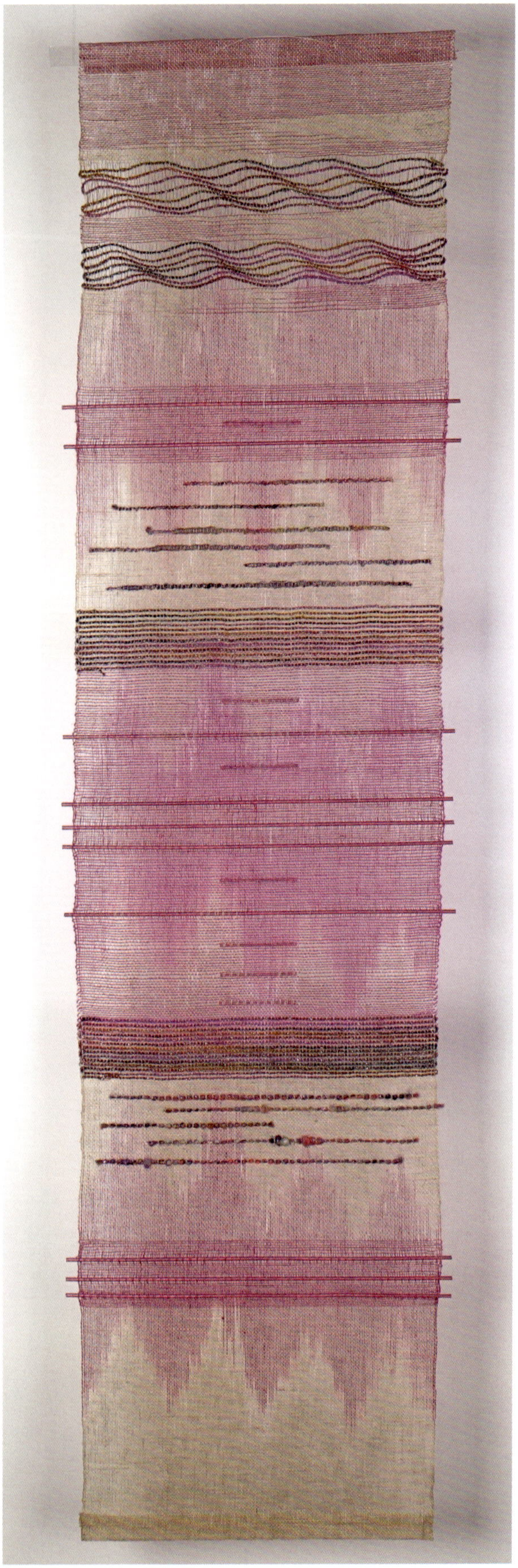

Rebecca Smith. *Rhythms*, 2024. Linen, mixed wefts, painted wood dowels, faux ikat: 12 × 48 inches.

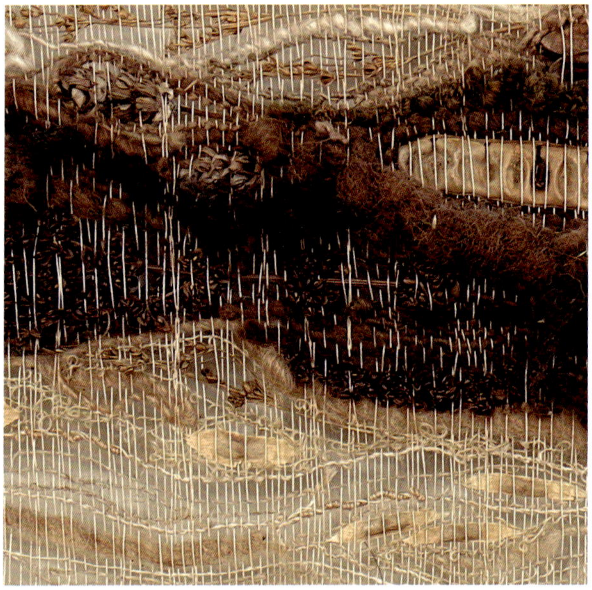

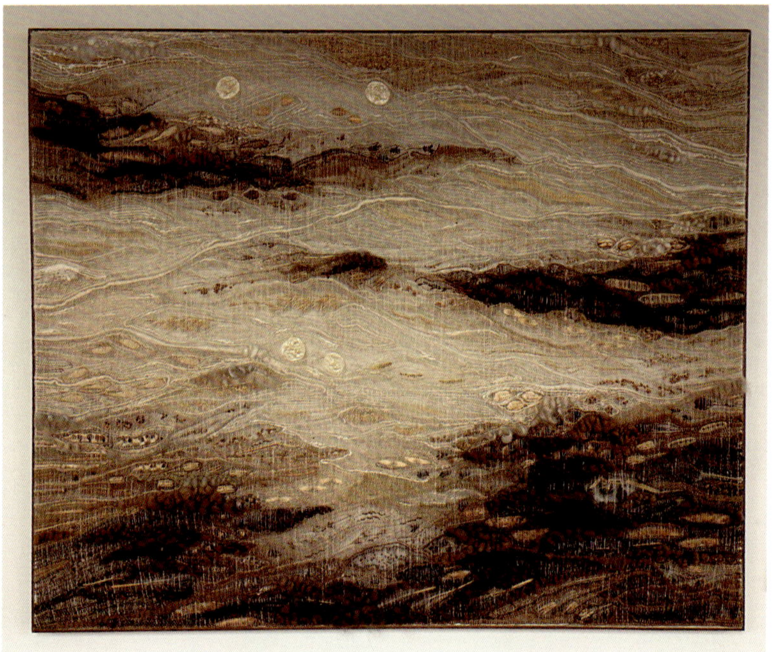

Betty Williams, untitled, circa 1975, and detail. (*top*). Photo: Rebecca Smith.

Inclusions of thick or odd-shaped materials lend themselves well to the free-form style of weaving. These materials often have unusual shapes that are hard to corral into straight rows of weaving. The contouring possible with free-form weft is perfect to outline inserted objects.

A weaver who excelled at using thick yarns and natural materials in transparency weaving was Betty Williams. Williams's work was included in Doramay Keasbey's book *Sheer Delight*. Her masterful compositions bring together naturally dyed wool roving with elements from nature. A close look at the detail reveals that various sizes of yarn weft encapsulate the natural inclusions within a framework of free-form plain weave.

Highly textured yarns and natural materials can add a lot of interest to a transparent weaving. The key to incorporating thick yarns or nonyarn materials is to make sure they are (1) not too heavy for the weaving to support, and (2) not so thick they distort the ground weft.

You might question whether the natural materials used in Williams's work will stay intact over time. Williams did take some precautions to ensure their longevity. The plant materials in the weft were naturally dried, and some were treated with glycerin. Once they were finished, she sprayed the pieces with a coating of Krylon lacquer.[3] This piece was woven sometime around 1975 and photographed in 2025. After fifty years, it is still looking good!

Lace Weaves

Several lace structures could potentially be introduced into the weaving of transparent textiles. Leno weave stands apart, however. Interest in ancient gauze weaves—precursors to leno—has been a recurring theme among many prominent weavers of transparent textiles. Lenore Tawney and several of her contemporaries found inspiration in ancient Peruvian gauze.[4]

Leno lace can be worked into the ground weave across an entire row or confined to just a section of the row. To weave leno lace, warp ends are crossed, and the weft is passed through the opening in the cross. The smallest unit for leno lace is to cross one warp over another. Larger bundles can be crossed as well. Let's look at an example for crossing four and four, or eight warp ends in total:

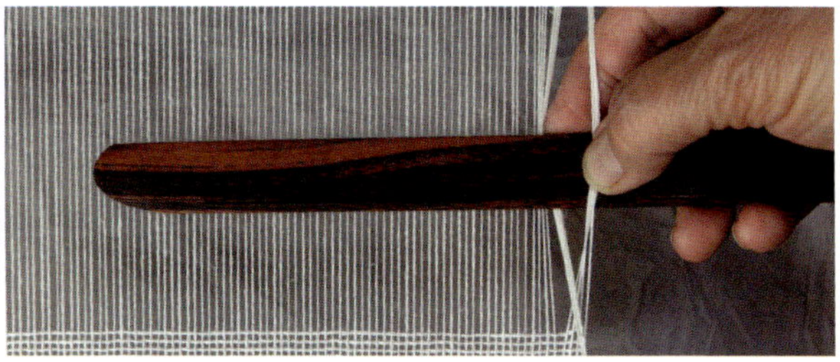

Begin on the right side of the warp if you are right-handed. Pick up the outer four warps and pull them to the left as you move the next four warps under them to the right. Place a pickup stick into the opening.

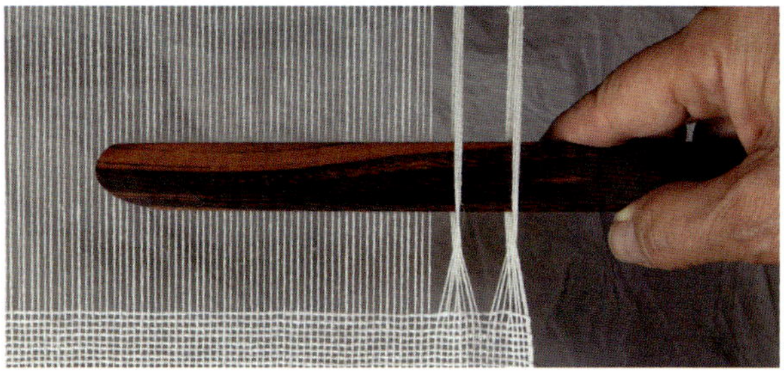

Continue crossing pairs of four warps and inserting the pickup stick as you work across the warp.

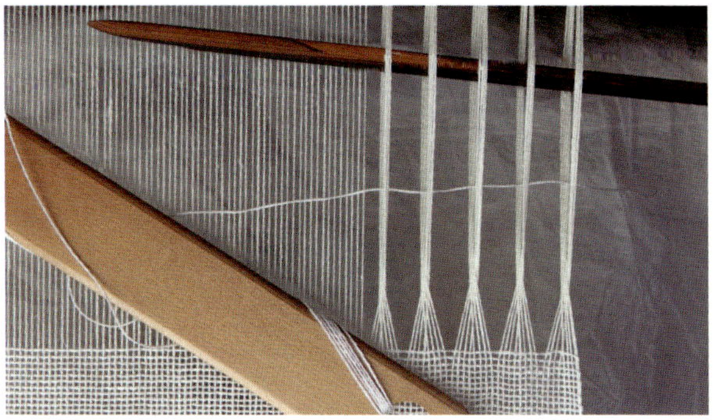

Turn the pickup stick on its side and pass the weft through the space created. A boat shuttle won't fit through space. Instead, cut a couple of yards from the boat shuttle and wrap it onto a stick shuttle or into a butterfly. Pull the weft tight enough to hold the warps in the twisted position.

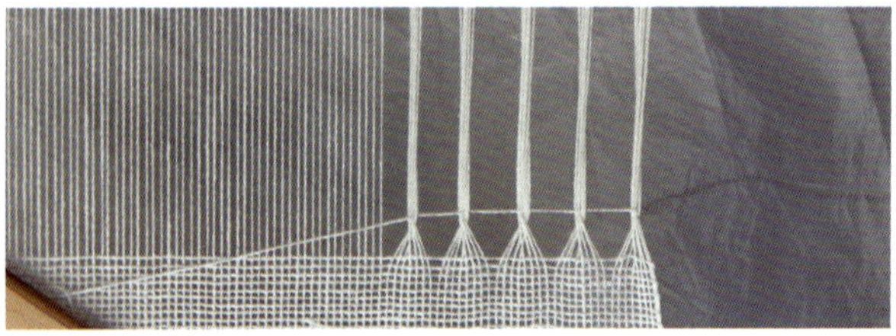

Press the weft into place, using the beater.

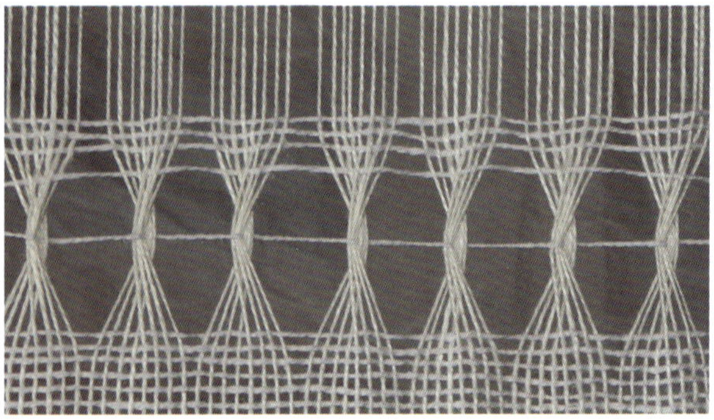

Weave a shot of plain weave from left to right and press into place. Try to leave the same amount of open space above the cross as below. This completes the first row of leno lace. You can continue to weave plain weave or weave another row of leno.

Weaving leno lace on linen can be tricky because the warp has no elasticity. If you experience trouble getting the twists to stay in place, try loosening the tension on the warp.

Adding Beads to Transparency Weaving

The addition of seed beads offers an interesting dimension for transparency weaving. The reflective surface of seed beads adds sparkle to the weaving similar to what can be accomplished with metallic threads. Randomly spaced beads make tiny points of light, whereas groups of beads will make a bigger visual impact.

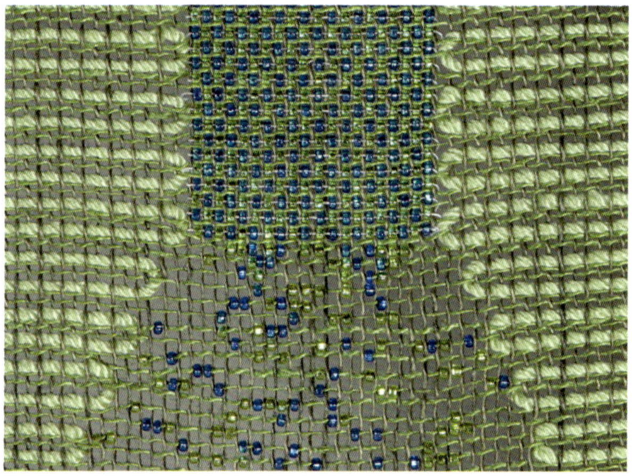

Rebecca Smith. *Time Framed* (detail). Showing solid rows of beads and randomly placed beads.

The detail of *Time Framed* shows two ways to add beads in a transparency. At the top, beads are densely woven in solid rows to imitate grains of sand

ONE WEAVER, THREE WEFT INNOVATIONS

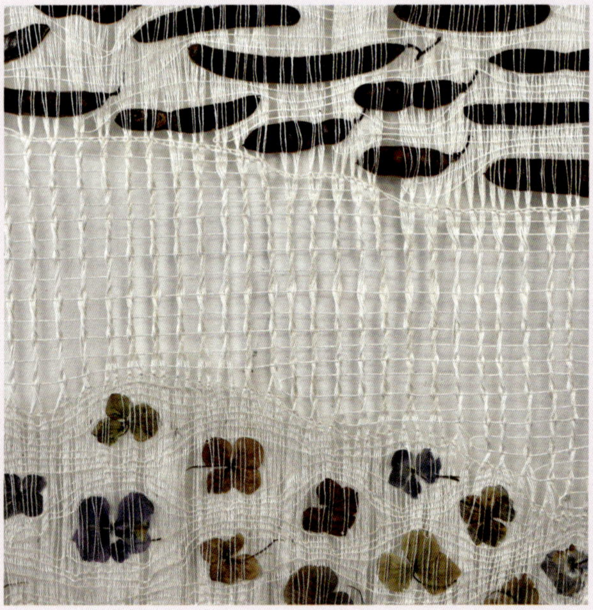

Canadian weaver Kathleen Morris has captured the essence of innovation in her open-weave transparent hangings. Examples shown on page 26 illustrate Morris's use of three of the weft innovations presented above: free-form weft, leno lace, and inclusions of natural materials. Morris intersperses free-form weft with leno lace to define space around the natural materials that form the focus of her work.

Kathleen Morris. *imbibe like roots* (detail). Courtesy of the artist.

in the neck of an hourglass. Below that, randomly placed beads suggest the grains of sand as they fall through the hourglass. Randomly placed beads are part of the ground weft, while woven rows of beads lie between rows of weft. Detailed instructions for each method are given below.

Random Placement

Random placement is done by threading the beads onto the ground weft. Either a stick shuttle or a boat shuttle with bobbin can be used. After winding ground weft onto the shuttle or bobbin, unwind several inches and begin loading beads onto the thread. Load as many as you think you will need, keeping in mind that once you start weaving, you will have to cut the thread if you need to add more beads. Use a big-eye needle: The entire needle is the eye, making it possible to easily thread the linen warp yarn.

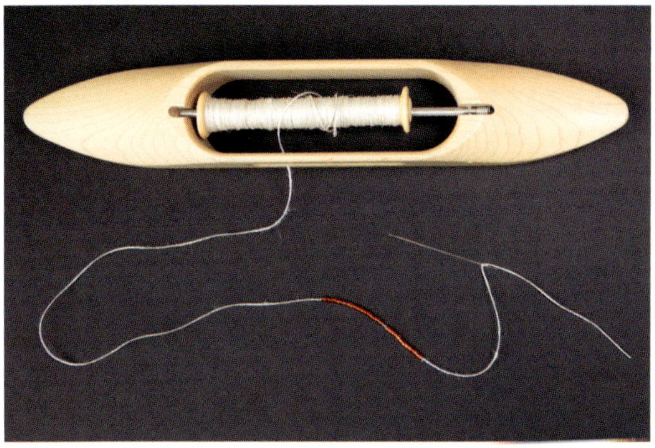
Beads strung onto ground weft

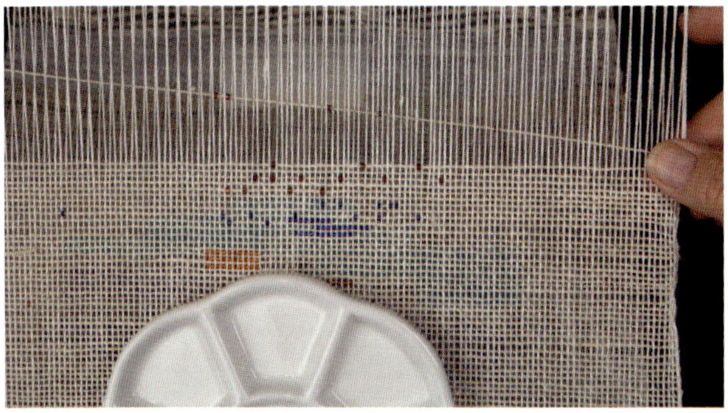
Randomly placing beads in open shed

Pass the shuttle through the warp, then move individual beads into the spaces between warps where you want them. Push the unused beads out of the shed toward the shuttle. Beat, change the shed, and repeat. At each row of weaving, place as many beads as desired to create a scatter effect. Unused beads can be pushed farther up the weft and saved for future use, or you can cut the weft to remove them if you are done beading.

Short rows of beads can also be woven, using the random placement method. A ½-inch row of sparkly beads, for example, is an interesting effect. The random placement method *could* be used to weave solid rows, but it is difficult—as well as tedious and frustrating—to make a whole row of beads stay in place as you change the shed. It would be better to use the row-weaving method below.

Solid Bead Rows

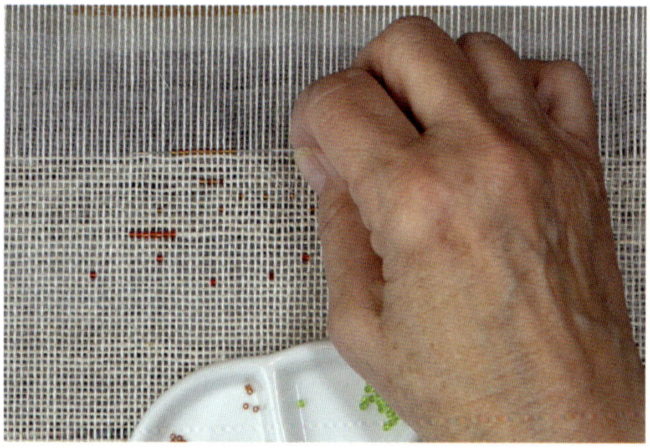
Beads woven using beading needle and thread

You will need a beading needle and beading thread to weave rows of beads (see suggestions in "Resources," on page 154). Bead weaving is done on a neutral or closed shed. The warp is sandwiched between two rows of bead thread that hold the beads in place between each warp.

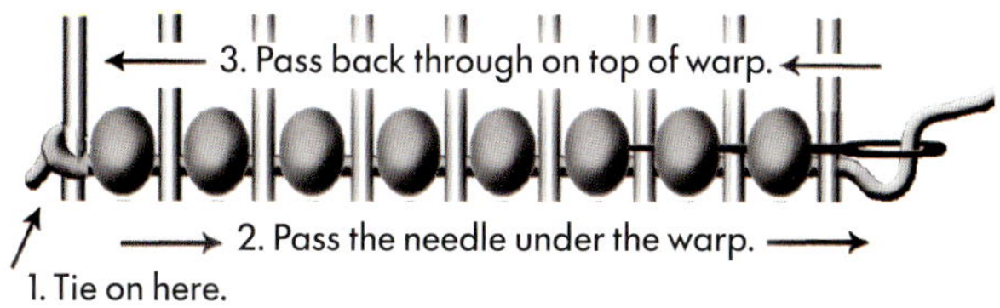

Follow these steps (see illustration):

You will need a piece of bead thread that is twice the length of the beaded row times the number of rows you will weave, plus enough extra to tie knots and leave tails at each end. Or you can just cut 30 inches of bead thread and add more when needed.

1. If you are right-handed, tie the end of the bead thread to the warp on the left side of the area that will be beaded. Load beads for the first row onto the thread, one bead for every space between the warps.

2. Take the needle and beading thread (loaded with beads) behind the warp; come back to the front to the right of the last warp in your beaded area.

3. From underneath, press the beads up into the spaces between the warps. On the top side, pass the needle through the beads on top of the warp, being careful not to snag the warp with the needle. It's easier if you try to pass through only a few beads at a time, rather than the whole row at once.

Once the first row is finished, you can continue to weave additional beaded rows. Weave ground weft between each row. Load enough beads onto the thread for only one row at a time.

If you are left-handed, reverse the direction of the weaving. The ideal is to weave back through the beads on top of the warp using your dominant hand.

Always add new thread at the end of a row rather than in the middle, since that would cause a gap between beads where you tie on a new length of thread. When you come to the end of the final row of beading, secure the beading thread around the warp with a double knot. To hide the thread's tail, use the needle to pass the tail back through three or four beads, then trim the tail. Hide the tail at the beginning of the beaded section in the same way.

Bead Size

The best size of bead to use will depend on the warp sett, and on whether they will be grouped together or randomly placed. Beads should fit easily in the open spaces of the ground weave. There are three variables to consider in choosing the correct beads to use:

- The width of the bead (bead width is measured in the direction that the hole runs): Beads that are too wide for the space will push the warps out of alignment.
- The height of the bead: Beads that are too tall will push rows of ground weft out of alignment.
- The size of the bead's hole: You must be able to thread the ground weft through the hole in the bead for random placement.

A special class of seed beads called Delica beads meet all these criteria. Delica beads are cylindrical rather than round. Because of this, the hole is bigger than in a comparably sized seed bead. When woven, they lie in flat rows like yarn.

Delica beads come in a wide array of colors, but only a few sizes are small enough to fit the open spaces in the ground weave. From smallest to largest, the useful sizes are 15, 11, and 10. The chart shows the best bead size for each use.

	Delica Bead Size		
	15	11	10
Warp and Sett			
16/1 @ 15 epi	Beaded rows	Random	n/a
16/2 @ 12 epi	n/a	Beaded rows	Random

Bead Finish

Seed beads come in a variety of finishes that affect the strength of their color and their sparkle. While transparent beads may sound ideal for transparency weaving, that is not correct. Transparent beads tend to lose their vibrancy when light shines through them. Matte beads have a flat finish, so they lack sparkle. Several other finishes—silver lined, color lined, and metallic—will give good results. Beads designated as cut have a hexagonal surface rather than a uniform flat surface. These beads tend to have a lot of sparkle.

WARP VARIATIONS

The traditional approach to transparency weaving assumed that the warp performed a supporting role. Together with the ground weft, the warp was not intended to draw attention to itself. A neutral-colored warp and matching ground weft provided the background that supported the star of the show: the inlay. In this section, we will look at two methods to draw more attention to the warp.

Variations in Denting and Spacing

Attention can be drawn to the warp by interrupting the even spacing of the warp in the reed. Uneven denting (e.g., 1-2-1-2-1-2 to sley for 12 epi in an eight-dent reed) will be a nuisance if your aim is to weave inlay in either a geometric or pictorial pattern. These types of design rely on uniform spacing of warp ends. But uneven denting can offer an interesting background for an abstract design that doesn't rely on evenly spaced warps. Along with uneven spacing of the warps, you might try warps of different thickness or color to offset the uniformity of the warp.

Skipping dents altogether opens further options for exploring transparency designs. Leaving several contiguous dents empty will create floats of ground weft across the empty spaces that lack warp. Whether these floats are long or short, they will lend an interesting aspect to the design. You might even make them the focus of the design. Continuing a design motif across the open dents is one idea for skipped dents. Combining open denting with free-form weft or a wave beater might open a rich vein of unique transparency designs!

Dyeing Warps for Special Effects

In tapestry weaving, the warp is rarely seen, so I never had much reason to pay attention to it. When I began to weave transparencies, I was elated with the potential for making warp variations part of the design. In my earliest transparencies, I dyed the warp in a color gradient from top to bottom. Later I began to use a design approach that I call faux ikat since it gives an ikat effect without truly being ikat.

Linen is a cellulose fiber, which means it can be dyed in the same manner as cotton, using fiber-reactive dyes commonly known as Procion MX dyes. Many online sources are available for learning how to work with fiber-reactive dyes (see "Resources," on page 154). These dyes require only soda ash as a fixative and require no heat. Some approaches will have you soak the fiber in a soda ash solution prior to dyeing, while others will tell you to mix the soda ash in with the dye solution. The key factor is that once the dye and soda ash are combined, they begin to react with each other. Mixing soda ash in the dye solution will force you to work more quickly, since the reaction time is limited.

There are a few things to keep in mind as you wind your warp and dye it:

- The final 10–20 inches at each end of the warp will be included in loom waste, so don't worry about dyeing these areas, and don't include them in the layout for where your colors will go.
- Do not tie tight chokes around the warp, since these will prevent the dye from penetrating and will result in a white stripe. The initial choke that you tie for warping front to back (see page 40) may present a problem. If so, tie the choke closer to the end of the warp and move it to its proper position after dyeing the warp.
- In place of the other chokes, tie loose figure eights to keep the warp ends under control.

Lay the warp out on a surface to prepare to dye it. Apply the dye with a foam brush or other implement that can soak up a lot of dye. The dye is applied heavily to make sure all the warp ends get soaked. Cover the warp with plastic and let it rest for twenty-four hours or so to make sure the dye is set. Rinse until all the unabsorbed dye has run out of the yarn.

Color Gradation

A warp dyed with a color gradation from top to bottom will give a subtle but rich background for the inlay design. *Past Tense* is a perfect example of this. You need only two colors to make a good color gradation, but you can use more. Two dye colors applied side by side will naturally bleed into each other, often mixing together to create a third color. At the border between the two colors, you can simply let the dyes flow into each other, or you can make a mixture of the two colors to get a hue that is midway between the two. The latter approach will give more subtle color transitions between colors.

Be sure to dye enough ground weft to weave each color zone. Weaving a single color of ground weft across all the color zones in the warp would mute the effect of the dyed warps. Where the warp begins to transition to a new color, use the color-blending technique described on page 101 to soften the effect of changing to a new weft color.

DYE SAFETY

Procion MX dyes are relatively safe for both you and the environment. They do not contain heavy metals or other toxic substances. Soda ash is a strong alkali that can cause eye, skin, and respiratory irritation. A few precautions can make your dye practice safer:

For you:

- Wear a mask or respirator while mixing the dyes. In powdered form, the dye is easily airborne, and breathing it could cause lung issues.
- Wear gloves to prevent staining your skin.
- Never use the same pots or utensils for cooking and for dye preparation.

For the environment:

- Minimize water usage. Low-water immersion and long soaks when rinsing are two strategies that can reduce water waste.
- Dilute spent dye solutions before pouring them into the sewer system.

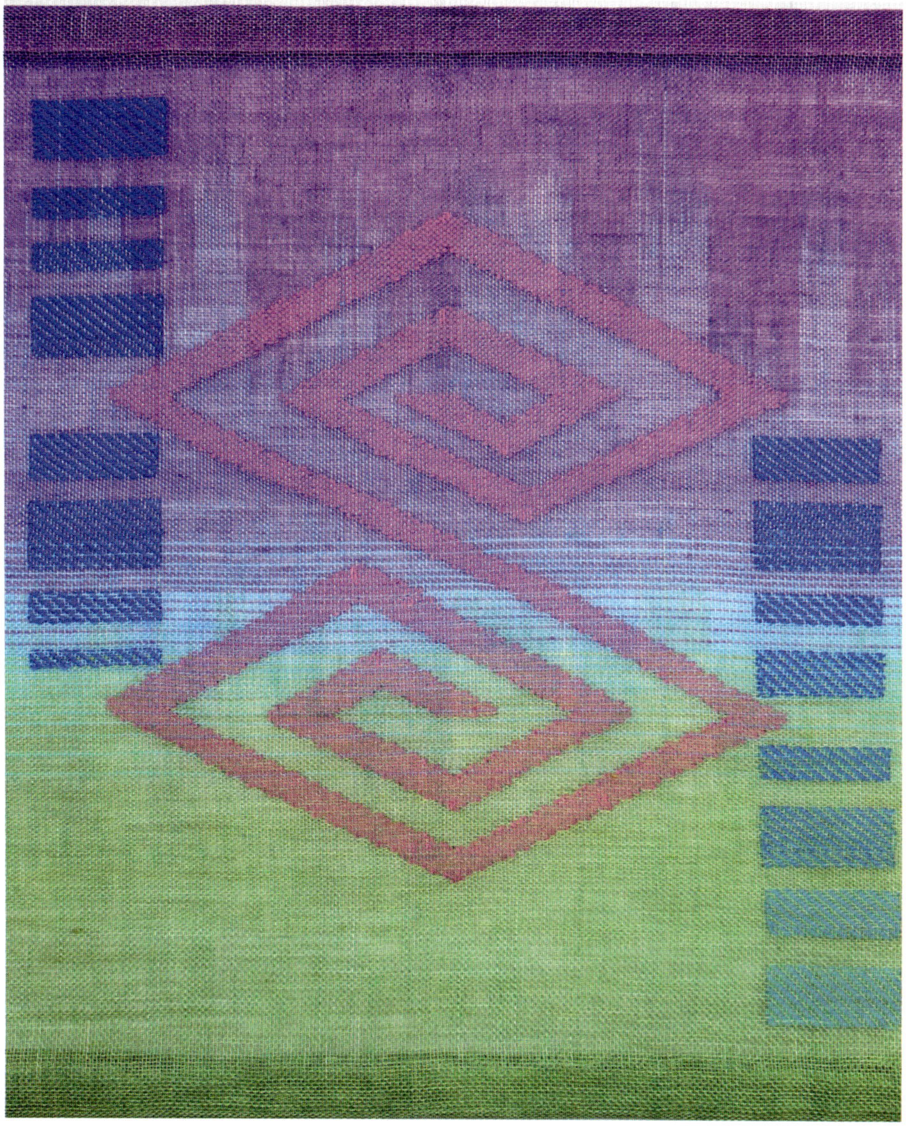

Rebecca Smith. *Past Tense*, 2018. Linen, wool, painted warp: 18 × 18 inches. Color blending helps to transition between weft colors.

Faux Ikat

Ikat is a term applied to the technique of wrapping parts of the warp or weft to prevent those areas from absorbing the dye. It is generally used when yarns are dyed in a vat. When the dye is applied to yarn while it is lying on a table, a similar effect can be achieved by simply not applying dye to some areas. This effect is called faux ikat since it achieves a similar effect to ikat, but by taking a different approach to achieving that effect.

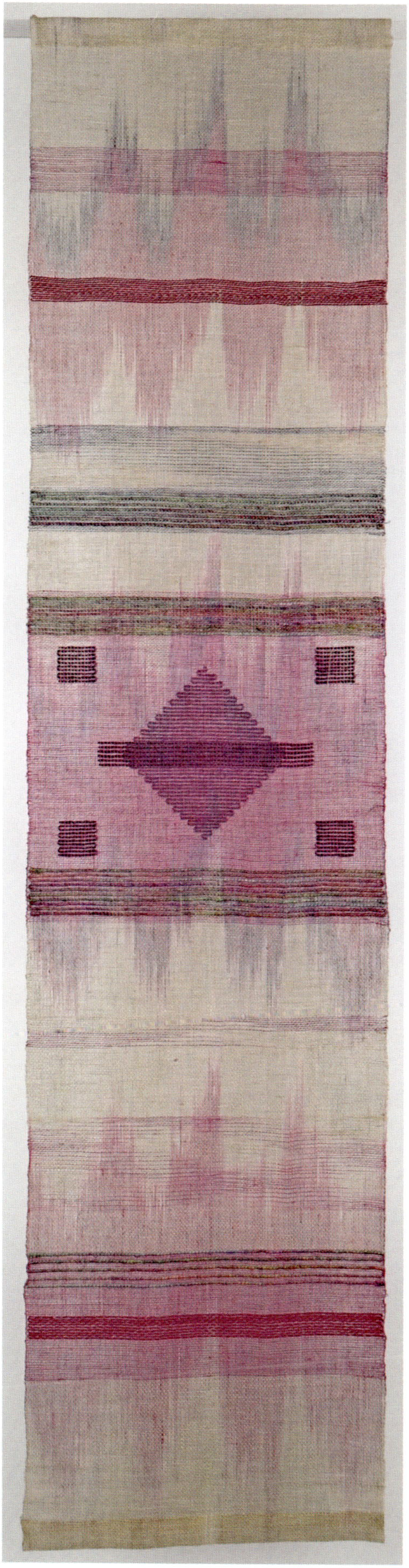

RIGHT: Rebecca Smith. *Heartland*, 2024. Linen, wool, faux ikat warp and weft: 12 × 48 inches.

The steps for dyeing faux ikat are the same as described above for dyeing a color gradation. Instead of dyeing the entire warp, the warp is dyed in stripes. The area between the stripes can be left undyed or can be dyed in a different color.

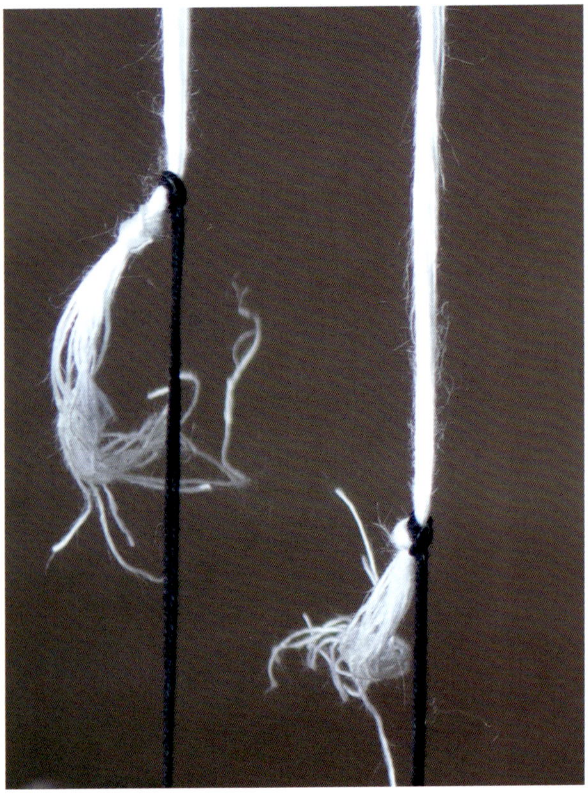

ABOVE & BELOW: Warps are offset with cord ties of varying lengths.

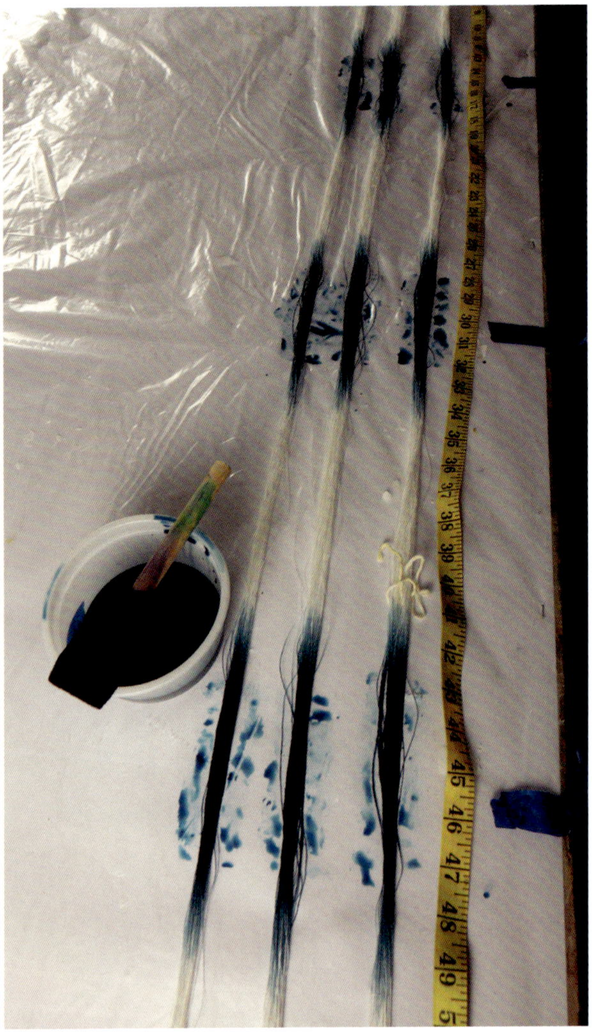

A warp wound in three bouts is laid out for dyeing. A tape measure is laid alongside the warp, and blue tape is used to mark the center of each dyed stripe.

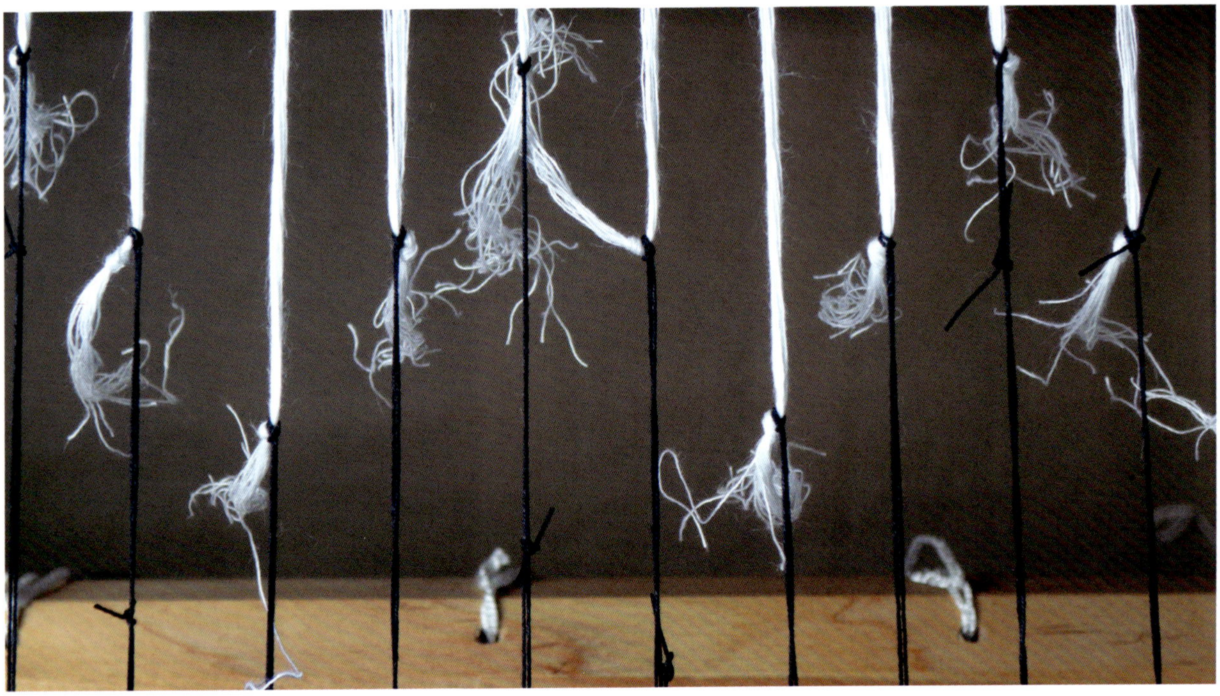

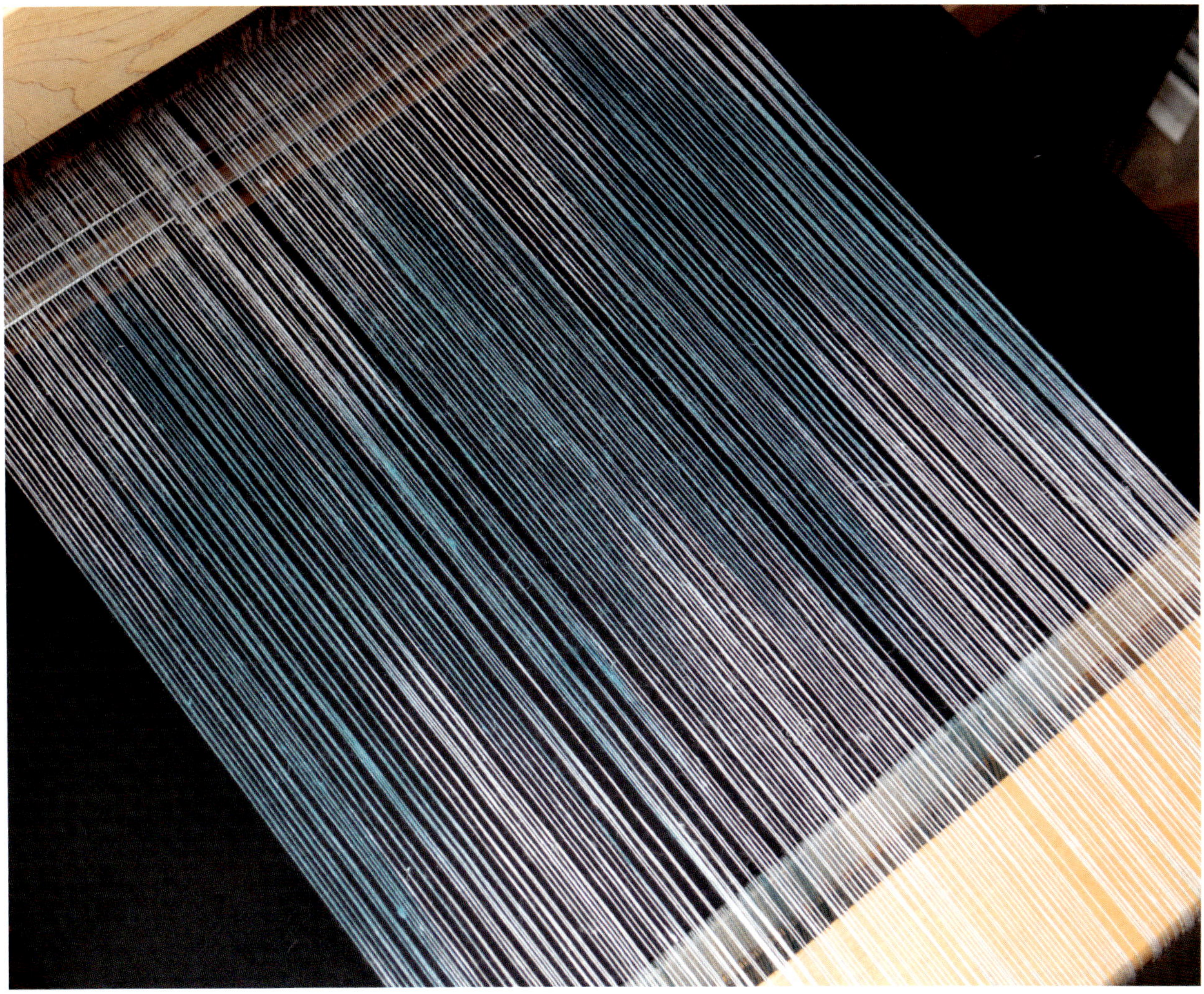

The dyed stripes are turned into jagged designs that characterize ikat by offsetting warps during the warping process. A simple yet effective method to offset warps is to use cords that are cut to different lengths.[5] Tie cords to the back apron rod in a pattern that is based on their lengths.

Tie overhand knots in 1-inch groups of warps. Use a lark's head knot to connect the cords to each group of knots (see close-up photo). As they are wound onto the warp beam, the warps will shift position to mimic the pattern established by the tie-on cords.

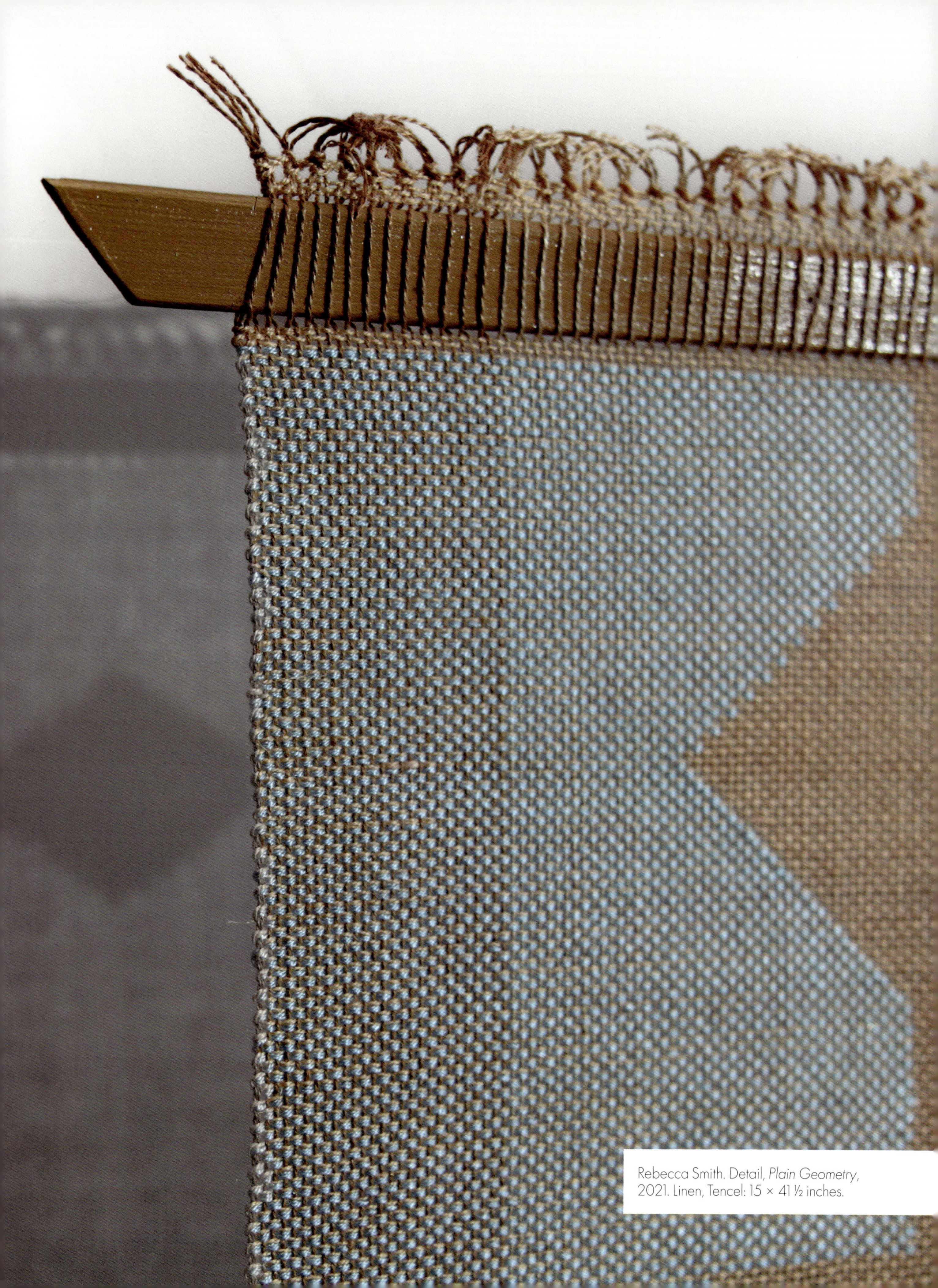

Rebecca Smith. Detail, *Plain Geometry*, 2021. Linen, Tencel: 15 × 41 ½ inches.

Chapter 9

FINISH AND DISPLAY YOUR TRANSPARENCY

OFF-LOOM FINISHING

Once your transparency is off the loom, you must take steps to even out its appearance and deal with weft tails. The first step of finishing is to treat the finished weaving to a bit of damp heat and pressure from an iron. Right off the loom, your transparency may have indentations from the cloth beam. Damp heat and pressure will even out the surface. Do the damp finishing before you trim off your weft tails. The damp heat will open the fibers so that they cling to each other, helping to prevent the ends of the inlay from popping loose.

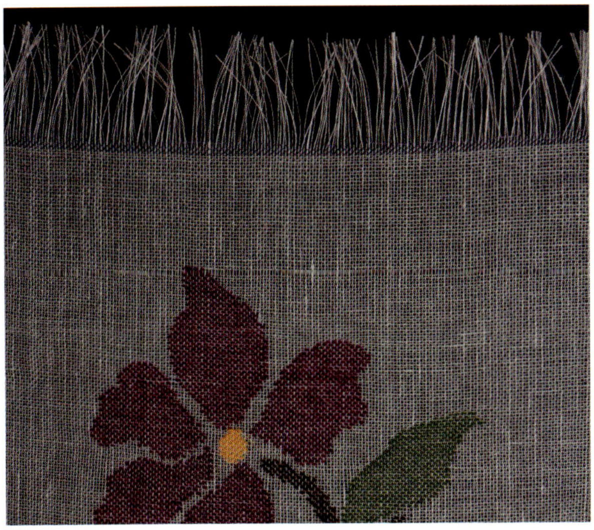

A slight curve along the top edge of the piece means this piece must be blocked.

Damp finishing can be used to block the weaving in order to correct inconsistencies in the width or length. Once it is off the loom, you may find that the top end of the weaving curves in a smile shape. This is generally due to looser warp tension at the outer edges. This can happen when the inlay is concentrated in the middle of the warp, creating greater tension for the warps that go over and under the inlay weft. Also check for inconsistencies in the width: To some extent, these can be corrected with damp finishing.

Method for Damp Finishing

You will need a waterproof surface to work on, a foam pad, about ½ inch thick and slightly bigger than the piece, white towel(s), stainless-steel straight pins, and an iron.

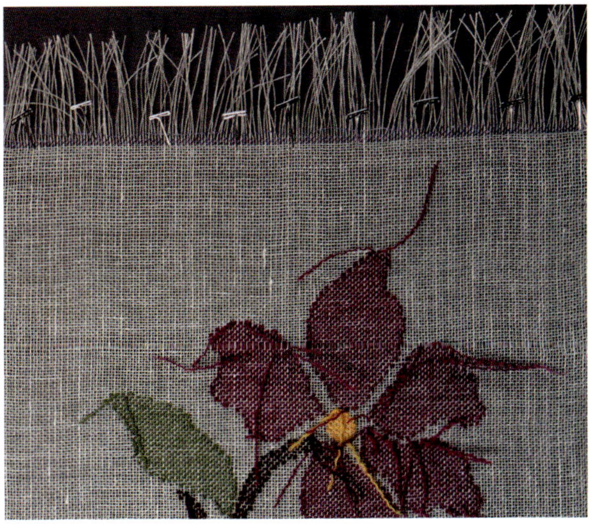

Pins inserted to hold the edge straight for blocking

1. Lay the piece working side up on the padded surface. If it needs blocking, align the top edge in a straight line. Insert pins every ½ inch to maintain the straight edge. Work the loose cloth at the sides down toward the bottom. Place occasional pins along the side edges to hold it in place. If the sides need blocking, place pins every ½ inch in the sections that need to be blocked. Pin the bottom edge in a straight line.

2. Soak the towels, then wring them out by hand to remove most of the water. Place the towels over the weaving. Completely cover the weaving with one layer of towels.

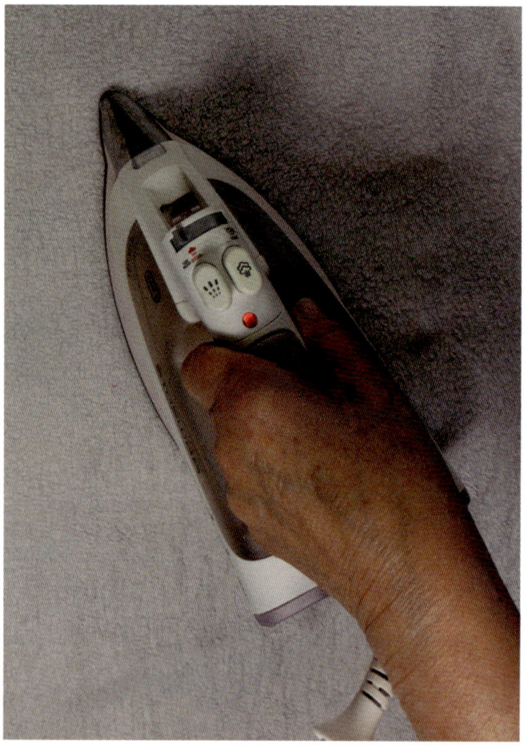

Steam ironing through the towel to force moisture and heat into the weaving

3. Set the iron to high on a steam setting. While applying pressure, iron the entire surface of the weaving through the towel. This forces moisture and heat down into the cloth.

4. Leave the towel in place for at least twenty-four hours. If it hasn't begun to dry out after that time due to humidity, remove the towel and let the weaving dry naturally.

5. Remove the pins. Admire your work.

6. The next step is to trim the weft ends. These can be trimmed close to the surface of the weaving.

Sewing Your Hem

If you opted to create a hem in preparation for inserting a rod, follow these steps:

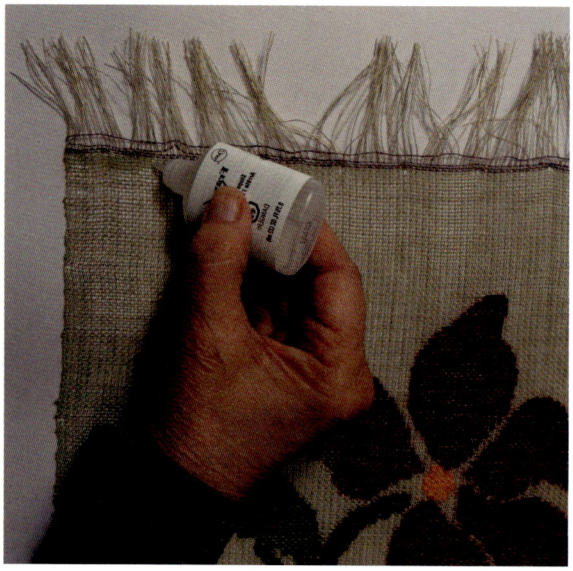

1. Run a line of Fray Check along the line where the header ends and the ground weft for the body of the piece begins. Let it dry, then trim away the header along the line.

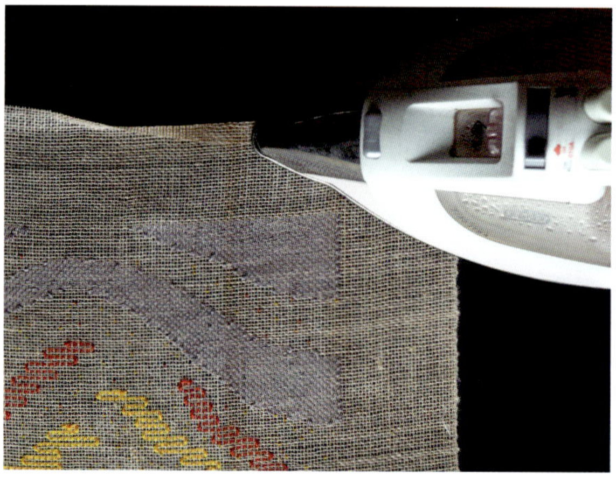

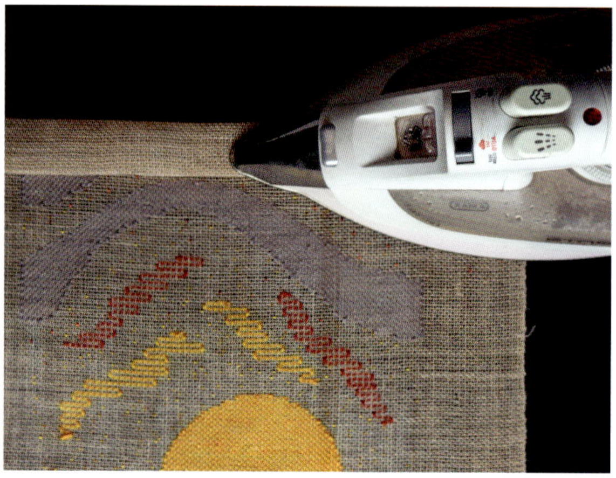

2. Working with the back of the transparency up, turn under ¼ inch and iron a crease. Then turn under a hem that is wide enough to accommodate the size of the rod that you plan to use. The hem should be approximately twice the width of the rod. For instance, if using a ⅝-inch wide acrylic rod, the hem should be 1 to 1¼ inches wide; if using a ¾-inch-wide wooden slat, make the hem 1½ inches wide. Iron a crease and pin into place if necessary.

3. Hand stitch the hem into place, using a hemstitch that is invisible on the front. Using sewing thread that matches the color of the ground weave, anchor the thread in the hem with a knot, then pass the needle under a single warp of the transparency and come back through the edge of the hem. Work your way across the width, making a stitch every ¼ inch, then secure the end of the thread. Leave the ends of the pocket open.

DISPLAYING YOUR TRANSPARENCY

There are many ways to display your transparency. Some methods are better than others for taking advantage of the transparent quality of the weaving. If simply hung from a nail or picture hook, the weaving will rest against the wall, and the transparency effect will be lost. Below we will look at a variety of mechanisms for hanging the weaving a few inches from the wall to take advantage of the transparency and potentially create some shadows.

For simplicity, let's group the various methods presented below into three categories:

- Hanging by a string
- Hanging from a support
- Mounting in a frame

Hanging by a String

Hanging by a string requires you to attach a supporting rod to the weaving. In the design phase (see chapter 4), we discussed the need to plan ahead for your display method by either weaving a hem, hemstitching the edges, or weaving a border (see page 59). Both hemming or hemstitching prepare the transparency to be hung from a support rod. For this purpose, you need to prepare a suitable rod to support the transparency. Wood or acrylic are the most common materials to use for a rod, although you may opt for other suitable materials. A flat rod is preferable to a round dowel because round dowels, whether wood or acrylic, tend to bend under the weight of the weaving.

Preparing the Rod

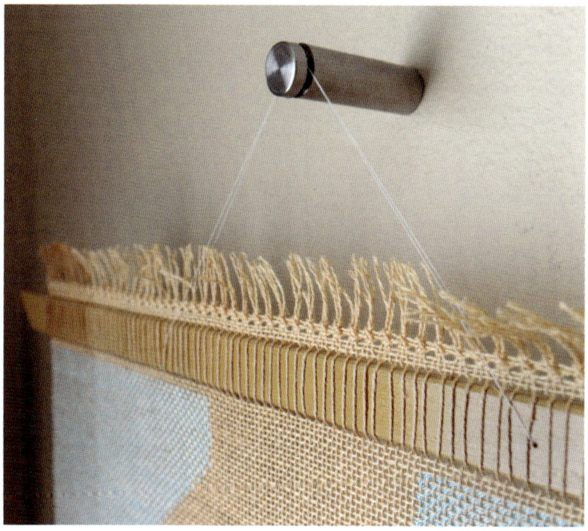

Hemstitched finish with support rod woven in: Monofilament passes front to back through holes drilled in the rod. Shown hanging from a single standoff screw.

The rod should be cut to a length that is 3 inches wider than the width of the transparency. This ensures that the entire piece will be supported, and allows space at both ends for drilling holes if needed.

A wood rod should be painted or coated with polyurethane to seal the wood, which contains fiber-damaging acids. Painting the wood gives you an opportunity to match the color of the rod to the transparency, which can have a nice effect.

Holes must be drilled in the rod in order to hang it from a string. Drill a pair of ⅛-inch-diameter holes. There are two options for where to drill holes:

- Drill a hole near each end of the rod.
- Drill a hole one-third of the way in from each end of the rod.

The second option works better for wide pieces (20 inches or wider) since it distributes the weight more evenly and lessens the chance that the rod will bend forward or backward under the weight.

Inserting the Rod

If you opted to hemstitch the ends of the transparency combined with weaving in a rod near each end, your rod is now ready to be woven in. If you have prepared a hem for the rod, carefully feed it through the sleeve created by the hem, trying not to snag the delicate threads.

Attaching String or Monofilament

Monofilament is a clear string most often made from nylon. It is commonly used for fishing but is also available from craft retailers. It is often used in galleries for hanging work because it tends to disappear into the background.

Cut a piece of string or monofilament to a length that is three times the distance between the holes. Pass the piece from front to back through both holes that you predrilled in the rod, then bring up both ends of the line to tie together. This will create a double line for hanging, one supporting from the front and one supporting from the back of the rod. Secure the knot with a dab of quick-drying glue.

Hanging from the Ceiling or Wall

You can make the most of the transparent quality of the weaving by hanging it away from a wall. Hang it from the ceiling in front of a window (avoid direct sun exposure) or other locations where it is out of the flow of traffic.

Hanging from a single hook will allow the piece to turn with the movement of air in the room. Hanging from two hooks will stabilize the position so that the same side is always facing the same direction.

Transparencies can be hung from a wall by using the same support rod options discussed above. However, as mentioned above, if the weaving hangs against the wall, it will lose its transparent features. Several methods are available to put some distance between the weaving and the wall. The simplest of these methods is to use a long nail or screw that is only partially driven into the wall, leaving the rest of its length to stand out horizontally from the wall.

MAGNETIC HANGERS

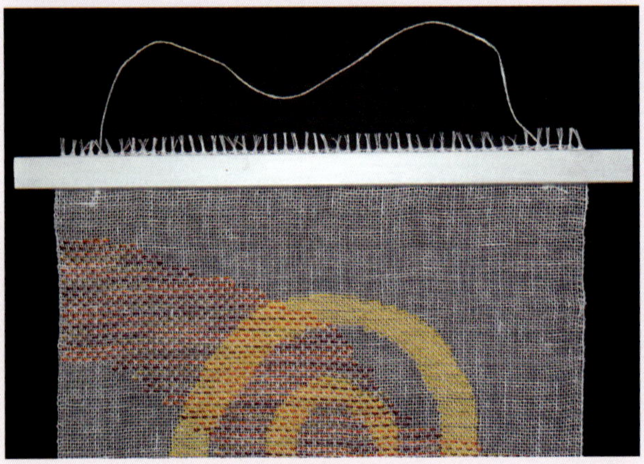

Magnetic hanger combined with hemstitched edge.

Magnetic poster hangers offer an alternative form of rod to support your transparency. Magnetic hangers use compression to hold lightweight, thin objects. They are adaptable to holding transparencies, but because the magnets are positioned near the outer ends, the transparency may pull loose at the center. To avoid this, add hemstitching to your weave plan. The hemstitched edge adds just enough bulk so that the weaving can't slip out of the hanger. An alternative solution would be to attach the weaving to the wood on the inside of the hanger, either with tape, glue, or even staples.

A piece of hardware called a standoff screw is specifically designed for this purpose. Standoff screws come in various widths and lengths. The one shown here is 2½ inches long by ⅝ inches wide. The base of the screw is attached to the wall, then the outer screw is inserted, creating a groove. Simply hang the string from this groove.

Hanging from a Support

A second class of display options involve hanging the transparency from a support. These methods have the advantage that they hold the transparency away from the wall so that the transparent and shadow features can be seen. To use a support, you must still use a hanging rod, as discussed above, but you do not need to drill holes or attach a string. Instead, the transparency is held away from the wall by the support.

One such support is the standoff screw introduced above. To treat the standoff screw as a support rather than just a hook, use a pair of them. The easiest way to hang a transparency from a pair of standoff screws is to simply rest the rod in the grooves of the standoff screws. A more secure method is to drill a hole at each end of the support rod large enough to accommodate the standoff screw. The base of the standoff screw is attached to the wall, then the screw is inserted through the hole in the rod and screwed into the base. Once mounted, the transparency hangs about 2 inches from the wall, far enough out to be able to see the shadows behind it.

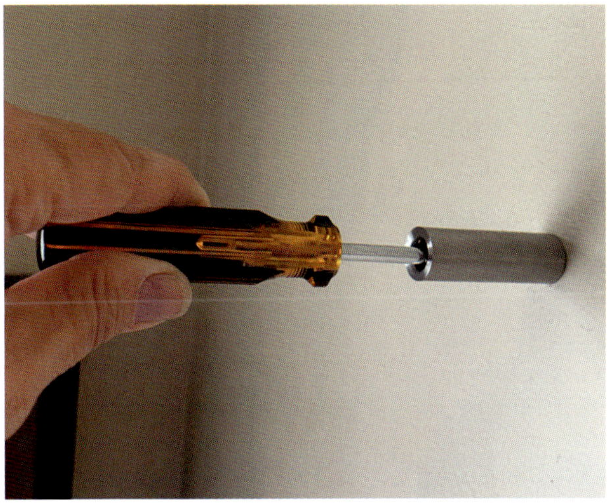

Base of standoff screw is attached to the wall.

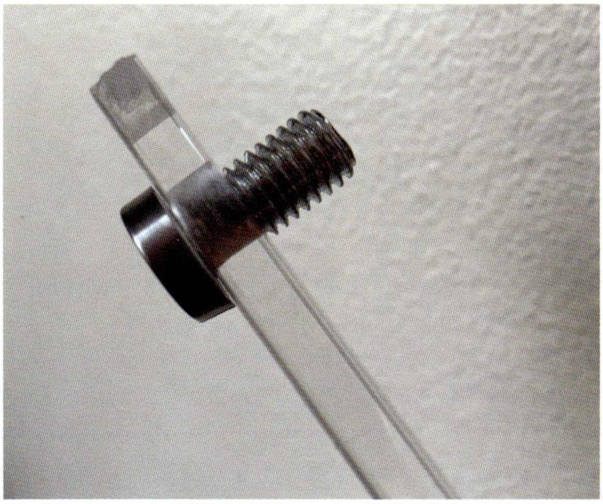

Front screw is inserted through the acrylic rod before screwing into base.

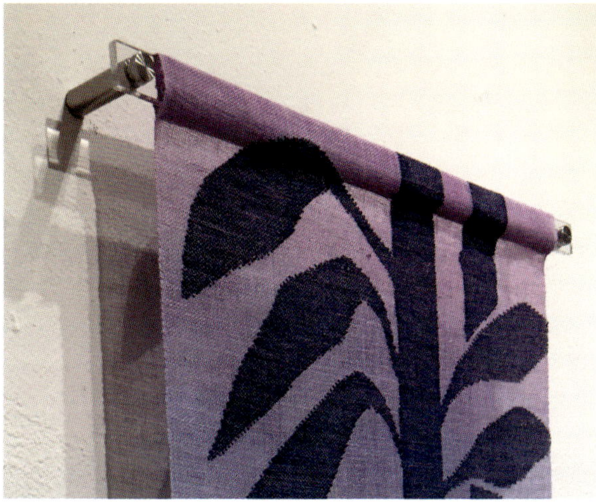

Hemmed finish with acrylic rod inserted. Shown mounted on a pair of standoff screws.

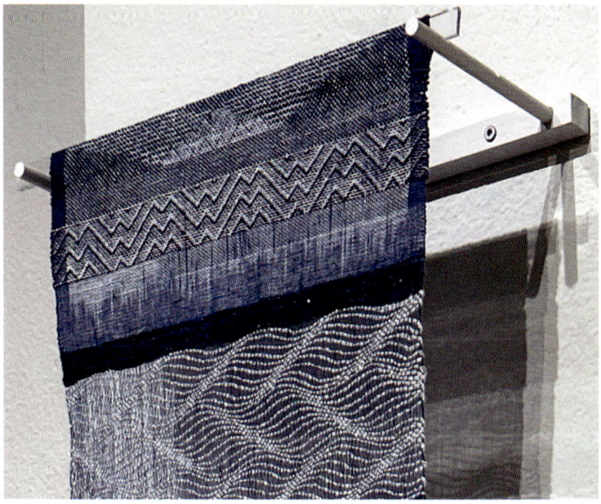

Custom-made support device.

You might also build your own support device. The custom-made support pictured above is made using a dowel and a length of 1-by-1-inch wood. The dowels fit snugly into holes drilled into the wood support. Notches cut in the top side of the dowel allow the transparency's support rod to stand on its edge. The length of the dowel and placement of the notches can be changed to allow the transparency to hang at various distances from the wall. Here it is shown holding the weaving 6 inches from the wall. Notice the great shadows.

Mounting in a Frame

An alternative to free-hanging transparency display methods is a display that requires the transparency to be mounted in a rigid format. Framing is one obvious alternative, but traditional picture framing is not the only, or always the best, solution for displaying a woven piece of art. Let's look at a few ideas that have worked for transparency weavers.

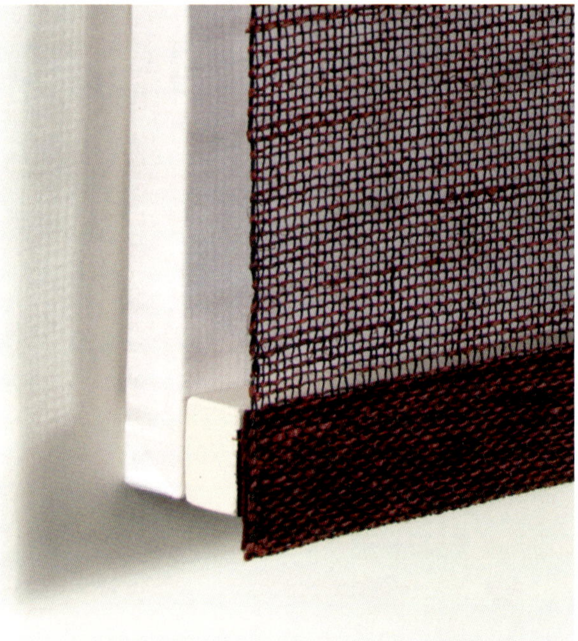

Corner of *30 Little Squares*, showing twill tape and Velcro.

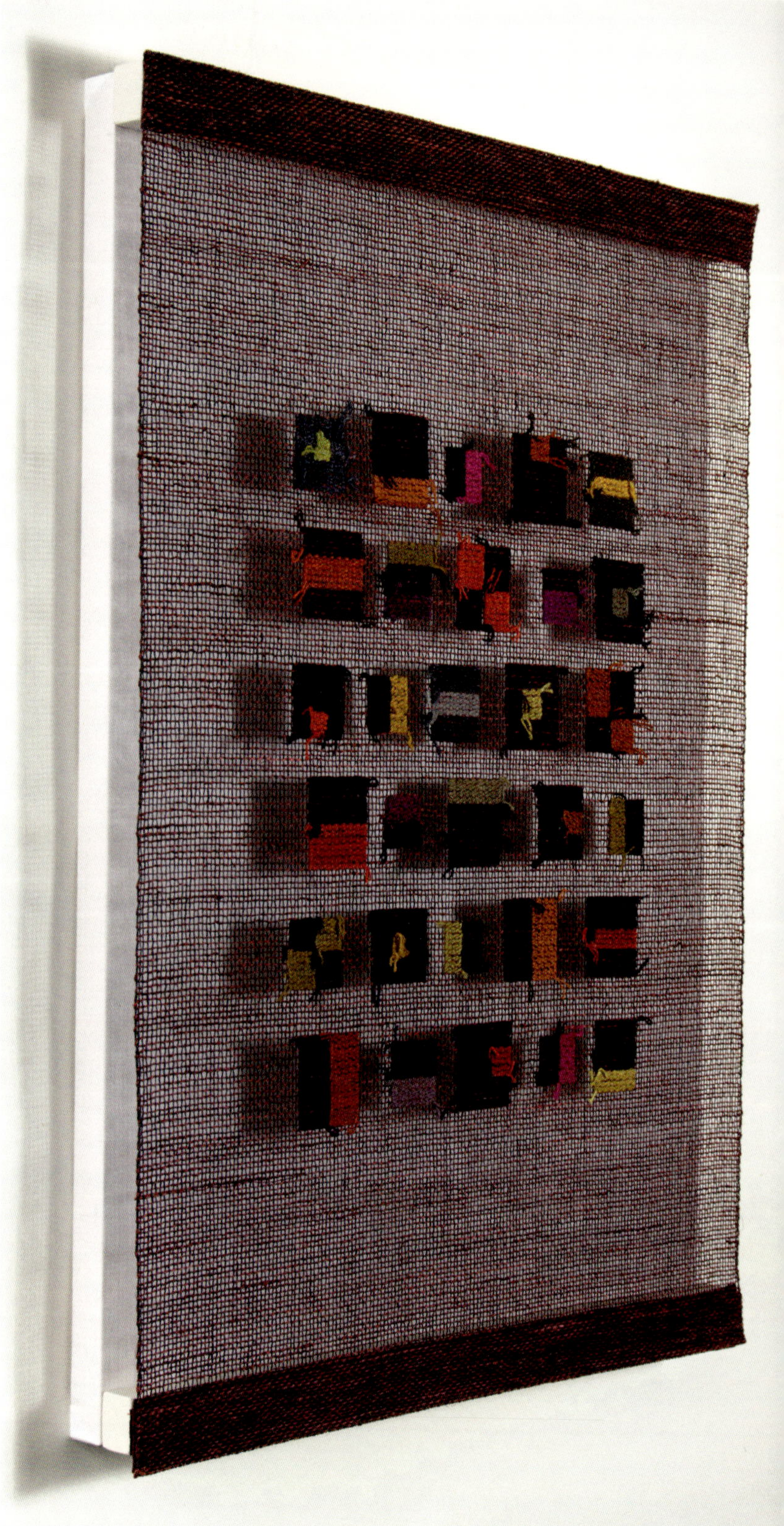

Morgan Clifford. *30 Little Squares*, 2011. Linen, silk: 17 × 24 × 2 inches. Courtesy of the artist.

Morgan Clifford is meticulous about the way she displays her transparent or gauze weavings. They are mounted away from the wall to give the pieces some presence and, ideally, shadows.

A hem is turned under along the bottom and top edges. Velcro is sewn to a strip of cotton twill tape that has been dyed a color to match the ground weave. The twill tape is then sewn to the hem on the backside of the weaving at each end.

The other side of the Velcro is attached to strips of 1-by-2-inch wood. The wood strips can be directly attached to the wall or mounted on a cloth-covered frame that has been attached to the wall. Measurements are crucial to getting the weaving to hang taut between the strips of Velcro. The overall size of the fabric-covered frame should be slightly smaller than the size of the weaving, so that it doesn't extend beyond the edges of the weaving.

While labor intensive, Clifford's method is less intrusive of the physical integrity of the weaving than other rigid framing techniques. It's possible to mount a transparency onto stretcher bars the way a canvas painting is mounted, and then secure it to a floater frame that conceals the edges. However, the delicate weave structure could be damaged by the stretching itself, not to mention the staples used to hold it under tension. It might be best to take the weaving to a professional framer for this type of framing. If your edges are uneven, this solution may be a good option to hide those edges.

Another solution for framing your transparency is to encapsulate it between two sheets of glass or acrylic in a float frame (not to be confused with the *floater* frame referred to above!). This is a workable solution especially for small transparencies. Float frames are typically designed to hold photographs. The sheer weave of a transparency is thin enough to be used in many float frames.

There are two approaches to mounting a transparency in a float frame. For the first approach, choose a frame that has the same dimensions, but is a tad smaller than the weaving. The off-the-shelf frame I used for Project 2 was slightly smaller than the weaving. This helped me to be able to pull the weaving taut at the edges. The excess fabric was then neatly tucked in around the back edge.

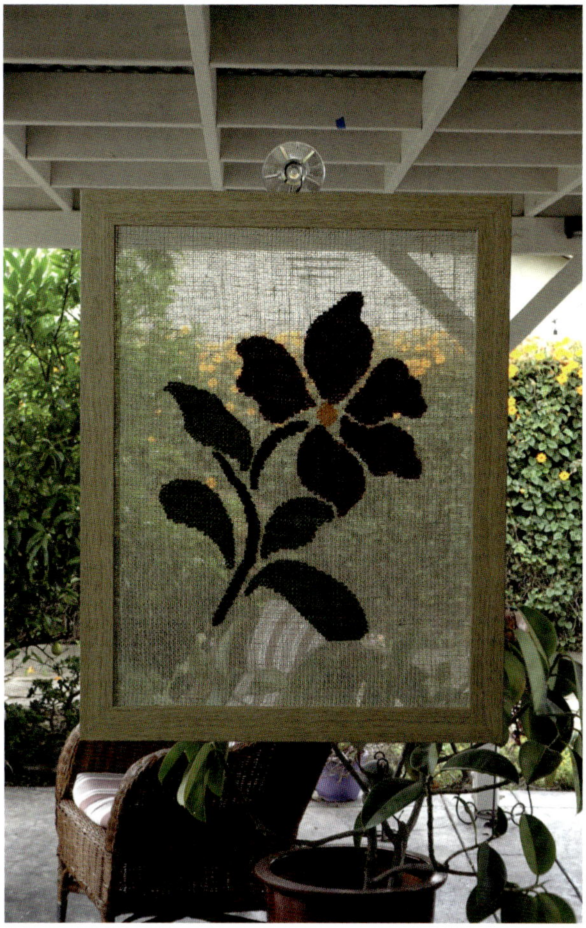

Project 2 mounted in an off-the-shelf float frame, hanging on patio door

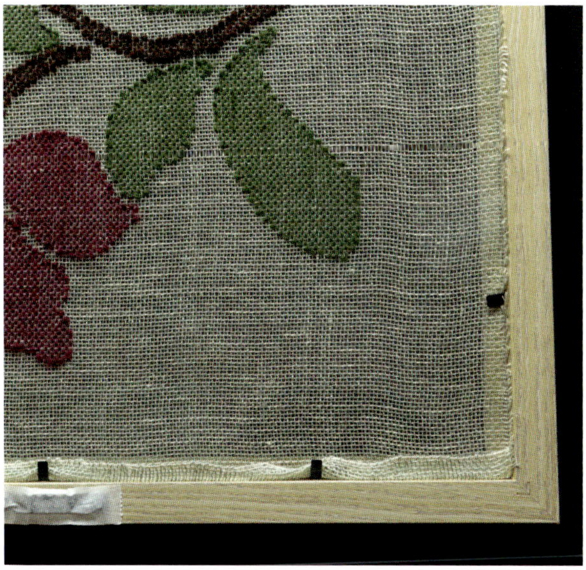

On the backside of the float frame, the extra fabric is neatly tucked in.

The second approach to mounting a transparency in a float frame is to choose a frame that is larger than the weaving. All four edges of the piece will be visible, so ideally you have nice straight edges. Hems and hemstitching would both be too bulky, so either leave a raw edge or pull out a few rows of weft to create a small fringe. The raw edges will be protected from unraveling once the piece is in the frame.

Center the weaving in the float frame. It should remain in place, but if you find that it slips, apply a small amount of double-sided tape or clear-drying glue (Superglue works for this) along the top edge on the backside of the weaving.

A typical float frame will hold the transparency about ½ inch away from the wall. It may not be possible to see shadows at this distance. However, if the ground weave is a color that contrasts with the color of the wall, the structure of the weaving should give a nice impression.

This is not an exhaustive list of possible ways to hang a transparency; nor are the foregoing chapters an exhaustive list of possibilities for weaving transparencies. Weavers are creative people, and that creativity can be applied to how things are displayed as much as to the weaving itself.

Please enjoy the work you have created on your journey through this book. It is my pleasure to teach others what I have learned through my years as a weaver. I wish you much success in your exploration of transparency weaving.

CREATE A FOUR-SIDED FRINGE

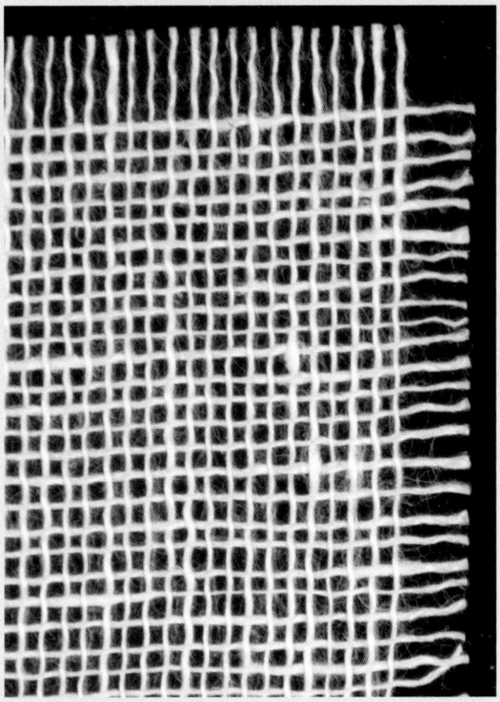

Fringe is created on all four sides by removing rows of warp and weft.

A four-sided fringe is created by pulling out rows of weft along the top and bottom, as well as removing several warps from each side. This is a good solution if the side edges are less than perfect.

Carefully cut away the outer warp on each side, which will also cut through the ground weft. Yikes, you might say, that sounds dangerous! Work carefully and it will be fine.

After the edges are trimmed, begin pulling away the ground weft from each end. Also pull away warp threads from each side. Once you are happy with the size of the piece, trim the fringe to an equal length on all four sides. About ¼ to ½ inch looks good.

Place the weaving in a float frame to safeguard from unraveling.

Or try this alternative: Before trimming the edges, hemstitch all four sides where you want the new border to be, using sewing thread to make the hemstitching as inconspicuous as possible. Remove the warps and ground weft that are outside of the hemstitched border and trim the fringe.

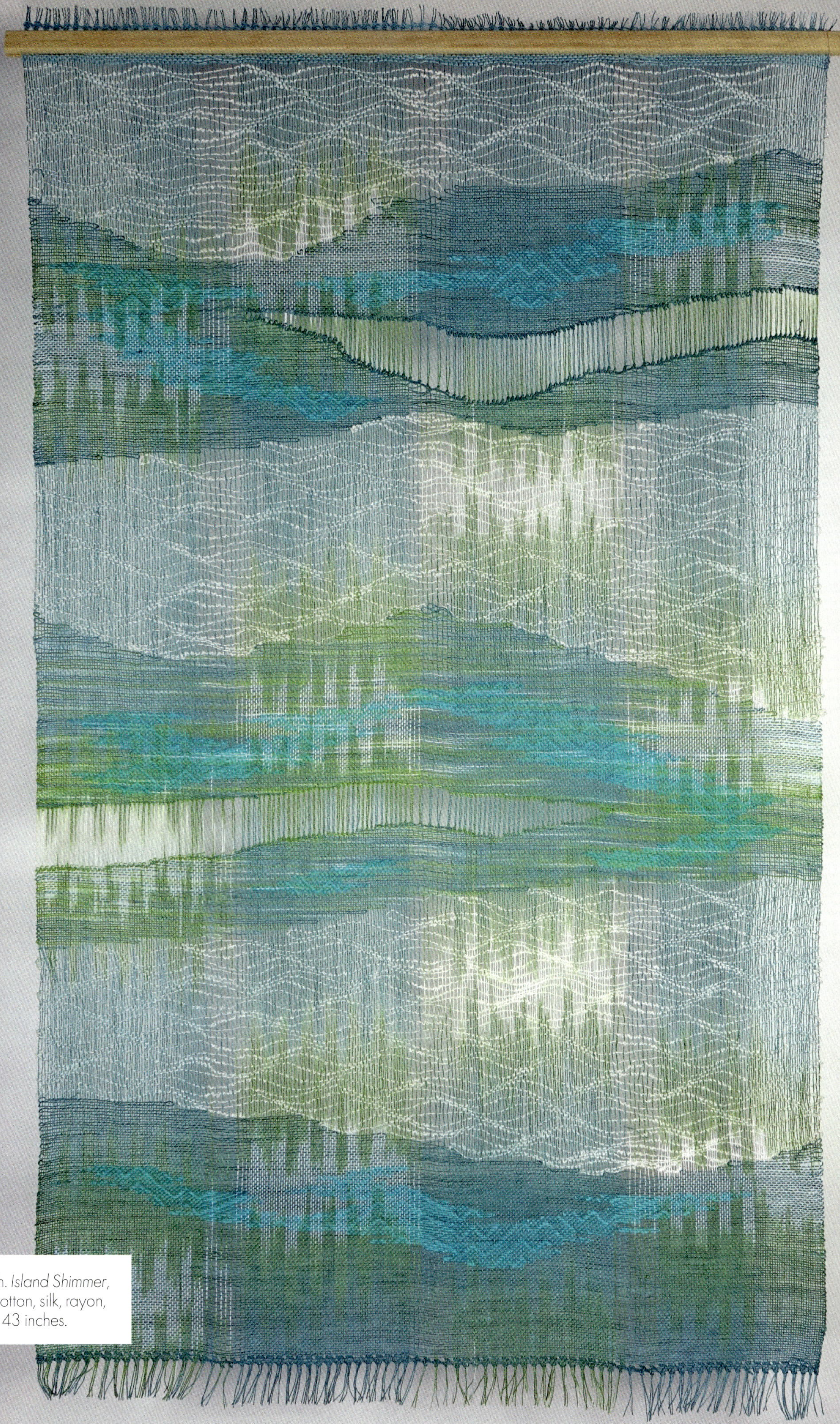

Rebecca Smith. *Island Shimmer*, 2026. Linen, cotton, silk, rayon, metallic: 26 × 43 inches.

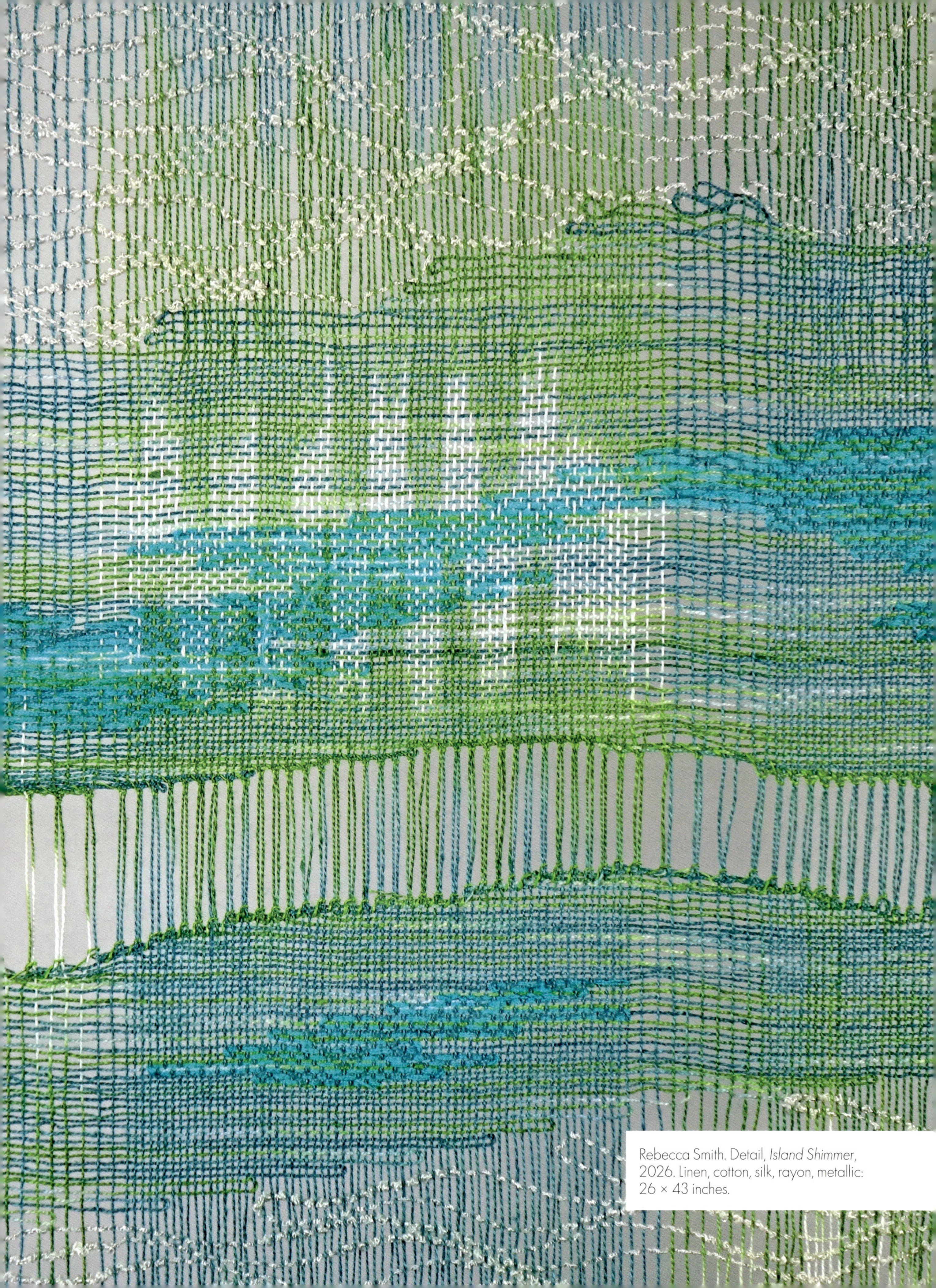

Rebecca Smith. Detail, *Island Shimmer*, 2026. Linen, cotton, silk, rayon, metallic: 26 × 43 inches.

Chapter 10
PROJECTS

PREPARING FOR THE PROJECTS

These six projects are an opportunity for you to practice the skills introduced in chapters 5 through 8. As you work sequentially through the projects, you will build your skills from basic to advanced. All the projects can be woven on the same warp. Warp and weft specifications are given below.

Cartoons for the six projects are provided in the appendix, pages 156–161. They are also available for download at www.schiffercraft.com/Transparency. Feel free to increase the dimensions of the cartoons. In some cases, this will make it easier to weave the finer details. Increase the warp width to accommodate larger cartoons.

Likewise, you may want to substitute 16/2 linen and a sett of 12 ends per inch. In this case, the cartoon and project dimensions should be scaled up by at least 25% to be able to weave enough detail at a coarser sett.

Equipment

Recommended equipment includes a four-shaft loom with a minimum 15 inches of weaving width, 15- or 16-dent reed (reed substitution is not possible), and a boat shuttle. (*See* note above about substituting with 16/2 linen, for which you would change to a 12-dent reed.)

Yarns

Warp: 16/1 linen in natural or other light color

Ground weft: 16/1 linen to match warp color

Inlay weft: any fine yarn that fits easily between rows of ground weft (*see* page 36)

Weave Structure

Plain weave

Sett

15 or 16 ends per inch, doubled at the selvedges in both heddle and reed.

Warp Length

If you warp your loom for multiple projects, allow 1 yard per project plus 1 yard for loom waste.

Width in Reed: 13 inches

Use an uneven number of warps; expect ½-inch draw-in.

Other Supplies

Pins or magnets for cartoon; Fray Check. Display supplies are specified with each project.

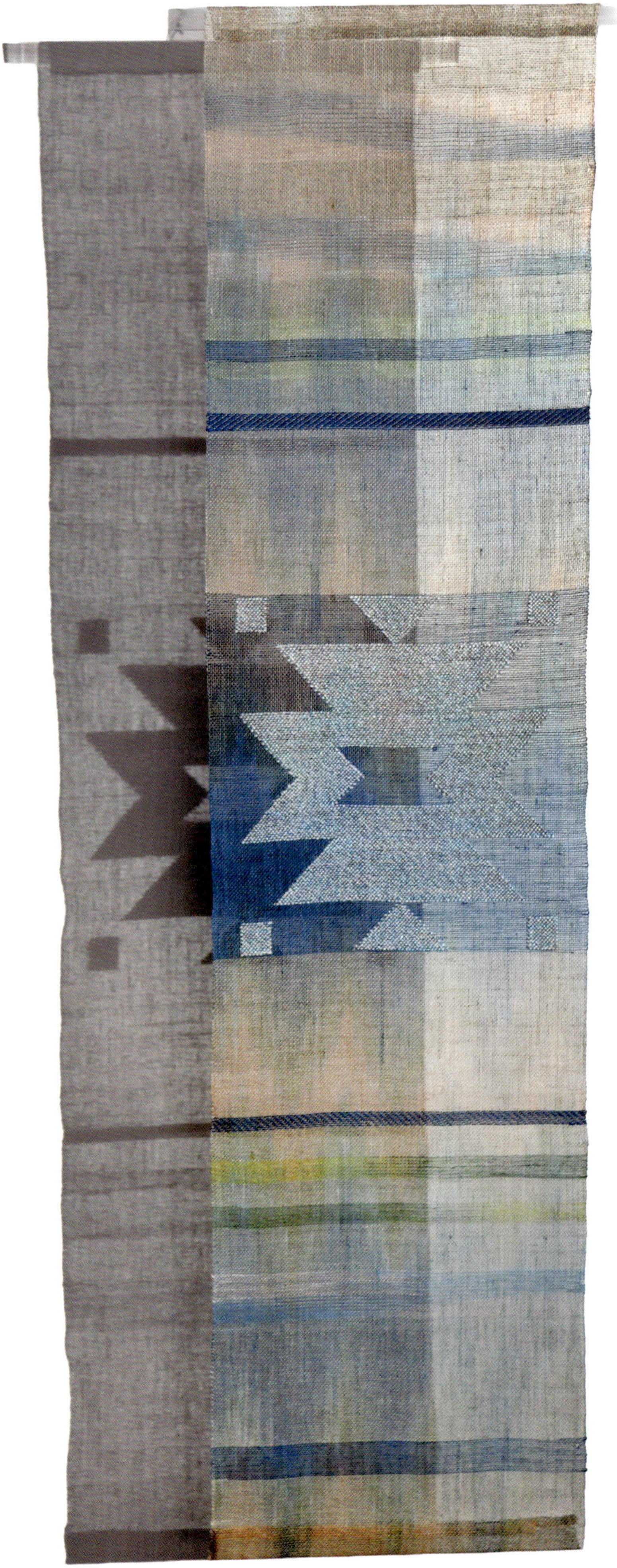

Rebecca Smith. *Seeing Blue*, 2023. Linen, wool, acrylic: 12 × 48 inches.

Project 1

GEOMETRIC DESIGN

Geometric shapes evoke historical textiles and the cultures that wove them. The central motif for this project can be found in textiles from diverse cultures, including Navajo rugs and Middle Eastern kilims.

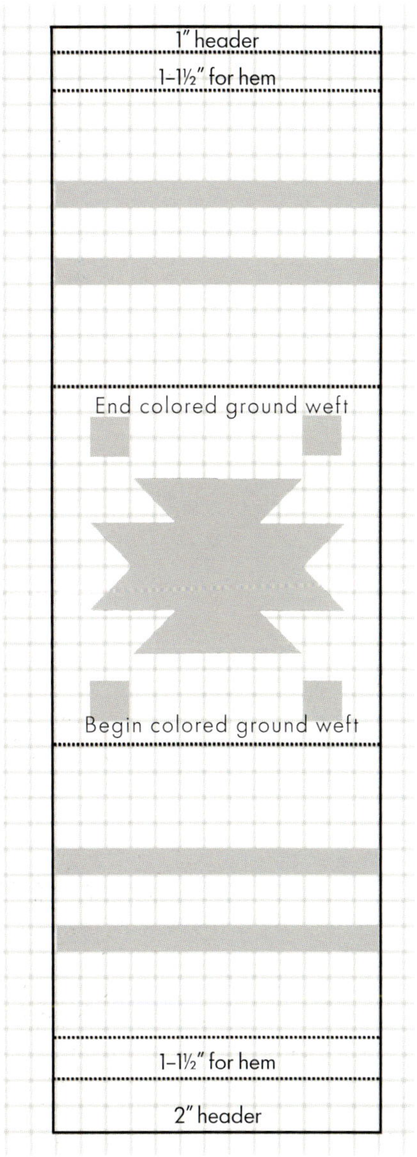

Project 1 weaving plan

Weaving straight edges is a straightforward weaving exercise, making this the perfect subject for your first transparency project. This project draws on techniques introduced in chapter 5. It challenges you to weave diagonal edges that move in two directions: right to left and left to right, and to weave more than one diagonal at the same time. Does that sound like enough of a challenge for your first project?

DESIGN

The design is a simplified version of a larger work (see *Seeing Blue* on facing page). A cartoon for the central geometric motif is provided on page 157 in the appendix.

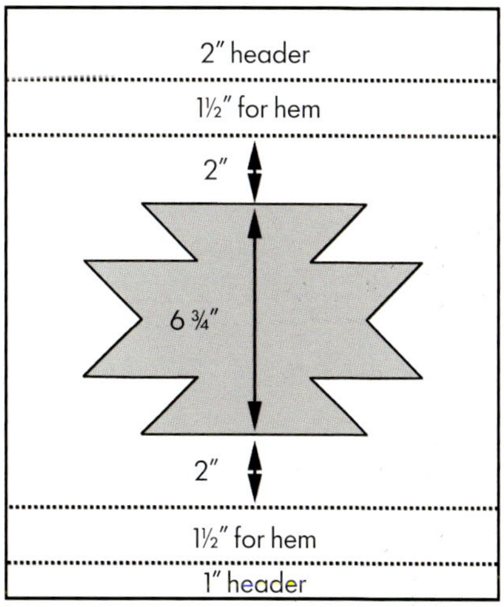

Simplified plan

OPTION FOR SIMPLIFYING

You may further simplify the design by weaving only the central motif (see simplified plan).

YARNS AND COLORS

Warp: 16/1 linen in natural or other light color

Ground weft: 16/1 linen to match warp color; additional dark color for central block

Inlay weft: any yarn that fits easily between rows of ground weft (see page 36)

OTHER SUPPLIES

Pins or magnets to attach cartoon; Fray Check; two wood or acrylic rods for display, approximately 5/8 inches wide by 14 inches long; monofilament or other thread approximately 30 inches long.

DIMENSIONS

Woven width: 12½ inches

Woven length: 40 inches, not including the header; expect 3%–5% shrinkage off the loom

Finished size: 12–12½ inches wide by 36 inches long

WEAVING

Follow the weaving plan shown here, reading from the bottom up.

Weave a 2-inch header with waste yarn to space the warps and establish the actual weaving width (expect about ½-inch draw-in).

Weave 1½ inches of ground weft for the hem.

There is a 10-inch border before the central motif begins. You can be creative in how you fill this space. Two stripes are shown in the weaving plan. Consider these options for the stripes:

- Stripes woven in a pattern weave (see pages 86 and 89)
- Stripes using a textured or variegated yarn

When you reach the central motif, switch to a colored ground weft to highlight the area. After weaving the small squares, attach the cartoon of the geometric shape.

CALCULATING THE ANGLE

How do you weave the correct angle to match the angle on the design? This issue is discussed on page 69. Let's apply that principle to the angles in Project 1. Did you notice that all the angles in this design are the same? The formula for determining the woven angle is the following:

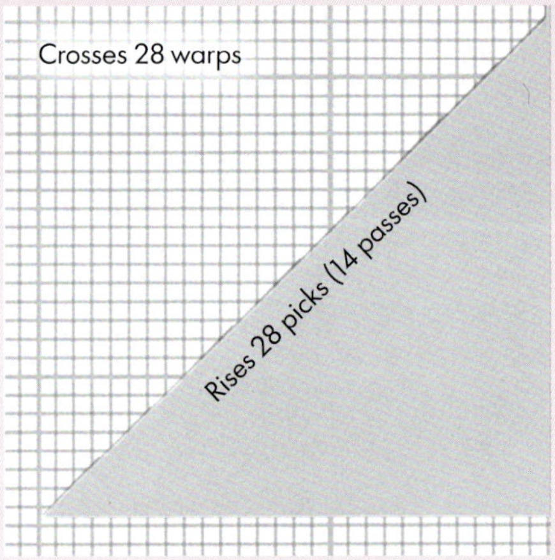

28 warps / 14 passes = 2 warps per turn

- Passes per inch / epi = passes per warp

In this example, the diagonal edge crosses 28 warps and rises 28 picks or 14 passes. Applying the formula,

- 14 passes / 28 warps = 0.5 *turns per warp*

Since this is a shallow angle with less than one turn per warp, we reverse the formula:

- 28 warps / 14 passes = 2 *warps per turn*. This indicates that a warp is skipped between turns.

Note the difference between turns per warp and warps per turn.

ATTACH THE CARTOON

Trace or print the cartoon provided on page 157. Attach the cartoon to the back of the weaving, using pins, sewing thread, or magnets. Center the cartoon so it starts and ends an equal number of warps from each side. Align the bottom of the design with the fell line of your weaving. Pushing the cartoon up against the weaving from underneath the warp will give you an accurate view of where the edges of the shapes should be woven.

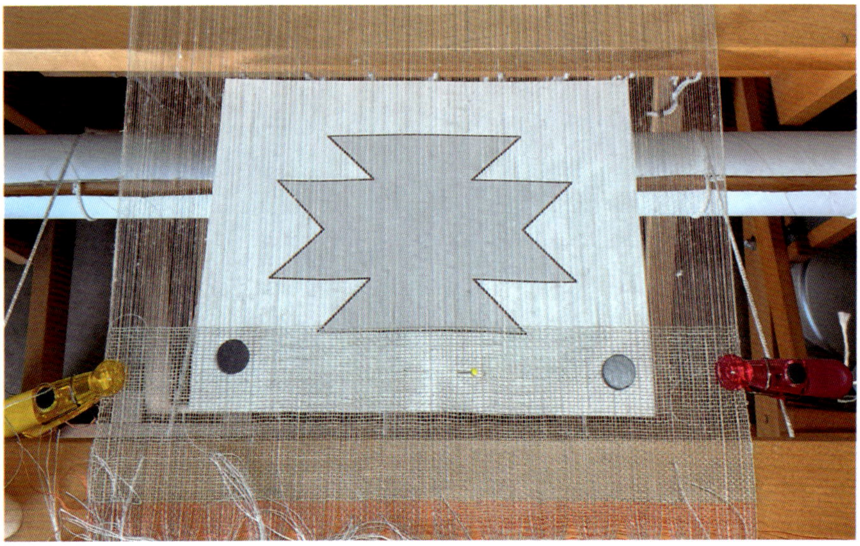

WEAVE THE GEOMETRIC MOTIF

Weave the geometric shape following the lines on the cartoon. Follow each shot of inlay with a shot of ground weft. All the diagonal segments in the design are the exact same angle. Once you determine how to weave that angle, just be consistent. See the inset for tips on calculating the angle.

After completing the geometric shape, weave the remainder of the weaving plan to match the first half. Weave 1½ inches for the hem, then weave a header of 1 to 2 inches.

FINISHING

Follow the instructions in chapter 9 for steam finishing, sewing the hem, and preparing the wood or acrylic hanging rod.

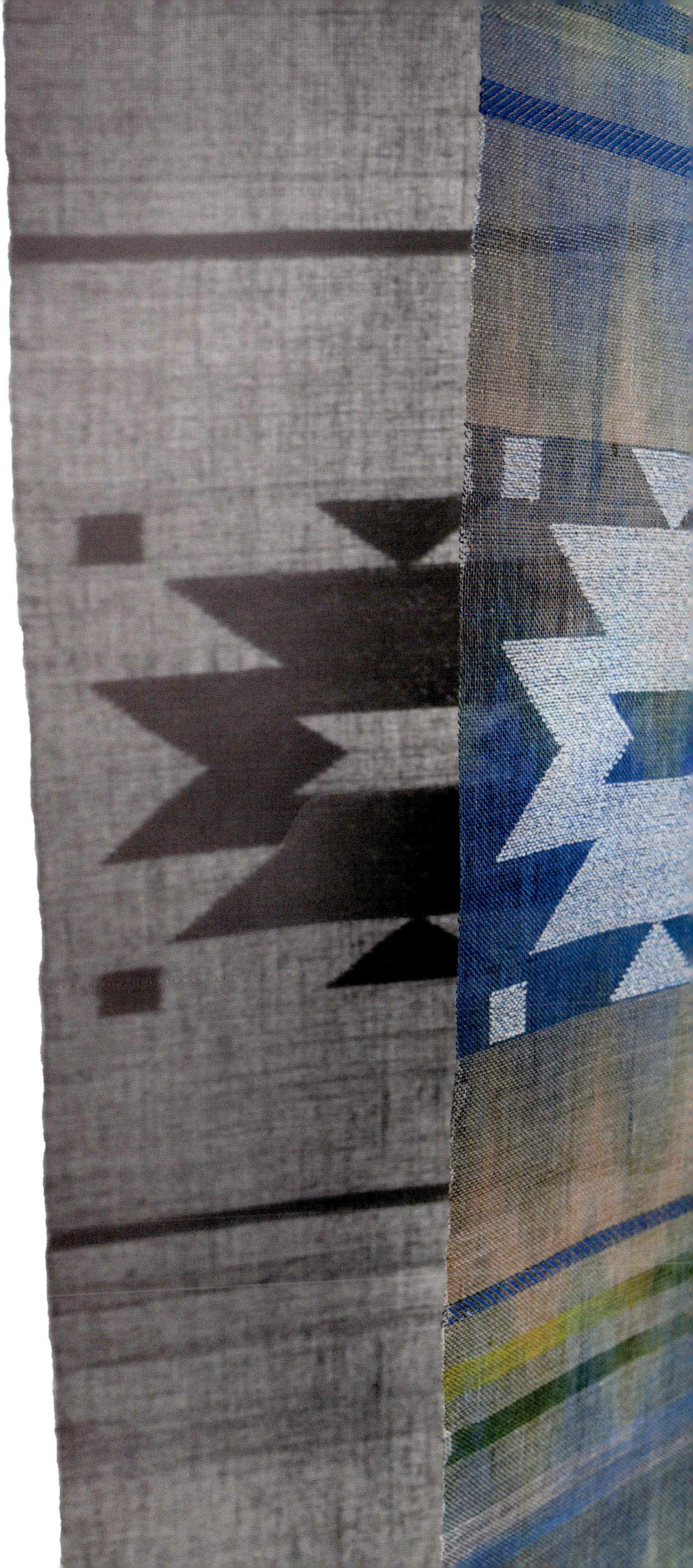

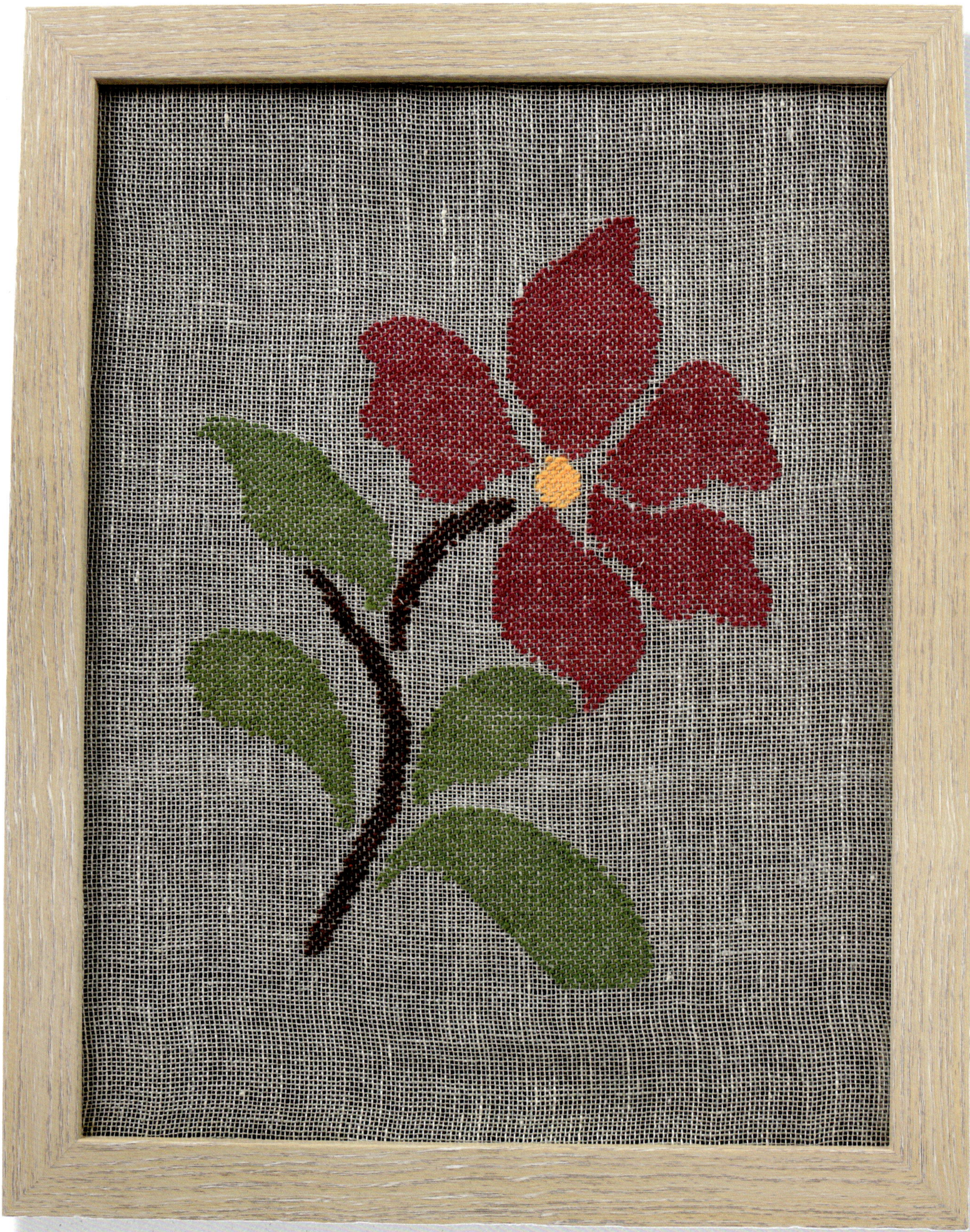

Project 2

FLORAL IMAGERY

Figurative or pictorial designs are largely made up of shapes with curvy edges. Some subjects, such as flowers, are very forgiving if you don't precisely follow the lines on the cartoon. You can go off script quite a bit and still end up with convincing shapes. For that reason, this project is a good first introduction to weaving curves.

This project uses techniques introduced in chapter 6. It challenges you to follow a cartoon to weave several curvy shapes, with multiple shapes weaving at the same time. If you find this too daunting for your level of experience, see the options below for modifying the design.

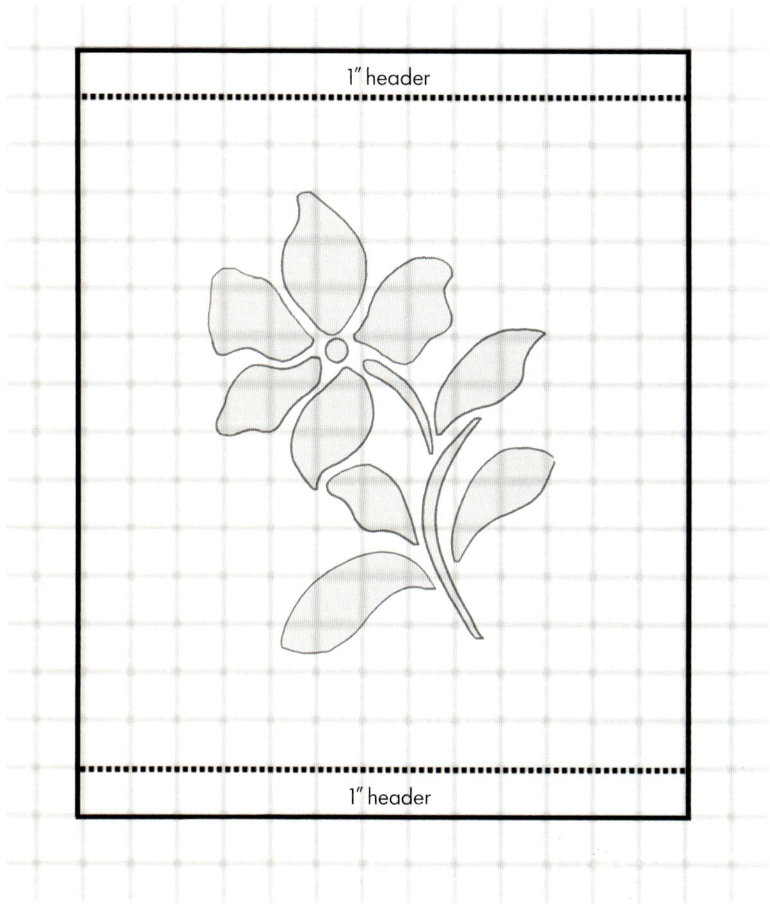

Project 2 weaving plan

DESIGN

The cartoon for this project is provided on page 158 in the appendix. Trace it or print it on plain white paper.

OPTIONS FOR SIMPLIFYING

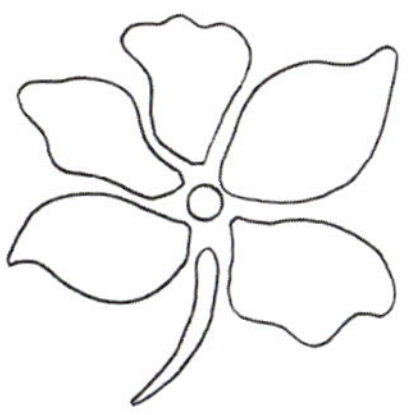

Simplified cartoon showing only the flower and stem

Simplify the cartoon in several possible ways:

Option 1: Weave only the flower and the stem, leaving out the leaves.

Option 2: Turn the cartoon so that the flower is more vertical. This gives you more horizontal shapes to weave.

Option 3: Smooth out the shapes so that there are fewer ins and outs.

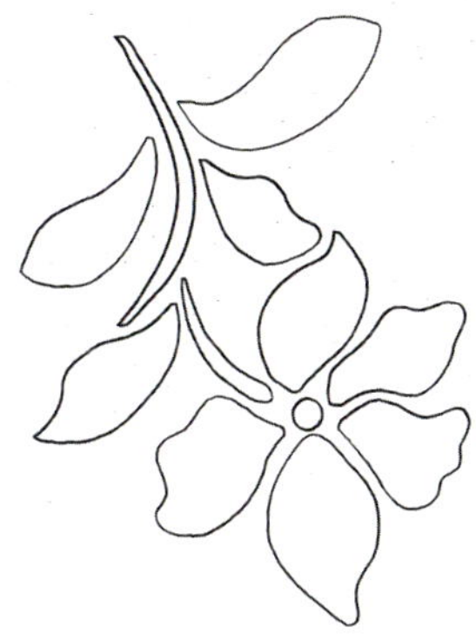

Turn the cartoon upside down.

Option 4: Weave it upside down. Most of the shapes have wider tops than bottoms, so it would be easier to begin the new wefts if you weave the image upside down.

Option 5: Enlarge the design. Increase the width of your warp and upsize the cartoon to more comfortable proportions.

YARNS AND COLORS

Warp: 16/1 linen in natural or other light color

Ground weft: 16/1 linen to match warp color

Inlay weft: four colors of a yarn that fits easily between rows of ground weft (see page 36)

OTHER SUPPLIES

Pins or magnets to attach cartoon; Fray Check; 11-by-14-inch float frame

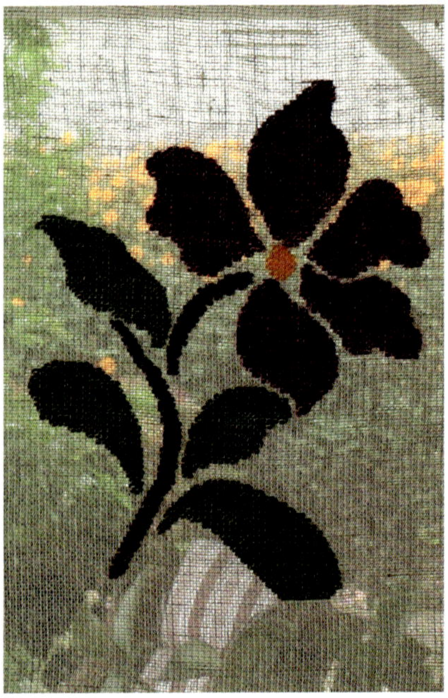

DIMENSIONS

Woven width: 12½ inches

Woven length: 14½ inches, not including the header

Finished size: 12–12½ inches wide by 14 inches long

WEAVING

Follow the weaving plan, reading from the bottom up.

Weave a 1-to-2-inch header with waste yarn to space the warps and establish the actual weaving width (expect about ½-inch draw-in).

Weave 2½ inches of ground weft only for a border.

ATTACH THE CARTOON

The cartoon for this project is provided on page 158 in the appendix. Trace it or print it on plain white paper.

Attach the cartoon to the back of the weaving, using pins, sewing thread, or magnets. Center the cartoon so there is an equal border on each side of the flower design. Align the bottom of the lowest leaf with the fell line of your border. Pushing the cartoon up against the weaving from underneath the warp will give you an accurate view of where the edges of the shapes should be woven.

WEAVE THE FLOWER

Add each new shape as you come to it. Continually push the cartoon against the weaving from below to help guide you in choosing turning points. When you are ready to advance the warp, move the pins or magnets holding the cartoon closer to the fell line of the weaving, being careful not to let it shift position.

When you have completely woven the design, weave a 2½-inch border of ground weft. Weave several picks of header in a distinct color from the ground weft to give a clear demarcation of the end of your weaving.

FINISHING

Follow the instructions in chapter 9 for steam finishing. Block if necessary.

This project can be displayed in a float frame. See instructions for using a float frame on page 125. Place the weaving between two sheets of acrylic or glass and place in the float frame. If the weaving is bigger than the acrylic, tuck it neatly along the edges or trim if necessary, using Fray Check to prevent unraveling.

Watch for these key points while weaving:

1. Begin weaving the lowest leaf on the cartoon.

2. When you reach the bottom of the stem, begin weaving that shape. Both shapes will weave simultaneously.

3. Some of the shapes begin with two sections that later join. Review the instructions on page 77 for joining two sections into a single shape.

4. Here the shape divides into two sections. Review page 79 if needed.

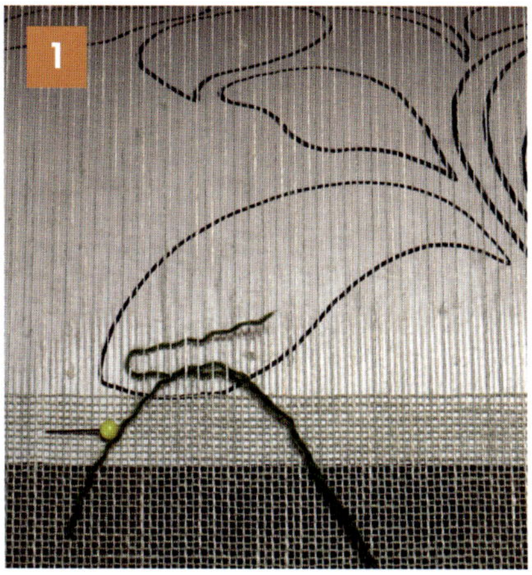

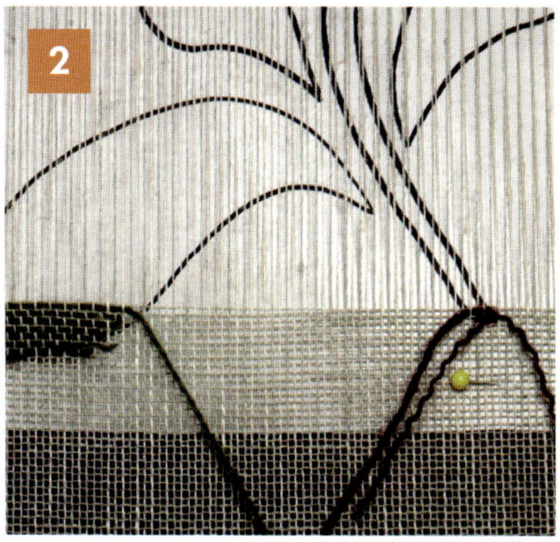

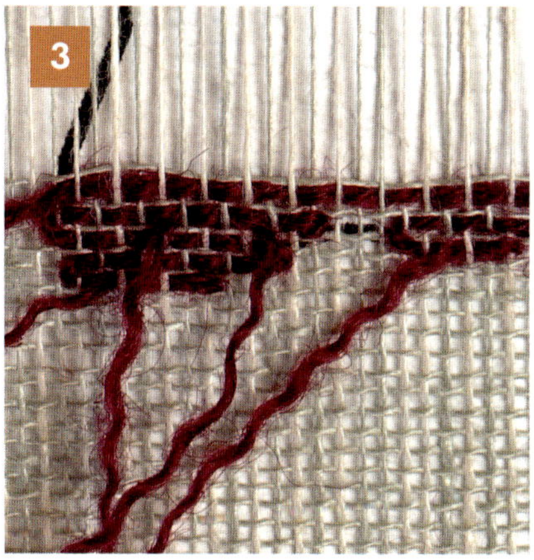

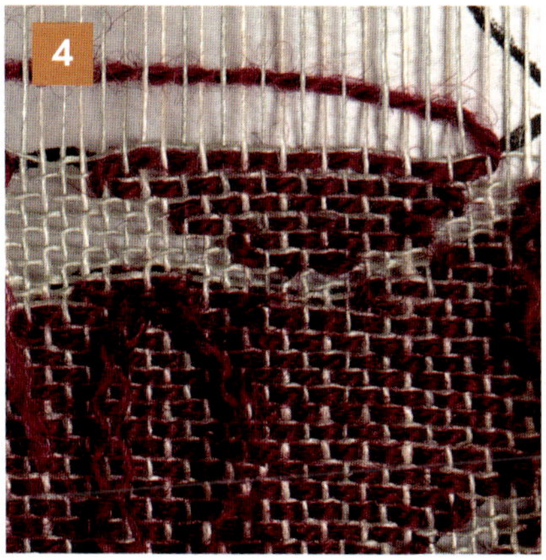

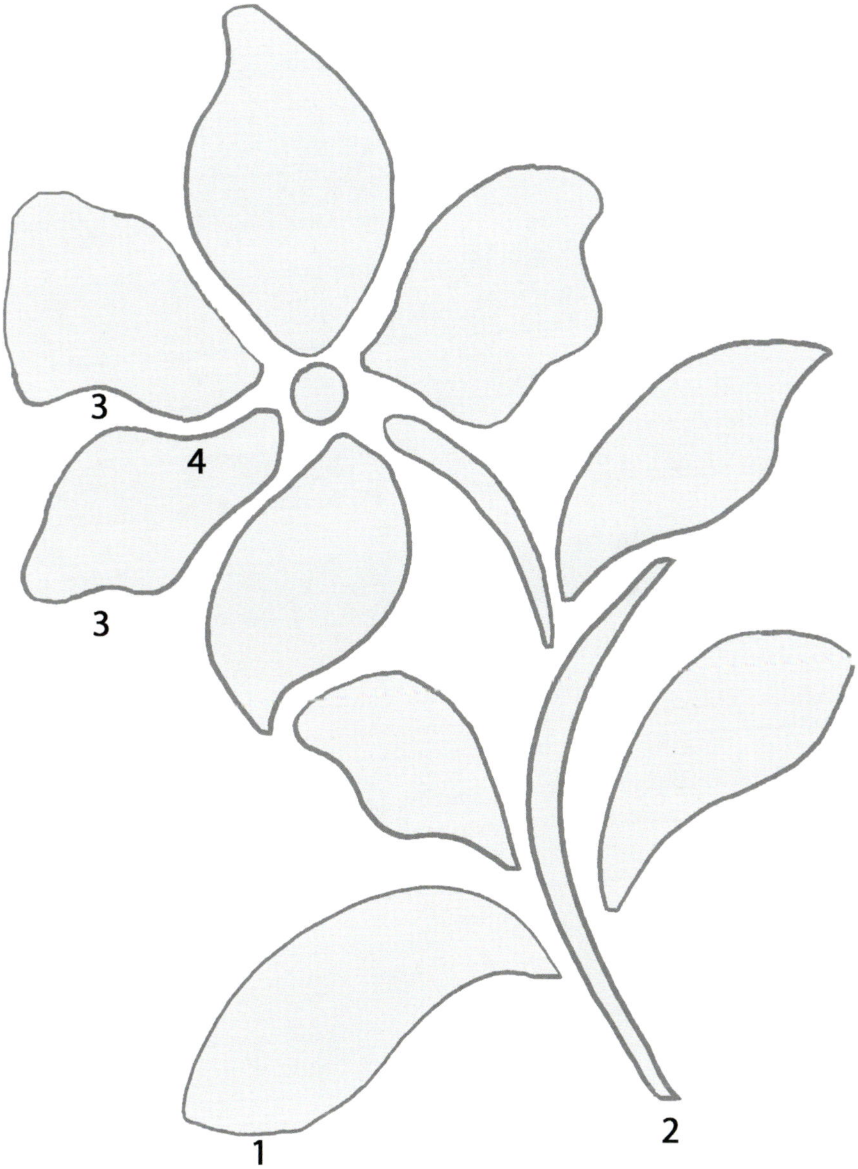

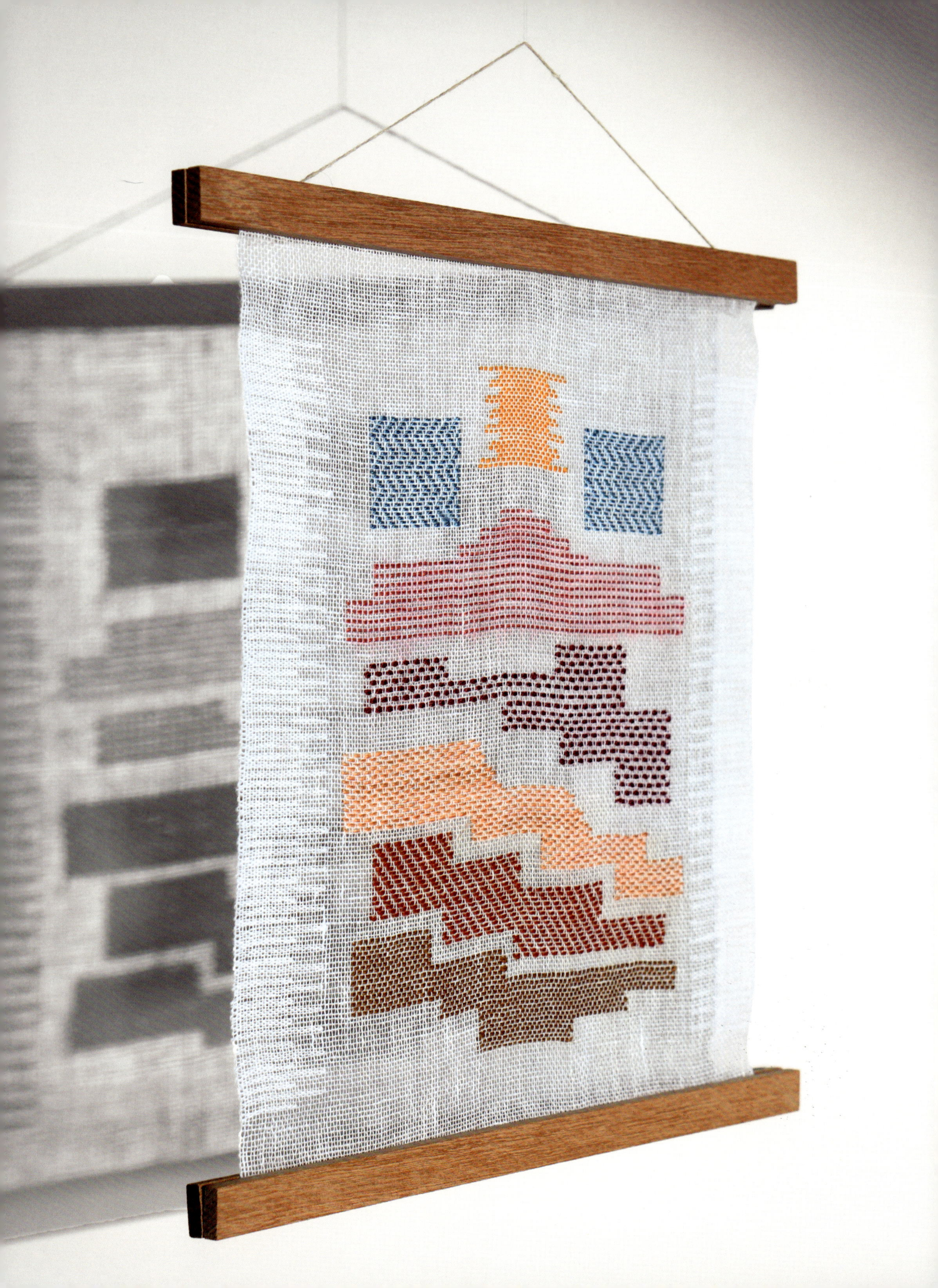

Project 3

INLAY PATTERNS

Using weave patterns for inlay other than plain weave can add visual interest to a transparency. This project will give you practical experience in weaving several patterns. Challenges include remembering to change the shed back to plain weave for the ground weft and weaving straight vertical edges on all the shapes. A special (optional) border is also suggested for this project (see below).

The display plan for this project is up to you. There is enough border specified in the weave plan to sew a hem for inserting an acrylic or wood rod for hanging. Or add hemstitching to the top and bottom and use a magnetic hanger.

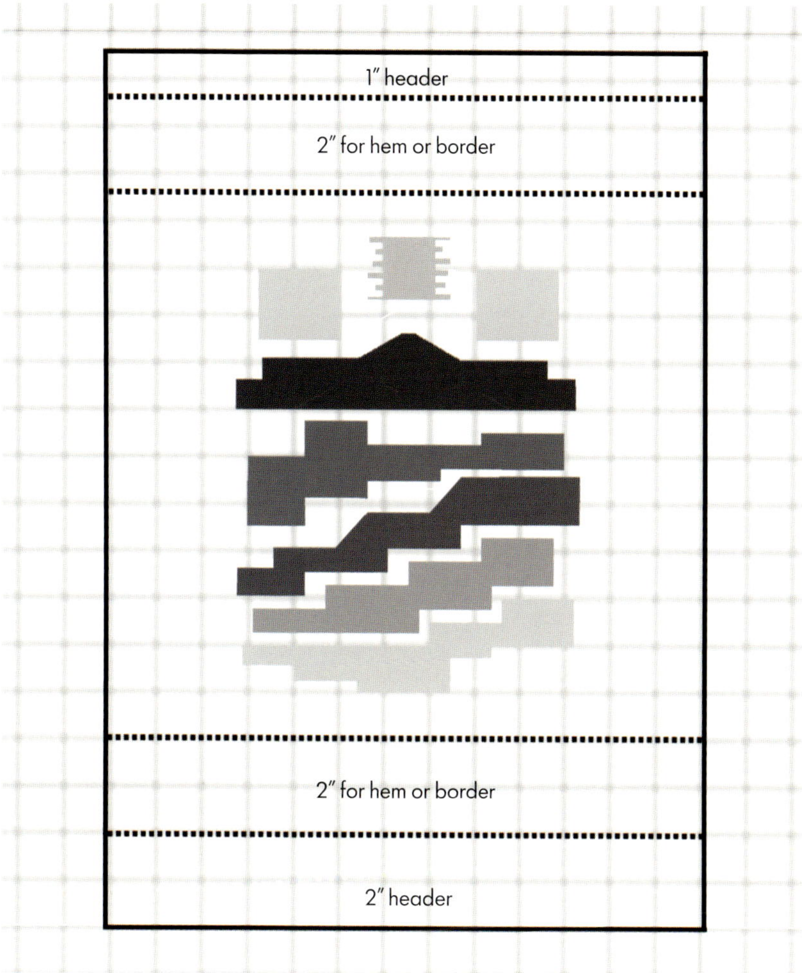

Project 3 weaving plan

DESIGN

The cartoon for this project is provided on page 159 in the appendix. Trace it or print it on plain white paper.

YARNS AND COLORS

Warp: 16/2 linen in natural or other light color

Ground weft: 16/2 linen to match warp color

Inlay weft: several colors of fine yarn that fit easily between rows of ground weft (see page 36)

OTHER SUPPLIES

Pins, sewing thread, or magnets for cartoon; Fray Check. Optional supplies for display: two pieces of acrylic or wood approximately ⅝ inch high and 3 inches longer than the width of the weaving, or magnetic hanger; monofilament line or other string

DIMENSIONS

Woven width: 12½ inches

Woven length: 15–15½ inches, not including the header

Finished size: 12–12½ inches wide by 12½ inches long

WEAVING

Follow the weaving plan shown here, reading from the bottom up.

Weave a 1-to-2-inch header with waste yarn to space the warps and establish the actual weaving width (expect about ½-inch draw-in). Use a color that contrasts with the ground weft to indicate where the piece begins.

Weave 2 inches of ground weft for a border or hem.

Weave an additional 1 inch of ground weft before attaching the cartoon.

ATTACH THE CARTOON

Attach the cartoon to the back of the weaving, using pins, sewing thread, or magnets. Center the cartoon so there is an equal border on each side of the design. Align the bottom of the lowest shape with the fell line of the weaving. Pushing the cartoon up against the weaving from underneath the warp will give you an accurate view of where the edges of the shapes should be woven.

WEAVE THE SHAPES

Each shape on the cartoon is woven in a different weave pattern. Make your own choices about which patterns to use, or follow the patterns used in the sample, as indicated below.

To weave the straight vertical edges at the sides of each shape, turn on the same warp each time. Some weave patterns, such as 2/2 twill, make this challenging when the warp you need to turn on is in the down position. The solution is to turn around the correct warp even if it is in the down position.

When you have finished weaving the design, weave an additional 1 inch of ground weft, then repeat the hem/border to match the other end. Finish by weaving several picks of header in a distinct color from the ground weft to give a clear demarcation of the end of your weaving.

FINISHING

Follow the instructions for steam finishing in chapter 9. Block if necessary.

Apply Fray Check along the weft separating the weaving from the header at both ends. When dry, trim away the header. Depending on your choice of display method, you may need to sew a hem and use a support rod, as instructed on page 121, or attach a magnetic hanger if you have hemstitched the ends.

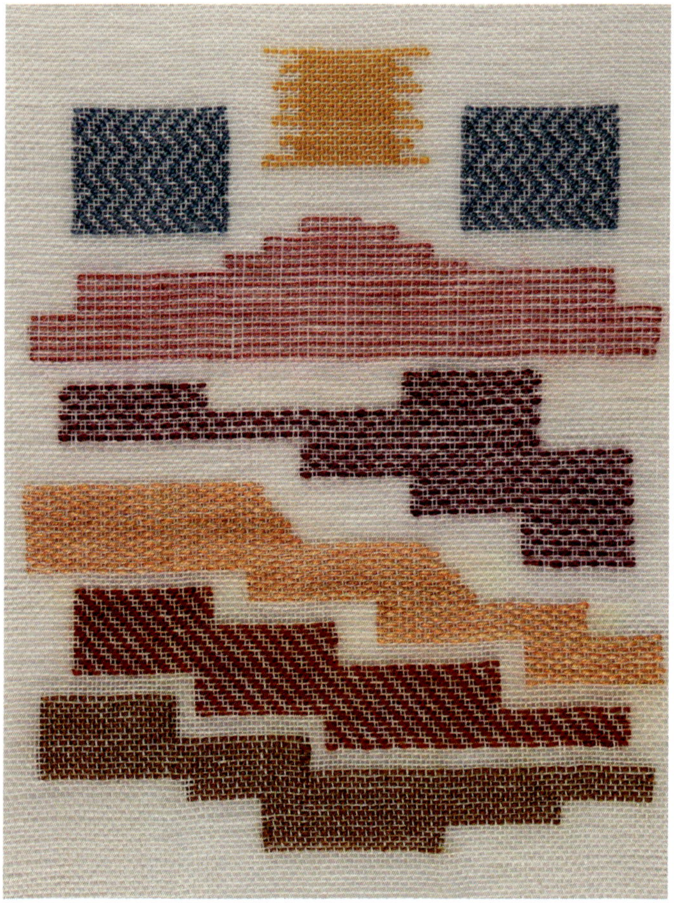

WEAVING A SIDE BORDER WITH GROUND WEFT

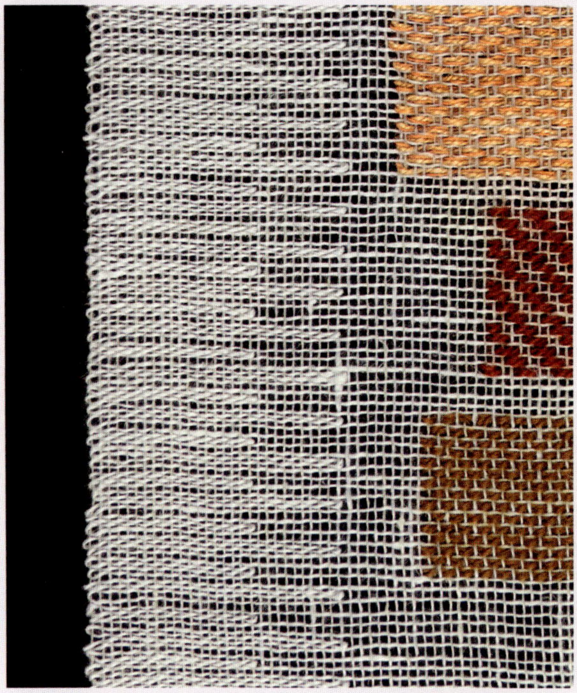

Try weaving a border by using the ground weft. This helps equalize the warp tension, since all the inlay patterns are in the middle of the warp. The staggered border shown here fits nicely with the Southwest flavor of the design. I learned this technique from Ruth Ronan when she was a student in my workshop at HGA's Convergence 2024.

Weave the ground weft 1 or 2 inches in from the edge, change the shed and weave back to the edge; change the shed again, then weave the entire row of ground weft. Repeat this sequence each time you weave a row of ground weft. Staggering the distance of the turning point from the edge is optional. In the project sample, the turning point alternates between ten and fifteen warps from the edge.

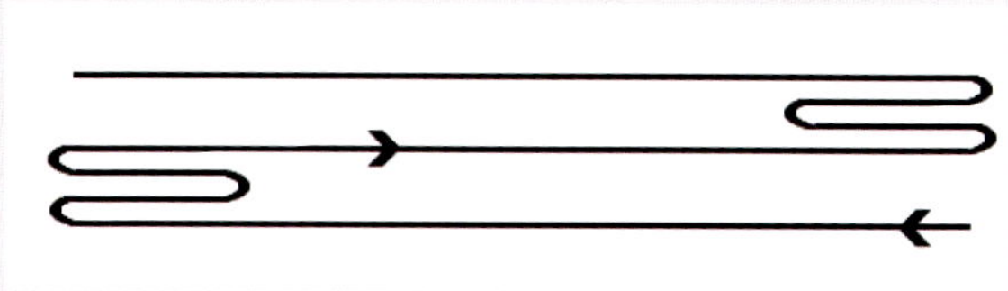

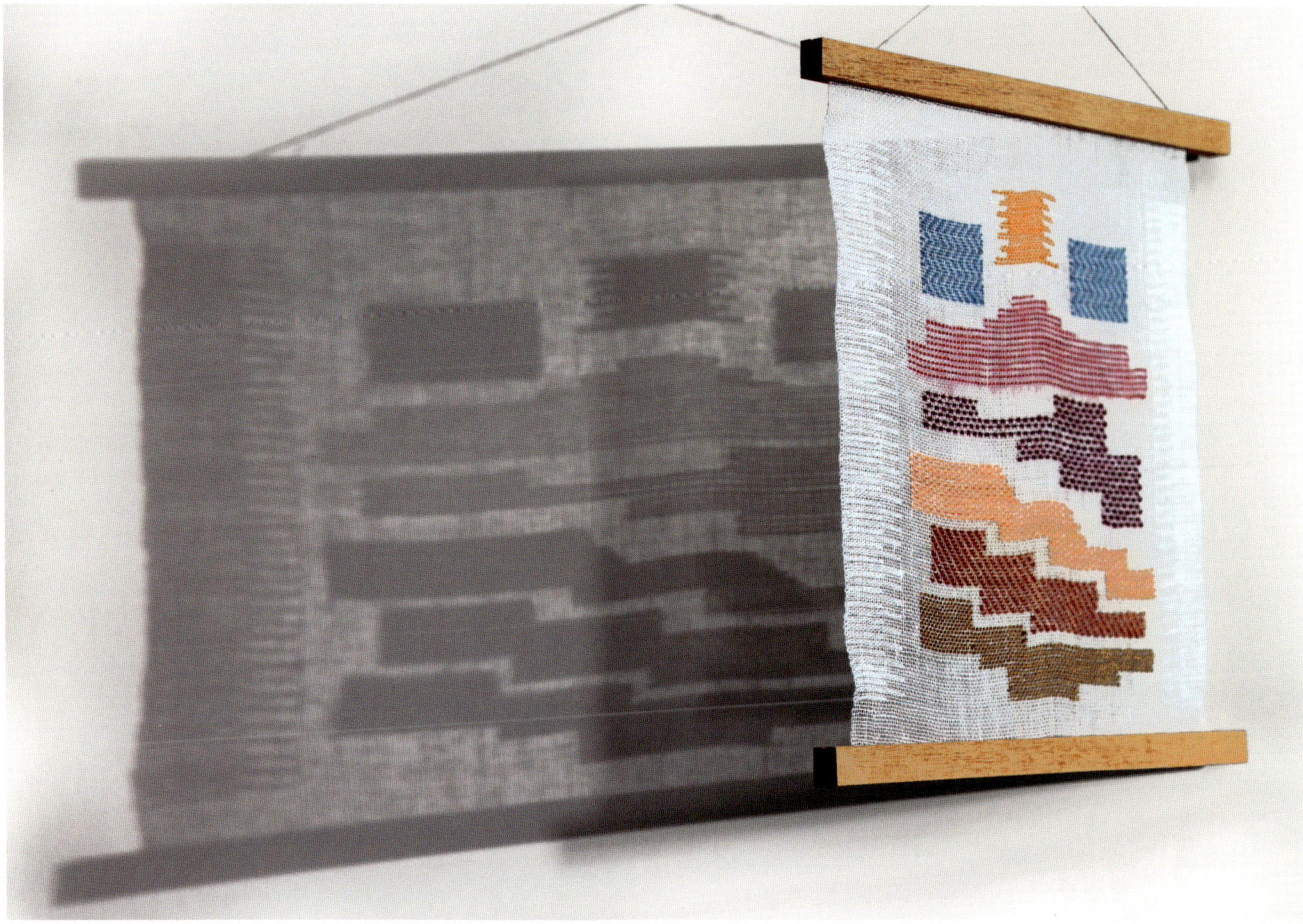

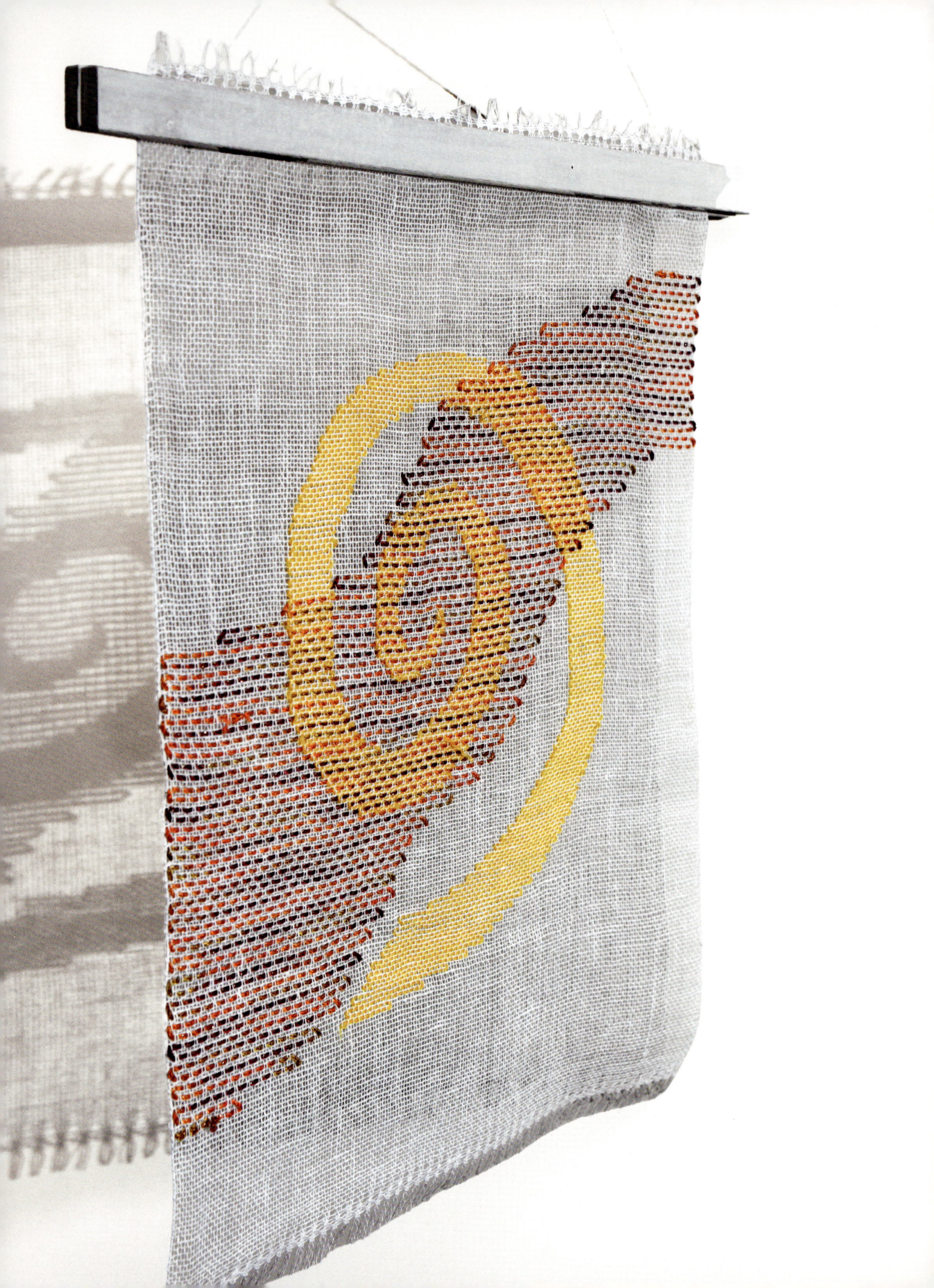

Project 4

OVERLAPPING SHAPES

The next step in your weaving journey is to weave overlapping shapes in different weave patterns. This project draws on skills presented in chapter 7.

This design features a cloud shape wafting over a spiral. The spiral is intentionally imperfect, freeing you up to not worry about weaving perfect curves! Even so, weaving the spiral will be challenging, and I suggest that you weave it in plain weave. Choose any other pattern you wish for the cloud shape. Where the two shapes cross, weave both patterns simultaneously.

The display plan for this piece is to hemstitch the ends and use a magnetic hanger.

OPTION FOR SIMPLIFYING

If weaving two different patterns proves to be too difficult, use plain weave for both shapes instead.

DESIGN

The cartoon for this project is provided on page 160 in the appendix. Trace it or print it on plain white paper.

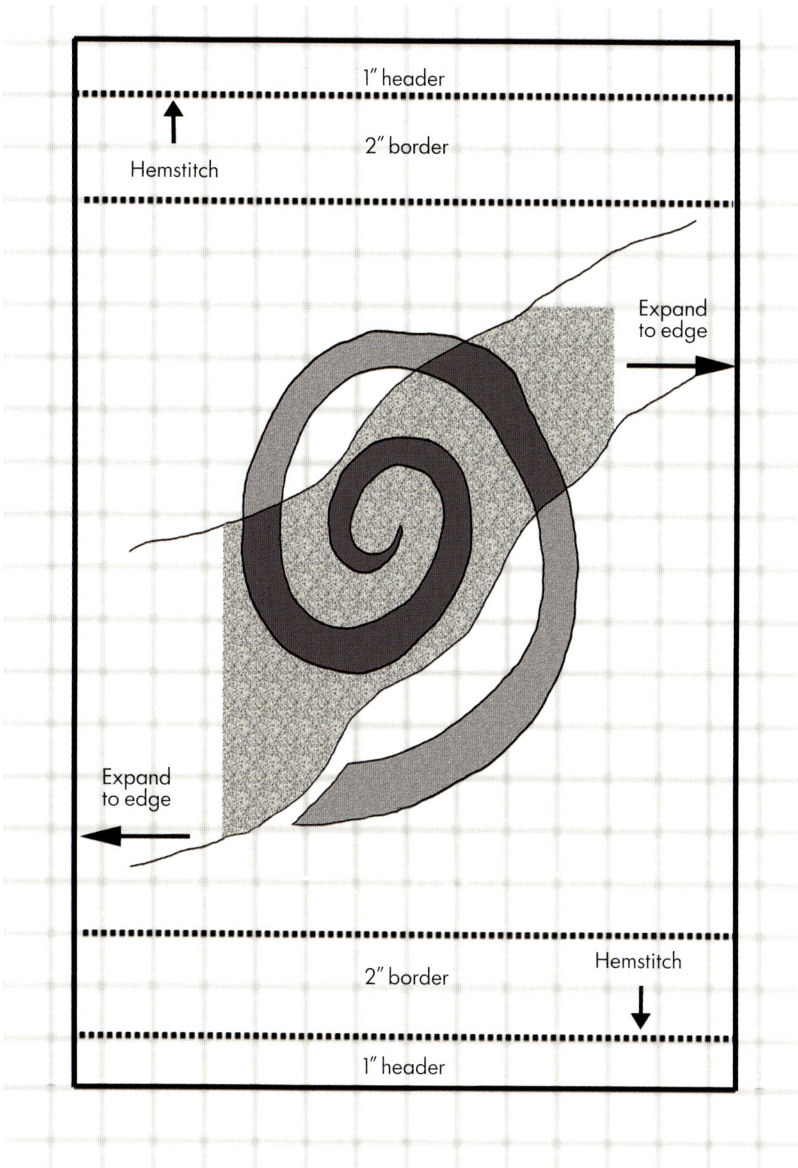

Project 4 weaving plan

YARNS

Warp: 16/1 linen in natural or other light color

Ground weft: 16/1 linen to match warp color

Inlay weft: two contrasting colors of a fine yarn that fits easily between rows of ground weft (see page 36). A lighter color for the cloud will help suggest that it is floating over the spiral.

A LESSON IN UPSCALING A CARTOON

The cartoon for this project is drawn to fit the 8½-by-11-inch page format of this book. The actual cartoon (see page 160) is slightly smaller due to the margins: It measures about 7½ inches wide by 10 inches long. Yet, the weave plan calls for a 12½-inch-wide warp. How can you adapt a 7½-wide cartoon to weave the design 12½ inches wide? The simple answer is shown on the weaving plan: Expand the cloud shape so that it weaves all the way to the edge.

Or you can opt to upscale the cartoon to fit the weaving width. This is a situation that you will undoubtedly encounter in the future, so why not practice it here? To upscale the cartoon, divide the desired width by the actual width of the cartoon. In this case, this is 12½ divided by 7½, which yields 1.67. If you have a computer program that can enlarge images, increase the scanned cartoon by 167%. This will give you new dimensions of 12.5 by 16.7 inches. After adding the 2-inch borders on each end, the new woven dimensions will be 12½ by (roughly) 20½ inches, not including the headers.

OTHER SUPPLIES

Pins or magnets to attach cartoon; magnetic hanger

DIMENSIONS

Woven width: 12½ inches

Woven length: 18 inches, not including the headers

Finished size: 12 inches wide by 18 inches long

WEAVING

Follow the weaving plan shown here, reading from the bottom up.

- Weave a 1-to-2-inch header with waste yarn to space the warps and establish the actual weaving width (expect about ½-inch draw-in).
- Hemstitch the edge.
- Weave 2 inches of ground weft for a border.

ATTACH THE CARTOON

Attach the cartoon to the back of the weaving, using pins, sewing thread, or magnets.

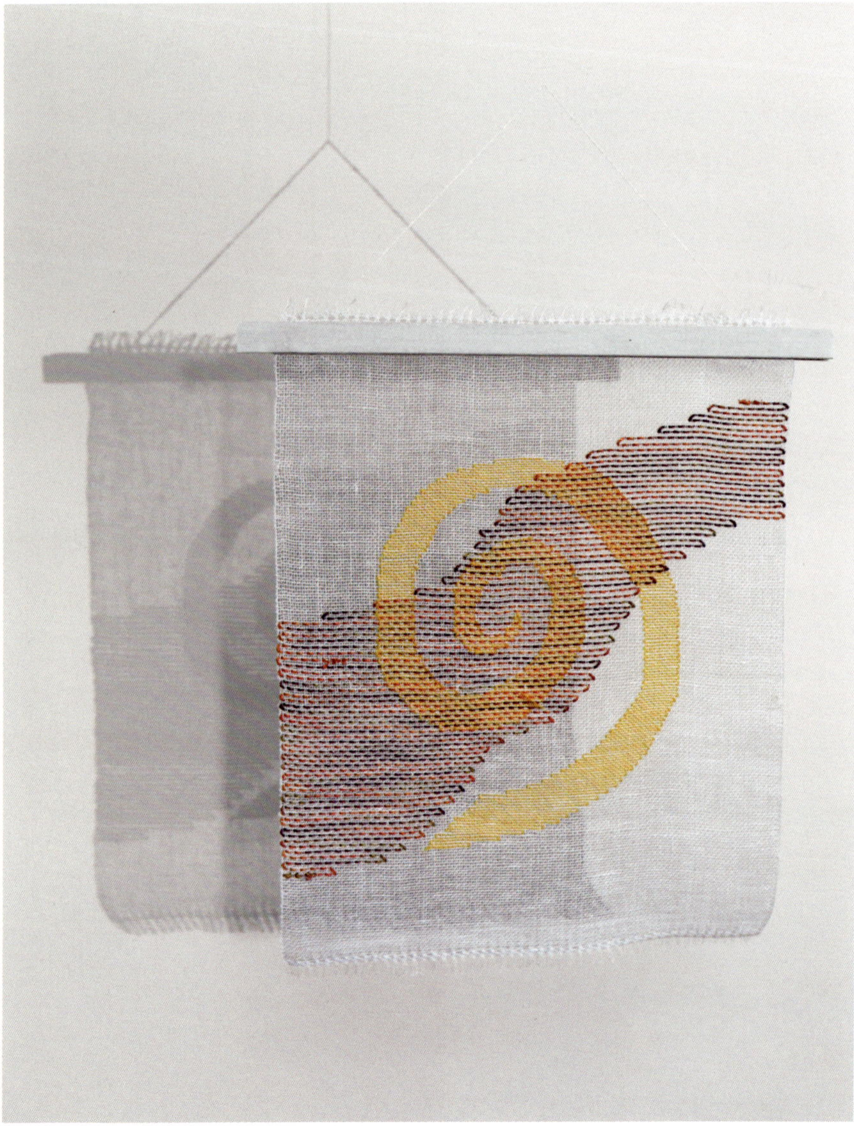

WEAVE THE SHAPES

Weave the design, using plain weave for the spiral and a different pattern for the cloud.

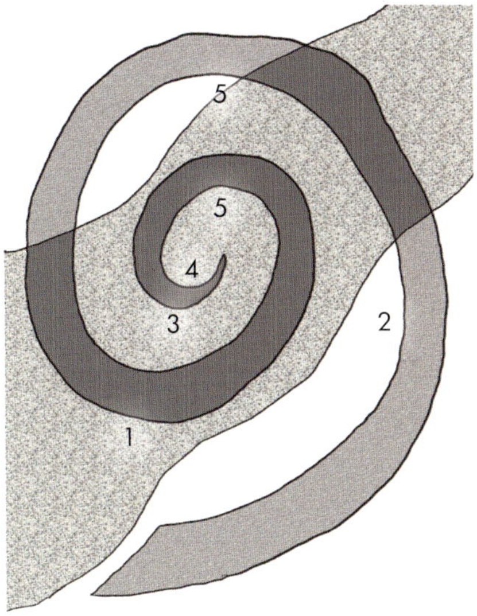

There are several critical points in the weaving to be aware of:

1. Begin weaving the spiral shape where it overlaps with the cloud. Weave both shapes within their respective areas, maintaining a consistent weaving order as discussed on page 93.

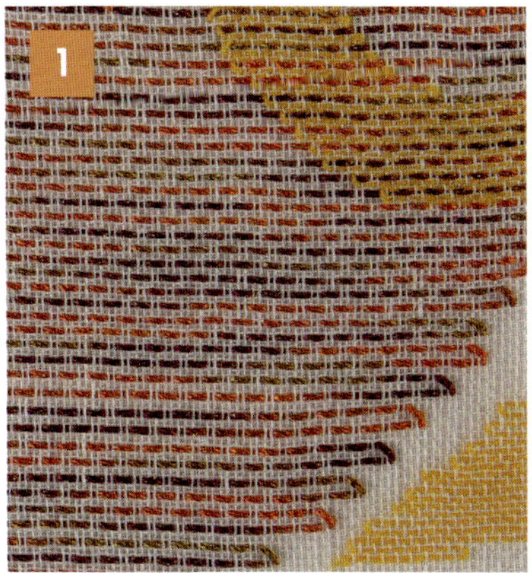

2. It's a common mistake to begin bending this curve back to the left too soon. There are several rows where the inlay turns on the same warp. In the sample shown here, there are sixteen turns on the same warp on the right side of the shape, and twelve on the left side. Moving the turning point too soon will cause the curve to bend sooner than you want it to.
3. Don't forget to begin the inlay shapes when you come to them in the cartoon. It's *so* easy to weave beyond this point and have to unweave back to where the shape begins.
4. When a single shape splits into two sections, you must add a new weft. Review page 79 for how to do this.
5. Review page 77 for how to join two parts of a shape into one.

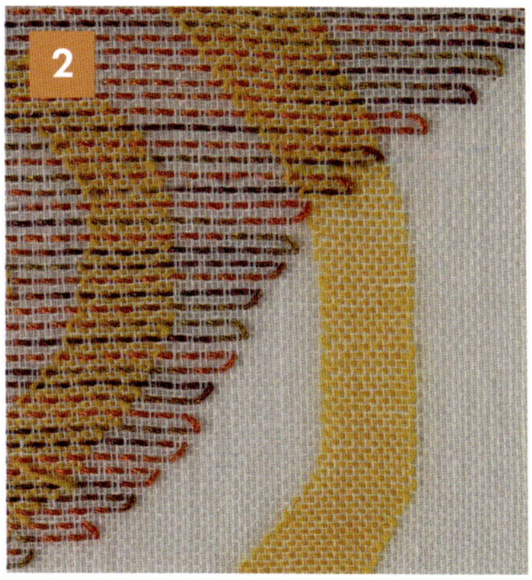

In instances where the inlay weft weaves to the edge of the warp, a trick is to never turn around the outer warp. If the inlay weft is allowed to turn around the outside warp, it creates a slight bulge. The thicker the yarn, the bigger the bulge. To keep the edges looking straight, always turn the inlay weft on the warp before the outer warp. This will keep the edges of the weaving straight. The ground weft continues to weave to the outer edge.

When you have completely woven the design, weave a 2-inch border of ground weft. Hemstitch the edge, then weave the header.

FINISHING

Follow the instructions in chapter 9 for steam finishing. Block if necessary.

At both ends, trim away the header, leaving ½ inch beyond the hemstitching. Unravel the remaining header weft, leaving a ½-inch warp fringe.

For this project, a magnetic hanger was painted white to match the ground weave. The hanger is placed just inside the hemstitching on both the top and bottom. The ½-inch fringe extends beyond the magnetic hanger.

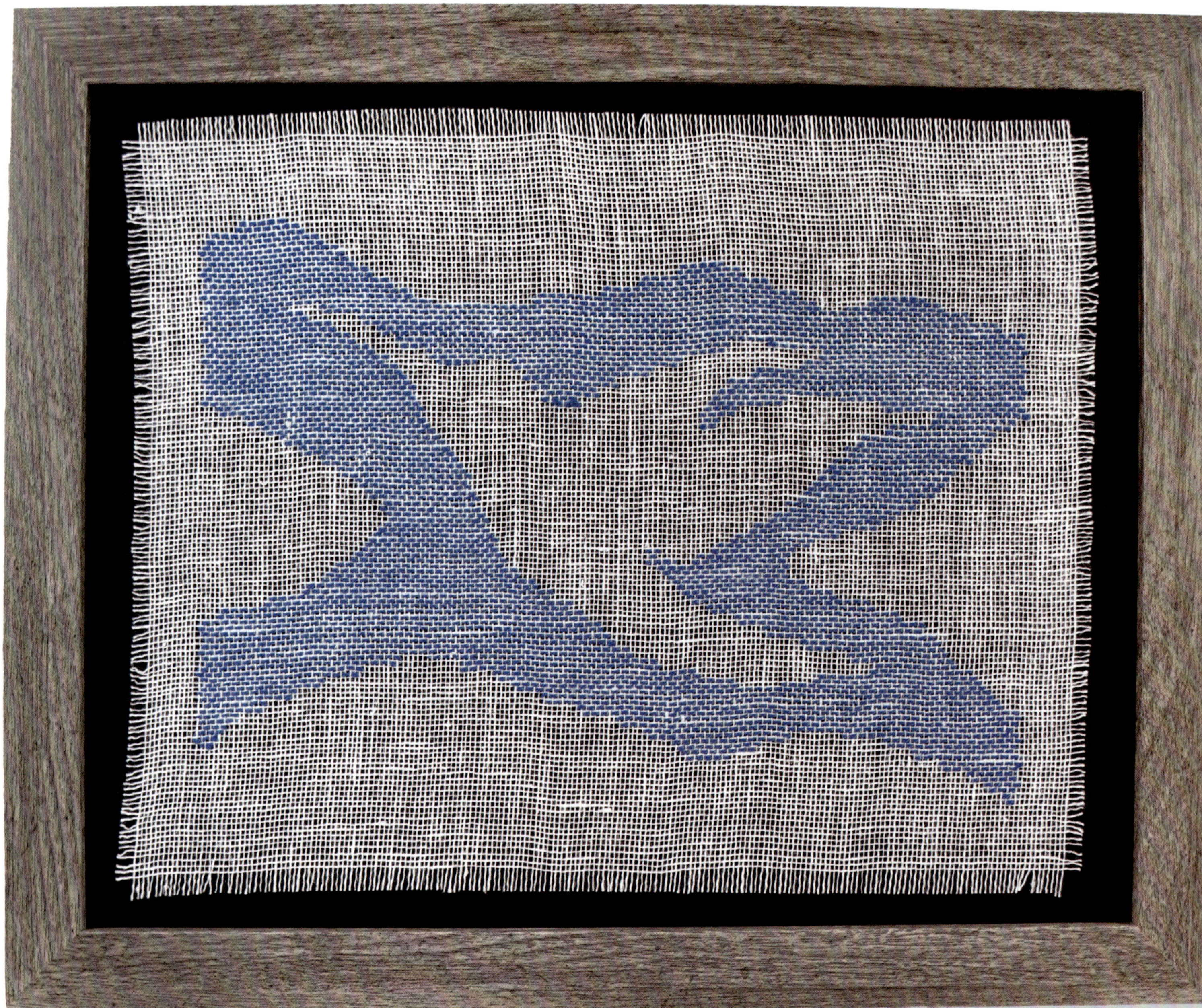

Project 5

REVERSE IMAGERY

The subject matter of the design does not always have to be the part that is woven with inlay. By reversing positive and negative space—making the subject matter the transparent part of the image— the viewer is invited to look into and through the weaving rather than focusing on the surface of the woven cloth.

The idea of reversing the positive and negative parts of a design was introduced in chapter 8. The weaving technique remains virtually the same as it is when the object of the design is woven with inlay. You just have to reverse your thinking about where the inlay will go.

The simple imagery in this project is a hummingbird outlined by blue sky. In keeping with the airborne vision of the hummingbird, the display plan is to create a four-sided fringe and display the piece in a float frame.

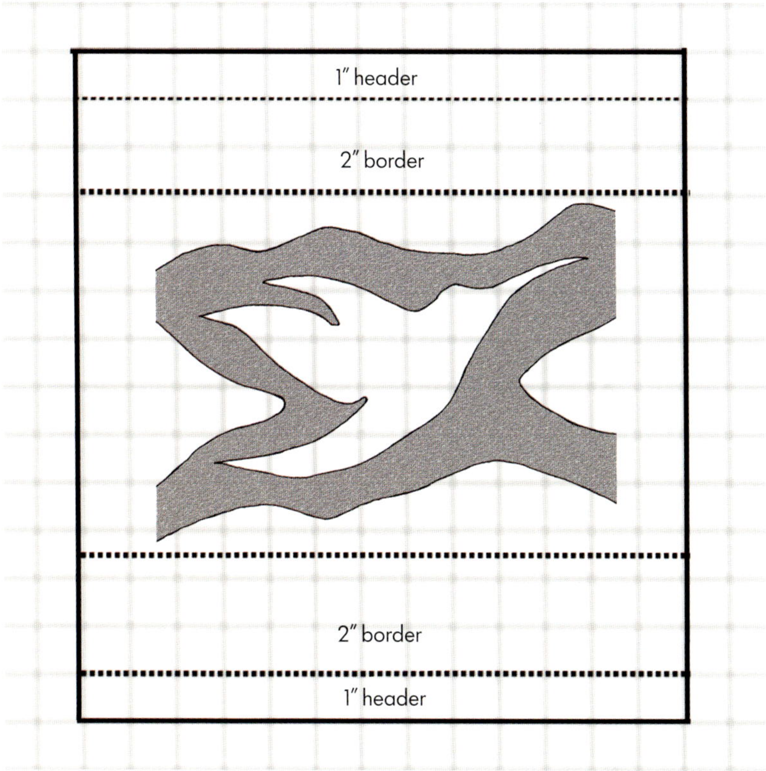

Project 5 weaving plan

DESIGN

The cartoon for this project is provided on page 161 in the appendix. Trace it or print it on plain white paper.

YARNS AND COLORS

Warp: 16/1 linen in natural or other light color

Ground weft: 16/1 linen to match warp color

Inlay weft: a single color of yarn that fits easily between rows of ground weft (see page 36)

OTHER SUPPLIES

Pins, sewing thread, or magnets to attach cartoon; 11-by-14-inch float frame; Fray Check (optional)

DIMENSIONS

Woven width: 12½ inches

Woven length: 12 inches, not including the header

Finished size: approximately 11 inches wide by 9 inches long

WEAVING

Follow the weaving plan shown here, reading from the bottom up.

Weave a 1-to-2-inch header with waste yarn to space the warps and establish the actual weaving width (expect about ½-inch draw-in).

Weave 2 inches of ground weft for a border.

ATTACH THE CARTOON

Attach the cartoon to the back of the weaving, using pins, sewing thread, or magnets. The cartoon measures 10 inches wide. Center the cartoon so there is an equal border on each side of the design. Place the lowest part of the sky shape just above the fell line. Pushing the cartoon up against the weaving from underneath the warp will give you an accurate view of where the edges of the shapes should be woven.

WEAVE THE DESIGN

Weave the sky around the outline of the hummingbird, using the knowledge you gained in chapter 6 for weaving curved shapes. Note these key points in the weaving:

1. Avoid creating a gap along long vertical edges by alternating turns between two warps to create a serrated edge.

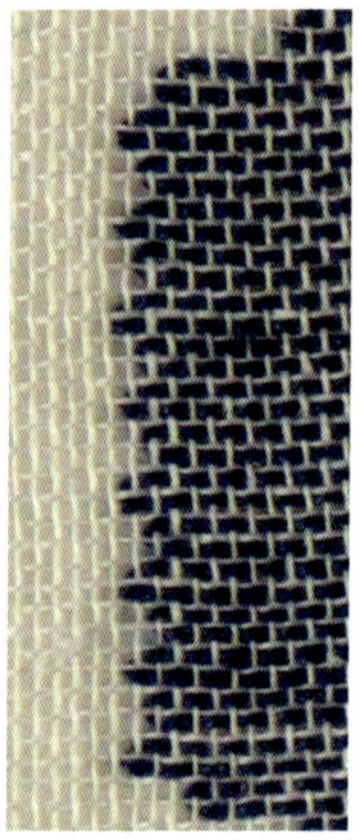

Serrated edge

2. Along the bottom edge of the sky there are points where two parts of the shape merge into one. Review the instructions on page 77.
3. Conversely, there are several points where a single shape splits into two parts. At the base of the wing, there is a small notch of 2 to 3 rows that needs to be woven with a separate piece of weft. Review instructions on page 79 for splitting shapes.

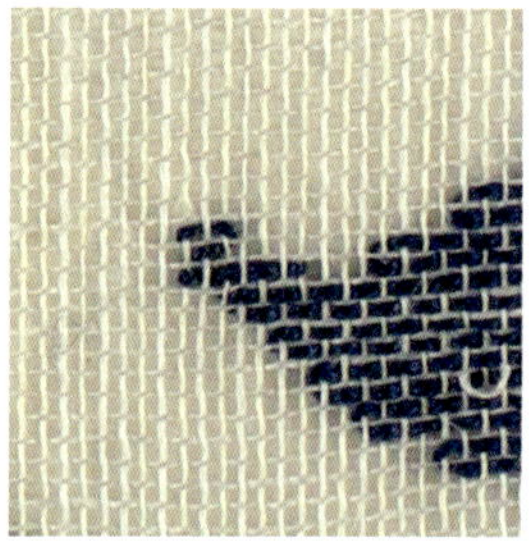

Small notch at the base of the wing

When you have completely woven the design, weave a 2-inch border of ground weft. Weave several picks of header in a distinct color from the ground weft to give a clear demarcation of the end of your weaving.

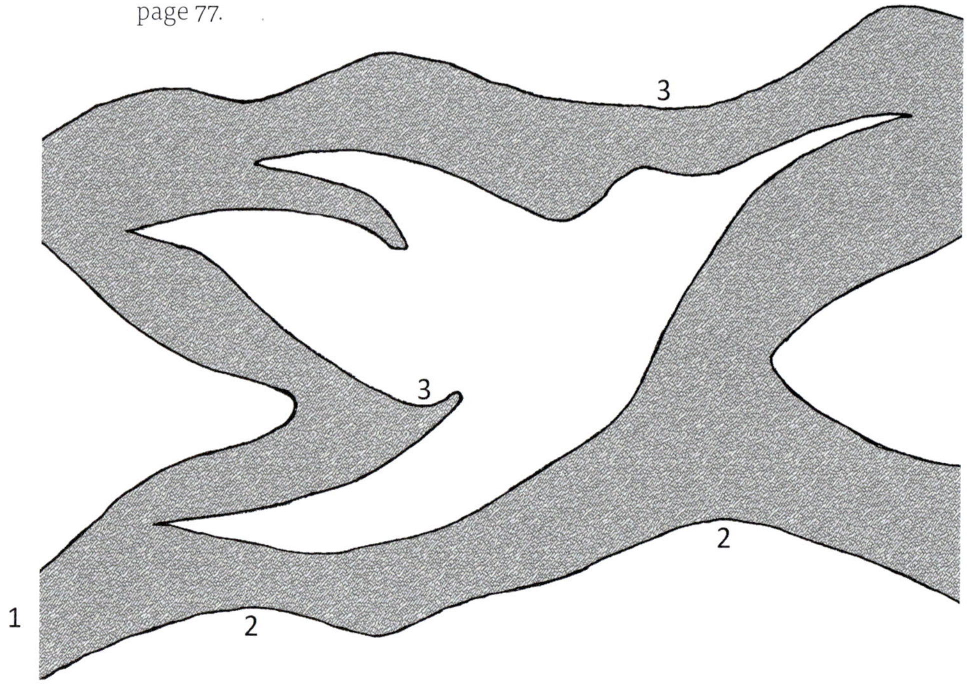

FINISHING

Follow the instructions in chapter 9 for steam finishing. Block if necessary.

The four-sided fringe is created by pulling out rows of weft along the top and bottom, as well as removing several warps from each side. Carefully cut away the outer warp on each side, which will also cut through the ground weft.

After the edges are trimmed, begin pulling away the ground weft from each end until the total height is about 9 inches. Also pull away warp threads from each side until the width is about 11 inches. You can remove more if you want less border around the sky shape. Once you are happy with the size of the piece, trim the fringe to an equal length on all four sides. About ¼ to ½ inch looks good.

If handled carefully, the edges should not unravel. However, if you do experience unraveling, place a little Fray Check along the edges to stabilize them.

Place the weaving between the two pieces of acrylic or glass that came with your float frame. Admire your work!

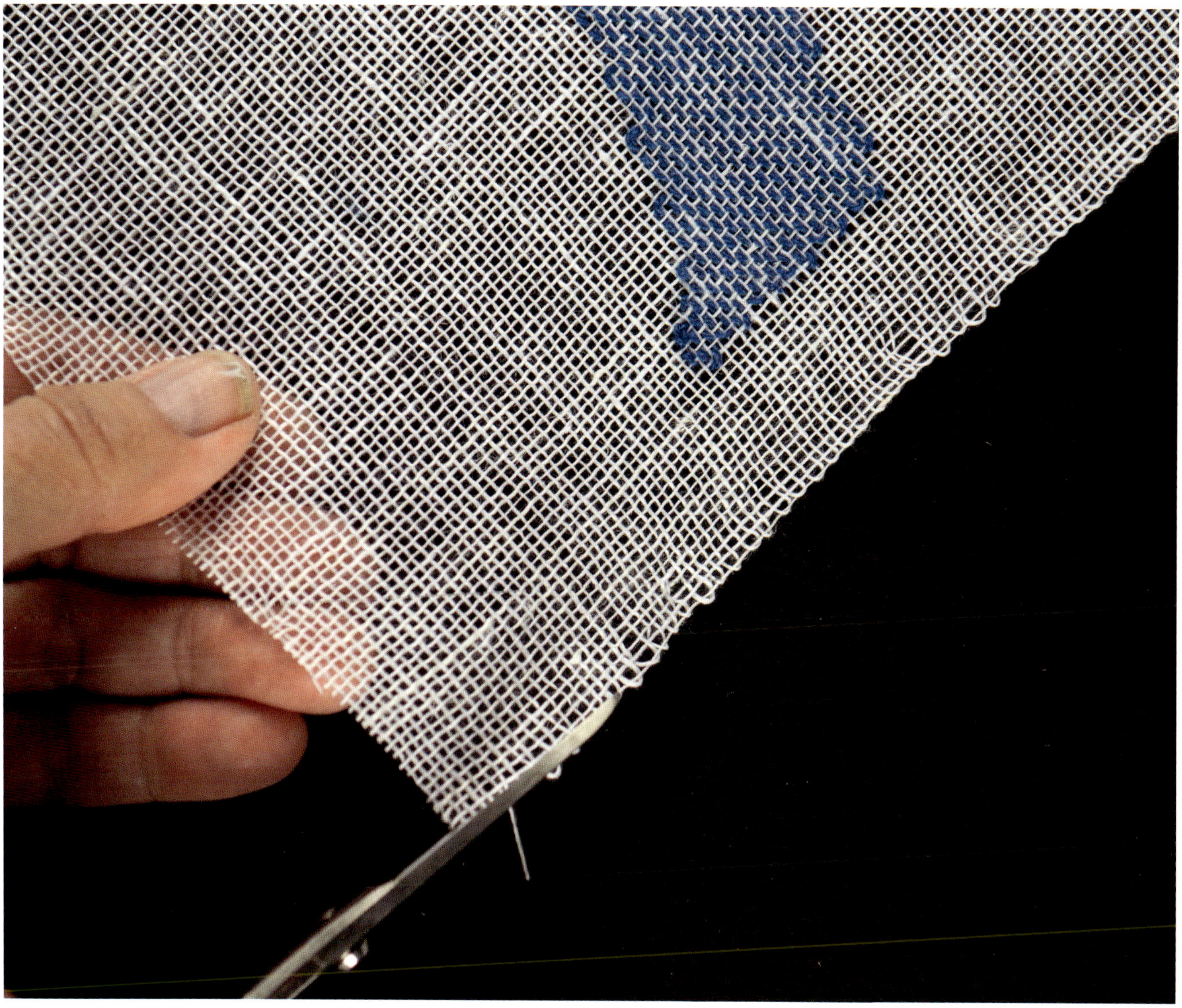

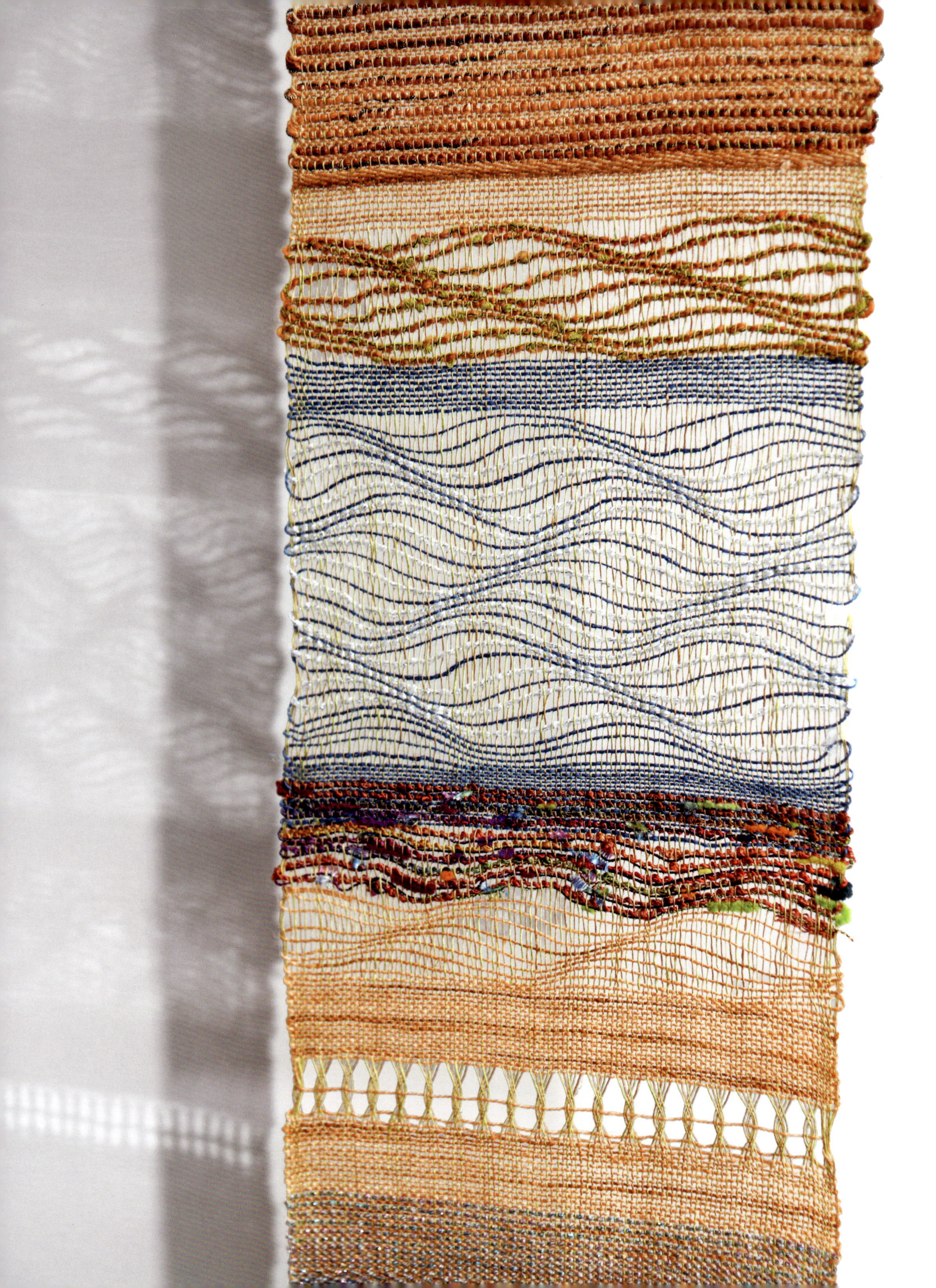

Project 6

LACY WAVY BANNER

This project is pure fun! It draws on skills presented in chapter 8 for weaving leno lace and using a wave beater. A few ideas are given below to add variety in the use of these two elements, but there is no set pattern to follow.

The display plan for this piece is to hemstitch the ends and insert dowels into the weaving as support rods.

DESIGN

The design for this project is open ended. Alternating sections of plain weave, leno lace, and waves make a visually interesting design. Six suggested design elements are indicated on the weaving plan. Corresponding woven examples can be seen on the following page.

YARNS

Warp: 16/1 linen in any color or even a combination of colors

Ground weft: 16/2 linen in any color(s). Note: ground weft is heavier linen than the warp.

Inlay weft: Be as creative as you like in choosing weft yarns to use. An assortment of textures, hues, and value contrasts make this a successful project.

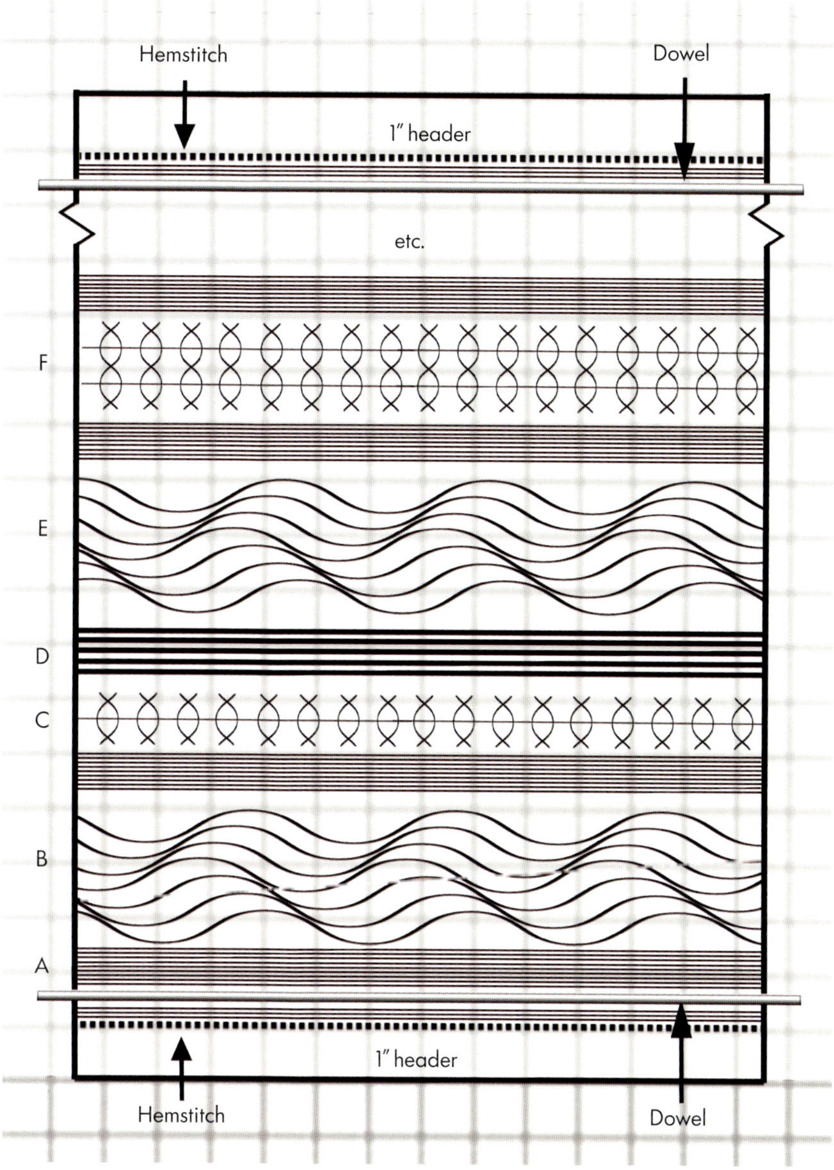

Project 6 weaving plan

OTHER SUPPLIES

Two ¼-inch dowels cut 2 inches wider than the warp, painted or coated with polyurethane; monofilament line

DIMENSIONS

Woven width: any width (the sample shown above is 6½ inches wide)

Woven length: any length (the sample is 47 inches long)

Finished size: expect minor draw-in and shrinkage

WEAVING

Follow the weaving plan on the previous page, reading from the bottom up.

- Weave a 1-to-2-inch header with waste yarn to space the warps and establish the actual weaving width (expect about ½-inch draw-in).
- Hemstitch the edge.
- Weave three rows of ground weft, then insert the dowel. Continue weaving a few more rows of ground weft.

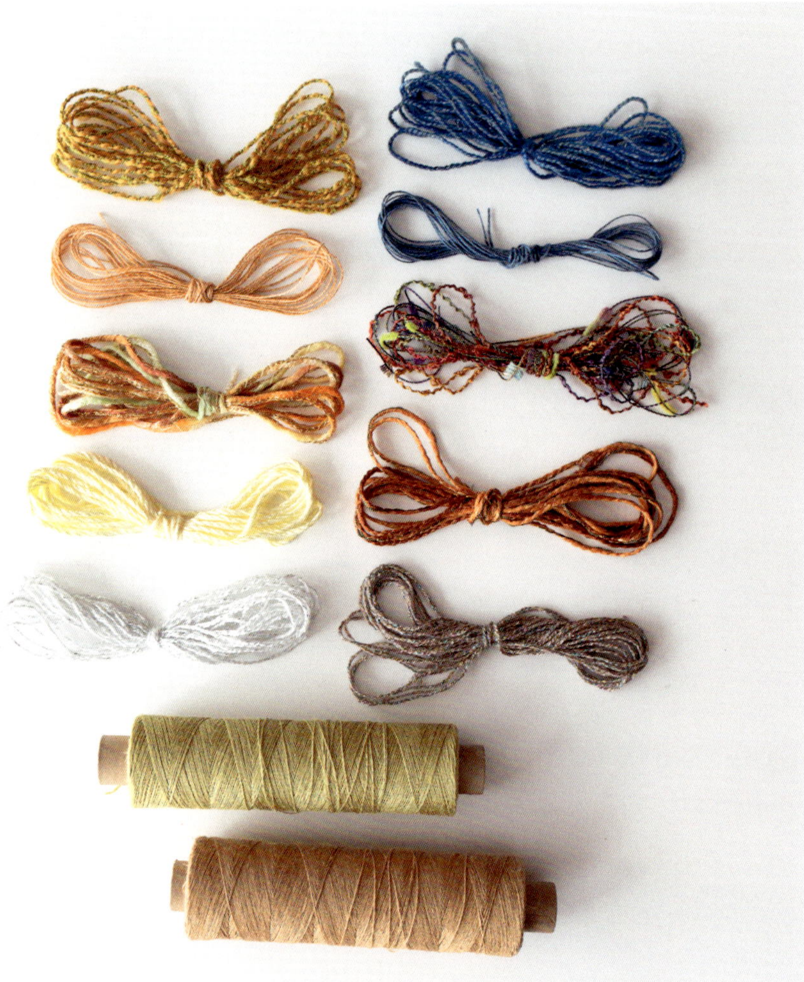

Yarns used to create my *Lacy Wavy Banner*

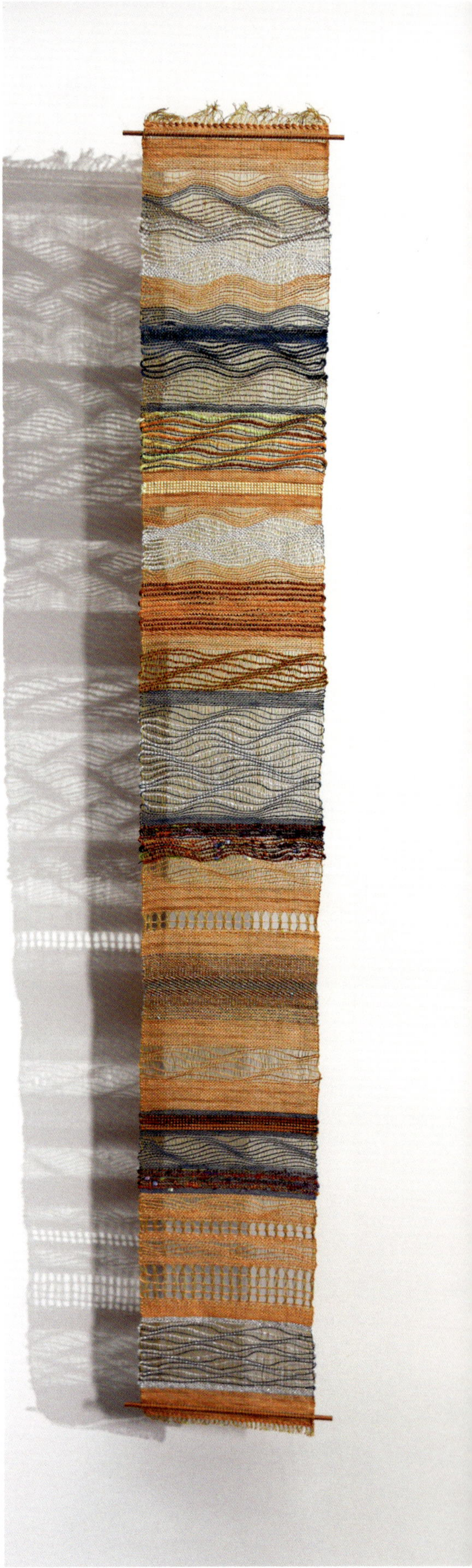

WEAVE THE DESIGN

Weave the body of the piece, choosing from these suggested design elements, or make up your own variations. The order is up to you: There are no wrong answers!

When your pattern weaving is complete, weave a few rows of ground weft, then insert the dowel. Weave three more rows of ground weft. Hemstitch the edge. Weaving a header is optional. The hemstitching is sufficient to hold the weft in place.

A. Rows of 16/2 linen ground weft

B. Wave pattern using a single yarn

C. Single row of leno lace

D. 16/2 linen ground weft with heavier inlay weft woven every second row

E. Wave pattern alternating with two yarn colors

F. Multiple rows of leno lace

FINISHING

Follow the instructions for steam finishing in chapter 9. Block if necessary. Attach monofilament to the dowel at the top for hanging.

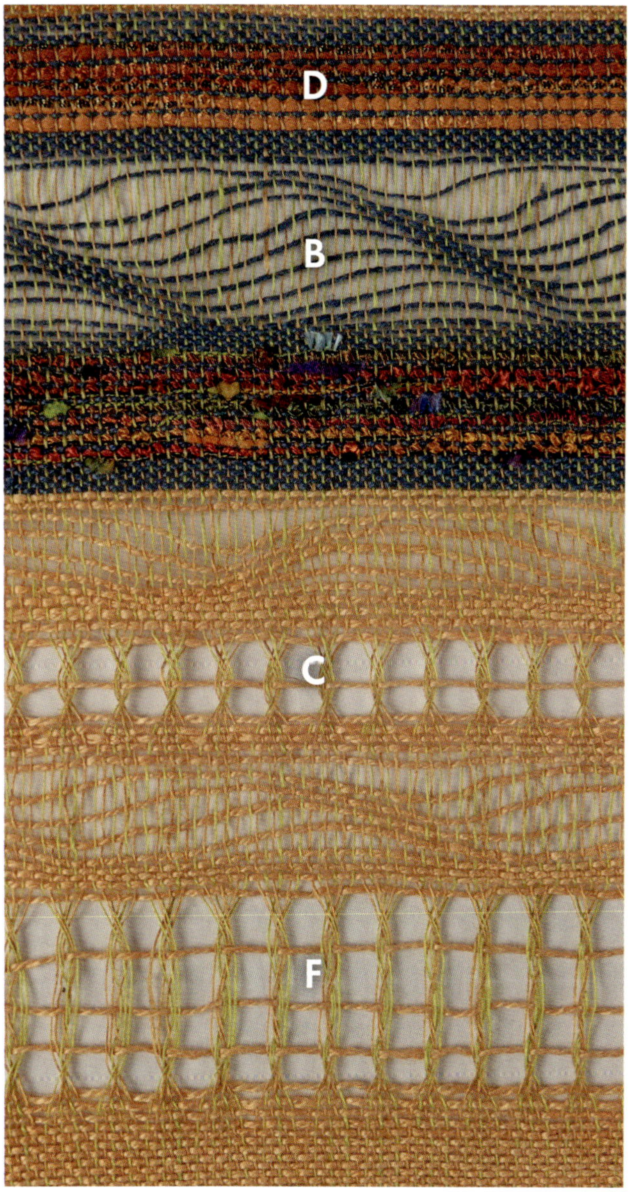

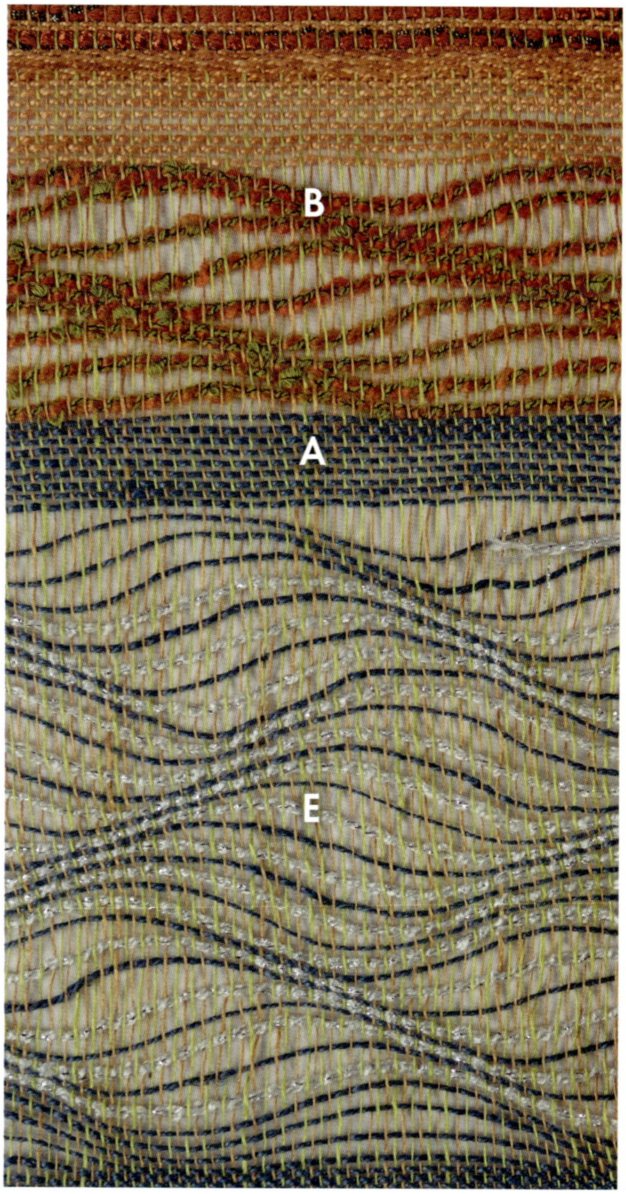

RESOURCES

linen yarn: A popular brand of linen is Bockens Lingarn from Sweden. It is available in both 16/1 and 16/2 in a variety of colors. It can be purchased from many online retailers for weaving supplies.

beads: Light-reflecting seed beads with appropriate width, height, and hole size. I use Miyuki Delica™ beads, available from many online retailers.

beading needles: Big Eye needles are best for threading beads on the weft for random placement. They are available at most crafting stores. To weave rows of beads using beading thread, I use Japanese thin beading needles that are 2⅛ inches long.

beading thread: I recommend Berkley Fireline®, which is available at most craft and beading stores as well as online. Choose either clear or smoke in 6 or 8 lb. weight.

dowel support device: "Angel wings" is the name of the device that I use. Search "angel wings for warping" on the internet.

Procion MX dyes: The main producer of Procion MX dyes is Jacquard Products. Other brands such as Dharma Trading Co. and PRO Chemical and Dye also sell Procion MX-type dyes under their own names. Because the original patent has expired, many manufacturers around the world now produce these dyes.

GLOSSARY

apron rod (apron bar): A removable rod or bar at the warp or cloth beam used to attach warp, historically via a fabric apron but now often via cords or direct lashing.

balanced weave: A weave in which the number of warp ends per inch equals the number of weft picks per inch, producing a uniform texture.

balanced weave pattern: A weave structure that weaves over and under the same number of warps so that the pattern shows equally on both the front and back of the weaving.

beater: A loom component used to press the weft yarn into place; crucial for controlling the spacing of ground weft in transparency weaving.

blocking: Restoring straight edges on the finished weaving by pinning in place and applying moisture and heat.

bobbin: A tool for holding inlay weft. A tapestry bobbin is an elongated, pointed tool used by tapestry weavers. A kumihimo bobbin is a plastic disk with an opening for holding yarn.

bubbling: Forming an arced shape with the weft before it is beaten in; prevents drawing in by placing adequate weft yarn in the shed.

butterfly: A method of wrapping inlay yarn into a small bundle for ease of manipulation during weaving.

cartoon: A full-scale design or drawing placed behind the warp to guide pictorial or geometric pattern placement.

damp finishing: The process of laying out the finished weaving and applying heat and moisture. Used to remove loom marks, soften threads, and blocking when necessary.

draw-in: Unintended narrowing of the fabric as it is woven.

end(s) per inch (EPI): A measurement indicating the number of warp threads per inch across the width of the weaving.

false satin: A four-shaft adaptation of satin weave; similar to twill but uses a different treadling sequence to avoid forming a diagonal pattern.

faux ikat: A warp-dyeing technique that mimics ikat without resist wrapping.

fell: The most recent weft pick pressed into place by the beater.

float: A weft thread that skips over two or more adjacent warps to show more prominently on the surface of the weaving.

float frame: A picture frame designed to display an item by holding it under pressure between two sheets of glass or acrylic.

floating selvedge: An extra warp thread at each edge of the warp used to create neater selvedges; usually unnecessary in transparency weaving when the ground weft is woven in plain weave.

ground cloth: The base layer of sheer cloth in transparency weaving, woven with light beat and widely spaced warps to allow light through.

half tapestry: A generic term referring to techniques that weave patterned inlay weft, much as in tapestry, but with a continuous ground weft that forms the structure of the cloth. Also known by the Swedish term halv gobeläng.

hatching: Blending two adjoining color areas by having the two colors take turns weaving into the zone between them. Also, shifting the turning point at the edge of a shape to create a jagged or wispy edge.

header: Several rows of weaving that help spread the warps evenly, establish the weaving width, and prevent unraveling of the weft.

hemstitch: A decorative edge treatment intended to prevent the weft from unraveling.

inlay density: The thickness of the inlay weft. Inlay density determines how much light is allowed to pass through the weaving.

inlay weft: Heavier or decorative weft added to the ground cloth to create opaque design elements in a transparency.

kuultokudos: A Finnish weaving style of translucent fabrics, popular in mid-twentieth-century Finland, foundational to modern transparency weaving.

leno lace: A lacelike weave where pairs of warp threads are twisted around each other to lock in the weft.

line linen: A type of linen yarn made from long, smooth fibers; preferred for warps in transparency weaving due to its strength and minimal stretch.

meet and separate: A method where two wefts weaving adjacent areas move in opposite directions, avoiding overlap in the same shed.

MMF technique: Weaving method developed by Swedish textile designer Märta Måås-Fjetterström in the early twentieth century that weaves inlay in the same shed as the ground weft.

negative space: The part of a design that surrounds the object or positive space.

open warp: A weaving style in which the warps are more widely spaced than they would be for weaving solid cloth.

pass: Two picks of the weft thread through the warp, over and back.

pick (also shot): Drawing of the weft through the shed one time, left to right or right to left.

picks per inch (PPI): The number of weft picks within an inch of weaving.

plain weave: The simplest weave structure where each weft thread passes over and under alternate warp threads.

row of weaving: Nontechnical term referring to a single pick or shot of weft.

ryssväv: The Swedish name for an unbalanced inlay technique in which the weft travels over three and under one warp end. Also called Russian weave.

selvedge: The finished edge of a woven fabric that runs parallel to the warp.

sett: The number of warp threads per inch, determining the density of the weave.

shed: The separation of warp ends created by separating the shafts, creating a space for the weft to pass through.

shim: Material (cardboard, mat board, etc.) inserted under warps to correct tension disparities during weaving.

shot: A single passage of the weft through the warp, also called a pick.

side weights: Weights attached to the edges of the weaving to help prevent draw-in. Side weights are an alternative to using a temple.

supplemental weft: A nonstructural weft added for decorative effect, such as inlay; can be removed without compromising fabric integrity.

take-up: Shortening of the warp as it interlaces with the weft.

tapestry weaving: A weft-faced weaving technique where the design is built directly into the cloth structure using colored wefts.

temple: A tool used to maintain the full width of the weaving, helping to prevent draw-in.

Theo Moorman technique: A weaving technique developed by British weaver Theo Moorman in the mid-twentieth century. The technique uses tie-down warps to hold inlay in place on the surface of the ground weave.

tie-down warp: Warps on one or more shafts whose role is to hold the inlay in place.

transparency weaving: A weaving technique combining sheer ground cloth with opaque design elements, allowing light to pass through the background.

turns per warp: Number of times the inlay weft turns around each warp to form a diagonal or curved shape.

twill: One of the basic weave structures (plain weave and satin are the other two). Floats in successive sheds are offset by one warp to form diagonal patterns.

unbalanced weave pattern: A weave structure that does not cover the same number of warps on both sides of the weaving; a good example is 1/3 twill, which goes under one warp and over three on the working side and has the opposite effect on the reverse side of the weaving.

warp: The vertical threads stretched on a loom through which the weft is woven.

warp beam: Part of the loom where the warp threads are wound before weaving begins.

warp sticks: Flat pieces of wood or cardboard placed between layers of the warp as it is wound onto the warp beam.

warps per turn: Indicates the number of warps to move away from the last turn to make the next turn when weaving shallow diagonal edges.

wave beater: Curved edge tool used instead of the loom's beater to place the weft in wavy patterns.

weave pattern or structure: Loom-controlled sequence of raising shafts to create interlacements of warp and weft that are distinguished from plain weave.

weft: The horizontal threads interwoven with the warp to make fabric.

working side: The side of the weaving that faces up while working on a floor or table loom. The working side is generally considered the back of the transparency.

CARTOONS

These resources are available for download at www.schiffercraft.com/Transparency.

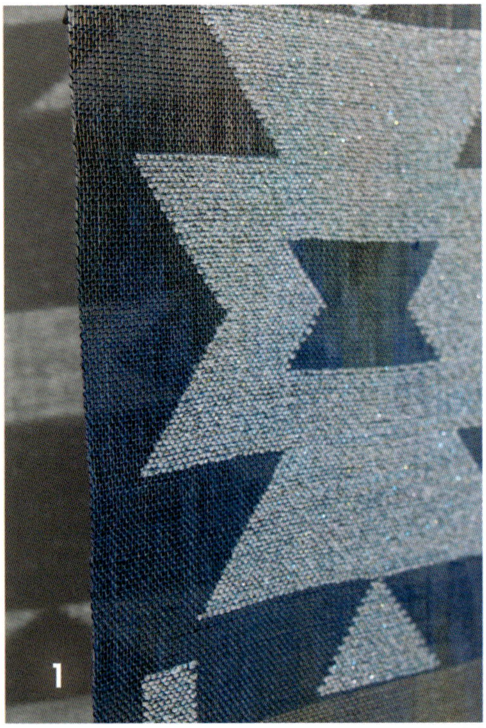

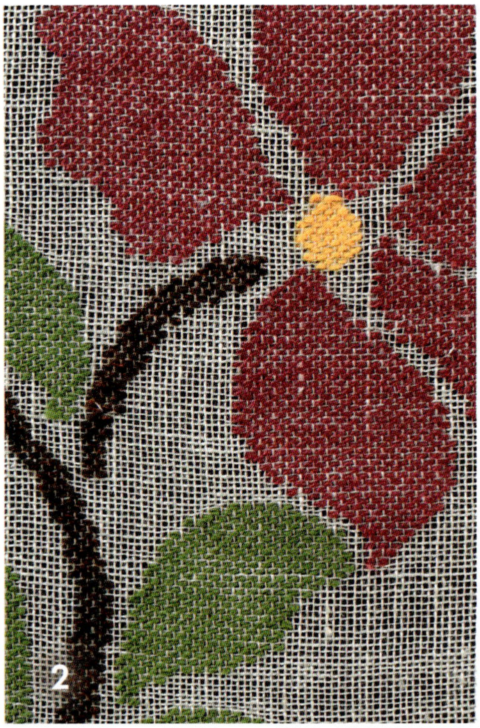

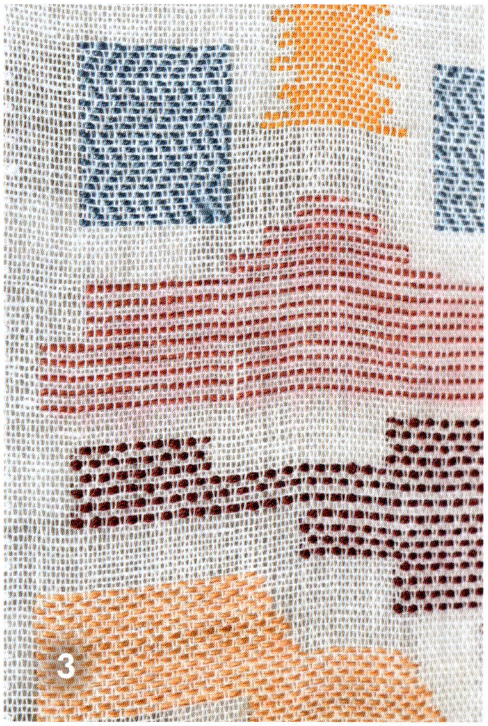

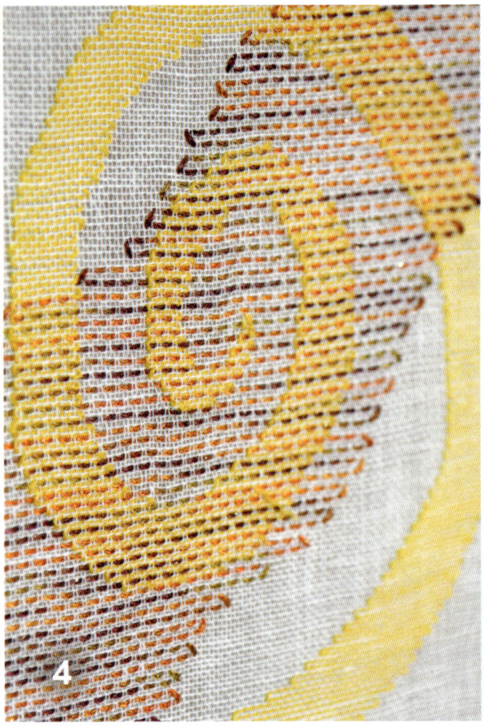

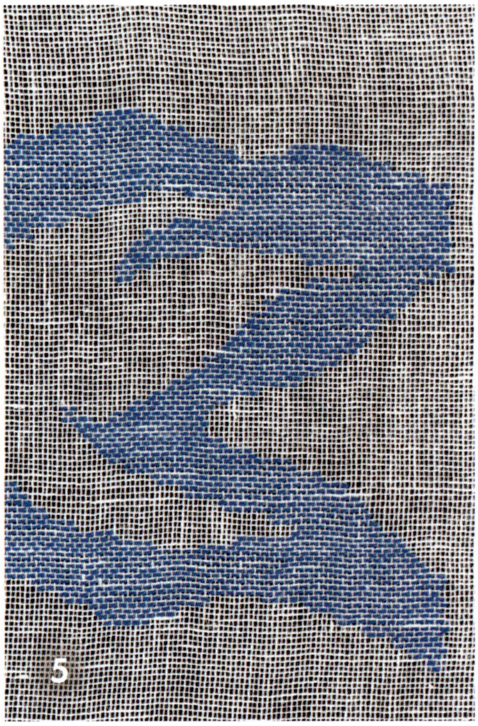

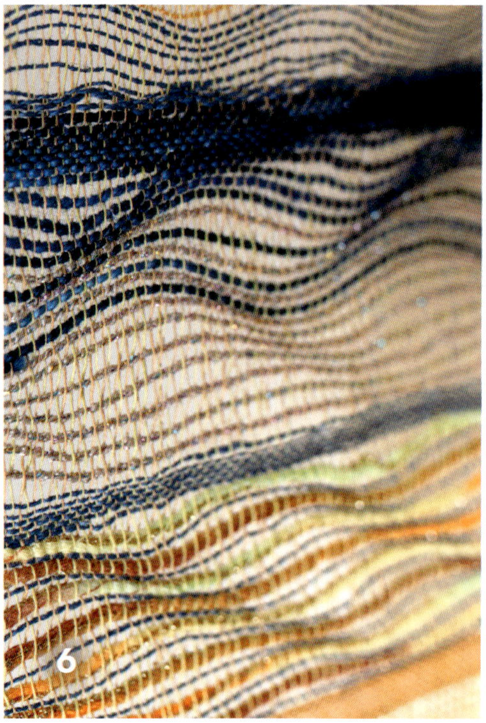

CARTOON FOR PROJECT 1

CARTOON FOR PROJECT 2

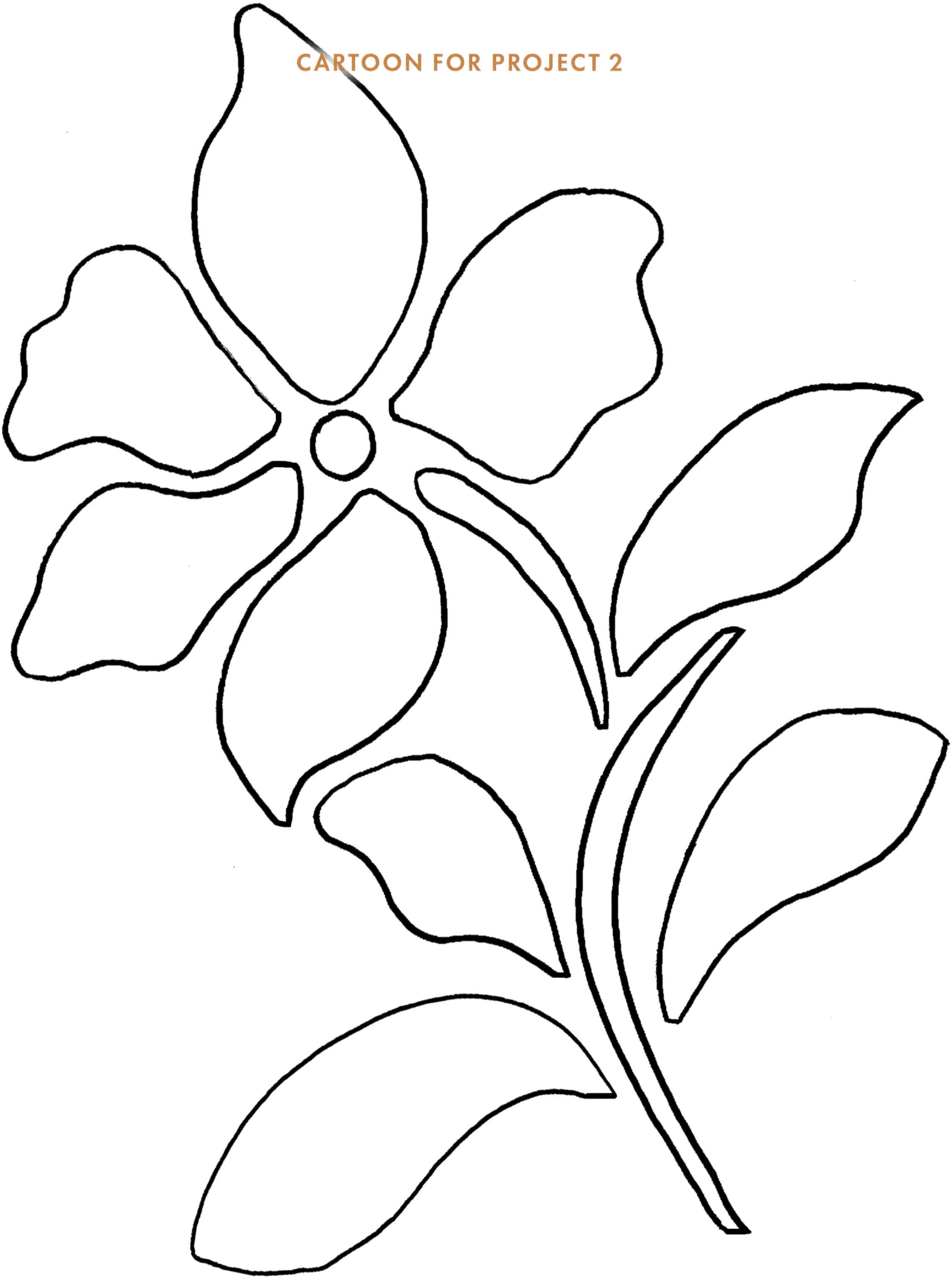

CARTOON FOR PROJECT 3

For project as described, enlarge to be 9.5" high.

CARTOON FOR PROJECT 4

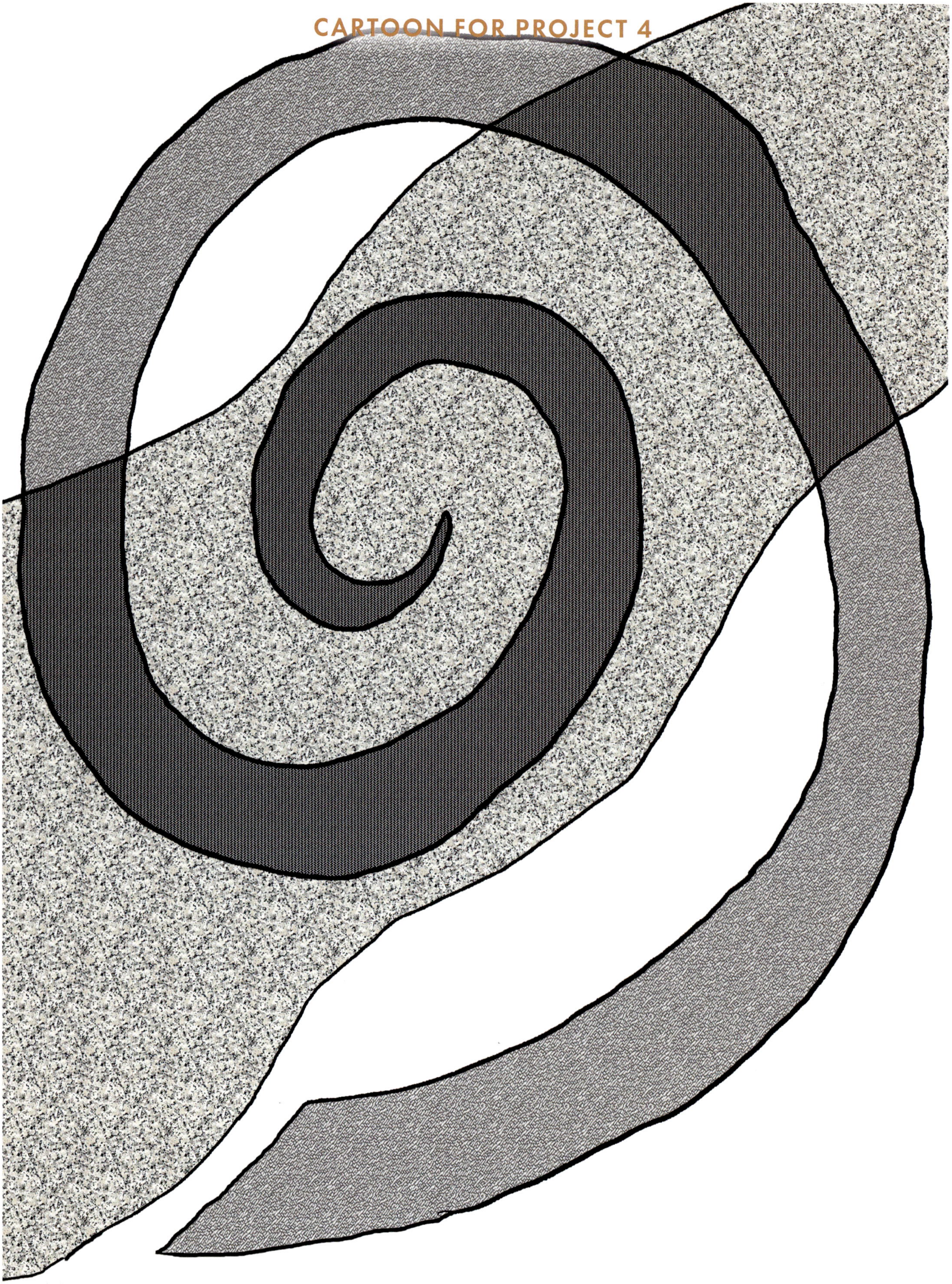

CARTOON FOR PROJECT 5

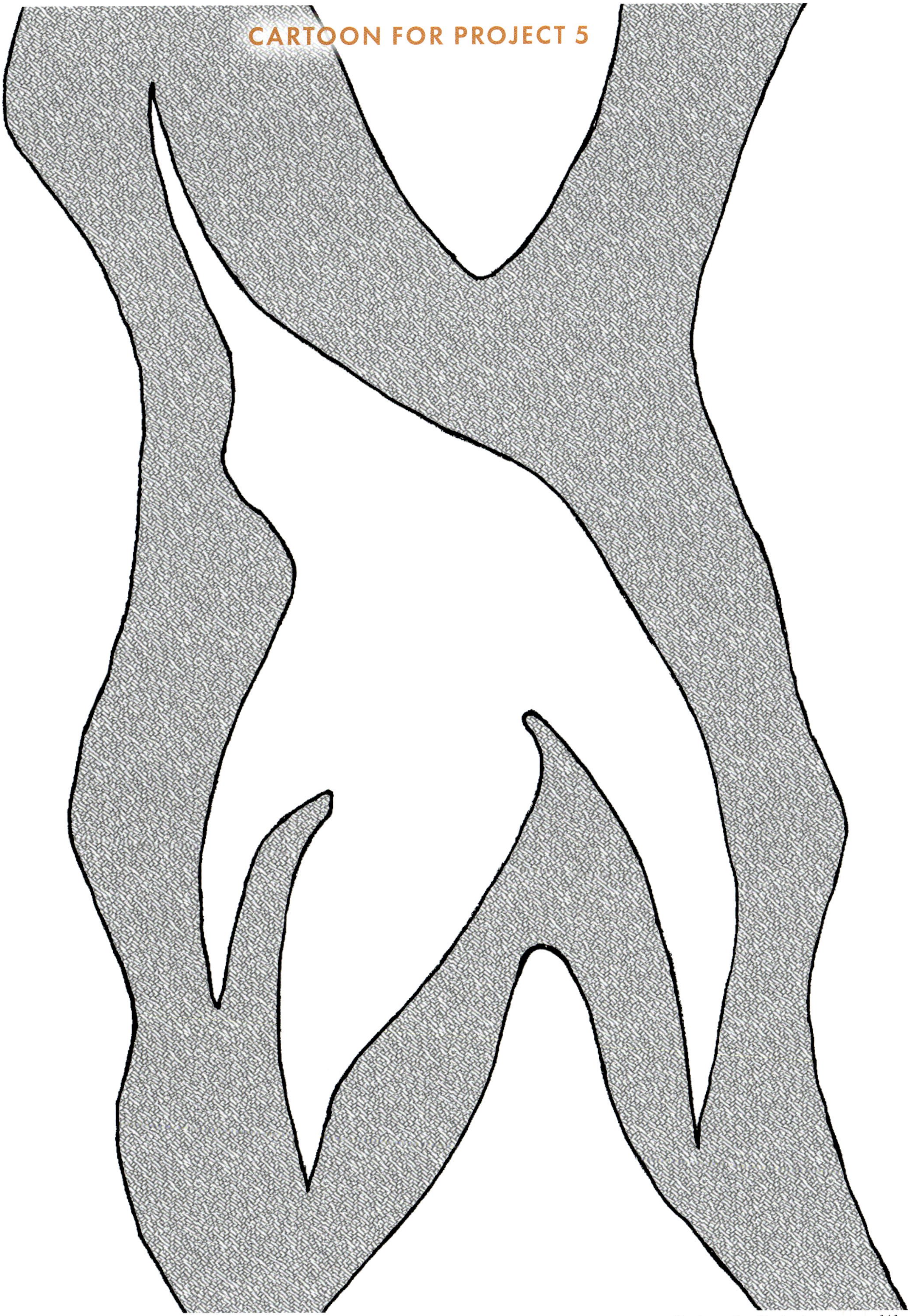

APPENDIX 1: GRAPH PAPER FOR 12 ENDS PER INCH

1 inch

APPENDIX 2: GRAPH PAPER FOR 16 ENDS PER INCH

1 inch

APPENDIX 3: GRAPH PAPER FOR 15 ENDS PER INCH

1 inch

APPENDIX 4: TEMPLATE FOR WAVE BEATER

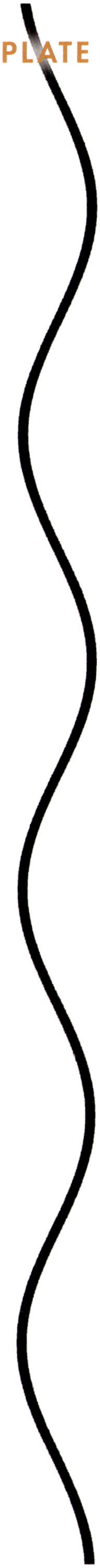

1 inch

NOTES

Introduction

1. Doramay Keasbey, *Sheer Delight—Handwoven Transparencies* (Petaluma, CA: Stellar, 1990).
2. Annie Gottlieb and Barbara Sher, *Wishcraft: How to Get What You Really Want* (New York: Random House, 1986).

Chapter 1

1. Märta Måås-Fjetterström AB, "Weaving Techniques: Wall Hangings and Tapestries," accessed August 14, 2025, https://mmf.se/pages/knotted-pile.
2. Anne Whidden, "A Look at 'Half-Tapestry' in Ryssväv: Agda Österberg," *theswedishrugblog*, February 28, 2020, theswed ishrugblog.wordpress.com, accessed April 26, 2025.
3. Sari Jantunen, *Kuultokudos* (Jyväskylä, Finland: Finnish Crafts Museum, 2021), 18.
4. Ibid., 27.
5. Conversation with Inger Harrison Seitz, June 23, 2025.
6. Theo Moorman, *Weaving as an Art Form: A Personal Statement* (West Chester, PA: Schiffer, 1975).
7. Ibid., 20.
8. Ibid., 21.
9. Ibid., 89.
10. Karen Patterson, *Lenore Tawney: Mirror of the Universe* (New York: John Michael Kohler Art Center in association with University of Chicago Press, 2019), 56ff.
11. Ibid., 54.
12. Warren Seelig, "Thinking Lenore Tawney," in Kathleen Nugent Mangan, Sid Sachs, Warren Seelig, and T'ai Smith, *Lenore Tawney: Wholly Unlooked For* (Baltimore: Maryland Institute College of Art, 2013), 19 (cited in Patterson, *Lenore Tawney: Mirror of the Universe*, 55).
13. Helena Vento, email communication, March 24, 2025.
14. Muriel Beckett, "Through Thick and Thin—a Weaver's Journey," *Journal for Weavers, Spinners and Dyers* 294 (Summer 2025): 26–29.
15. Boisali Biswas, "Artist Statement," 26th International Open, Woman Made Gallery, Chicago, March 2025.
16. Lili Blumenau, *Creative Design in Wall Hangings* (New York: Crown, 1967), 148–158.
17. Email conversation with Morgan Clifford, March 20, 2025.
18. Quote from https://cyndybarbone.com/current-work-2/, viewed on July 14, 2025.

Chapter 8

1. Keasbey, *Sheer Delight*, 2.
2. Patterson, *Lenore Tawney*, 59.
3. Information accompanying the piece, which was hanging at the Weaving and Fiber Arts Center in Rochester, NY, where I photographed it in May 2025.
4. Patterson, *Lenore Tawney*, 118.
5. See also Mary Zicafoose, *Ikat: The Essential Handbook to Weaving Resist-Dyed Cloth* (Loveland, CO: Interweave, 2020).

SELECTED BIBLIOGRAPHY

Beckett, Muriel. "Through Thick and Thin—a Weaver's Journey." *Journal for Weavers, Spinners and Dyers* 294 (Summer 2025): 26–29.

Blumenau, Lili. *Creative Design in Wall Hangings: Weaving Patterns Based on Primitive and Medieval Art*. New York: Crown, 1967.

Cyrus, Ulla. *Manual of Swedish Hand Weaving*. Boston: Charles T. Branford, Boston, 1956.

Gottlieb, Annie, and Barbara Sher. *Wishcraft: How to Get What You Really Want*. New York: Random House, 1986.

Itten, Johannes. *The Elements of Color*. New York: John Wiley and Sons, 1970.

Jantunen, Sari. *Kuultokudos*. Jyväskylä, Finland: Craft Museum of Finland, 2021.

Keasbey, Doramay. *Sheer Delight—Handwoven Transparencies*. Petaluma, CA: Stellar, 1990.

Lancaster, Daryl. *Warping from Front to Back*. Digital monograph, July 2023. Available from Daryl Lancaster's website.

Moorman, Theo. *Weaving as an Art Form: A Personal Statement*. West Chester, PA: Schiffer, 1975.

Patterson, Karen. *Lenore Tawney: Mirror of the Universe*. New York: John Michael Kohler Arts Center in association with University of Chicago Press, 2019.

Whidden, Anne. "A Look at 'Half-Tapestry' in Ryssväv: Agda Österberg." *theswedishrugblog*, February 28, 2020. the swedishrugblog.wordpress.com. Accessed April 26, 2025.

Zicafoose, Mary. *Ikat: The Essential Handbook to Weaving Resist-Dyed Cloth*. Loveland, CO: Interweave, 2020.

INDEX

Note: Page numbers in *italics* indicate projects, and page numbers in (*parentheses*) indicate cartoons for projects.

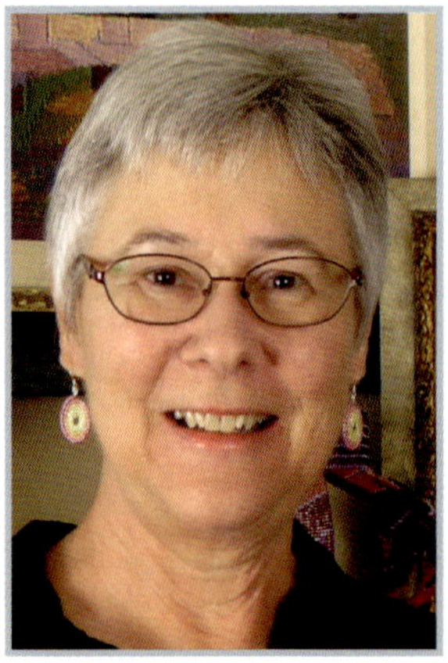

Rebecca Smith is a professional weaver and instructor who has been working at the loom for the past 40+ years. Her work has been included in juried exhibitions across the United States, and she teaches her innovative weaving techniques throughout the country. She is a member of the fiber art organization California Fibers, as well as a board member and creative leader of the San Diego Creative Weavers' Guild. www.rebeccasmithtapestry.com